# Inclusive Education in South African Further and Higher Education

# Inclusive Education in South African Further and Higher Education: Reflections on Equity, Access, and Inclusion

EDITED BY

**TSEDISO MICHAEL MAKOELLE**
*Nazarbayev University, Kazakhstan*

AND

**CINA P. MOSITO**
*Nelson Mandela University, South Africa*

United Kingdom – North America – Japan – India – Malaysia – China

Emerald Publishing Limited
Emerald Publishing, Floor 5, Northspring, 21-23 Wellington Street, Leeds LS1 4DL.

First edition 2025

Editorial matter and selection © 2025 Tsediso Michael Makoelle and Cina P. Mosito.
Individual chapters © 2025 The authors.
Published under exclusive licence by Emerald Publishing Limited.

**Reprints and permissions service**
Contact: www.copyright.com

No part of this book may be reproduced, stored in a retrieval system, transmitted in any form or by any means electronic, mechanical, photocopying, recording or otherwise without either the prior written permission of the publisher or a licence permitting restricted copying issued in the UK by The Copyright Licensing Agency and in the USA by The Copyright Clearance Center. Any opinions expressed in the chapters are those of the authors. Whilst Emerald makes every effort to ensure the quality and accuracy of its content, Emerald makes no representation implied or otherwise, as to the chapters' suitability and application and disclaims any warranties, express or implied, to their use.

**British Library Cataloguing in Publication Data**
A catalogue record for this book is available from the British Library

ISBN: 978-1-83608-945-2 (Print)
ISBN: 978-1-83608-944-5 (Online)
ISBN: 978-1-83608-946-9 (Epub)

Printed and bound by CPI Group (UK) Ltd, Croydon, CR0 4YY

**Erratum:** It has come to the attention of the publisher that the book (2025), "Prelims", Makoelle, T.M. and Mosito, C.P. (Ed.) Inclusive Education in South African Further and Higher Education: Reflections on Equity, Access, and Inclusion, Emerald Publishing Limited, Leeds, pp. i–xix. https://doi.org/10.1108/978-1-83608-944-520251046, incorrectly listed the biographical information for the author Heloise Sathorar on the 'About the Contributors' page. This error was introduced in the production process and has now been corrected in the print and online versions. The publisher sincerely apologizes for this error and for any inconvenience caused.

INVESTOR IN PEOPLE

# Contents

List of Figures and Tables — *vii*

About the Editors — *ix*

About the Contributors — *xi*

Preface — *xvii*

Acknowledgements — *xix*

**Chapter 1   Introduction: Towards an Inclusive Higher Education**
*Tsediso Michael Makoelle and Cina P. Mosito* — *1*

**Chapter 2   The Historical Development of Inclusive Education in South Africa: Higher Education Perspectives**
*Thinavhudzulo Norman Mafumo, Michael Mbongiseni Buthelezi and Mohammed Xolile Ntshangase* — *15*

**Chapter 3   Education Barriers in Higher Education**
*Sanet Deysel* — *35*

**Chapter 4   Higher Education Curriculum and Inclusion**
*Zandisile Mawethu Sitoyi and Johannes Buthelezi* — *53*

**Chapter 5   Strategies of Support for Inclusive Teaching and Learning in Higher Education**
*Thabo Makhalemele and Appolonia Masunungure* — *69*

**Chapter 6   Inclusive Assessment in Higher Education**
*Heloise Sathorar and Deidre Geduld* — *85*

vi    Contents

**Chapter 7    Decolonisation of Higher Education, Indigenous Knowledge, and Inclusion**
*Xolani Khalo and Benjamin Damoah*                    101

**Chapter 8    A Critical Review of Pre-service Teacher Education and Inclusion in the South African Higher Education Context**
*Cina P. Mosito and Lulama Mdodana-Zide*              117

**Chapter 9    Mentoring Pre-service Teachers for Inclusive Pedagogies**
*Tsediso Michael Makoelle*                            131

**Chapter 10    Exploring the Value of Critical Disability Theory in Public Technical and Vocational and Training Colleges in South Africa**
*Lucky Maluleke and Anelisa Pezisa*                   143

**Chapter 11    African Women Leaders in Universities: Using Memory in the Establishment of Leadership Practices**
*Siphokazi Tau and Dikeledi A. Mokoena*               161

**Chapter 12    Embracing the Melting Pot in Teacher Training: Language and Inclusion in Education**
*Erasmos Charamba and Shalom Ndhlovana*               177

**Chapter 13    Beyond Rhetoric: Reimagining Inclusive Education for Sexual and Gender Diversity in South African Higher Learning Institutions**
*Obakeng Kagola and Anthony Brown*                    191

**Chapter 14    Leveraging Assistive Technologies to Advocate for Accessibility for Students with Disabilities, an Inclusive Curriculum Practice**
*Mohau Ben Manyarela, Mochina Mphuthi and Ntsoaki Joyce Malebo*                         209

**Chapter 15    Inclusion in Higher Education During Natural Disruptions: Lessons from the COVID-19 Pandemic**
*Maitumeleng Albertina Nthontho and Pontsho Moepya*   229

**Chapter 16    Conclusion**
*Tsediso Michael Makoelle*                            245

# List of Figures and Tables

## Figures

| | | |
|---|---|---|
| Fig 1.1. | Summary of Higher Education Programmes and Inclusive Education Modules. | 4 |
| Fig 1.2. | Organising Areas of Inclusive Education in HE. | 5 |
| Fig 3.1. | Educational Barriers in Higher Education. | 48 |
| Fig 5.1. | Systematic Review Methodology. | 71 |
| Fig 6.1. | Main Aspects That Contribute to Inclusive Assessment Practices in Higher Education. | 87 |
| Fig 7.1. | Main Factors That Contribute to the Transformation of the Higher Education System. | 103 |
| Fig 9.1. | Mentoring Framework for Pre-service Teacher Practicum. | 138 |
| Fig 16.1. | Inclusive Further and Higher Education Cardinal Pillars. | 246 |

## Tables

| | | |
|---|---|---|
| Table 2.1. | Summary of Participants. | 28 |
| Table 3.1. | Differences Between School and University Experiences. | 39 |
| Table 5.1. | Examples of Universal Design for Learning (UDL) Principles. | 73 |
| Table 8.1. | Inclusive Education Policy Development in South Africa. | 124 |
| Table 11.1. | Summary of Participants. | 164 |
| Table 14.1. | Search Terms Used. | 213 |
| Table 14.2. | Search Strings. | 214 |
| Table 14.3. | Data Extraction and Analysis Table. | 217 |

# About the Editors

**Tsediso Michael Makoelle** (DEd, PhD) is a Full Professor at Nazarbayev University (NU) Graduate School of Education (GSE). He is a distinguished scholar who was awarded the prestigious Nelson Mandela Scholarship from the UK. His teaching and research experience of over 30 years focussed on secondary education as a school teacher, head of department, vice principal, and principal. In higher education, he has notably been a Lecturer and Senior Lecturer at the Cape Peninsula University of Technology, Cape Town, the University of Johannesburg, and Centre Coordinator at the University of Free State, South Africa. He has worked at NUGSE for nearly 10 years as an Associate Professor, Director of Doctoral Studies, General Director for Research, and Vice Dean for Research. He is a Visiting Fellow at the International Laboratory of the Social Integration Research of National Research University Higher School of Economics, Moscow, Russia.

**Cina P. Mosito** is an Associate Professor of Inclusive Education at Nelson Mandela University, South Africa. Her research and teaching focuses on understanding and supporting child development and learning in diverse circumstances, as well as mainstreaming inclusive education in initial teacher education and continuing professional development of teachers. She has contributed to the roll-out of a British Council-sponsored project, the Teaching for All programme in the Western Cape and Eastern Cape provinces. She is also a principal investigator in Understanding Teacher Pedagogy in South Africa, a longitudinal study that is being conducted by a consortium of 12 universities, in partnership with the National Education Collaboration Trust.

# About the Contributors

**Anthony Brown** is a Professor in the Department of Educational Psychology at Stellenbosch University. He promotes inclusive, safe, and supportive learning spaces for all in education. His pioneering work spotlights the experiences of LGBTIQ+ students in parts of Southern African learning institutions and promotes evidence-based strategies to nurture their academic success and socio-emotional well-being.

**Johannes Buthelezi** is a PhD alumnus from the University of Johannesburg and previously held a New Generation Academic Programme (nGAP) position at the Cape Peninsular University of Technology. A high school teacher by training, he worked with the school-based support teams to create safe learning environments for learners with LGBTQ identities. Working with young adults helped him understand the challenges, prejudice, and discrimination that learners face in schools. This led to his PhD in Inclusive Education as an nGAP scholar on the inclusion of students with transgender identities, emphasising the crucial role played by lecturers, security guards, and administrators in supporting students with diverse sexual orientations and gender expressions. He currently holds the position of Lecturer in the Faculty of Education at the University of Free State, where he continues to engage with distinct challenges that LGBTQ individuals encounter within the education system and actively advocates for adopting more inclusive policies and practices. He is also teaching subjects like Social Justice Education and Inclusive Education.

**Michael Mbongiseni Buthelezi** has a PhD in Educational Psychology from the University of KwaZulu-Natal. He is a Lecturer in the Department of Education Studies at the University of Limpopo. He has taught at all levels of education: primary school, high school, technical and vocational education training college, and university. As an Etutor at UNISA, he has taught several modules from 2014 to date. He has also served as National Evaluator for 9 years in Evaluation & Accreditation Unit at UMALUSI before he became an Accreditation Council Committee member at UMALUSI. His research includes student development, inclusive education, sustainable learning, psychosocial support, and rural development. He has published academic research papers in national and international journals. He has also presented at national and international conferences. He is currently supervising Bed Hons, PGCE, and masters' students.

xii   About the Contributors

**Erasmus Charamba** (PhD) is a Researcher at the University of Limerick who writes on issues of multilingualism, translanguaging, literacy, and science education. He has published substantially in these areas, including as a guest editor of two accredited journals and an edited book. He also supervises masters' and PhD students.

**Benjamin Damoah** (PhD) is a Research Fellow at the University of Fort Hare. He is a distinguished environmental scientist with expertise in environmental education, climate change, and sustainable development. He has co-supervised masters' and PhD candidates and has published over 30 peer-reviewed articles. He has been instrumental in shaping environmental policies through participation in local and international conferences.

**Sanet Deysel** (PhD) is a Lecturer in Inclusive Education in Initial Teacher Education at Nelson Mandela University. Her areas of interest and research are inclusive education, barriers to learning, and learner support. She is keenly interested in community engagement and employed a Participatory Action Learning and Action Research methodology during her PhD studies.

**Deidre Geduld** is an Associate Professor in the Department for the BEd Foundation, Primary School (Gr R-3) at Nelson Mandela University. Her research interests include teaching and learning in the early years, inclusive education, eco pedagogy, humanising pedagogy, teacher education curriculum design, community schooling and engagement within communities of practice, and critical participatory approach to research.

**Obakeng Kagola** is a Lecturer in the Faculty of Education at Sol Plaatje University. The author is a transdisciplinary researcher with a specific focus on gender and childhood sexualities, men and masculinity studies, and the use of participatory and visual methodologies as a design and pedagogy. The author aims to promote inclusive, safe, and supportive learning environments in education.

**Xolani Khalo** is a Senior Lecturer and a Head of School in the School of Further and Continuing Education at the University of Fort Hare, South Africa. His research area of interest is in education for sustainable development, and inclusivity and diversity issues in education. He has published 15 peer-reviewed articles, supervised PhD and MEd student to completion, and presented in 13 local and international conferences.

**Thinavhudzulo Norman Mafumo** is an Associate Professor of Education Policy Studies at the University of Limpopo. He is holding PhD in Education Policy Studies from Stellenbosch University. He is currently teaching philosophy of education, education policy studies, and education management and law. His publications and writings are on social justice, education policy, and education management.

**Thabo Makhalemele** (PhD) is an Associate Professor in Learner Support and Deputy Director of the School of Psycho-Social Education, Faculty of Education, North-West University, Vaal Campus, South Africa. His fields of study are educational psychology, inclusive education, and learner support. He teaches various modules at both undergraduate and postgraduate levels. Additionally, he supervises MEd and PhD students and has reviewed manuscripts for national and international journals. His research interests are learner support and inclusive education. He has published articles in peer-reviewed journals, contributed chapters in edited books, and participated in funded national and international research projects.

**Ntsoaki Joyce Malebo** is a PhD graduate with experience in Higher Education and Leadership Development and an NRF grant holder. She leads units responsible for academic staff and student development including the Disability Unit at the Central University of Technology, Free State. She is a Former Lead of the Academic Development Leadership Scholarly Group within HELTASA. She actively participates in academic programme reviews internally and at peer institutions nationally and internationally. She coordinates the Erasmus plus funded iKudu project focussing Collaborative Online International Learning to internationalise curriculum, collaborating with South African and European universities. Throughout her career, she has held several senior positions, including Research Manager, Head of Department, and Assistant Dean of Teaching and Learning. She leads the Siyaphumelela student success project at the Central University of Technology, Free State. She has presented her work at local and international conferences and published in peer-reviewed journals.

**Lucky Maluleke** is a dedicated academic with a PhD in Education, currently serving as a Lecturer at Nelson Mandela University. His research expertise is centred around technical and vocational education and training (TVET), career development, and teacher development. Through his work, he contributes to the advancement of educational practices that empower individuals in vocational fields, ensuring they are equipped with the skills and knowledge necessary for success in their careers. His commitment to teacher development further highlights his role in shaping the next generation of educators, making a significant impact on the broader education landscape. His current research project focusses on the career development of lecturers in TVET Colleges in South Africa.

**Mohau Ben Manyarela** is the Head of the Disability Unit (Deputy Director: Disability Unit) at the Central University of Technology (CUT). As a novice researcher, his focus lies in inclusive education, educational technology, assistive technology, and disability studies. He completed his master's degree at the CUT, an honours degree in curriculum studies at the University of the Free State, and an undergraduate degree in information technology from CUT. He is currently completing a Postgraduate Diploma in Higher Education at Rhodes University. In his role at CUT, he is dedicated to enhancing accessibility, inclusive practices, and support for students with disabilities. He leverages technology and innovative practices to create an inclusive academic environment, ensuring that all students have the opportunity to succeed. His work reflects a deep commitment to promoting equity and inclusivity in higher education.

**Appolonia Masunungure** (PhD) is a Senior Lecturer at the School of Psycho-Social Education, Faculty of Education, and North-West University, South Africa. Her fields of study are educational psychology, inclusive education, and learner support. She teaches various modules at both undergraduate and postgraduate levels. She is currently supervising postgraduate students in the inclusive education strand. Her research interests are equity, access, social justice, and inclusion in education. She is a COMBER executive committee member.

**Lulama Mdodana-Zide** is a Lecturer and Teaching Practice Subject Head at the University of the Free State (UFS), Qwaqwa Campus, in the Faculty of Education within the Department of Curriculum Studies and Higher Education. She holds a PhD in Continuing Teacher Professional Development. Prior to joining the UFS academic community, she worked in the SA Department of Education (DBE) as an Educator, Head of Department, and Senior Education Specialist. She is responsible for teaching undergraduate students and supervising postgraduate students (honours, masters, and PhDs) in Education Management and Leadership as well as in Curriculum Studies. Her research focusses on Continuing Professional Development for teachers with a further specialty in Educational Leadership and Management Professional Development. She has published and presented on various platforms locally and internationally.

**Pontsho Moepya** is currently a Lecturer and Doctoral candidate in the Department of Education Management, Law Policy, Faculty of Education, and University of Pretoria. She is a recipient of the DSE-NRF postgraduate scholarships and a member of the prestigious Golden Key UP Society.

**Dikeledi A. Mokoena** is a lecturer in the Department of Anthropology and Development Studies at the University of Johannesburg. She teaches Gender and Development as well as Development, Governance and Research. Her work and publications are informed by African Feminism, Decoloniality and African-centered perspectives. Dr Mokoena has coordinated multi-country research projects and has won several awards including the NIHSS catalytic research programme for the development of an Encyclopaedia of African Feminisms. Dr Mokena holds a PhD in Political Science and has 9 years of lecturing experience. She has facilitated leadership programmes for international institutions such as the Africa Union's Women, Gender and Youth division for a couple of years. Her research interests include African politics, gender and feminist political economy.

**Mochina Mphuthi** is an eLearning Support Officer at the Center for E-learning and Educational Technologies. He is also a Part-time Lecturer specialising in Economic and Management Sciences, Economics Education, and Academic Literacy. He holds an honours degree in Education Management and has research interests in pre-service teachers, curriculum practice, eLearning and educational technology, and transformation in higher education. He has published numerous articles, book chapters, and presented at conferences both nationally and internationally.

**Shalom Ndhlovana** is a master's student and a Tutor at the University of the Witwatersrand. She writes on issues of language education and multilingualism. Her recent articles showcase the pivotal role language plays in education.

**Maitumeleng Albertina Nthontho** is currently a C2 rated Research Professor at the Education and Human Rights in Diversity (Edu-HRight) Research Unit, North-West University, Potchefstroom campus. She served the University of Pretoria for the past eight years as a Lecturer, Senior Lecturer and an Associate Professor. Professor Nthontho is a recipient of Margaret Mcnamara and the African Union scholarships. She mentored the nGAP Lecturer, supervised over 20 PhD and master's students to completion and she published over 50 research papers.

**Mohammed Xolile Ntshangase** is a Lecturer of Philosophy of Education and Psychology of Education from 2018 in the University of Limpopo. He holds a master degree in Philosophy (with a doctoral degree pending) from the University of KwaZulu-Natal. He has published works in the areas of African philosophy, educational psychology and gender studies, as well as political philosophy.

**Anelisa Pezisa** is an emerging Academic and Assistant Lecturer, currently pursuing her PhD in Social Development Professions at Nelson Mandela University. Her research interest is online work-integrated learning, with a focus on the implications for developing key competencies for social work education during emergencies, for example, COVID-19. Her academic qualifications include Bachelor of Social Work, Honours and Masters in Development Studies. She is actively involved in student engagement initiatives and volunteers with local organisations. She recently presented at the 2021 HELTASA (un)conference and co-authored a forthcoming book chapter on academic development and student assistance.

**Heloise Sathorar** is the Executive Dean of the Faculty of Education at Nelson Mandela University. She is also an Associate Professor and her research interests include critical pedagogy, humanising pedagogy, teacher education, higher education, and critical community engagement. Her most recent work is Leading for Sustainability and Empowerment: Reflecting on the Power of Collaboration and Humanising Pedagogy.

**Zandisile Mawethu Sitoyi** is an New Generation Academic Programme Lecturer at Cape Peninsula University of Technology in the Academic Staff Development Department. He is a PhD candidate in Educational Psychology and Inclusive Education at the University of the Western Cape (UWC). He is a member of the Golden Key Society and has a MEd (Cum Laude) from UWC.

**Siphokazi Tau** is an interdisciplinary African feminist researcher. She integrates African feminisms, higher education transformation, cultural memory, leadership studies and the interplay of power and culture. Her scholarly work centers on African women's lived realities, leadership dynamics, and institutional cultures in postcolonial contexts. She is pursuing a Ph.D. in Education (Higher Education Studies), at the University of Johannesburg. She holds an MA in Political Science and has experience in lecturing and designing decolonial courses.

# Preface

The advent of the new political dispensation in South Africa in 1994 has seen the new government embark on the transformation of education, in particular, the higher education sector. The Higher Education Act No. 101 of 1997 (DoE, 1997) was the first step in the process of redressing the imbalances of the past as a result of the apartheid policy advocating for separate development for different racial groups. The unequal provision of education for different races perpetuated class differences and made quality higher and further education inaccessible to Africans, coloureds, and Indians. In order to ensure the equitable distribution of resources in higher education, the Ministry of Education embarked on several processes, among others, the university measures and the establishment of further education and training institutions. Regarding the university managers, the traditionally non-white higher education institutions were absorbed by the traditionally white-only institutions that were well-resourced. However, issues of access and exclusion, such as epistemic access, lack of support for students with disability, and student dropout persisted. Reorganisation of higher education institutions with the establishment of inclusion university councils, transformation offices, and institutional forums were measures put in place to accelerate redress, inclusion, access, and equity in these institutions of higher learning.

While the adoption of White Paper 6 in 2001 has seen more concerted effort in ensuring inclusion and social justice in secondary education, implementing inclusion in higher and further education took time to kick start. As a result of the implementation of inclusion in secondary education, the throughput of students from this level to the tertiary level has seen an increase in the number of students with disabilities in higher and further education. It is estimated that 1% of students in colleges and universities are with either a disability or special needs. As a result, colleges and universities face the major task of ensuring that higher and further education is accessible, equitable, and inclusive. Institutions of higher learning are focussed on redress, and processes such as decolonisation of curriculum, transformation of institutional cultures, and other related transformational endeavours are all aimed at making higher and further education inclusive.

Therefore, the idea of this book was born of the need to take stock of the developments regarding the implementation of inclusive education and the general process of ensuring access, equity, inclusion, and social justice in the South African higher and further education landscape. The editorial of this book, first, Tsediso Michael Makoelle, Professor of Inclusive Education and School Leadership, brings a wealth of international experience in both higher and secondary education that could contribute to a deeper understanding of inclusion in higher and further education. Second, Cina P. Mosito, an Associate Professor of Inclusive Education with extensive experience in South African higher education teacher education, brings a depth of knowledge in the sphere of inclusive pedagogy.

As a result, this volume gives a reflective account of how sound institutions of higher learning in South Africa have responded so far to the mandate to ensure equity, access, and inclusion as promulgated in the relevant policies (2013 Education White for Post School Education, 2001 Education White Paper 6, and 1997 White Paper 3).

The volume provides an analysis of the South African higher education system's response to the concepts of equity, access, and inclusion, and highlights how these concepts have evolved, been enacted, and practised in the higher education institutions of South Africa since 2001. It also highlights some challenges, successes, and opportunities that prevail in those institutions of higher learning as a result of their attempts to make higher education accessible in order to widen the participation of all students in teaching and learning. Therefore, this volume makes an interesting read for educationists, higher education scholars, students, researchers, policymakers, and civil society organisations.

*Tsediso Michael Makoelle and Cina P. Mosito*

# Reference

Department of Education (DoE). (1997). Higher Education Act no 101 of 1997. Government Printers.

# Acknowledgements

We wish to acknowledge the contributing authors and their respective affiliated universities, which provided them with the time and resources to ensure the completion of this book.

# Chapter 1

# Introduction: Towards an Inclusive Higher Education

Tsediso Michael Makoelle[a] and Cina P. Mosito[b]

[a]Nazarbayev University, Kazakhstan
[b]Nelson Mandela University, South Africa

## Abstract

This introduction provides an overview of the book's content by providing an introductory orientation on inclusive education in higher education (HE) internationally. The background of inclusion in HE within the South African context is provided. The introduction also provides the conceptual framework on which the book is based, as well as the methodology. The executive summary of the book is provided to give a snapshot of the focus of the chapters' contents.

*Keywords*: Inclusive higher education; inclusive education; inclusion; equity; access; social justice

## Inclusive Education in HE

According to Moriña (2017), the need for inclusive HE systems has increased as diverse students, including those with special needs and disability from secondary education, are now enrolled in institutions of higher learning to pursue HE. However, the implementation of inclusive education in institutions of higher learning is not without its challenges. It is influenced by several variables such as finance, resources, faculty preparedness competence, etc. The fact that some institutions are autonomous and subscribe to academic freedom might either be an enabler or a hindrance to the implementation of inclusive education.

---

Inclusive Education in South African Further and Higher Education:
Reflections on Equity, Access, and Inclusion, 1–13
Copyright © 2025 by Tsediso Michael Makoelle and Cina P. Mosito
Published under exclusive licence by Emerald Publishing Limited
doi:10.1108/978-1-83608-944-520251003

The emphasis on throughputs and completion rates at institutions of higher learning may pose a risk for neglect of students who are at risk or need additional support to make a success in their learning. The increasing levels of diversity at the institutions of higher learning might pose a serious barrier to effective inclusion and access. Moriña (2017) postulates that although institutions of higher learning have become more diverse, the focus of inclusion in HE is still heavily directed towards students with disabilities. In their work, Salha and Albadawi (2021) stress the need for a participatory process in the implantation of inclusive education in institutions of higher learning. They believe that all stakeholders, including students, should be part of the discussions. Svendby (2024) believes that inclusion in HE institutions has to be obligatory and that it should be infused into the curriculum and the training of lecturers and instructors. The institutions are paced at the centre for the attainment of sustainable development goal 4 of the 2030 agenda to ensure inclusive and equitable quality education and promote lifelong learning for all. Therefore, the implementation of inclusion in institutions of higher learning calls for renewal of academic planning, pedagogical and curriculum design, infrastructure redesign, deployment of assistive technologies, and the development of an inclusive culture, which may widen and broaden the participation of diverse students in teaching and learning (Makoelle, 2022).

## The South African Context

Following the Higher Education Act (DOE, 1997), the adoption of the notion of inclusive education led to the adoption of relevant policies: Education White Paper for Post-School Education (DHET, 2013), Education White Paper 6 (DOE, 2001), and White Paper 3 (CHE, 1997). These policy frameworks aim to redress the past exclusive practices within the South African Education system. They are also oriented towards understanding and implementing inclusion from access, equity, and inclusion, as well as social justice and human rights perspectives. The historical context of apartheid continues to bear the hallmarks in HE. South African HE landscape experiences multiple barriers, and institutions of higher learning have embarked on the transformation process towards inclusion to redress past inequities. The institutions of higher learning are in the process of revising the curriculum and exploring different strategies to support students with diverse needs. The institutions of higher learning are grappling with the management of diversity, including gender, language, technology, and leadership, and how those impact access, equity, and inclusion. Institutions of higher learning are implementing inclusion amidst the process of decolonisation of the curriculum in HE and attempting to incorporate indigenous pieces of knowledge and Afro-centric knowledge in the HE curriculum. The technical and vocational education and training institutions (TVETs) are being positioned as centred on youth skills development.

The post-apartheid era saw the South African government promulgate a range of policies for building an inclusive education system. One of these policies, White Paper 6: Building an Inclusive Education and Training System, outlines how the education and training system must transform itself to contribute to establishing a caring and humane society, how it must change to accommodate the full range of learning needs and the mechanisms that should be put in place (DOE, 2001). According to the White Paper 6 section 2.2.2.3, it was required that institutions of further and HE establish institutional-level support teams. As a result, in section 2.2.5, institutions of higher learning were mandated to develop institutional plans to increase the enrolment of students with special needs. In this process, physical access was to be prioritised, and more resources were to be invested to support students with disabilities and special needs in HE. Then in year 2023, which is 22 years later, it is important to review the process of the implementation of inclusive education by institutions of further and HE since the adoption of the White Paper in 2001.

The process of the implementation of inclusive education by further and HE institutions came into the fore amidst the university merging process, which was championed by the then Minister of Education, the late Mr Kader Asmal in 2004. According to Baloyi (2015), the merger was not only aimed at changing facilities and buildings but also to ensure that the doors of teaching and learning were open to all, regardless of ethnicity, race, and other barriers. To achieve epistemic access, universities had to undergo language changes, review their admissions policies, and enrol more students from disadvantaged rural backgrounds. The government restructured HE funding to ensure that there was a process by institutions of higher learning to redress the imbalances and injustices of exclusion that occurred in the past.

However, in 2015, the *fee-must-fall* campaign, which was student-led, took centre stage in demanding a reduction in the high cost of HE. In 2016, government announced that tuition would not be increased, but in 2017, fee increases were capped at 8%. Students viewed high fees at institutions of higher learning as a barrier to the education of mostly disadvantaged black majority students. Most sources point out that the drop rate of students in South African universities in various years/levels of study varies from 30% to 60% (Ntema, 2022). As a result, the indication is that inclusion, equity, and access have not been sufficiently addressed despite all institutional efforts. While universities are investing in first-year preparatory programmes, it seems as though the problem of students dropping away will not go away soon (Hlalele & Alexander, 2012). It is important to note that while the White Paper was aimed at redressing past injustices, it was not specific about strategies to accomplish this goal.

Through initial teacher education programmes, HE in South Africa is also tasked with preparing prospective teachers to graduate with knowledge, skills, and attitudes for inclusive teaching. In their report entitled 'The State of Inclusive Education in South Africa: Implications for Teacher Education and Training Programmes' Majoko et al. (2018) postulate that inclusive education is not well represented in teacher education courses. Fig. 1.1 illustrates the distribution of teacher education courses at South African universities with teacher education programmes.

While some universities have taken measures to incorporate courses on inclusive education in these teacher education programmes, the indication is that they are still lacking. As a consequence in this report, it is recommended that institutions of teacher training incorporate more courses on inclusive education within

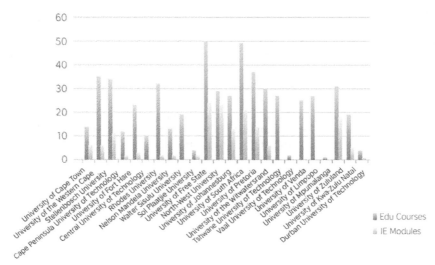

Fig. 1.1. Summary of Higher Education Programmes and Inclusive Education Modules. *Source*: Adapted from Majoko et al. (2018, p. 53).

the teacher education curriculum. Therefore, it becomes critical to understand how well institutions of higher learning in South Africa have responded so far to the mandate to ensure equity, access, and inclusion as promulgated in different policies (1995 White Paper on Education and Training, 1997 White Paper 3 A programme for Transformation of Higher Education, and 2001 Education White Paper 6).

It is also important to provide an analysis of the South African HE system's response to the concepts of equity, access, and inclusion, highlighting how these concepts have evolved, been enacted, and practised in the HE institutions of South Africa since 2001. It further highlights some challenges, successes, and opportunities that prevail in those institutions of higher learning as a result of their attempts to make HE accessible and widen the participation of all students in teaching and learning.

## Conceptual Framework

Our approach to the discussions in this volume is inspired by the systems and ecological approach, which was used in many studies on inclusive education and support (Tahir et al., 2019) (in Schools) (Hewett et al., 2019) (in HE) which depart from the underlying assumptions that inclusion is nested within and across various interdependent components. In this volume, Bronfenbrenner's

Bioecological Systems Theory is adopted as it assumes an interplay between the one who needs to be supported or included and the conditions surrounding him/her in the immediate environment or ecology. The theory was meant for the child's development through the support of the systems in the environment, i.e. the microsystem – composed of the support structures which are closest to the child, e.g. family; mesosystem – composed of connecting structures between microsystems, e.g. school; exosystem – made up of the broader societal structures, e.g. parents workplace; macrosystem – composed of values, customs, and traditions of the society; and chronosystem – denoting time and its relationship with the children development in the environment. While this theory was meant for the child's development and support, we adopted it as authors in this volume assume that educationally, at any given pedagogical moment, there is a child, student, and learner at all levels of education, including higher and further education that need support based on their educational need that might have been identified. Therefore, to address the educational needs of all students, the environmental systems are crucial.

The discussions in the chapters are organised into five strategic areas for inclusive education in the HE landscape. The organising areas anchored in various chapters are policy, human and physical aspects (leadership, gender, infrastructure, and technology), teaching and learning (curriculum, barriers, and assessment), philosophical aspects (decolonisation, indigenisation, and transformation), and organisational aspects (teacher education, TVET, and universities). Fig. 1.2 depicts how the thoughts and ideas in this volume are presented.

## *Policy*

We recognise that HE is governed through a set of policies and principles. It is therefore important that while an understanding of policies is important, contributions from this volume are aimed at advancing new research and thus knowledge that could influence policy debates, conceptualisation, formulation, enactment, and consequently the implementation.

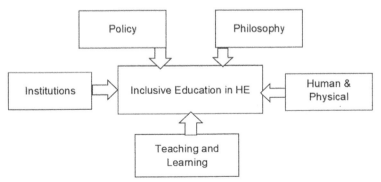

Fig. 1.2. Organising Areas of Inclusive Education in HE.

### Philosophical Aspects

We are mindful that the implementation of inclusive education in HE coincided with the process of redress of the past imbalances of apartheid and the exclusion of other sections of society from benefiting from the fruits of HE as an economically empowering tool. In this volume, care is given that inclusive education comes amidst the processes of decolonising the curriculum and HE practices and the indigenisation process whereby indigenous knowledge systems are considered central to the decolonisation process.

### Institutions

While inclusive education was originally targeted at primary and secondary education, we recognise that it is a multi-level phenomenon hence in this volume more focus is devoted to inclusive education in teacher training, TVET, and university education. We also recognise that it is multidisciplinary and that the principles of inclusivity cut across all education sectors and are geared towards equity, access, and social justice.

### Human and Physical Resources

Inclusion is a collaborative endeavour that most often relies on human interactions and the provision of resources. In this volume, we elaborate on the need for leadership that may promote inclusion in HE. We are aware that HE is experiencing transformation due to gender issues, that HE institutions are grappling with the inclusion of women in leadership roles, and that admission of female students in some disciplines has taken a priority as an equity goal.

The provision and allocation of technology to aid inclusion through the use of relevant assistive devices has in many ways become part of the universal learning design, which has proved to be important for inclusion in HE. We also focus on the necessary adaptations of infrastructure to ensure mobility and institutional access and the creation of an enabling environment for inclusion in HE.

### Teaching and Learning

For inclusive education to succeed, teaching and learning is central. In this volume, we elaborate on issues of epistemic access and support for teaching and learning. We do this by highlighting the significance of inclusive curriculum and how it is critical for inclusive learning. In this volume, barriers to inclusive HE are illuminated both from the perspective of teaching, learning, and environment. The notion of inclusive assessment in HE is conceptualised in the context of inclusive HE.

## Methodology

The methodological approaches in this volume are informed by the social justice approach to equity, equality, and inclusion. As Adams et al. (2022) postulate that there are five critical elements of social justice education practice, i.e.

considering the roles of facilitators and participants in the learning community; fostering an inclusive learning community; centring an analysis of systems of oppression and how they operate in society and the classroom; defining goals, learning objectives, and evaluation mechanisms; and utilising collaborative and active learning. (p. 1)

To unravel these five principles, the authors, through different chapters, scope the extent of inclusion, exclusion, equity, equality and access, and quantitative approaches are applied, while qualitative methods are applied to understand the social constructions. The chapters adopt various lenses based on the area they are exploring. In this volume, frameworks within decolonising, disability, transformative, and critical emancipatory paradigms are employed.

Therefore, all the lenses adopted in this volume contribute towards the attainment of the following objectives:

- Analyse the current state of equity, access, equality, and inclusion in the South African further and HE.
- Identify some successes, opportunities, and challenges of inclusion in further and HE.
- Discuss implications for studies and make recommendations going forward.

The following is an executive summary of each chapter and aspects that address the objectives of this volume.

## Executive Summary

### Chapter 2: The Historical Development of Inclusive Education in South Africa: Higher Education Perspectives

This chapter provides theoretical orientation and principles of inclusion and how those relate to the HE context. This is done from a human rights and social justice perspective. A comprehensive account of the development of inclusive education in South Africa is provided with discussions centred on how inclusion is conceptualised, enacted, and practised within the HE sector. The chapter also provides context with reference to HE, including policy development, challenges, successes, and opportunities.

### Chapter 3: Education Barriers in Higher Education

According to Maree (2014) while the burden of access and success of students is based squarely on HE institutions, there needs to be a comprehensive intervention that focusses on both schools and universities to improve throughputs. This chapter highlights the barriers that affect the access and inclusion of diverse students in institutions of higher learning. These are discussed from the perspectives of institutional barriers (Grant, 2015) infrastructures, curriculum delivery, student attributes epistemic processes, and others.

### Chapter 4: Higher Education Curriculum and Inclusion

Stentiford and Koutsouris (2022) postulate that the notion of inclusive curriculum is understood differently in HE based on the conceptions of those involved. However, there is consensus about what inclusive curriculum should seek to achieve, i.e. to provide support to those experiencing exclusion or barriers to educational success. In this chapter, the notion of curriculum is conceptualised, and the concept of an inclusive curriculum is explained. The nuances of inclusive curriculum development, delivery, and assessment are foregrounded. The chapter provides an analysis of inclusive curriculum practices in the South African HE context and thus makes recommendations about how an inclusive curriculum could be developed.

### Chapter 5: Strategies of Support for Inclusive Teaching and Learning in Higher Education

There are different approaches towards inclusive teaching and learning. The Universal Design for Learning is one of the prominent approaches to how teaching and learning can be configured. Hockings et al. (2012) advocate for open education resources. In this chapter, the notion of an inclusive teaching strategy is conceptualised, and strategies used for enhancing equity and inclusion to support diverse students are unpacked. These are discussed in the context of South African HE. The chapter makes some recommendations about relevant and appropriate strategies in the South African context.

### Chapter 6: Inclusive Assessment in Higher Education

Bain (2023, p. 1) 'defines inclusive assessment as the provision of assessments that allow all students to do well without receiving alternative or adapted assessments'. Bain further avers that assessment should be considered part of a more comprehensive and broader aspect of pedagogy and may not be treated in isolation. This chapter, therefore, conceptualises the notion of inclusive assessment and illuminates how it is operationalised, enacted, and practised within the South African HE context. Challenges, successes, and opportunities for inclusive assessments are highlighted.

### Chapter 7: Decolonisation of Higher Education, Indigenous Knowledge, and Inclusion

There is a view that decolonising HE and its curriculum may include the introduction of indigenous knowledge. This view purports that cultural artefacts mediate knowledge, and, as such, to include the marginalised; they need to see themselves in the curriculum. However, in the literature, some believe decolonising the curriculum might disrupt the academic project (Senekal & Lenz, 2020). This chapter highlights those contestations of decolonising and brings the debate to the fore. The chapter takes stock of the extent of decolonisation and its impact on epistemic access, ensuring equity and casing inclusion, particularly for the previously marginalised.

## Chapter 8: A Critical Review of Pre-service Teacher Education and Inclusion in the South African Higher Education Context

There is consensus in the literature that pre-service teacher preparation is important for ensuring teachers are ready for inclusive teaching (Harvey Yssel et al., 2010). There have been efforts in South African HE to incorporate courses on inclusive education into the teacher education programmes (Majoko et al., 2018). This chapter analyses teacher education and its impact on teacher preparation for inclusive pedagogy. The chapter also highlights some challenges this process has encountered and what has been achieved so far, and it makes suggestions for going forward.

## Chapter 9: Mentoring Pre-service Teachers for Inclusive Pedagogies

Mentoring has been used as a training method for pre-service teachers (Hobson, 2016). During the pre-service teacher practicum, school teachers are appointed to mentor the pre-service teacher in teaching and learning. This chapter is devoted to analysing the extent to which mentoring during the practicum prepares pre-service teachers for inclusive teaching. It analyses the partnership of teacher training institutions of higher learning and schools, identifies practices that promote inclusion, and makes recommendations about how institutions of higher learning may enhance this process.

## Chapter 10: Exploring the Value of Critical Disability Theory in Public Technical and Vocational and Training Colleges in South Africa

According to Delubom et al. (2020, p. 1)

> TVET South African colleges experience challenges such as inadequate infrastructure, funding, lecturer-training, and staff shortage to support students with disabilities. It was recommended that TVET colleges establish Disability Service Units and recruit trained lecturers, or they must train current lecturers to facilitate the learning process of disabled students.

This view is also supported by Ntombela (2019). This chapter, therefore, unpacks the state of inclusion, equity, and access at the South African TVET colleges, highlights some challenges and recommends how TVET colleges may enable inclusion in their context.

## Chapter 11: African Women Leaders in Universities: Using Memory in the Establishment of Leadership Practices

According to Ntombela (2013), how the university is organised and led could profoundly influence the success of inclusion. Leadership for inclusion is of the essence for institutions of higher learning to be able to ensure access, equity, and inclusion. Bipath et al. (2021) state that in implementing inclusive education, leadership is required to coordinate, facilitate, monitor, and evaluate the process. This chapter conceptualises leadership for inclusion and reviews the leadership practices that have enabled or disabled processes of ensuring access, equity, and inclusion within the South African HE context. Recommendations about effective inclusive leadership, operational, organisational, and strategic, have been made.

### Chapter 12: Embracing the Melting Pot in Teacher Training: Language and Inclusion in Education

Cele (2021) laments that the HE policy has not yielded the expected results regarding access, equity, and inclusion. This view is echoed by Nudelman (2015), who sees policy documents as merely symbolic and do not address the underdevelopment of local languages in ensuring epistemic access. This is based on his argument that most students are still finding it hard to access education. This chapter provides a comprehensive analysis of the language policy debate in South Africa's HE system. Interesting determinations are made about the current state of language and its influence on inclusion and access or exclusion.

### Chapter 13: Beyond Rhetoric: Reimagining Inclusive Education for Sexual and Gender Diversity in South African Higher Learning Institutions

According to Hlatshwayo et al. (2022) and Akala (2018), although there have been efforts to empower women in institutions of higher learning in South African universities, women continue to be underrepresented significantly in senior roles. The policy pronouncements seem to have not translated into tangible outcomes. Akala and Divala (2016) postulate that although enrolment of women in South African HE has increased, the systemic disadvantages have not been dealt with; thus, the achievement of equity, access, and inclusion has not materialised. Therefore, this chapter analyses the issue of gender and its impact on access, equity, and inclusion. Some lessons are drawn to make recommendations regarding gender in South African HE.

### Chapter 14: Leveraging Assistive Technologies to Advocate for Accessibility for Students with Disabilities, an Inclusive Curriculum Practice

Technology has become a critical tool to support teaching and learning (Ng'ambi et al., 2016) within South African HE in the age of the 4th Industrial Revolution (Moloi & Salawu, 2020). According to Kajee (2010, p. 1),

> Policy documents such as the Green Paper on Higher Education (Department of Education, 1996), as well as the Education White Paper (Council on Higher Education, 1997) expound the need for a resource-based approach to teaching and learning and

recommend the use of technology to encourage South Africa to join the competitive global economic market.

This chapter analyses the impact of technology and digitisation to assess their role in enabling access, equity. and inclusion in South African HE.

### *Chapter 15: Inclusion in Higher Education During Natural Disruptions: Lessons from the COVID-19 Pandemic*

Van Schalkwyk and Canares (2022) postulate that although technology became important during the COVID-19 Pandemic, there were, however, several challenges experienced by both faculty and students in their application. However, there is a view that institutions of higher learning need to invest more in assistive technologies that can enable the inclusion of students with disabilities (Lyner-Cleophas, 2019). This chapter, therefore, analyses the impact of the pandemic on access, equity, and inclusion. This analysis unpacks the process during and after the pandemic. Lessons are drawn regarding how institutions of higher learning may enable inclusion during disruptions.

### *Chapter 16: Conclusion*

Drawing lessons and conclusions provides reflections on the findings and conclusions from the previous chapters. This is done by providing a comprehensive synthesis of the seven cardinal pillars of inclusion in further and HE that emerged from the discussions in this volume. Based on the research outcomes presented in this volume, lessons and recommendations are made presenting successes, opportunities, benefits and challenges of inclusive further and HE in South Africa.

## References

Adams, M., Briggs, R. R., & Shlasko, D. (2022). Pedagogical foundations for social justice education. In M. Adams, L. A. Bell, D. J. Goodman, D. Shlasko, R. R. Briggs & R. Pacheco (Eds.), *Teaching for diversity and social justice* (pp. 27–55). Routledge.

Akala, B. (2018). Challenging gender equality in South African transformation policies – A case of the white paper: A programme for the transformation of higher education. *South African Journal of Higher Education, 32*(3), 226–248.

Akala, B., & Divala, J. J. (2016). Gender equity tensions in South Africa's post-apartheid higher education: In defence of differentiation. *South African Journal of Higher Education, 30*(1), 1–16.

Bain, K. (2023). Inclusive assessment in higher education: What does the literature tells us on how to define and design inclusive assessments? *Journal of Learning Development in Higher Education, 27*, 1–23.

Baloyi, M. C. (2015). *Mergers in South African higher education: Realization of policy intentions* [Doctoral dissertation]. University of South Africa.

Bipath, K., Tebekana, J., & Venketsamy, R. (2021). Leadership in implementing inclusive education policy in early childhood education and care playrooms in South Africa. *Education Sciences, 11*(12), 815.

Cele, N. (2021). Understanding language policy as a tool for access and social inclusion in South African Higher Education: A critical policy analysis perspective. *South African Journal of Higher Education*, *35*(6), 25–46.
Council of Higher Education. (1997). *Education White Paper 3: A programme for the transformation of higher education*. Government Printers.
Delubom, N. E., Marongwe, N., & Buka, A. M. (2020). Managers' challenges on implementing inclusive education: Technical vocational education and training colleges. *Cypriot Journal of Educational Sciences*, *15*(6), 1508–1519.
DHET. (2013). *White paper for post-school education and training: Building an expanded effective and integrated post-school system*. Government Printers.
Grant, M. J. (2015). *Institutional barriers to learning: A case study of a university in KwaZulu Natal* [Master thesis]. University of KwaZulu-Natal.
Harvey, M. W., Yssel, N., Bauserman, A. D., & Merbler, J. B. (2010). Preservice teacher preparation for inclusion: An exploration of higher education teacher-training institutions. *Remedial and Special Education*, *31*(1), 24–33.
Hewett, R., Douglas, G., McLinden, M., & Keil, S. (2019). Developing an inclusive learning environment for students with visual impairment in higher education: Progressive mutual accommodation and learner experiences in the United Kingdom. In M. R. Coleman & M. Shevlin (Eds.), *Postsecondary educational opportunities for students with special education needs* (pp. 90–109). Routledge.
Hlalele, D., & Alexander, G. (2012). University access and social justice. *South African Journal of Higher Education*, *2*(3), 487–502.
Hlatshwayo, L. P., Mashaba, B., Mathuloe, O., & Yende, S. J. (2022). Being a woman is not a barrier to achieving successful leadership in South African Higher Education. *African Journal of Gender, Society & Development*, *11*(4), 7.
Hobson, A. J. (2016). Judge mentoring and how to avert it: Introducing ONSIDE mentoring for beginning teachers. *International Journal of Mentoring and Coaching in Education*, *5*(2), 87–110.
Hockings, C., Brett, P., & Terentjevs, M. (2012). Making a difference — Inclusive learning and teaching in higher education through open educational resources. *Distance Education*, *33*(2), 237–252.
Kajee, L. (2010). Disability, social inclusion and technological positioning in a South African Higher Education institution: Carmen's story. *Language Learning Journal*, *38*(3), 379–392.
Lyner-Cleophas, M. (2019). Assistive technology enables inclusion in higher education: The role of Higher and Further Education Disability Services Association. *African Journal of Disability*, *8*(1), 1–6.
Majoko, T., Phasha, N., Brown, A., Soni, T. D., Duku, N., Febana, Z., Maharajh, L. R., Mkra, Z. P., Mngomezulu, S., Moodly, S., Mosito, C. P., & Ndlovu, S. (2018). *The state of inclusive education in South Africa and the implications for teacher training programmes*. British Council.
Makoelle, T. M. (2022). Social justice in higher education: A quest for equity, inclusion and epistemic access. In A. P. Ndofirepi, F. Maringe, S. Vurayai, & G. Erima (Eds.), *Decolonising African University knowledges, Volume 1: Voices on diversity and plurality* (1st ed., pp. 214–217). Routledge. https://doi.org/10.4324/9781003228233
Maree, J. G. (2014). *Barriers to access to and success in higher education: Intervention guidelines*. https://repository.up.ac.za/bitstream/handle/2263/41129/Maree_Barriers_2014.pdf?sequence=1&isAllowed=y
Moloi, T., & Salawu, M. (2020). *Institutionalizing technologies in South African universities: The imperatives in the Fourth Industrial Revolution era*. https://www.etdpseta.org.za/education/sites/default/files/2021-09/Institutionalizing%20Technologies%20in%20South%20African%20Universities.pdf

Moriña, A. (2017). Inclusive education in higher education: Challenges and opportunities. *European Journal of Special Needs Education, 32*(1), 3–17. https://doi.org/10.1080/08856257.2016.1254964

Ng'ambi, D., Brown, C., Bozalek, V., Gachago, D., & Wood, D. (2016). Technology enhanced teaching and learning in South African higher education – A rear view of a 20 year journey. *British Journal of Educational Technology, 47*(5), 843–858.

Ntema, R. P. (2022). Profiling students on risk of dropout at a university in South Africa, *Journal of Student Affairs in Africa, 10*(2), 179–194.

Ntombela, G. N. N. (2019). *The dynamics of inclusive education in further education and training in South Africa: A case study of two technical and vocational education and training colleges in Pietermaritzburg* [Doctoral dissertation]. University of Kwazulu-Natal, Durban.

Ntombela, S. (2013). Inclusive education and training in South African Higher Education: Mapping the experiences of a student with physical disability at university. *Africa Education Review, 10*(3), 483–501.

Nudelman, C. (2015). *Language in South Africa's higher education transformation: A study of language policies at four universities* [Master thesis]. University of Cape Town.

Salha, M. O. & Albadawi, B. (2021). Lead inclusive education in higher education: Challenges and opportunities. *Multicultural Education, 7*(11), 97–105.

Senekal, Q., & Lenz, R. (2020). Decolonising the South African Higher Education curriculum: An investigation into the challenges. *International Journal of Social Sciences and Humanity Studies, 12*(1), 146–160.

South Africa Department of Education (DoE). (1995). *White paper on education and training*. Government Printers.

South Africa DoE. (1996). *Green paper on higher education transformation*. Department of Education.

Department of Education of South Africa (1997). *The Higher Education Act 101 of 197*. Government Printers.

Department of Education. (2001). *The Education White Paper 6 on Inclusive Education*. Government Printers.

South Africa Ministry of Education. (1997). *Draft white paper on higher education* (No. 17944). Government Printers.

Stentiford, L., & Koutsouris, G. (2022). Critically considering the inclusive curriculum in higher education. *British Journal of Sociology of Education, 43*(8), 1250–1272.

Svendby, R. B. (2024). Inclusive teaching in higher education: Challenges of diversity in learning situations from the lecturer perspective, *Social Sciences, 13*(3), 140. https://doi.org/10.3390/socsci13030140

Tahir, K., Doelger, B., & Hynes, M. (2019). A case study on the ecology of inclusive education in the United States. *Journal for Leadership and Instruction, 18*(1), 17–24.

van Schalkwyk, F., & Canares, M. (2022). *Higher education, ICTs and inclusion: Assessing the impact of the COVID-19 pandemic.* https://osf.io/preprints/socarxiv/gd6jc

Chapter 2

# The Historical Development of Inclusive Education in South Africa: Higher Education Perspectives

*Thinavhudzulo Norman Mafumo, Michael Mbongiseni Buthelezi and Mohammed Xolile Ntshangase*

University of Limpopo, South Africa

## Abstract

This chapter analyses the historical development of inclusive education within the context of higher education. This study was conducted through interpretative qualitative research using unstructured and semi-structured interviews, focus groups, and observation. Data were analysed using a qualitative approach interpretive design. Among the main findings of the study is that there are many students who experience barriers to learning, such as learning and social and emotional problems, which could negatively influence their optimal learning and academic achievement. We, therefore, recommend expanding the debate about the inclusive educational system in South Africa to even include the issue of inequality in general among South Africans because there are those who were previously disadvantaged by the government system while others were favoured.

*Keywords*: Inclusive education; higher education; accessibility; teaching and learning support; infrastructure, exclusion

## Introduction

When the National party came into power in 1948, it introduced apartheid education system. Apartheid education system's main aim was to promote a separate

---

Inclusive Education in South African Further and Higher Education:
Reflections on Equity, Access, and Inclusion, 15–34
Copyright © 2025 by Thinavhudzulo Norman Mafumo, Michael Mbongiseni Buthelezi and Mohammed Xolile Ntshangase
Published under exclusive licence by Emerald Publishing Limited
doi:10.1108/978-1-83608-944-520251005

education system in South Africa which not only divided education system into races but also on the disabilities and abilities (Thobejane, 2013). The purpose of this chapter is to argue that South African education system was divided into the following racial categories: white, coloured, Indians as well as Blacks only education sub-systems as Gumede and Biyase (2016) argue, and as democracy gets matured people now have knowledge of how wrong that system was.

Exclusion in general and exclusion in education in particular, which was pioneered and promoted by the apartheid government in South Africa, was a widely discussed thorny issue in the discourse of education development in South Africa from the early 1980s (Mekoa, 2018). Although exclusion discussions focussed mainly on how students were deprived of getting an education due to social exclusion, after the inception of democracy, there was a shift in the focus of education. According to Walton and Engelbrecht (2022), the shift focussed on the conceptualisation, development, and formation of equitable rights and access to education irrespective of different racial groupings and ethnic groupings without forgetting different disabilities. In the early 1990s, exclusion was thoroughly debated in the deliberations of global education, and South Africa was not immune from these deliberations, as Matolo and Rambuda (2021) argue. Rapatsa (2022) adds that exclusion became a popular concept in education engagement because of its characteristics of promoting social injustices in societies, schools, and higher education institutions (HEIs). The deliberations were initiated with the sole intention of initiating the processes of addressing the social ills/social injustices promoted by exclusion, such as racial discrimination, ethnic discrimination, as well as ability and disability discrimination (Mutanga, 2023). According to Maseko (2024), these suppressive deliberations led to the contrary views that envisage conceptualisation, development, and promotion of inclusion in general and inclusion in education. Therefore, through the review of the literature, this chapter explored the historical implementation of inclusive education within the higher education context. The review traces inclusion developments in higher education since 1994. The following research questions guided the study: how has inclusive education evolved within the higher education context of South Africa? What were the challenges and successes from 1994 to 2024? Therefore, by answering these research questions, the chapter seeks to analyse the historical development of inclusive education within the higher education context.

## *Context*

When the Democratic Government of National Unity came into power in 1994 after the first democratic elections in South Africa, consultative processes phased out exclusion and promoted inclusion. According to Engelbrecht (2020), this resulted in the development of green papers and white papers such as Education White Paper 6: Special Needs Education: Building an Inclusive Education and Training System (EWP 6). All these consultative and policy development processes involved South Africans from different racial and dis[ability] groupings and backgrounds and they were conducted to redress the apartheid social injustices. According to Hungwe (2022), this effort was necessary to promote equality and equity among South Africans from different racial groupings as well as people with different dis[abilities], towards building one unitary South Africa.

The strenuous efforts by the first South African Democratic Government of developing and implementing the above policies resulted in the drives to offset the historical disadvantages or imbalances and discriminatory education system, which in turn came with a range of enabling provisions that enhance access to and ensure the increasing enrolment of learners in schools and universities in South Africa. These processes were aimed at the inclusion of all students in South African higher education irrespective of their (students) racial groupings and dis (abilities). Therefore, inclusion is the process of addressing and responding to the diversity of needs of all students by increasing their participation and integration in the teaching and learning process. Furthermore, Inclusive education can be considered an approach to make education universal irrespective of different racial categories and any disability to maintain equity in education. It promotes that learners and students from different racial categories and different special needs can be included in the education system without any differentiation.

> An inclusive education was adopted in South Africa where all children and students can learn together within a seamless system of support that addresses not only disabilities but also range barriers of learning arising from poverty, inequality and other social conditions. (Department of Education, 2001a)

This chapter argues that the inclusive education journey in the South African education system remains a good dream to be realised because it is one of those injustices that cannot be entirely redressed at once. However, if South Africa could conceptualise and develop the practical part of inclusive education, the journey could strengthen social cohesion, which could later strengthen the South African dream of promoting social justice in the South African education system, as Ntshangase and Mafumo (2024) argue. In the case of South Africa, inclusion in education goes beyond only opening educational institutions to all races and differential abilities, but as Pillay and Shipalana (2023) argue, this should extend to the issues of infrastructural support. Furthermore, the concept of inclusion involves the process of modifying the way institutions of higher education support and address the diverse needs of each learner in the institutions.

EWP 6 (South Africa Department of Education, 2001, p. 31) briefly mentions student inclusion in higher education when it states the following: 'The ministry, therefore, expects institutions to indicate in their institutional plans the strategies and steps, with the relevant time frames, they intend taking to increase the enrolment of these learners.'

When this policy was published, it did not state who should take responsibility for equalising access to higher education for students who experience barriers to learning. It also does not provide clear guidelines on the steps that should be taken to make HEIs inclusive, nor does it state any goals that HEIs should work towards achieving.

Changing the South African education system to an inclusive education practice started with the establishment of the National Commission on Special Needs in Education and Training (NCSNET) in 1996, along with the National Committee on Education Support Services (NCESS) in 1997. The report, 'Quality education for All: Overcoming barriers to learning' (created by the joint NCSNET and NCESS) emphasised the need for a paradigm shift, from a focus on learners with special needs to a systemic approach in identifying and addressing barriers to learning (Engelbrecht, 2006). The viewpoint of both the NCSNET and NCESS was that barriers to learning should not be perceived as residing only in the individual but within the learning system as well (Green, 2001, p. 13) (cf. 2.6.1). The issue of human rights moved to the forefront of all policy-making and subsequently the documents that followed focussed on the integration of special and ordinary education. In 2001, Education White Paper 6: Special Needs Education, building an inclusive education and training system, was published. This document became the foundation on which inclusive education in South Africa would be built and placed inclusive education and its focus on addressing barriers to learning, at the core of education transformation in South Africa. The key focus of EWP 6 (South Africa Department of Education, 2001, p. 6) is on acknowledging that all children and youth can learn and that all children and youth need support.

In many countries and publications, the phrases 'special needs' and disabilities are still used; however, the accepted term in South Africa is 'barriers to learning' (South Africa Department of Education, 2001). According to Howell (as referenced in Walton et al., 2009, p. 107) this term is preferable to 'special needs', which signifies a medical or deficit approach to educational difficulties and locates the problem within the learner, rather than the system. Donald et al. (2006, p. 3) define a barrier to learning as 'any factor that is a hindrance or obstacle to a student's ability to learn'. Barriers to learning may be best understood as resulting from a complex interplay of learners and their contexts, including the reality of impairments or disabilities, socio-economic restraints, and wider societal factors including values, attitudes, policies, and institutions (Walton et al., 2009, p. 3). Thus, if a student has some impairment or disability, the barrier lies in the interaction between the student and the different contexts (home, university, peer group, wider society) in which he finds himself. The focus should shift from 'fixing' the student to addressing the barriers that prevent the student from achieving academic success. The Screening, Identification, Assessment and Support strategy manual (South Africa Department of Education, 2008, p. 8) describes barriers to learning as difficulties that arise within the education system as a whole, the learning site and/or within the learner himself, which complicate access to learning and development for learners. Thus, there are intrinsic factors located within the student, and extrinsic factors located outside the student that could have an impact on academic achievement. Intrinsic barriers to learning refer to factors that are located within the student that have an impact on students' learning and academic performance. Intrinsic barriers to learning include physical, sensory, neurological and developmental impairments, chronic illness, psycho-social disturbances, and differing intellectual ability (Walton et al., 2009, p. 107). In contrast, extrinsic barriers to learning refer to factors that arise outside the student. Especially in a developing country such as South Africa, these barriers are prominent (Nel et al., 2012, p. 15).

Education in South Africa has always been dominated by unequal access to education, which resulted in unequal opportunities at school and in the workplace. To date, the situation is still more or less the same. According to Mohamed (2020, p. 2), the South African education system continues to be persistently subjected to stark inequalities and prolonged underperformance of learners that have deep roots in the legacy of apartheid and are still not addressed by the current government. In other words, education is still not transformed even with the development of 'equal education for all' policies. People and children with barriers to learning are the most affected. Some have no access to education and the level of poverty affects them the most. There has been utmost mistreatment, neglect, and lack of resources and facilities for Black learners especially those with special needs (Muthukrishna & Schoeman, 2000, p. 316). This is informed by the resistance of officials and teachers to implement change (Snyder, 2017, p. 2). This results in low success rate because teachers still use the same teaching methods for all learners despite learners having different educational needs. In addition, many learners are still not identified and teachers are still not supported and trained. Learners are treated the same despite being different and their needs are different.

Students with physical disabilities have a long-standing history of facing more challenges in accessing higher education compared to students without physical disabilities. The case is severe in underdeveloped countries due to varied factors such as stigma, prior exclusion from primary and secondary education, social isolation, and resource constraints (Datta et al., 2019; Lord & Stein, 2018). To this end, Bicket and Wall (2009) reported that some universities in the United Kingdom (UK) were failing to provide accessible accommodation or facilities to students with disabilities. It was discovered that about 40% of the 78 HEIs surveyed did not have accessible rooms to cater for students with disabilities, thus resulting in students having to live at home. This is one of many challenges faced by students with disabilities in both developed and developing countries (Mutanga & Walker, 2017). Students with physical impairments are part of a HEI's student population, but they have special needs arising from their impairments. Riddell et al. (2005) pointed out that the legal duties of HEIs towards students with disabilities have increased over the years. Countries like the UK, which includes England, Scotland, and Wales, passed laws and policies that force HEIs to take responsibility by providing reasonable facilities, which enable students with physical impairments to gain equal access to higher education (Matthews, 2009). This background shows that quite a number of countries, among others Australia, the United States of America, and African countries such as Uganda and South Africa, struggle to provide equal access for students with disabilities to HEIs (Foundation of Tertiary Institutions of the Northern Metropolis, 2011; Harpur & Stein, 2019). This is confusing in the context of South Africa, where the country unreservedly signed and adopted the 1990 World Declaration on Education for All in Jomtien, which seeks to ensure a universal 'access to education for all children, youth and adults, as well as the promotion of equality' (Mutanga, 2018, p. 229).

In the next section, the focus is on international policies and legislation related to persons with disabilities.

## *South African Policies Perspective*

In South Africa, after 1994, the Supreme Law was developed (the Constitution of South Africa, 1996 (section 29 (1) (b)), the Bill of Rights), which promotes the values of human rights and prohibits all forms of discrimination. It entrenches the right of equality and access to equal education for all persons and provides for measures to address past imbalances (Republic of South Africa, 1996). Chapter 2 (the Bill of Rights) of the Constitution of South Africa also promotes equality which mandates the state not to discriminate directly or indirectly against anyone in terms of race, gender, sex, pregnancy, marital status, ethnic origin, colour, sexual orientation, age, disability, religion, belief, culture, language, and birth (Republic of South Africa, 1996). This was followed by many policies, which aimed to address all forms of discrimination, especially against marginalised persons. In noting the anti-discrimination notions as mentioned in the Constitution of the Republic of South Africa, the South African higher policy frameworks emphasise the issue of redress of past inequalities and transforming the higher education system to serve a social order and marginalised persons including people with disabilities. It also addresses the goals and strategic objectives which promote the provision of increasing access to higher education to all irrespective of race, gender, age, class, or disability (Department of Education, 1997). The state provided the guidance and guidelines to government departments to create conducive environments for persons with disabilities (Handbook on Reasonable Accommodation for Persons with Disabilities in the Public Service, 2007). This handbook provides information on reasonable accommodation and accessibility in terms of the physical environment of the institution. The Department of Education formulated policy such as The National Plan for Higher Education (Department of Education, 2001b), which emphasises the inclusion of students with disability into mainstream education and specifies the expected number of students with disability to be enrolled at a certain time within higher education (Department of Education, 2001b). Another important policy framework developed in 2018 was the Strategic Policy Framework on Disability for the Post-School Education and Training System (Department of Higher Education and Training (DHET), 2018, p. 15). The aim of this policy is to:

- create an inclusive PSET system for people with disabilities;
- guide PSET institutions in the creation of an enabling environment for people with disabilities;
- provide the DHET with a monitoring and evaluation instrument to ensure that disability compliance is mainstreamed in all PSET institutions;
- realise the goals of the White Paper on the Rights of Persons with Disabilities in PSET institutions; and
- ensure the mainstreaming of people with disabilities in the PSET system.

The Department of Social Development developed the White Paper on the Rights of Persons with Disabilities (WPRPD) (Department of Social Development, 2015). The purpose of this WPRPD, to mention a few, is to:

- provide a mainstreaming trajectory for realising the rights of persons with disabilities through the development of targeted interventions that remove barriers and apply the principles of universal design;

- provide clarity on and guide the development of standard operating procedures;
- stipulate norms and standards for the removal of discriminatory barriers that perpetuate the exclusion and segregation of persons with disabilities;
- stipulate norms and standards to remove discriminatory barriers which exclude and segregate persons with disabilities;
- broadly outline the responsibilities and accountabilities of the various stakeholders involved in providing barrier-free, appropriate, effective, efficient, and coordinated service delivery to persons with disabilities;
- provide the framework for a uniform and coordinated approach by all government institutions in the mainstreaming of disability across all planning, design, budgeting, implementation, and monitoring of services; and
- guide gender mainstreaming to ensure that women with disabilities enjoy equitable access to all women empowerment and gender equality legislation, policies, and programmes (Bucholz, 2017).

In spite of all these measures from policies and regulations, further challenges remain. Scholars such as Bucholz (2017, p. 24) highlight that 'despite the call for transformation and equity in these policies, the majority of students with physical impairments remain subjected to different challenges'. In this section, we discuss previous studies conducted on the experiences of students with physical impairments, regarding the accessibility to higher education, inadequate and inaccessible infrastructure, learning and institutional support, stigmatisation, and discrimination.

## *Lessons from Existing Research*

A need for inclusion in higher and further education has influenced a wide variety of research. This section highlights the prominent research themes.

*Accessibility to Higher Education*

When most countries address the issue of persons with disabilities, they apply the inclusion and integration principles (Jali, 2009). The inclusion principle emphasises equity while integration is a way of incorporating those members who are excluded or a marginalised group such as persons with disabilities back into the society (Jali, 2009). The exclusion principle promotes that those students with physical disabilities be excluded in the learning environment. The aim of inclusion education is to promote oneness within students because it embraces the diversity introduced by students with physical impairments in the learning environment (Jali, 2009). The principle of equity encourages fair opportunities to enter higher education programmes and to succeed, while the integration principle promotes the acceptance of all learners in the regular classrooms (Collins et al., 2018; Du Plessis, 2013; Jali, 2009). During colonialism in African countries, access to higher education was restricted to able-bodied persons by colonial authorities (Teferra & Altbachl, 2004) and the persons with disabilities were not even considered (Subrayen, 2011). In a study conducted by Gidley et al. (2010), they found that Australian Higher Education is based on concepts related to access, participation, and success imperatives. This emphasised the inclusion of students with physical impairments in the mainstream of higher education. The South African government encourages HEIs to recruit students with disability, to see the committed implementation of policies that encourage inclusion of students with disability into the mainstream. The Education White Paper 3: A Programme for Transformation of Higher Education (Department of Education, 1997) promotes the provision of increased access to higher education irrespective of race, gender, age, class, or disability.

The inclusive education view incorporates equality of opportunities for every person. Mittler (2000) defines inclusion as a radical reform of the school in terms of access, curriculum, assessment, and grouping of learners. Howell (2005) indicates that, due to inclusive education, the number of students with physical impairments who were previously marginalised has increased enrolment in HEIs. Social redress should include the provision of resources to education institutions who deal with the learning needs of students with disability.

*Inadequate and Inaccessible Infrastructure*

Donald et al. (2002) describe mobility as an ability to move around. According to Donald et al. (2002), physical disabilities may range from the loss of a limb or limbs to conditions where the muscles are affected so that the person cannot adequately control body position or movement. As a result, students with physical disabilities need accessible infrastructure such as library, tuition block, lecture halls, accommodation, administration block, toilets, and safe and appropriate learning environment (Mutanga & Walker, 2017). The HEIs should ensure that their buildings' infrastructure, such as doors, office administration block, lifts, lecture halls, cafeteria library, and accommodation are accessible to everyone, as some students with physical impairments use crutches and wheelchairs. It has been noted that, most often, the HEIs' infrastructure is not designed to be user-friendly for students with physical impairment or those with special needs, thus restricting easy access (Ahmad, 2016; Allen & Cowdery, 2009; Buthelezi, 2014; Engelbrecht & De Beer, 2014; Maotoana, 2014; Mosia & Phasha, 2017; Mutanga, 2017). They also further state that this challenge manifests itself when students with physical impairments go about their activities of daily living at HEIs. This challenge addressed by the South African government by drawing up The South African National Plan in Higher Education (Department of Education, 2001b) requests institutions of higher education to provide suitable infrastructure for students with disability. There are a number of challenges faced by students with impairments based on inaccessible infrastructure, such as multiple storey buildings with no lifts for physically challenged students (Buthelezi, 2014). Other buildings have no ramps for wheelchair users, which makes it difficult for wheelchair users to access the tuition block, lecture halls, and computer labs. Even lecture halls need to be redesigned to allow a safe and appropriate learning environment for students with impairments, especially wheelchair users (Allen & Cowdery, 2009). Furniture such as desks need to be adjusted lower to suit wheelchair users since they do not move to the normal chairs. Another challenge is that the ablution facilities are not at all user friendly for persons with disabilities. Donald et al. (2002) argue that there must be accessible ablution facilities for wheelchair users to move around easily and the toilet seat must be of a similar height to a standard wheelchair to facilitate transfer from the wheelchair to the toilet seat. Administration buildings should be designed for wheelchair users to move through or to turn around, and passages and public spaces must not be obstructed in any way. Reception desks should be low enough so that a person of short stature or a person using a wheelchair can comfortably see the receptionist (Department of Public Service and Administration, 2007). All doorways should be sufficiently wide to admit a person using a wheelchair. Knoll (2009) highlights that education institutions should make their learning environments more accessible and welcoming, especially to people with disabilities to promote full participation.

*Learning Support*

The main objective of HEIs is to empower and equip students with the necessary knowledge and to ensure that particular knowledge is accessible to all students. The HEIs have a mandate to disseminate knowledge through different learning methods and support such as assistive aids, support from the HEIs staff, academic programmes, special examination venues, and student development programmes.

*Assistive Aids and Technology as Learning Support Resources*  HEIs should have assistive aids to enhance education for students with impairments. They should have video tapes, Braille, hearing aids, internet access and information available in large print, as well as awareness and good liaison among the institutional stakeholders (Van Jaarsveldt & Ndeya-Ndereya, 2015). Pudaruth et al. (2017) highlighted that students with disabilities should be empowered to become more active users of technology. They should be assisted to make informed decisions about technology, which will benefit their learning processes both on and off campus. The use of assistive technology, for example, Optical Character Recognition, which scans text to be read aloud by the computer's sound card, or speech recognition for converting the spoken word to printed word on the computer screen, supports meaningful and accessible learning (Chataika, 2019). Mutanga (2017) illustrates that though assistive technology heightens admittance to learning for students with disability, at times, it eliminates other students because it is designed for specific kinds of people. Some software, for example, could not read mathematical and scientific signs or graphics material (Mokiwa & Phasha, 2012).

*Staff Support to Enhance Learning Outcomes*  The role of lecturing staff, non-lecturing staff, and administration staff is vital. Therefore, training of the staff at the HEIs is needed to be able to handle students with impairment. Students with physical impairments receive different responses from lecturing staff and non-lecturing staff ranging from helpful to unsupportive (Holloway, 2001). A study conducted by Mutanga and Walker (2017) indicates that some lecturing staff distanced themselves from providing necessary support to students with disabilities because of negative attitudes. They further state that those who distanced themselves displayed a lack of involvement with students with disabilities and tended to refer them to the Disability Unit or Student Support Services at the institution. In an earlier study, Haywood (2014) mentions that lecturing staff reveal their lack of disability awareness resulting in the non-visibility of appropriate academic reasonable accommodations for students with impairment. This lack of support from the staff resulted in suffering and discrimination within the educational institution. In returning to Mutanga and Walker (2017), where they explored the academic lives of students with disabilities at South African Universities from the lecturers' perspectives, their study reveals that some lecturers do not understand diversity and, as a result, they eliminate students with disabilities in their teaching and learning activities. Their study also concurs with Buthelezi (2014) who found that lecturing staff lack professional training in dealing with diversity matters and particularly disability issues.

*Institutional Support*   According to the Education White Paper 6: Special Needs Education: Building an Inclusive Education and Training System (Department of Education, 2001a), students with disabilities should have equal opportunities within society and should be given the necessary support to enable them to exercise their rights. It further states that all students have equal rights to education and students with physical impairments have the right to receive the support needed for them to acquire knowledge. The Education White Paper 6: Special Needs Education: Building an Inclusive Education and Training System (Department of Education, 2001a) also outlines the inclusion of students with disabilities such that each HEI should draft its own institutional plan to support students with disabilities (Department of Education, 2001b). This means that each educational institution should develop their own Disability Unit or Student Support Office, which will deal with the needs, matters, and support of students with disabilities (Gumbi et al., 2015). This unit should cater for both students and staff and provide some of the required services (Mutanga, 2017). The question of how the academic and administration staff who are disabled receive support in the HEIs remains unanswered. Engelbrecht and De Beer (2014) noted that in some HEIs, even though students with disabilities disclosed their disability, the institution did not have any mechanism for routinely providing such information to student support services. Ahmad (2016) concurs with Engelbrecht and De Beer (2014) that disabled student services offered at the HEIs do not have relevant support services pertaining to specific disabilities.

*Support Offered by the Disability Units and Student Support Services*

The main function of Disability Units is to assist in identifying and helping students with disability and allow people with disabilities to voice their concerns (Ntombela, 2013). It also assists students with physical impairments to communicate their frustration and misperceptions about them and their disability as well as to facilitate and coordinate specific support services for students with disabilities (Gobalakrishnan, 2013). In instances where Disability Units did not perform according to students' needs, students with disability felt unwelcome at their institutions (Mutanga, 2017). Disability Units or student support services must ensure equal opportunities for students with disabilities in teaching and learning (Shevlin et al., 2004). They must also ensure that the needs of the students with impairments such as special exam venues, library, student residence, IT technician, orientation and mobility practitioner, braille assistant practitioner, and the librarian are available. The challenge of the disability unit or support services is that students do not receive expected help such as emotional support and counselling due to untrained staff or non-functioning of the offices (Buthelezi, 2014; Maotoana, 2014; Moodley & Mchunu, 2019). Naidoo (2010) concurs with Maotoana (2014) that even though disability units are there, the facilities and services offered are insufficient to assist students with disabilities. Another challenge is that not all disability units cater for all types of impairments at HEIs. Mutanga (2017) notes that, in newer and smaller disability units, it is primarily only those students with visual or mobility challenges who are catered for.

*Stigmatisation and Discrimination*

While there is a distinction between the concepts of stigma and discrimination, it has proven difficult to strike the exact difference (Deacon et al., 2009). Therefore, it is vitally important to separate the two concepts since both present a challenge to people with disability. Stigmatisation and discrimination can be experienced in and outside the HEIs (Goffman, 1963). Goffman (1963) defined stigma as a discrediting attribute assigned by society to those who differ in some custom from society's expectations. While discrimination refers to treating people from the same group differently, with some getting worse treatment than others (unfair or unequal treatment) (Larson, 2012). Deacon (2006) argues that stigma and discrimination are different processes, which can happen without following the other. Mnisi (2014) states that stigmatisation can happen where there is no active discrimination happening. According to Abbey et al. (2011), discrimination can occur when the stigmatisation has occurred by concrete behaviour such as exclusion and rejection. Deacon (2006, p. 421) concurs that 'stigma as something that results in discrimination'. For instance, stigma interferes with social interaction where society does not fully accept persons with physical disabilities due to certain physical attributes that are different from able-bodied persons. As a result, people with disability in that particular society experience exclusion and discrimination from fully participating (Harris & Enfield, 2003). Stigmatisation can manifest as an aversion to avoidance, social rejection, discounting, discrediting, dehumanisation, and depersonalisation of others into stereotypic caricatures (Dovidio et al., 2000).

In HEIs, students with physical impairments experience stigmatisation because of their disability. For instance, no one is prepared to listen to their opinions because they are disabled (Pudaruth et al., 2017). Maotoana (2014) adds that those people with disability are exposed to discrimination because they are from minority populations. As a result, students with impairments may choose at times not to declare their disability for administrative convenience, for identity reasons, to pass as 'normal', or to avoid possible stigma and discrimination (Riddell & Weedon, 2014). Another challenge faced by students with impairment is negative attitudes displayed by staff and peers (Seale et al., 2008; Subrayen, 2011). It is worth noting that students with impairments develop emotional and psychological problems due to a lack of support from the HEI (Gorter, 2009). In the following section, scholarly evidence is provided on the experiences of institutional and learning support available for students with physical disabilities in higher education.

## Methodology

The researchers hereby base the chapter on the review of literature from 1994, when SA gained a democratic government, to the present. They are tracing higher education inclusion developments over a period of 30 years, with the hope of arriving at some understanding of the achievements and gaps.

### *An Interpretative Research Paradigm*

A paradigm is a worldview and a framework that guides research (Mackenzie & Knipe, 2006). The interpretivist paradigm is also known as Constructivist paradigm. It emphasises understanding of both the individual and their interpretation of their world (Kivunja & Kuyini, 2017; Thanh & Thanh, 2015). The interpretivist paradigm is helpful when attempting to understand the experiences, perceptions, values, and cultural norms of participants in their social settings (Babbie & Mouton, 2001). The reality in interpretivist paradigm is socially constructed (Bogdan & Biklen, 1998). It allows for multiple reconstructions of the ideas, or that the data could lead to more than one conclusion (Bertram & Christiansen, 2014). The knowledge and conclusion are subjective. This means that the information is collected on the participant's experience from their perspective (Willing, 2001). Creswell (2003) concurs that the interpretive paradigm researcher relies upon the participants' views of the situation being studied while Winberg (1997) emphasises that interpretive paradigm displays how an individual interprets their reality. 'This is why sometimes this paradigm has been called the Constructivist paradigm' (Kivunja & Kuyini, 2017, p. 33). Cohen and Manion (1994) emphasise that it is the world of human experience that interpretive researchers understand. It is for that reason we used interpretive paradigm, which aims to understand the world of human experience from an individual perspective (Cohen & Manion, 1994; Cohen et al., 2011). It was deemed suitable for this study since the reality to be studied was from the participants' subjective experiences, opinions, and views regarding their equity and access which means that they shared their individual experiences about their social context. This also blended well with the qualitative techniques which were used in this study.

### *Qualitative Research Design*

Kothari (2004) explains that a research design is both a plan and a strategy. The plan specifies relevant sources and types of information and the strategy specifies the approach to use when gathering and analysing data. In this chapter, we used the qualitative approach interpretive design.

Qualitative research was suitable for this study because it aimed to explore, discover, develop an understanding, describe and report on the study and gain an understanding of underlying reasons, opinions, and motivations (Creswell, 2013). The research problem required the researchers to allow the students with learning barriers to draw from their own experiences. Jali (2009) states that qualitative research is relevant to studying social relations because it helps the researchers to understand the actions and meaning of different societies and settings. Qualitative research analyses people's individual and collective social actions, beliefs, thoughts and perceptions (White, 2005). The reality is socially constructed in qualitative research (Mertens, 2005). Thompson (1992) concurs that qualitative research is a collection of approaches to enquiry, all of which rely on verbal, visual and auditory data (tape recorder). From the above discussion, it is clear that qualitative research focusses on lived human experiences and the interpretations of the environment in which they live (Silverman, 1993). Therefore, qualitative research was appropriate for this study.

### *Data Generation Tools*

Qualitative data collection methods vary using unstructured or semi-structured techniques. Qualitative uses methods such as focus groups, individual interviews, description and observations. Qualitative research uses a small sample of participants as it is indulging in in-depth investigation and participants are selected to fulfil a given quota (Miles et al., 1994). Researchers identified two suitable data generation tools to be used to collect qualitative data and answer the research questions posed. Semi-structured interviews and observation were used to collect data. Observations were used once as the participants were observed in terms of their emotions and feelings while they related or described their lived experiences. The reason for the once-off observation is that it brought the painful and sad reality of educational exclusion which would not be nice to be timeously repeated as it risks traumatising the participants.

### *Selection of Participants*

The selection of participants in this study was done as shown in Table 2.1.

## Findings

The analysis of data from focus groups, individual interviews, description, and observations yielded the following themes: Accessibility to higher education, inadequate and inaccessible infrastructure, institutional support, and stigmatisation and discrimination. Many students, including persons with disabilities, still encounter barriers to full and equitable participation in teaching and learning, and many institutions still have far to go in improving their accessibility services and supports. Higher education should be available and accessible to all students regardless of

Table 2.1. Summary of Participants.

| Type of Data Collection | Participants | Selection Method | Number |
| --- | --- | --- | --- |
| *Focus groups* | Students | Purposive sampling | 18 |
| *Unstructured and semi-structured interviews* | Instructors | Purposive sampling | 15 |

physical, sensory, mental, or emotional abilities (McCormack, 2023). There is still no provision of resources to education institution to deal with the learning needs of students with disability. There are a number of challenges faced by students with impairments based on inaccessible infrastructure, such as multiple storey buildings with no lifts for physically challenged students (Buthelezi, 2014). Students with physical impairments have the right to receive the support needed for them to acquire knowledge. Ahmad (2016) concurs with Engelbrecht and De Beer (2014) that disabled student services offered at the HEIs do not have relevant support services pertaining to specific disabilities. Students with disability experience exclusion and discrimination from full participating (Harris & Enfield, 2003).

## Discussion

### Inclusion Achievements and Gaps in Higher Education

*Difficulty in Transforming the System*

Since this study shows that the issue of inclusion in higher education has been one of the difficult transformative aspects in this democratic era, South Africa has battled for some time with this issue like other third world countries. Many scholars like Abbey et al. (2011) give forth a fully-fledged narrative of the struggles for social justice against racism, discrimination of disabled people, and many other forms of manifest injustice in South Africa. All these could not happen without the education system included, hence the South African education system pre-1994 was laden with unimaginable levels of inequality, lack of discussion about equity, lack of access to higher education, and many other forms of exclusion that according to Thobejane (2013) made a life of black disabled person unbearable. The issue of exclusivity in higher education during apartheid though was caused by the government of that time who was against inclusivity of any form as that was a vivid threat to the kind of what was then 'a wanted state' (Maseko, 2024).

*Lack of Inclusive Policy Implementation*

Although one cannot clap and celebrate that post-1994 government was interested in democracy, cries about inclusion in higher education system of South Africa have not ended. Hungwe (2022) and Maseko (2024) argue that many South African people think that inclusion in higher education system means that everyone must be allowed to go the institutions of higher learning and have space to study, while it actually means more than that. To be clear, the case of educational inclusive educational system in the history of South Africa shows that inclusivity is still a mirage or a dream if the debate would be only limited to the ability and being allowed to go to any institution and learn. According to Mutanga (2023) there are additional factors like access to the institution itself, and he narrates the cases of poverty, lack of resources, lack of facilities, unequal quality of education in differently historicised institutions, and many more.

Among many issues, this chapter strictly argues that conceptualising inclusive educational system with all major elements of exclusive educational system still involved mystifies the whole process of striving for inclusive education system in South Africa. However, researchers like Walton and Engelbrecht (2022) acknowledge that some work continues to be done in South Africa to create an inclusive educational system like drafting some statutes like Education White Paper 6, but the question is how much of that actually gets implemented. So, in an existentially differentiated state in terms of abilities, races, classes, skills, and so on, it really becomes difficult to emerge to a complete state of having a functional inclusive educational system.

## Conclusion

This chapter has highlighted that inclusion in higher education is well supported by policy with a slow pacing on moving policy intends to implementation. The post-apartheid government managed to enact educational system regulations like Education White Paper 6, which do not cover other aspects and also lack implementation in everyday life. Limited research has been done on the inclusion of students with barriers to learning in South African HEIs. From the researchers' own experience in working with students at a university, there are many students who experience barriers to learning, such as learning, social, and emotional problems, which could negatively influence their optimal learning and academic achievement. Although a support centre is in place at the university where the researchers are teaching, from the researchers' own experience, it does not function adequately to meet the needs of all students who experience various barriers to learning. This could be due to factors such as a shortage of trained staff, the time that it takes to effectively help a student and the inability to cope with the volume of referrals. The support structure for students with learning barriers in South African universities is situated within student services and even though a high number of institutions do provide support services for students with learning barriers, the range of support seems to be limited to blindness, deafness, and paraplegia. This study may recommend expanding the debate about inclusive educational system in South Africa to even include the issue of inequality in general among South Africans, because there are those that were previously disadvantaged by government system while others were favoured. Access to education must be the first point when debating about the inclusive educational system in South Africa because that will quickly lead to availability of supportive infrastructure (to accommodate differential abilities), inequality of educational institutions due to different backgrounds, affluence to even succeed in the group that gains access in higher education. Throughput must be second point in the inclusive educational system debates in South Africa because it speaks to the real issues of having access to higher education and have not support when inside. Support in this case refers to educational enablers which include hunger due to home poverty because studying in poverty might be as difficult as climbing the stairways with a wheelchair.

## References

Abbey, S., Charbonneau, M., Tranulis, C., Moss, P., Baici, W., Dabby, L., Gautam, M., & Paré, M. (2011). Stigma and discrimination. *Canadian Journal of Psychiatry, 56*(10), 1–9.

Ahmad, W. (2016). Higher education for persons with disabilities in India: Challenges and concerns. *Journal of Disability Management and Rehabilitation, 2*(1), 1–4.

Allen, K. E., & Cowdery, G. E. (2009). *The exceptional child: Inclusion in early childhood education* (6th ed.). Thomson/Delmar Learning.

Babbie, E., & Mouton, J. (2001). *The practice of social research*. Oxford University Press.

Bertram, C., & Christiansen, I. (2014). *Understanding research: An introduction to reading research*. Van Schaik.

Bicket, D., & Wall, M. (2009). BBC News in the United States: A super-alternative' news medium emerges. *Media, Culture & Society, 31*(3), 365–384.

Bogdan, R., & Biklen, S. K. (1998). *Qualitative research for education: An introduction to theories and methods*. Allyn and Bacon, Inc.

Bucholz, A. W. (2017). *The experiences of a student with cerebral palsy at a higher education institution: A case study* [Thesis presented in partial fulfilment of the requirements for the degree of Master of Education in Educational Support in the Faculty of Education at Stellenbosch University].

Buthelezi, M. M. (2014). *Exploring challenges experienced by physically challenged students at a Further Education and Training College in KwaZulu-Natal Province* [Masters dissertation, University of South Africa].

Chataika, T. (2019). *The Routledge handbook of disability in southern Africa*. Routledge.

Cohen, L., & Manion, L. (1994). *Research methods in education*. Routledge.

Cohen, L., Manion, L., & Morrison, K. (2011). *Research methods in education*. Routledge.

Collins, A., Azmat, F., & Rentschler, R. (2018). 'Bringing everyone on the same journey': Revisiting inclusion in higher education. *Studies in Higher Education, 44*(8), 1–13.

Constitution of South Africa. (1996). *Constitution of South Africa*. GovernmentPrinters.

Creswell, J. W. (2003). *Research design: Qualitative, quantitative, and mixed methods design*. SAGE.

Creswell, J. W. (2013). *Research design: Qualitative, quantitative, and mixed methods approaches* (4th Ed.). SAGE Publications, Inc.

Datta, P., Halder, S., Talukdar, J., & Aspland, T. (2019). Barriers and enablers to inclusion of university students with disabilities in India and Australia. In S. Halder, V. Argyropoulos, (Eds.), *Inclusion, equity and access for individuals with disabilities*. Palgrave Macmillan. https://doi.org/10.1007/978-981-13-5962-0_26

Deacon, H. (2006). Towards a sustainable theory of health-related stigma: Lessons from the HIV/AIDS literature. *Journal of Community & Applied Social Psychology, 16*(6), 418–425.

Deacon, S. H., Wade-Woolley, L., & Kirby, J. R. (2009). Flexibility in young second-language learners: Examining the language specificity of orthographic processing. *Journal of Research in Reading, 32*(2), 215–229.

Department of Education. (1997). *Education White Paper 3: A program for the transformation of higher education*. Government Printers.

Department of Education. (2001a). *Education White Paper 6: Special Needs Education: Building an inclusive education and training system.* Government Printers.
Department of Education. (2001b). *National plan for higher education.* Government Printers.
Department of Education. (2001c). *Special needs education: Building an inclusive education and training system* [Education White Paper 6]. https://www.gov.za/sites/default/files/gcis_document/201409/educ61.pdf
Department of Higher Education and Training (DHET). (2018). *Strategic disability policy framework in the post-school education and training system.* Retrieved on February 3, 2024, from http://www.dhet.gov.za/SiteAssets/Gazettes/Approved%20Strategic%20Disability%2 0Policy%20Framework%20Layout220518.pdf
Department of Public Service and Administration. (2007). *Handbook on reasonable accommodation for people with disabilities in the public service* https://www.gov.za/sites/default/files/gcis_document/201409/dpsaannualreport20062007.pdf.
Department of Social Development. (2015). *The white paper on the rights of persons with disabilities* (WPRPD). Retrieved October 17, 2019. https://www.gcis.gov.za/sites/default/files/docs/resourcecentre/yearbook/SocialDevelopment-SAYB1516.pdf
Donald, D., Lazarus, S., & Lolwana, P. (2002). *Educational psychology in social context* (2nd ed.). Oxford University Press.
Donald, D., Lazarus, S., & Lolwana, P. (2006). *Educational psychology in social context* (3rd ed.). Oxford University Press.
Dovidio, J. F., Major, B., & Crocker, J. (2000). Stigma: Introduction and overview. In T. F. Heatherton, R. E. Kleck, M. R. Hebl, & J. G. Hull (Eds.), *The social psychology of stigma* (pp. 1–26). Guilford Press.
Du Plessis, P. (2013). Legislation and policies: Progress towards the right to inclusive education. *De Jure, 46*(1), 76–92.
Engelbrecht, L., & De Beer, J. J. (2014). Access constraints experienced by physically disabled students at a South African higher education institution. *Africa Education Review, 11*(4), 544–562.
Engelbrecht, P. (2006). The implementation of inclusive education in South Africa after ten years of democracy. *European Journal of Psychology of Education, 21*(3), 253–264.
Engelbrecht, P. (2020). Inclusive education: Developments and challenges in South Africa. *Prospects, 49*(3–4), 219–232.
Foundation of Tertiary Institutions of the Northern Metropolis. (2011). *Disability in Higher Education.* Project Report.
Gidley, J. (2010). An other view of integral futures: De/reconstructing the IF brand, futures: *The Journal of Policy, Planning and Futures Studies, 42*(2), 125–133.
Gobalakrishnan, C. (2013). Problem faced by physically challenged persons and their awareness towards welfare measures. *International Journal of Innovative Research & Development Supreme Court*, 2017, The Supreme Court of Mauritius: Legislations alphabetical. Retrieved May 7, 2019, from https://supremecourt.govmu.org/_Layouts/CLIS.DMS/Act/ActGroup.aspx
Goffman, E. (1963). *Stigma.* Spectrum.
Gorter, J. W. (2009). Determinants of students' attitudes towards peers with disabilities. *Developmental Medicine & Child Neurology, 15*(6), 417–418.
Green, L. (2001). Theoretical and contextual background. In P. Engelbrecht & L. Green (Eds.), *Promoting learner development: Preventing and working with barriers to learning* (pp. 3–15). Van Schaik.
Gumbi, D., Cekiso, M., Gqweta, Z., Makiwane, B., Majeke, L., Bojanyana, N., Dlava, B., & Wakaba, L. (2015). An exploration of challenges related to inclusion of students with disabilities at a university of technology in South Africa. *International Journal of Educational Sciences, 8*(2), 261–266.

Gumede, V., & Biyase, M. (2016). Educational reforms and curriculum transformation in post-apartheid South Africa. *Environmental Economics, 7*(2), 69–76.

Harris, A., & Enfield, S. (2003). *Disability, equality and human rights: A training manual for development and humanitarian organisations.* Oxfam GB.

Harpur, P., & Stein, M. A. (2019). Children with disabilities, human rights and sustainable development. In G. Fenton-Glynn (Ed.), *Children's rights and sustainable development: Interpreting the UNCRC for future generations. Treaty implementation for sustainable development* (pp. 139–164). Cambridge University Press.

Haywood, C. (2014). *The opinions of lecturers at a university of technology regarding their role in supporting students experiencing barriers to learning* [Master's thesis, North West University, South Africa].

Holloway, S. (2001). The experience of higher education from the perspective of disabled students. *Disability & Society, 18*(4), 597–615.

Hungwe, J. P. (2022). A 'requiem' for global citizenship education in higher education? An analysis of the exclusive nationalistic response to the COVID-19 pandemic. *Citizenship Teaching & Learning, 17*(1), 109–122. https://doi.org/10.1386/ctl_00084_1

Jali, L. (2009). *Experiences of students with physical impairments studying at Durban University of Technology* [Submitted in partial fulfilment of the academic requirements for the degree of Masters in Higher Education. Centre for Higher Education Studies. Faculty of Education. UKZN].

Kivunja, C., & Kuyini, A. B. J. I. J. O. H. E. (2017). Understanding and applying research paradigms in educational contexts. *International Journal of Higher Education, 6*(5), 26–41.

Knoll, K. R. (2009). Feminist disability studies pedagogy. *Feminist Teacher, 19*(2), 122–133.

Kothari, C. R. (2004). *Research methodology: Methods and techniques.* New Age International.

Larson, L. K. (2012). Larson on employment discrimination. *Employee Health AIDS Discrimination, 10.* Retrieved June 25, 2019, from http://www.lexisnexis.com/store/catalog/booktemplate/productdetail.jsp?pageName=relatedProducts&prodId=10110

Lord, J. E., & Stein, M. A. (2018). Pursuing inclusive higher education in Egypt and beyond through the Convention on the Rights of Persons with Disabilities. *Social Inclusion, 6*(4), 230–240.

Mackenzie, N., & Knipe, S. (2006). Research dilemmas: Paradigms, methods and methodology. *Issues in Educational Research, 16*(2), 193–205.

Maotoana, M. R. (2014). *The challenges experienced by students with physical disability* [SWPD's at the University of Limpopo (Turfloop Campus). University of Limpopo].

Maseko, N. T. (2024). Current inclusive education debates in South Africa and the world over. In Maguvhe M., Mpya. N, & Sadiki, M. (Eds.), *Handbook of research on inclusive and accessible education* (pp. 78–91). IGI Global. https//doi.org/10.4018/979-8-3693-1147-9.ch006

Matolo, M. F., & Rambuda, A. M. (2021). Factors impacting the application of an inclusive education policy on screening, identification, assessment, and support of the learners at schools in South Africa. *International Journal of Learning, Teaching and Educational Research, 20*(9), 207–221.

Matthews, N. (2009). Teaching the 'invisible' disabled students in the classroom: disclosure, inclusion and the social model of disability. *Teaching in Higher Education, 14*(3), 229–239. https://doi.org/10.1080/13562510902898809

McCormack, M. (2023). *Diversity, equity, and inclusion (DEI).* EDUCAUSE.

Mekoa, I. (2018). Challenges facing higher education in South Africa: A change from apartheid education to democratic education. *African Renaissance, 15*(2), 227–246. https://hdl.handle.net/10520/EJC-10c9ce8b9a

Mertens, D. M. (2005). *Research methods in education and psychology: Integrating diversity with quantitative and qualitative approaches* (2nd ed.). SAGE.

Miles, M. B., Huberman, A. M., Huberman, M. A., & Huberman, M. (1994). *Qualitative data analysis: An expanded sourcebook.* SAGE.

Mittler, P. (2000). *Working towards inclusive education: social contexts.* David Fulton Publishers.

Mnisi, T. E. (2014). *Digital storytelling to explore HIV-and AIDS-related stigma with secondary school learners in a rural community in KwaZulu-Natal.* Nelson Mandela Metropolitan University.

Mohamed, S. (2020). *South Africa: Broken and unequal education perpetuating poverty and inequality.* Amnesty International.

Mokiwa, S. A., & Phasha, T. N. (2012). Using ICT at an open distance learning (ODL) institution in South Africa: The learning experiences of students with visual impairments. *Africa Education Review, 9*(1), 136–151.

Moodley, S., & Mchunu, G. (2019). Current access and recruitment practices in nursing education institutions in KwaZulu-Natal: A case study of student nurses with disabilities. *African Journal of Disability (Online), 8,* 1–9.

Mosia, P. A., & Phasha, N. (2017). Access to curriculum for students with disabilities at higher education institutions: How does the National University of Lesotho fare? *African Journal of Disability (Online), 6,* 1–13.

Mutanga, O. (2017). Students with disabilities' experience in South African higher education – A synthesis of literature. *South African Journal of Higher Education, 31*(1), 135–154.

Mutanga, O. (2018). Inclusion of students with disabilities in South African higher education. *International Journal of Disability, Development and Education, 65*(2), 229–249. https://doi.org/10.1080/1034912X.2017.1368460

Mutanga, O. (Ed.). (2023). *Ubuntu philosophy and disabilities in Sub-Saharan Africa* (1st Ed.). Routledge.

Mutanga, O., & Walker, M. (2017). Exploration of the academic lives of students with disabilities at South African universities: Lecturers' perspectives. *African Journal of Disability (Online), 6,* 1–9.

Muthukrishna, N., & Schoeman, M. (2000). From "special needs" to "quality education for all": A participatory, problem-centred approach to policy development in South Africa. *International Journal of Inclusive Education, 4*(4), 315–335. https://doi.org/10.1080/13603110050168023

Naidoo, A. (2010). *Students with disabilities' perceptions and experiences of the Disability Unit at the University of KwaZulu-Natal, Howard College Campus.* University of KwaZulu-Natal.

Nel, N., Nel, M., & Hugo, A. (2012). *Learner support in a diverse classroom: A guide for foundation, intermediate and senior phase teachers of language and mathematics.* Van Schaik.

Ntombela, S. (2013). Inclusive education and training in South African higher education: Mapping the experiences of a student with physical disability at university. *Africa Education Review, 10*(3), 483–501.

Ntshangase, M. X., & Mafumo, T. N. (2024). A philosophical critique of possible reasons that lead to barriers against social cohesion. *International Journal of Social Science Research and Review, 7*(1), 463–473. http://dx.doi.org/10.47814/ijssrr.v7i1.1947

Pillay, R. M., & Shipalana, M. L. (2023). The effects of school infrastructure on curriculum policy implementation. *International Journal of Social Science Research and Review, 6*(8), 167–182. https://doi.org/10.47814/ijssrr.v6i8.1550

Pudaruth, S., Gunputh, R. P., & Singh, U. G. (2017). Forgotten, excluded or included? Students with disabilities: A case study at the University of Mauritius. *African Journal of Disability, 6,* a359. https://doi.org/10.4102/ajod.v6i0.359

Rapatsa, M. (2022). Social identity and social exclusivity: South Africa's middle-class strata in a perpetual struggle for integration. *Social Sciences and Education Research Review, 9*(2), 133–139.

Republic of South Africa. (1996). *The Constitution of the Republic of South Africa*. Government Printers.

Riddell, S., Tinklin, T. & Wilson, A. (2005). *Disabled students in higher education*. Routledge.

Riddell, S., & Weedon, E. (2014). Disabled students in higher education: Discourses of disability and the negotiation of identity. *International Journal of Educational Research, 63*, 38–46.

Seale, J., Wald, M., & Draffan, E. A. (2008). Disabled learners' experiences of E-learning. In J. Luca, & E. Weippl (Eds.), *Proceedings of ED-MEDIA 2008--World Conference on Educational Multimedia, Hypermedia, & Telecommunications* (pp. 6374–6383). Association for the Advancement of Computing in Education (AACE). Retrieved May 14, 2024. https://www.learntechlib.org/primary/p/29268/

Shevlin, M., Kenny, M., & McNeela, E. (2004). Participation in higher education for students with disabilities: An Irish perspective. *Disability & Society, 19*(1), 15–30.

Silverman, D. (1993). *Interpreting qualitative data*. SAGE.

Snyder, M. H. (2017). Adaptation in theory and practice. *The Oxford Handbook of Adaptation Studies* (p. 101).

South Africa Department of Education. (2001). *Education White Paper 6. Special needs education: Building an inclusive education and training system*. Government Printer.

South Africa Department of Education. (2008). *Operational manual to the national strategy on screening, identification, assessment and support*. Government Printer.

Subrayen, R. (2011). *Social exclusion among students with visual impairments at UKZN Edgewood and Howard College Campuses* [Unpublished Doctoral thesis]. University of KwaZulu-Natal, Durban.

Teferra, D., & Altbachl, P. G. (2004). African higher education: Challenges for the 21st century. *Higher Education, 47*(1), 21–50.

Thanh, N. C., & Thanh, T. J. A. J. o. E. S. (2015). The interconnection between interpretivist paradigm and qualitative methods in education, *1*(2), 24–27.

Thobejane, T. D. (2013). History of apartheid education and the problems of reconstruction in South Africa. *Sociology Study, 3*(1), 1–12.

Thompson, A. G. (1992). Teachers' beliefs and conceptions: A synthesis of the research. In D. A. Grouws (Ed.), *Handbook of research on mathematics teaching and learning*. MacMillan.

Van Jaarsveldt, D. E., & Ndeya-Ndereya, C. N., (2015). "It's not my problem": Exploring lecturers' distancing behaviour towards students with disabilities. *Disability and Society, 30*(2), 199–212. https://doi.org/10.1080/09687599.2014.994701

Walton, E., & Engelbrecht, P. (2022). Inclusive education in South Africa: Path dependencies and emergences. *International Journal of Inclusive Education, 28*(10), 2138–2156. https://doi.org/10.1080/13603116.2022.2061608

Walton, E., Nel, N., Hugo, A., & Mulller, H. (2009). The extent and practice of inclusion in independent schools in South Africa. *South African Journal of Education, 29*(1), 1–13.

White, C. (2005). *Research: A practical guide*. Ithuthuko Investment (Publishing).

Willing, C. (2001). *Introducing qualitative research in psychology: Adventures in theory and method*. Open University Press.

Winberg, C. (1997). *Learning how to research and evaluate* (pp. 153–160). Uswe.Wordnetweb.princeton.edu/perl/webwn

# Chapter 3

# Education Barriers in Higher Education

*Sanet Deysel*

*Nelson Mandela University, South Africa*

## Abstract

This literature review chapter comprehensively analyses barriers to higher education in the South African context. Educational barrier is conceptualised, and then various barriers are discussed, including academic, financial, language, cultural, technological, support, services, teaching and learning, and beliefs. Among the lessons learned from this review chapter is that the higher education landscape has changed significantly over the last few years and follows a more inclusive approach towards access for students. Consequently, higher education comprises a diverse student population. Within this higher education landscape, myriad barriers exist preventing student success. Therefore, the main recommendation is that a multifaceted approach is required to counter the education barriers in higher education. Specific support systems are needed to alleviate barriers in higher education and ensure student success.

*Keywords*: Education barrier; higher education; teaching and learning; institutional-related barriers; student-related barriers

## Introduction

The South African higher education landscape in the 1960s and early 1970s consisted of one specific group of students. Other race groups in South Africa were denied access to specific higher education institutions (HEIs) that employed exclusion as a means of instilling injustices and inequality. After the abolishment of apartheid in 1994, according to Mdepa and Tshiwula (2012), South Africa strived towards accepting and including all population groups within the higher education system. In light of this, South Africa reformed its student population to include a more diverse student population (Mouton et al., 2013). Therefore, at HEIs, students of different races and cultures from diverse backgrounds register to obtain a qualification in a particular area of specialisation that interests them.

Students from previously disadvantaged marginalised communities were exposed to substandard education because of apartheid (Chetty & Pather, 2015; Mdepa & Tshiwula, 2012). Rural and township schools before and even after apartheid and post-apartheid are marginalised. These unfunded schools lack essential resources, are poorly equipped and hinder learners from receiving a quality education that can prepare them for post-schooling (Van der Berg, 2016). The root cause of why first-year students need to prepare for post-secondary education is primarily attributed to the dismal state of schooling in South Africa. Stephen et al. (2004) stated that the education system for black students is inferior compared to that of white students, and therefore, black students are unprepared for post-school education.

According to Mdepa and Tshiwula (2012), quality education for all secondary school learners can assist HEIs in their aim to be more inclusive towards all students. Chetty and Pather (2015) concur with Mdepa and Tshiwula (2012) and further state that although HEIs strive for quality and equity, it requires the students' schooling to be equal and of a high standard to ensure a smooth transition between school and university. Maree (2015) also acknowledges the critical role of schools in students' success and argues for transforming both schools and universities to alleviate students' barriers at the university level. Most students at HEIs, because of exclusionary practices, need to be adequately equipped to deal with the academic challenges of university studies. Undoubtedly, adjusting from school to a higher learning educational institution is a defining moment for learners as they embark on a demanding journey that encourages critical thinking, independence, and responsibility. When first-year students have difficulty transitioning, the outcome is high dropout rates, low pass rates, and lower grade achievements.

Thus, the playing field at HEIs is unequal as students from low-income, marginalised, and disadvantaged communities must compete academically with those who have better schooling opportunities.

The question that begs to be answered is, how equipped are these learners to successfully navigate the corridors of higher learning? It will be easy for a few to cope as they may have been previously exposed to schools where they could navigate schooling. However, managing the academic and social demands would be challenging for most students from quintile one, two, and three schools (i.e., non-fee-paying schools in South Africa). It is, therefore, no surprise that the success rate at HEIs is below 20% (Mtshali, 2013), and the dropout rate at HEIs in 2013 was 55% (Council on Higher Education, 2018).

Students are expected to complete their qualification in the minimum period prescribed to the qualification. However, there are multiple education barriers that retard student success. These education barriers may result in students dropping out of higher education and, for many, result in students overcoming obstacles to succeed academically. Low academic success rates at HEIs are concerning, and the barriers that limit student success or poor performance need to be discussed, interrogated, investigated, and debated.

In this chapter, the barriers experienced by students are discussed. However, before discussing these barriers, the term educational barriers is defined, and the background to understanding the type of students currently enrolled at HEIs in South Africa is discussed. Therefore, the purpose of this chapter is to provide a conceptual understanding of educational barriers within the higher education context and thus make recommendations to address the impact of barriers.

## Methodology

In order to address the research purpose a systematic literature review was conducted as a research methodology. The aim of the review was mapped to achieve the following objectives:

- to conceptualise notions of educational barriers within the South African context;
- to identify different educational barriers in the South African higher education context; and
- to determine their impact and make recommendations about how educational barriers within the South African context can be addressed.

Empirical evidence was the main criterion for choosing the literature. Literature that was not evidence-based was not included. While the literature was reviewed for a study focussed on educational barriers in higher education, some of the reviewed work was inclined towards post-school education.

I consulted several databases, such as the Web of Science, Scopus, and Google Scholar. Internationally accredited journals, including the *International Journal of Inclusive Education*, were further sources of relevant information. I also consulted the Nelson Mandela University library and perused books, articles, theses, and electronic sources for relevant, up-to-date literature on the topic.

## Educational Barriers Defined

As articulated by several researchers, the definition of education barriers expresses the view that some aspect, albeit external or internal to the student, obstructs or limits the student's access to engage fully in academic learning activities to achieve academic success (Bailon, 2022). The aspects that hinder student progress may be, among other things, academic, social, financial, technological, and cultural. These barriers are not exclusive; several may function collectively to prevent academic success.

### *Knowing the Student*

Over 80% of students currently registered at HEIs are from the previously marginalised Black community in South Africa (Murray, 2016). These students are primarily from township or rural schools that are under-resourced. These circumstances impact the quality of education received and, therefore, would impact their performance at university. This means that most students come to university with limited knowledge, skills and values needed to excel academically. On the other hand, most students, comprised of a smaller group of students who attended schools with highly trained teachers and fully resourced schools, have skills that allow them to navigate the challenges at HEIs easily. For example, these students have been exposed to study techniques and have enhanced technology skills that are needed for a higher education student. Although these students might have an academic advantage in their studies, they also experience various psychosocial challenges.

### *First-year Students Entering HEIs*

Students entering HEIs hold preconceived ideas about student life. These ideas create excitement as there is the promise of freedom, independence, and fun. However, for the marginalised students' expectations soon fade when reality steps in and they soon discover that life at HEIs is not as envisaged. After this discovery, they experience anxiety. They are anxious about academia, accommodation issues, funding, transport, coping with the volume of work, new terminology, and new ways of learning. Other challenges, as identified by Kantanis (2000), are that making new friends is not easy, lecturing staff for support is not always accessible, the volume of work is vast, and some content is difficult to understand. All these aspects are new and very different from a school environment, and transitioning from school to a new environment creates a barrier to their academic success.

Nthabiseng et al. (2024) believe that the transition from school to higher education results in first-year students struggling to cope with the 'rigours of academics' (p. 113), which results in students dropping out and poor academic performance.

## Barriers Experienced by Students

Numerous barriers can significantly impact a student's successful academic performance in higher education. A Google search on barriers at HEI would produce a lengthy list that would include systemic inequalities, institutional, social, economic, mental, emotional, psychosocial, financial, support services, and others. Several barriers that significantly impede student academic progress at HEIs are academic readiness, academic barriers, financial barriers, financial literacy, language barriers, cultural barriers, technology barriers, lack of support services, housing insecurity, transport barriers, teaching and learning environment, and psychosocial barriers.

### *Academic Non-readiness*

One of the most common challenges university students face is balancing the academic material volume, keeping up with assignments and tests, and preparing for lectures (Rokhmani et al., 2019). According to Agherdien (2014), academic readiness considers how prepared a student is to meet the basic requirements to navigate higher education successfully. Students are challenged as there is a significant difference between what they experienced at secondary school and what they are exposed to at an HEI.

Conley (2008) tabulated the differences between secondary school and tertiary education (see Table 3.1).

The factors identified by Conley, namely pupil–teacher relationship, engagement, pace, preparation, responsibility, research, and academic ability, and the

Table 3.1. Differences Between School and University Experiences.

| Factors | Secondary School | Tertiary Education |
| --- | --- | --- |
| *Pupil–teacher relationship* | • Small classrooms and number of learners | • Large classrooms, bigger class groups, limited opportunity to get to know all the students |
| *Engagement* | • Learners are required to listen and input is not necessary | • Students are required to engage and reflect on the learning material |
| *Pace* | • Slower paced with less work to cover | • Fast paced and emphasises different aspects taught, larger content covered |
| *Preparation* | • Class preparation is not obligatory | • Prior lecture preparation is considered to be very important as the learner needs to come to class with an idea of what is to be expected |
| *Responsibility* | • Spoon-fed<br>• Learners are provided with all the information | • Ownership<br>• Learners need to take ownership over their studies to succeed. A high level of responsibility is expected |
| *Research* | • Limited information required<br>• Two research assignments throughout school<br>• Due dates far apart | • In depth information required<br>• Students are required to interpret, analyse, reach conclusions and make recommendations |
| *Academic ability* | • Basic skills | • Language and mathematical proficiency<br>• Solve complex problems |

*Source*: Conley (2008, pp. 5–6).

related description in the table indicate what is expected of the student at secondary school versus the requirement at the tertiary level. The differences are significant, and the transition from school regarding the factors is challenging for students, especially those from rural and township schools.

Regarding the pupil–teacher relationship, the student is familiar with the teacher at school, and the students know each other in the classroom. At the tertiary level, class size can be four times the size of school classrooms with little or no interaction among the students. At the tertiary level, more engagement is expected of the student than at the secondary. According to Conley, students are to engage and reflect on the learning material, an aspect that they do not practice at school.

## *Academic Barriers*

Steyn and Kamper (2011) identified study barriers as barriers in higher education. Many students need self-discipline to manage their studies and time. Some students also need help with study planning. Steyn and Kamper (2011) suggest the development of study organisation skills to alleviate this barrier. Steyn and Kamper (2011) state that self-discipline and time management skills predict student success in HEIs. Students who can employ self-control to learn independently and efficiently have an advantage over ill-disciplined students (Steyn & Kamper, 2011). Similarly, time management skills are evident in successful students, although many first-year students need help acquiring this skill.

Mseleku (2022) indicates responsibility, motivation, agency, courage, and ownership as further attributes of student success. These characteristics are necessary for students to be prepared for challenges that may result in barriers in their journey as students. Chiramba and Ndofirepi (2023) identified resilience as contributing to student success. Consequently, the two authors suggest that resilience be included in universities' curricula.

## *Financial Barriers*

The most prevalent barrier to South African students' accessing and remaining at an HEI is the financial constraints they experience. The lack of funding and poverty are among the most significant barriers to higher education. Mseleku (2022) refers to poverty as the most debilitating barrier to access to HEIs. According to Mseleku (2022), low-income families cannot support their children financially, so studying at a HEI is often not an option. Many families need the financial means to send their children to university.

Students at HEIs must face high tuition fees, textbooks, living expenses, laptops, data and internet access. These expenses create financial stress that has a negative impact as it limits their ability to concentrate on their academics. As mentioned previously, more than 80% of the students in higher education are from rural or township homes. These students are challenged to fund their tertiary education and rely on government funding or bursaries. However, funding sources are few. Furthermore, with the cost of tuition at HEIs being so exorbitant, many students need help to afford to study at an HEI. According to Malaza (2016), tuition fees increased by 27% in 2010 and 2012; these high increases are problematic because they limit access to higher education for the poor and middle class.

Mdepa and Tshiwula (2012) flagged the correlation between insufficient funding and the exclusion of students into the higher education landscape. However, the National Student Financial Aid Scheme (NSFAS) provides a solution to the financial woes of some students. Through loans provided by NSFAS, students obtain the financial means to access university. A proportion of the NSFAS loan can be converted into a bursary, subject to the student's academic success. Nonetheless, this arrangement poses considerable challenges to students who must budget all their living expenses, accommodation, and transport from the allocated money. According to Maree (2015), poverty remains a massive barrier in higher education as the existing financial measures fail to alleviate students' financial needs.

In October 2015, there was a student-led protest against the high fee increases. The purpose of the protest was twofold: first, to stop the fee increases and secondly, to increase funding to state-owned HEIs. The protest led to a 0% increase in fees in 2017.

Student funding is available through the NSFAS, which the government funds. However, the government's total funding must be more to award loans to deserving students (HESA, 2008).

## *Financial Illiteracy*

Although a lack of funding is one of the most significant barriers in higher education, students also indicated financial planning as a barrier (Chiramba & Ndofirepi, 2023). Students need to manage their funding money and experience challenges with this aspect. For many students, it will be the first time that they are living away from their homes and now have the responsibility to manage their finances. They need to gain experience creating a budget and will be anxious as the resources are limited (Chiramba & Ndofirepi, 2023).

A student with money problems experiences stress and needs help concentrating on their studies. A lack of funds halfway through the academic year may result in students dropping out, taking fewer modules in the second semester, or trying to find work to sustain themselves (Heckman, 2014).

Jessop et al. (2005) report that financial hardships are vast and can affect students' mental and physical health. Heckman (2014) concurs with Jessop et al. and elaborates that personal financial issues influence university students' stress. The emotional stress and anxiety experienced by students result in depression, poor academic performance, poor health, and a lack of resilience to complete their qualifications (Heckman, 2014).

With financial management experience, students can avoid financial challenges and will be able to budget and prioritise their expenditures. For many of the students at South African Universities, the issue may be that they need to receive more money to cover their expenses. Student expenses include accommodation, groceries, tuition fees, textbooks, transportation, and essential personal items.

## Language Barriers

Mdepa and Tshiwula (2012) and Steyn and Kamper (2011) consider language an educational barrier for many students. Maree (2015) states that many students need help conversing in English and fully understanding the language. However, Pym (2006) perceives language as an asset and encourages students to engage in their home language for understanding and insight. Although English is the Language of Learning and Teaching (LOLT) at many universities, the students are encouraged to conceptualise concepts using their mother tongue, while others can interpret and translate.

At HEI, the language of instruction is English, which may not be the student's mother tongue. Thus, students might face challenges in academic writing, verbal communication, or understanding course materials if English is not their first language. In addition, students may interpret instructions or expectations differently, leading to misunderstandings or misinterpretations. Thus, using English may pose a challenge when the student's vocabulary and pronunciation are not precise (Lipsky, 2018). According to Mudaly and Singh (2018), language and communication are the two factors that act as a barrier when teaching is given to students in a language they do not use at home as it is a 'language they hardly use and understand' (p. 56). Additionally, Mudaly and Singh (2018) claim that students at HEIs do not understand the content because there is a misalignment relation between the language used in the classroom and the language that students are not well-versed in. Because students do not have a command of the language, they have difficulty understanding the content and instruction, which will result in poor academic performance.

## Cultural Barriers

At the HEI, each student is unique, having their own set of values, norms, and beliefs, and they would want to ensure that their culture is being valued. Students will feel alienated when the culture at the HEI is inconsistent with their own cultural experiences (Smith-Maddox, 1998). Therefore, cultural factors are critical to student success and HEI retention. Students who feel that they are marginalised or underrepresented may experience negative emotions. Similarly, if lecturers stereotype students, they may feel inadequate and excluded. These emotions will impact their academic performance and overall well-being.

A further cultural barrier is the Eurocentric epistemologies still entrenched in HEIs (Badat, 2010; Soudien, 2008). One of the goals of the student protest movement of 2015 was that HEIs be decolonised, deracialised, and degendered. The movement achieved some success, and over the years since 2015, discussions to decolonise curricula at HEIs have been underway.

## Technology Barriers

In a study by Chiramba and Ndofirepi (2023), various students indicated the significant barriers they encounter regarding digital resources. Students indicated their limited access to computers during schooling; therefore, for some students, university is their first experience with a device of this nature. These students shared their initial frightening and unfamiliar experiences with the digital resources. In a similar study by Walker and Mathebula (2019), students echoed their challenges with technology and indicated that many needed access to devices pre-university. These students indicated they begin university with a backlog and must prepare for the digital challenges. Technological devices pose a barrier in the higher education context for many students, while the university landscape is embedded in the use of these devices.

Before the COVID-19 pandemic, even though lectures were face-to-face, all students at HEIs had to know how to submit assignments and perform tests through a platform used by the institution. For most students, using technology, like the laptop, which many could not access, would be challenging. For many, it may have been their first laptop use.

The COVID-19 pandemic forced the education sector to teach online. The most vulnerable students were severely handicapped, as many did not have devices to study online. The pandemic exposed the inequalities at HEIs (Knowles et al., 2023). Most of the universities were severely constrained because of the students' circumstances related to access to devices, internet availability, data, and access to students because of where they were located.

During COVID-19, students were sent home as learning and teaching was done online. Students were expected to continue with their learning using technology. This proved to be a challenge for many as many needed accesses to a device. Furthermore, internet access is required in the outlying rural areas. For students to effectively complete their work, they would need the money to purchase the necessary device and data and have internet access.

Since 2022, lectures at Mandela University have reverted to face-to-face. However, many lecturers present online classes because of large classes and limited classroom space. Loadshedding, unstable internet access, and limited workspaces are some barriers preventing students from joining their online courses.

Kara (2021) identified several barriers to working online. These include, among other things, the absence of peer support, little or no contact with lecturers, the content presentation being unclear and, therefore, difficult to understand, and an abundance of PowerPoint presentations. She further adds that lecturers set unreasonable time frames for assignment submissions. Furthermore, there was no feedback on the marked assignments. According to Kara, many students stated that the wording of the assignment questions was unclear.

The period during COVID-19 affected most students, and they were feeling the pressure of working online with many challenges out of their control. According to Kara, students were overwhelmed with online teaching and learning and the stresses of staying home.

D'Agostino (2022) reported that even students knowledgeable about technology faced external challenges. Her study found that at HEIs, there are insufficient computer laboratories for students, Wi-Fi is not always available, and hot spots are inadequate. Furthermore, she discovered that much-needed IT support for students was lacking. She further reported that because of the technology challenges students faced, more than half of the respondents in the study reported that they experienced stress (D' Agostino, 2022).

Knowles et al. (2023) contend that the HEIs failed the most vulnerable students despite their best efforts to support them during the COVID-19 pandemic.

## *Role of Support Services*

Without proper support services for students, HEI would face higher dropout rates and low throughput rates. According to Cloete (2016), to retain the marginalised and previously disadvantaged students at HEIs, support services play a significant role, and without the support services, the dropout rate would be severe.

Over the past few years, with more government funding (NSFAS) becoming available for those who qualify, more students from previously disadvantaged communities are registered at HEIs. However, according to Fisher (2011), these students must catch up to the advantaged students.

At HEIs, student support services contribute significantly to ensuring that students are not anxious and stressed. Academic support services should provide the student with assistance to enhance the student's chances of completing the qualification.

Student support should start at registration as they need to be guided on what courses they are to take. They also need to know how and where to access learning materials, the infrastructure layout, online learning, where to go for academic support, how to manage their time, and how to access library resources. According to Simpson (2012), support services should be all-encompassing to assist students in their studies and include academic advising, counselling, and tutoring resources. Access to support services provides valuable support for students to navigate their studies. Lack of support services can exacerbate feelings of isolation and frustration, ultimately hindering students' academic progress (Simpson, 2012).

## *Housing Insecurity*

Dr Blade Nzimande, the Minister of Education in Higher Education 2016, discussed the acute shortage of student housing at HEIs at a Student Housing Symposium. At this symposium, he reported that The Ministerial Review of Student Housing at Universities conducted in 2011 highlighted the severe shortage of student accommodation and revealed that only 18% of HEI students could be housed in university residences (Nzimande, 2016). He further stated that at HEIs, there was accommodation for only 5% of the most vulnerable first-year students who are away from home for the first time and expected to perform in a post-school environment (Nzimande, 2016).

The Ministerial Review of Student Housing at Universities reported that in 2016, the shortage of university accommodation would be 216,000 beds (Department of Higher Education and Training, 2011).

One of the reasons for the *Fees Must Fall* protests in 2015 and 2016 was the shortage of student accommodation, which had to be addressed. The state of student accommodation at most HEIs, according to Legodi (2019), is pathetic and dehumanising. He stated that the poor accommodation negatively impacted their academic success. He further noted that students often sublet in overcrowded accommodation off-campus that is more affordable. However, he states that this off-campus accommodation is not well-regulated, poses a health and safety risk, and can violate the student's fundamental rights.

Legodi (2019) highlights some catastrophic incidents that students endure at several HEIs. According to him, students at an HEI in South Africa went to a police station to demand safer living conditions since students were being raped, robbed and even shot at off-campus residences. At another university, Legodi reported that the rooms at residences are in a poor state, that the roof leaked when it rained, rooms were infested with bugs, and there was no hot water to bathe with.

To demand better living accommodations, students resort to student protests to draw attention to these unliveable and unbearable conditions. Students can only perform well under these circumstances.

## *Transport Barriers*

The rise in the number of students registered at HEI results in the need for more transport as there is an increase in the number of students living off-campus. The scarcity of on-campus residences results in a more significant percentage of students living off-campus. These off-campus accommodation sites may be university-managed or private. At Nelson Mandela University in Gqeberha, the distance of some University accommodations is away from campus. The university provides transport for these students. However, over the past few years, students have protested and demanded better transport services. The issues raised by the students are that the transport routes are decided by management, the service is unreliable as it does not always run on time, or the transport does not arrive, and the service ends too early. These reasons impact student performance.

According to Allen and Faber (2018), students have limited time and need all the time they have to focus on their studies. Tinto (1999) states that commuting is a deterrent as it prevents students from full participation in on-campus activities. Other incidences were also reported where students were robbed of their laptops, books and cell phones while walking to or from the bus stations.

The impact of poor or dysfunctional transport provision is problematic. Laby et al. (2021) reported that students who reside off-campus have lower academic success than students living on-campus. Furthermore, Mudau (2017) argues that residing off-campus reduces student commitment as students arrive on-campus exhausted and, therefore, have a shorter concentration span than their on-campus peers. Mudau (2017) also claims students do not participate in extra-mural activities and use the library because of inefficient transport. Mudau also states that off-campus students at the University of Johannesburg using university transport are anxious about being robbed on their way back to their residences.

Missing lectures and being robbed of their belongings because of inefficient transport provisions are barriers that do not augur well and limit students' academic performance.

## Teaching and Learning Environment

Mdepa and Tshiwula (2012) stated that many universities are still transforming to be more inclusive. Additionally, Pym (2006) states that this transformation process is often associated with the access of previously disadvantaged population groups. Pym (2006) further asserts that contrary to the diverse student population, all students are expected to do the same curriculum and content. In other words, a diverse student population is subject to the same module content and is expected to pass.

Additionally, are the current pedagogies used in HEIs to the advantage of diverse student populations? Lecturers should acknowledge, respect and value students' lived experiences and construct content in an accessible manner for all students. Pym (2006) discussed another barrier in the teaching and learning environment: the large number of students in lecture rooms. Furthermore, Pym (2006) identified that many lecturers are not educationalists, contributing to students' barriers to teaching and learning.

## Psychosocial Barriers

Students are confronted with various experiences and emotions during their tenure at HEIs (Steyn & Kamper, 2011). While dealing with many emotions, students must also navigate their academic challenges and adjust smoothly to university life. Students must deal with aspects regarding their emotional well-being. Steyn and Kamper (2011) explained the relationship between a positive self-image and a thriving university trajectory. Similarly, low self-esteem and a distorted self-image contribute to students' barriers in the higher education landscape (Steyn & Kamper, 2011). Chiramba and Ndofirepi (2023) discussed mental and emotional stressors as part of life in HEIs due to numerous experiences. These challenges have a significant detrimental impact on students' mental health and contribute to student barriers. Walker and Mathebula (2019) discussed the students' well-being extensively and suggested that HEIs prioritise the well-being of students. Students must find their place in the university and foster belonging within their family structure. Students must navigate the establishment of new relationships and retain their identity.

Van Breda (2017, p. 247) refers to the 'psychosocial vulnerabilities' of students. He indicates explicitly definite experiences as contributors to students' psychosocial vulnerabilities. These home, community, and university experiences include transitioning from school to HEIs and student's ability to manage their studies and time efficiently. Van Breda (2017) emphasises that lecturers need to realise that students are firstly humans and need to regard them as such. Although students face many academic challenges, it should be acknowledged that students also experience various psychosocial challenges. During the transition from school to university, students might experience university life as overwhelming.

In studies done (Van Breda, 2017), many students shared that they experienced traumatic incidences as part of their university life. Some of these incidences include occurrences of safety, gender-based violence, assault, domestic violence, and death of family members (Van Breda, 2017). These incidents all hurt the students' psychosocial well-being, which further harms the student's academic progress and development.

### *Lecturer and Student Beliefs and Perceptions*

Fraser and Killen (2005) conducted a study on the impact of lecturer and student perceptions on student success in higher education. Their research revealed that students' beliefs about factors that enhance their academic success often overshadow other contributors to student success and failure. Moreover, lecturers and students hold divergent beliefs about the factors that lead to success and failure at university. These differences can lead to confusion and even opposition, creating a significant barrier to education in higher institutions.

Students perceived unrealistic expectations from lecturers, too many lecturer demands on student time, boring lecturers, and misunderstandings regarding assessments as challenges that could lead to academic failure. In contrast to the students, the lecturers viewed the students' attributes as the biggest challenges that prevent student success.

The lecturers perceived the students' inability to plan and organise their time as one of the contributing factors to student failure. Both lecturers and students perceive students' self-discipline as a contributing attribute to student academic success. These educational barriers are exacerbated by the lecturers' and students' social and cultural differences, which are evident in the South African university context.

To overcome these challenges, Fraser and Killen (2005) suggested that lecturers and students should engage and communicate openly about their own beliefs and perceptions. This collaboration is not just a suggestion but a crucial step that the academic community must take to mitigate this barrier to learning and foster student success. It is a collective effort that should strive towards the development of strategies to ensure that students succeed academically. Furthermore, Fraser and Killen (2005) strongly believe that lecturers, as trusted collaborators, should support students throughout their journey in higher education to overcome educational barriers.

## Lessons Learned

Based on lessons learned from the review, I summarise findings regarding the challenges posed by education barriers and make recommendations on how they could be addressed. In order to discuss the lessons I decided to cluster them into five categories, i.e. Teaching and learning, support and services, institutional barriers, student-centred barriers, and instructor-centred barriers. Fig. 3.1 shows the identified clusters.

### *Teaching and Learning*

This review discussed academic readiness, academic barriers, technology barriers, language barriers, the language of instruction at HEIs, the relevance and delivery of the curriculum, and the various pedagogies used in higher education. Students

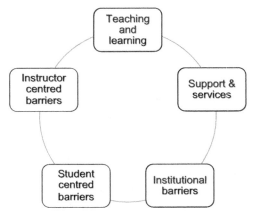

Fig. 3.1. Educational Barriers in Higher Education.

in higher education are expected to converse, learn, communicate, and show insight in a language of teaching (English) that often differs from their home language. Students within the higher education context are expected to do the same curriculum irrespective of diversity and other variables. Furthermore, students are exposed to pedagogies that are not necessarily student oriented and lack the advancement of student success. These challenges contribute to the dilemma in epistemic access at HEIs. Lessons learned from this cluster of findings are that HEIs should be sensitive towards the realities of epistemic access for students. Therefore, Xulu-Gama and Hadebe (2022) recommend that policies, and specifically the language policies, at HEIs be revised.

## *Support and Services*

It also became prudent that financial barriers, financial illiteracy, lack of support services, housing insecurity, and transport barriers were crucial in making higher education inaccessible. It is evident that educational barriers within HEIs hinder students' success and pose a significant obstacle. Inadequate support services, technological, accommodation, and transport barriers, individually or collectively, hamper academic success. Without adequate resources and support systems in place, students, especially the vulnerable and marginalised, cannot function effectively and will struggle to engage with their studies entirely. Simpson (2012) recommends that HEIs provide holistic support and services for students towards student success. Consequently, support should encompass all spheres of the student towards achieving their qualification.

## *Institutional-Related Barriers*

In this review, institutional-related barriers such as language barriers and cultural barriers are highlighted as possible challenges in the higher education context. It is evident that the culture of the student does not always align with the culture of the university, leading to failure in achieving success.

These institutional barriers affect the student's academic performance and cannot be accepted. A multifaceted approach is needed to address the barriers, led by student bodies, university leadership, and policymakers. These discussions must address removing the existing inequalities, providing decent, humane accommodation, improving the transport system, and providing adequate academic and support services. An environment must be created to allow every student to thrive and succeed academically.

### *Student-Centred Barriers*

Students from marginalised, low-income communities are worse affected by the barriers. Because of the poor quality of schooling and the lack of preparedness, they find it challenging to navigate the higher education landscape primarily because of limited financial resources, emotional and psychological support, and lack of financial literacy. The result is a gap between the masses of students and the privileged. Psychosocial barriers have a detrimental impact on student success. Students need to transition from school to the unfamiliar environment of a HEI. This adjustment and transition, together with navigating other challenges, lead to psychosocial barriers where the student's well-being is severely compromised. Therefore, Walker and Mathebula (2019) recommend that the well-being of students in HEI be prioritised. Thus, a concerted effort and focus are required to minimise the detrimental impact of psychosocial barriers on students.

### *Instructor-Based Barriers*

Student and lecturer beliefs and attitudes might differ marginally and constitute opposing views and opinions. These inconsistencies and challenges regarding beliefs and attitudes can include social and cultural differences, ultimately leading to the exclusion of students by lecturers. Lessons learned from these findings are that every student is unique and should be accepted and acknowledged as such. Each student has a set of beliefs and attitudes, and therefore, lecturers must refrain from stereotyping students. Therefore, Fraser and Killen (2005) recommend robust conversations and open communication between students and lecturers to promote acceptance and understanding of one another, paving the way towards student success.

## Conclusion

This chapter analysed the literature review to conceptualise the notion of educational barriers. It highlighted the challenges of school–university transition and educational barriers. Various educational barriers were discussed, and their impact on student learning was foregrounded. In this chapter, some lessons are drawn based on the analysis of the literature, and recommendations regarding how institutions of higher learning could address the educational barriers are made. While the higher education landscape of South Africa is evolving and changing based on the economic prospects of the country and the general higher education leadership, this chapter contributes to discussions about higher education access, equity, and inclusion.

## References

Agherdien, N. (2014). *Investigating student readiness for tertiary education.* [Unpublished thesis]. Nelson Mandela Metropolitan University.

Allen, J., & Faber, S. (2018). How time-use and transportation barriers limit on-campus participation of university students. *Travel Behaviour and Society. 13,* 174–182.

Badat, S. (2010). *The challenges of transformation in higher education.* Paper commissioned by the Development Bank of Southern Africa. https://www.ru.ac.za/media/rhodesuniversity/content/vc/documents/The_Challenges_of_Transformation_in_Higher_Eduaction_and_Training_Institutions_in_South_Africa.pdf

Bailon, A. (2022). *Barriers to learning.* Retrieved February 21, 2024, from https://www.edapp.com/blog/barriers-to-learning/.

Chetty, R., & Pather, S. (2015). Challenges in higher education in South Africa. In J. Condy, (Ed.), *Telling stories differently: Engaging 21st century students through digital storytelling* (Chap. 1). AfricanSunMedia.

Chiramba, O., & Ndofirepi, E. S. (2023). Access and success in higher education: Disadvantaged students' lived experiences beyond funding hurdles at a metropolitan South African university. *South African Journal of Higher Education, 37*(6), 56–75.

Cloete, N. (2016). *Free higher education another self-destructive South African policy.* Council for Higher Education.

Conley, D., (2008). *College readiness and high school-to-college success.* Educational Policy Improvement Center.

Council on Higher Education. (2018). *VitalStats public higher education 2016, Pretoria.* Retrieved from https://www.che.ac.za/sites/default/files/publications/CHE_Vital Stats_2016%20webv ersion_0.pdf

D' Agostino, S. (2022). Undergraduates' technology problems and needs. *Inside Higher Education,* 3 October 2022. Retrieved March 4, 2024, from https://www.insidehighered.com/news/2022/10/04/undergraduates-technology-problems-and-needs

Department of Higher Education and Training (2011). Report on the ministerial committee for the review of the provision of student housing at South African universities. https://www.gov.za/sites/default/files/gcis_document/201409/ministerial-committee-report-student-housing0.pdf

Fisher, G., & Scott, I. (2011). The role of higher education in closing the skills gap in South Africa. *Background Paper 3 for closing the skills and technology gap in South Africa.* The World Bank.

Fraser, W., & Killen, R. (2005). The perceptions of students and lecturers of some factors influencing academic performance at two South African universities. *Perspectives in Education, 23*(1), 25–40.

Heckman, S. (2014). *Factors related to financial stress among college students.* Retrieved March 4, 2014, from www.newprairiepress.org.

Higher Education South Africa (HESA). (2008). *Tuition fees: Higher education institutions in South Africa (Pretoria).* http://www.justice.gov.za/commissions/FeesHET/docs/2008-HESA-Report-TuitionFeesInSA.pdf

Jessop, D. C., Herbert, C., & Solomon, L. (2005). The impact of financial circumstances on student health. *British Journal of Health Psychology, 10*(Pt3), 421–439.

Kantanis, T. (2000). The role of social transition in students' adjustment to the first-year university. *Journal of Institutional Research, 9,* 100–110.

Kara, N. (2021). Enablers and barriers of online learning during the COVID-19 pandemic. *Journal of University Teaching and Learning Practice, 18*(4), ISS 4 (Art11).

Knowles, C., James, A., Khoza, L., Mtwa, Z., Roboji, M., & Shivambu, M. (2023). Problematising the South African Higher Education inequalities exposed during COVID-19 pandemic: Students' perspectives. *Critical Studies in Teaching and Learning, 11*(1), 1–21.

Laby, A. I., Shabalala, S., Molokwna, B., &. Van derWalt, J. (2021). *Transportation behaviours and challenges of non-resident students at a South African University*. https://www.researchgate.net/publication/359082403_Transportation_behaviours_and_challenges_of_non-resident_students_at_a_South_African_university

Legodi, L. T. (2019). *Student housing shortage is still a problem*. Retrieved March 5, 2024, from https://mg.co.za/article/2019-03-05-student-housing-shortage-still-a-problem/.

Lipsky, J. (2018). Dialects of Spanish and Portuguese. In C. Boberg, J. Nerbonne & D. Watt (Eds.), *Handbook of dialectology* (pp. 498–509). Wiley.

Malaza, D. (2016). *University of KwaZulu-Natal submission to the presidential commission on fees into higher education and training*. Retrieved March 2, 2024, from http://www.justice.gov.za/commissions/FeesHET/hearings/set1/day06-UKZN-Submission.pdf.

Maree, J. G. (2015). Barriers to access to and success in higher education: Intervention guidelines. *South African Journal of Education, 29*(1), 390–411.

Mdepa, W., & Tshiwula, L. (2012). Student diversity in South African higher education. *Widening Participation and Lifelong Learning, 13,* 19–33.

Mouton, N., Louw, G., & Strydom, G. (2013). Present-day dilemmas and challenges of the South African tertiary system. *International Business and Economics Research Journal, 12*(3), 285–300.

Mseleku, Z. (2022). Beyond hard barriers: Lack of aspiration as a soft barrier to access higher education amongst youth living in low-income housing estate. *South African Journal of Higher Education, 36*(6), 1–11.

Mtshali, N. (2013). Causes of low graduation rates exposed in news report. *Star Newspaper,* 12 June. https://www.iiemsa.co.za/news/causes-of-low-graduation-rates-exposed-in-new-report/

Mudaly, V., & Singh. K. (2018). Language: A barrier when teaching and learning business studies. *International Journal of Science and Research, 74*(9/1), 56–71.

Mudau, T. J. (2017). An exploration of the challenges faced by students residing off-campus in rural universities in South Africa. *Gender and Behaviour, 15*(4), 10568–10580.

Murray, M. (2016). Does poor quality schooling and/or teacher quality hurt black South African students enrolling for a degree at the University of KwaZulu-Natal? *PLoS ONE, 11*(4). https://doi.org/10.1371/journal.pone.0153091

Nthabiseng, S., Mphahlele, L., & Malatji, K. S. (2024). Transition from high school to university: Challenges faced by first-year B.Ed. students at a University of Technology in South Africa. *E-Journal of Humanities, Arts and Social Sciences, 5*(2), 112–122.

Nzimande, B. (2016). *Student housing matters*. Retrieved March 4, 2014, from https://www.dhet.gov.za/SiteAssets/Latest%20News/Independent%20Thinking%2010th%20Edition/ThinkingP1%20August%202016.pdf.

Pym, J. (2006). *The lost, the least and the last: A South African higher education case study exploring the possibility of defying the barriers to learning*. ResearchGate.

Rokhmani, T., Sujanto, B., & Luddin, R. (2019). The implementation of academic responsibility in higher education: A case study. *Integration of Education, 23*(3), 336–349.

Simpson, O. (2012). *Supporting students for success in online and distance education*. Routledge.

Smith-Maddox, R. (1998). Defining culture as a dimension of academic achievement: Implications for culturally responsive curriculum, instruction, and assessment. *Journal of Negro Education*, *67*(3), 302–317.

Soudien, C. (2008). *Transformation in higher education: A briefing paper*. Development Bank of South Africa.

Stephen, D., Welman, J., & Jordaan. W. (2004). English language proficiency as an indicator of academic performance at a tertiary institution. *SA Journal of Human Resource Management*, *2*(3), 42–53.

Steyn, M. G., & Kamper, G. D. (2011). Barriers to learning in South African higher education: Some photovoice perspectives. *Journal for New Generation Sciences*, *9*(1), 116–136.

Tinto, V. (1999). Taking student retention seriously: Rethinking the first year of college. *Nacada*, *19*(2), 5–9.

Van der Berg, S., Spaull, N., Wills, G., Gustafsson, M., & Kotzé, J. (2016). *Identifying binding constraints in education synthesis report for the programme to support pro-poor policy development (PsPPd)*. https://resep.sun.ac.za/wp-content/uploads/2017/10/PSPPD_BICiE-email-01062016.pdf

Van Breda, A. D. (2017). Students are humans too: Psychosocial vulnerability of first-year students at the University of Johannesburg. *South African Journal of Higher Education*, *31*(5), 246–262.

Walker, M., & Mathebula, M. (2019). Low-income rural youth migrating to urban universities in South Africa: Opportunities and inequalities. *Compare: A Journal of Comparative and International Education*, *50*(8), 1193–1209.

Xulu-Gama, N., & Hadebe, S. (2022). Language of instruction: A critical aspect of epistemological access to higher education in South Africa. *South African Journal of Higher Education*, *35*(5), 291–307.

Chapter 4

# Higher Education Curriculum and Inclusion

Zandisile Mawethu Sitoyi[a] and Johannes Buthelezi[b]

[a]Cape Peninsula University of Technology, South Africa
[b]University of the Free State, South Africa

## Abstract

South Africa's higher education system has undergone significant transformation since the end of apartheid in 1994, but challenges remain in creating an inclusive and equitable curriculum. This chapter examines the development of an inclusive curriculum in South African universities through the lens of the Glocal Engagement Framework (GEF). It provides a historical overview of the fragmented and discriminatory education policies under apartheid and the efforts towards reform post-apartheid. The chapter highlights the importance of curriculum inclusivity emphasised in international declarations like the Salamanca Statement and the African Charter on the Rights and Welfare of the Child. Drawing from a systematic literature review and analysis of university vision statements, it critiques the current state of curriculum inclusivity in South African higher education. Key issues identified include insufficient decolonisation and integration of indigenous knowledge (IK), language policies not fully promoting multilingualism, and persistent financial barriers to access for marginalised groups. The chapter culminates with recommendations for developing a truly inclusive curriculum aligned with the GEF dimensions of intellect, emotion, action, and morality. These include implementing work-integrated learning (WIL), decolonising curriculum content, strengthening language policies, reviewing graduate attributes, increasing financial support for disadvantaged students, and creating an enabling university environment that embraces diversity. Ultimately, the chapter calls for comprehensive curriculum transformation to realise the constitutional vision of accessible and equitable higher education in South Africa.

*Keywords*: Curriculum; assessment; inclusion; inclusive curriculum; higher education; globalisation

# Introduction

South Africa's journey from a fragmented society created by the apartheid system to one striving for inclusivity and equality is marked by significant challenges and complexities. The systemic racial divisions and inequalities, deliberately entrenched during the apartheid era (1948–1994), have left persisting scars on the nation's social, economic, and educational sectors (Le Grange, 2020). During the apartheid era, policies of separate development institutionalised racial segregation, most notably in the realm of higher education, where opportunities were stratified along racial lines (Ntshoe, 2017). The apartheid regime's educational policies did more than merely segregate; they entrenched a hierarchy that perpetuated social and economic disparities, particularly disadvantaging Black, Coloured, and Indian populations (Saurombe, 2018). The legacy of apartheid in education was profound, systematically depriving non-White populations of quality education and the skills necessary for upward mobility.

The curriculum itself was a tool of oppression, designed to maintain the status quo by limiting access to certain subjects and careers for Black and Coloured students (Van der Berg, 2007). The apartheid curriculum was not just about exclusion; it was about serving a political agenda that sought to reinforce ethnic divisions. Institutions that served marginalised communities were systematically under-resourced and offered curricula that were inferior and limiting compared to those available to White students (Beale, 1998). Even technical and vocational education, ostensibly provided to Black and Coloured students, was designed to keep them within certain occupational boundaries, perpetuating the cycle of economic disadvantage (McGrath, 2004). The exclusion was not merely a reflection of social attitudes but a deliberate strategy to marginalise these groups, effectively curtailing their economic and political agency.

Since the end of the apartheid system, South Africa has been on a challenging path towards educational reform, striving to redress these historical injustices. The contemporary South African education system, however, still grapples with the deep-rooted disparities created during the apartheid years (Le Grange, 2020). The journey towards an inclusive and equitable higher education system is ongoing, marked by both significant progress and persistent challenges (Ainscow, 2020). After 1994 elections, there has been a collaborative effort to transform the higher education landscape. Mergers of higher education institutions (HEIs) in 2005 and the inclusion of all nine African languages in curricula are some of the significant steps taken to address past injustices and promote inclusivity (Madadzhe, 2019; Mdepa & Tshiwula, 2012). These changes reflect a broader commitment to creating a higher education system that is not only inclusive but also reflective of South Africa's diverse society.

This chapter will explore the transformation of South Africa's higher education curriculum through the lens of the GEF. This framework provides a critical tool for assessing whether the current curriculum is truly inclusive and aligned with global and local (glocal) standards. We will begin by outlining the theoretical foundations of the GEF approach, followed by an examination of the methodology employed in this study. The chapter will then engage with both international and national literature on inclusion in higher education, offering a comprehensive perspective on how inclusivity can and should be implemented. Finally, we will analyse the graduate attributes and Vision 2030 statements of three South African universities, exploring how these institutions are navigating the complex landscape of curriculum transformation and inclusivity in the post-apartheid era.

## Glocal Engagement Framework

The GEF is a comprehensive approach to international higher education development (Patel et al., 2011). This framework was developed to offer a model for educational design, implementation, and assessment strategies that are pragmatic in nature (Patel, 2017; Patel et al., 2014). Pragmatism in education suggests that the education system should continuously evolve to meet the needs of students (Sharma et al., 2018). Consequently, GEF advocates for the creation of new values within the education system, as systems and theories should not remain fixed. This approach enables students to gain practical experience while studying. Therefore, universities in South Africa (and globally) emphasise WIL to provide students with practical experience (Dlamini, 2018). According to Dlamini et al. (2023), WIL is a global concept that describes an educational approach for undergraduate students to apply their theoretical knowledge in real-world professional practice relevant to their studies. Consequently, the curriculum should be flexible enough to accommodate the needs of all students so that they can be employed effectively. The GEF asserts that students should be taught problem-solving skills that they can use to address complex societal challenges (Patel, 2017). For example, they should be taught how to create employment opportunities for others, as societies often face the challenge of unemployment (Patel et al., 2014; Sharma et al., 2018).

The GEF comprises four dimensions: Intellect, Emotion, Action, and Morality (Patel et al., 2014). These dimensions are crucial components of the globalisation framework, as each ensures that the education system, including higher education, is fair, inclusive, and diverse (Patel, 2020; Patel et al., 2014). Therefore, this approach necessitates individuals, such as lecturers and administrators, to demonstrate knowledge and wisdom that can promote glocal perspectives or GEF dimensions. Patel (2017) suggests that those involved in higher education should possess all dimensions because intellect alone is insufficient to address the complexities of a glocal environment. Emotions should be managed carefully (Patel, 2020; Patel et al., 2014). This means those engaged in the learning process should exhibit sensitivity, understanding, intuition, and compassion when dealing with diversity in higher education (Patel, 2017). The GEF is an action-driven framework that requires individuals and groups to act (Patel, 2017). Through action, transformation in higher education will occur (Patel, 2020). Action entails a commitment and responsibility (Patel et al., 2014) to bring about social change in higher education. Morality is the final dimension critical to GEF, as it stipulates that students should be taught high standards of morality to ensure that challenges brought into the glocal space or dialog can be assessed on ethical grounds (Patel et al., 2014). This dimension mandates learning institutions to design a curriculum that educates university and college students on the responsibility to act with integrity, virtue, and fairness (Patel, 2017, 2020).

## Methodology

This systematic literature review aimed to analyse, evaluate, and consolidate the literature concerning South African higher education, particularly focussing on the nature of its curriculum (Cronin et al., 2008). The objective of this study was to determine how higher education has transformed its curriculum and the nature of assessments to accommodate the needs of students. In this chapter, existing literature reviews serve as primary data sources (Ramdhani et al., 2014). When reviewing the literature, scholars delineated the content of already available knowledge, effectively conveying the significance of existing research (Ramdhani et al., 2014). However, our approach differed in this chapter; rather than merely regurgitating the subject matter, we contributed to existing knowledge by synthesising available material and offering a scholarly critique (Okoli & Schabram, 2010). This was achieved by employing the GEF as a theoretical approach, allowing for an analysis of the status of South African higher education.

## Review Teams

For this chapter, there were two separate teams assigned to conduct the literature search. The second author of this chapter led the first team responsible for searching peer-reviewed journal articles on higher education curriculum and inclusion, both nationally and internationally. Subsequently, the second team, led by the first author, focussed on retrieving Vision 2030 statements from the sampled universities. The aim was to identify how these statements promote inclusion within the institutions and their impact on creating an inclusive curriculum within their institutions. The analysis was then conducted collaboratively by both teams.

Twenty peer-reviewed articles and the Vision 2030 statements from Cape Peninsula University of Technology (CPUT), Central University of Technology (CUT), and Walter Sisulu University (WSU) were reviewed to identify how they promote inclusive curriculum. We sampled these universities because they are historically disadvantaged and currently enrol students from disadvantaged backgrounds. The objective of this study was to investigate how the curriculum of these institutions addresses the needs of their student populations. We decided to use the original names of the sampled institutions because they are public institutions, and their Vision 2030 statements are publicly available. These Vision 2030 statements were obtained from the universities' official websites. Therefore, the information discussed in this paper is accessible to the public, and the use of the institutions' names is considered ethical.

## Method of Review

The literature review process was conducted in three phases, as stipulated by Thomas et al. (2015):

- *Establishing the Title of the Study*, therefore, 'Higher education curriculum and inclusion'.
- *Defining the Criteria*: We defined both inclusion and exclusion criteria for our literature search. For inclusion, we focussed on literature using keywords such as curriculum, inclusive assessment, inclusion, inclusive curriculum, higher education, and globalisation in higher education. Our exclusion criteria were equally important in refining our search. We excluded non-peer-reviewed sources; publications older than 20 years, unless they were addressing past injustices of the apartheid era; studies focussed solely on primary or secondary education; non-English language publications and opinion pieces or editorials without substantial empirical or theoretical grounding.
- *Establishing the Theoretical Approach*: This chapter used the GEF as a theoretical approach because we deemed it crucial for conducting this systematic literature review study.

## Historical Background of Higher Education

In 1948, the United Nations declared the Universal Declaration of Human Rights (UDHR) to ensure that nations become cognisant of human rights violations. The UDHR (1948), in Articles 1 and 2, states:

> All human beings are born free and equal in dignity and rights. Everyone is entitled to all the rights and freedoms set forth in this declaration, without distinction of any kind, such as race, colour, sex, language, religion, political or other opinion, national or social origin, property, birth or other status.

The declaration emphasises the significance of preserving the dignity of all human beings and promoting their human rights. The UDHR laid the foundation for promoting human dignity and rights globally. Furthermore, in 1990, the World Conference on Education for All in Jomtien, Thailand, marked a significant milestone in the global commitment to education (Florian, 2014). The conference resulted in the World Declaration on Education for All, which emphasised the significance of basic education for all learners in the world (UNESCO, 1990). This declaration promoted the concept of inclusive education by advocating for universal access to education and focussing on learning needs rather than merely providing access. It encouraged education systems to be more responsive to diverse learner needs, laying groundwork for curriculum reforms that would accommodate diverse learning styles and backgrounds (Florian, 2014).

The Salamanca Statement of 1994 stipulates that to achieve inclusion in educational institutions, the curriculum must be sufficiently flexible to accommodate the needs of every student (UNESCO, 1994). In transforming higher education and its curriculum, the Salamanca Declaration is often used as a guiding document influencing policies on curriculum, inclusion, and diversity (Mugambi, 2017). The Salamanca Statement (UNESCO, 1994) emphasises that acquiring knowledge extends beyond formal and theoretical instruction alone. The curriculum should adhere to high standards and cater to the needs of individuals, thus enabling their full participation in the educational system. Teaching should be connected to students' own experiences and practical enough to motivate them to become better citizens of the country (Stentiford & Koutsouris, 2022; UNESCO, 1994). Mugambi (2017) asserts that the development and implementation of policies that support inclusive education at all levels of education are significant and will assist in promoting education for all, as stipulated in the Salamanca Statement.

In 1999, the African Charter on the Rights and Welfare of the Child was adopted, specifically addressing the rights of children in the African context (Human Rights Law in Africa, 1999). Article 11 of this charter focusses on education, stating that every child has the right to education and emphasising the need to preserve and strengthen positive African morals, traditional values, and cultures (Lloyd, 2002). This charter is particularly relevant to curriculum development in African countries (Human Rights Law in Africa, 1999), including South Africa, as it calls for education that respects and promotes African cultural identity and values while preparing children for responsible life in a free society.

These international movements and declarations collectively align with the South African constitution, which emphasises the importance of accessible and equal education for all (Department of Justice, 1996). Therefore, providing an inclusive curriculum in higher education is mandatory and lawful. South Africa, as a democratic country, is obligated to adhere to the law, especially when aiming to create inclusive societies where people can live together without prejudice and discrimination. According to Ogude et al. (2005), the curriculum taught in higher education can contribute to creating a cohesive society by adhering to inclusive policies that eliminate discrimination against marginalised groups. Suppose lecturers do not possess the four GEFs dimensions, which require them to be intellectuals, emotionally intelligent, sympathetic, and willing to act in decolonising or transforming the curriculum. In that case, the curriculum will produce students who may struggle to thrive in the glocal world, where individuals capable of problem-solving are needed (Patel et al., 2014).

During the Apartheid regime, which was introduced in 1948 and ended in April 1994, deliberate racist policies and laws were enacted, legitimising numerous discriminatory practices (Madadzhe, 2019). For example, the system introduced the Extension of University Education Act No. 45 of 1959, which regulated the admission processes of non-Whites to higher education and was facilitated by the

Native Affairs Department (Beale, 1998). Magopeni and Tshiwula (2010) argue that non-Whites were admitted to colleges located in deep rural areas through this act. Furthermore, the Act prevented Black and Coloured people from attending tertiary education in urban areas with White students (Beale, 1998). It was a criminal offense for 'non-whites' to register at a white university without obtaining state permission (Beale, 1998; Magopeni & Tshiwula, 2010). In addition, the introduction of Bantu Education Act No. 47 of 1953 further segregated the education system in terms of race (Beale, 1998; Magopeni & Tshiwula, 2010). In other words, apartheid created four separate and distinct education departments that cater to Whites, Indians, Coloureds, and Blacks as was previously known. However, in recent literature it is termed Africans. In 1985, a total of 19 HEIs were designated for the exclusive use of white students, two were designed for Africans or Blacks students, six institutions were designated for Coloureds and two for Indian students (Bunting, 2006). White universities, such as the University of Cape Town, only accommodated English speakers. In contrast, universities like the University of Stellenbosch and the University of the Orange Free State exclusively admitted Afrikaans-speaking students (Madadzhe, 2019). Each institution had its own curriculum tailored to serve the needs of the apartheid system (Ogude et al., 2005).

While the higher education system in South Africa has seen significant restructuring since 1994, historical barriers still impede access to higher education. Despite the government's efforts, such as merging several institutions in 2005, these changes have not effectively addressed the underlying issues. Many students, particularly those from marginalised backgrounds, still need to work on exclusion due to financial constraints (Saurombe, 2018). The Council on Higher Education (CHE) (2016) and Saurombe (2018) share concerns that the current funding systems fail to support marginalised communities in accessing tertiary education. Moreover, efforts towards curriculum reform have not adequately reflected the diverse IK of South Africa's population (Muswede, 2017; Saurombe, 2018). Thus, while there have been revisions to the curriculum, these changes have not fully addressed the needs of all citizens, as IK remains largely absent (Stentiford & Koutsouris, 2022).

To rectify the injustices of the apartheid system, the South African government implemented policies and an education system aimed at safeguarding the dignity of all students, irrespective of their backgrounds, race, gender, or other differences (Madadzhe, 2019; Mdepa & Tshiwula, 2012). Although the policies and the new system of education are in place, challenges in higher education persist. To address these challenges, the government mandated that institutions of higher learning develop inclusive language policies for teaching and learning. South Africa has 11 official languages, nine of which are African languages. Before 1994, many universities operated with a single-language medium of instruction. However, following the post-1994 era, each institution was directed by the Language Policy for Higher Education (LPHE) of 2002 to incorporate one African language into their policies and offer courses teaching that language (Foley, 2004). Nonetheless, the issue of language of instruction poses significant challenges. Foley (2004) critiques the LPHE, suggesting that it fails to adequately address past injustices, particularly in its linguistic application. He highlights the diversity within African languages, such as Northern Sotho and Selobedo, which are dialects of Sepedi. Yet, in institutional policies, Northern Sotho tends to dominate, overlooking other dialects. Consequently, the language promoted in educational institutions may not accurately represent the entire population (Foley, 2004). Therefore, this chapter explores how the democratic government of South Africa has transformed the system and ensured the implementation of an inclusive curriculum in higher education.

## Decolonising Higher Education Curriculum

In South Africa, the issue of decolonisation began in 2015 when students from various institutions demanded the abolition of fees and decolonisation of the curriculum (Cini, 2019; Mheta et al., 2018). In this chapter, decolonisation should be interpreted as a process of rejecting colonial education, which was structured around colonialism (Fataar, 2018a). Therefore, decolonisation involves removing colonial legacies so that students can achieve their full potential and reclaim their humanity, which was suppressed by the colonial system (Fataar, 2018a). Before 2015, the curricula in South African institutions of higher learning were largely Eurocentric in nature (Mheta et al., 2018), thus failing to address the needs of African students. The content being taught did not align with the core values of African students (Saurombe, 2018). In addition, the assessment methods did not reflect the realities faced by African students. Another challenge was how lecturers presented the content; it did not resonate with the lived experiences of students, particularly those raised in Africa, such as B students. According to Mheta et al. (2018), the colonialism and apartheid system curricula denigrated and undermined IK systems. In other words, the knowledge systems practised in Africa before colonialism were disregarded by these two systems, resulting in an oppressive higher education environment. Saurombe (2018) asserts that the South African higher education system was shaped by colonial rule, primarily serving the goals of the colonial masters to undermine IK in any form.

Students from the University of Witwatersrand (WITS), Rhodes University, the University of Cape Town, and others demonstrated their dissatisfaction by protesting and calling for decolonising higher education. CPUT and WSU participated in the Fees-must-Fall movement, and their dissatisfaction was demonstrated by the South African media. According to Cini (2019), the Fees-Must-Fall movement results from the 10% increase in fees announced in October 2015 by Professor Adam Habib. The movement lasted 10 days, and students demanded decolonisation in higher education, including decolonisation of curricula (Booysen, 2016; Cini, 2019). According to Costandius et al. (2018), the protest played a critical role in decolonising the curriculum of a number of South African institutions of higher education. Greeff et al. (2021) have identified the following aspects that were critical for the movement:

- Raised public awareness for the need for financial aid and curriculum changes at universities.

- Some universities started decolonising their curricula.
- Seen as legitimate efforts towards social justice and decolonisation of tertiary education.

While the movement raised awareness and prompted some universities to start decolonisation efforts, Greeff et al. (2021) suggest the violent tactics and resulting financial/operational impacts could have slowed down or hindered the very changes the students were calling for. The volatile nature of some protests during Fees-Must-Fall was ultimately counterproductive to expediting curriculum transformation across universities (Costandius et al., 2018; Greeff et al., 2021).

## Graduate Attributes and Vision 2030 for Higher Education

One way to decolonise the curriculum in higher education is to introduce graduate attributes (Bester et al., 2018). South African universities have faced increasing pressure from industry to produce graduates who are prepared for the workforce, capable of adapting, problem-solving, and thinking critically to tackle the challenges of the 21st century (Faller et al., 2023, p. 95). In response, universities across the country have had to adapt their curriculum to meet the evolving demands of the job market (Cook, 2018, p. 57). However, universities should not solely focus on theoretical perspectives but also consider broader attributes beyond employability (Hill et al., 2016; Winberg et al., 2018). Graduates must be equipped with the knowledge and skills necessary to navigate an uncertain future and be responsible citizens (Bowden et al., 2000). Institutions of higher learning worldwide have established graduate attributes aligned with their vision and mission statements to produce graduates suitable for the contemporary world (Barrie, 2004). This aligns with the GEF, which promotes the respectful exchange of IK and perspectives among local and global communities (Patel, 2020).

In 2018, the CPUT developed Vision 2030, focussing on aspects of oneness and smartness that influence the university curriculum (Nhamo, 2020). This vision was crucial during and after the COVID-19 pandemic. It emphasised the use of technology for teaching to respond to the demands of the 21st century by enabling digital learning during lockdowns. To complement its vision and mission statement, CPUT identified four graduate attributes. CPUT identified graduate attributes that drive the institution's learning and teaching culture: technological capability and foresight, resilience and problem-solving capability, relational capability, and ethical capability. Therefore, these graduate attributes should be incorporated into the curriculum (Winberg et al., 2018). In this scenario, the curriculum will be inclusive, and academics will change their assessment to respond to these graduate attributes (Bester et al., 2018). The South African CHE (2013) considers graduate attributes essential, mandating institutions of learning to incorporate them across various disciplines and fields. Bester et al. (2018) argue that this is crucial as it enables modules or subjects in higher education to integrate values, attitudes, critical thinking, and ethical and professional behaviour into their curriculum, empowering graduates to apply what they have learned beyond the confines of the classroom.

Hence, CPUT encourages students to acknowledge different cultures and become global citizens through Vision 2030. Global citizenship requires students to solve societal challenges such as natural disasters, human perils, and conflicts related to religion, land, and family (Patel, 2020). In this glocalised learning space, real-life natural disasters and human peril situations serve as case studies for assessment. This approach aligns with Patel's et al. (2014) assessment as learning approach to curriculum design and implementation.

At WSU (2020), the vision statement comprises three main elements: impactful, technology-infused, and African. Impactful emphasises student success, while technology-infused encourages the use of technological tools in the classroom. Last, Africans acknowledge the diverse backgrounds of their students (WSU, 2020). Consequently, university graduates must possess the ability to access various opportunities in industry, the public sector, civil society, and entrepreneurial activities (WUSU, 2019). The university's 2030 vision commits to providing students with an enriching and liberating educational experience that prepares them for successful post-university careers.

Furthermore, the Vision 2030 document stipulates that the university must significantly impact by ensuring that its main activities (assessments) contribute to creating a just, equitable, and sustainable world (WSU, 2020). According to WSU (2020), the assertion that it is an African university reflects the institution's location, people, and dedication to the African context. Being an African university signifies Africa's contribution to global knowledge and acknowledges the socio-cultural richness from which the institution draws nourishment. The university recognises that knowledge institutions embody local and global attributes and must continually leverage the best attributes to fulfil their mandates (WSU, 2020). WSU's (2020) Vision 2030 aligns with globalisation, embracing indigenous histories, cultures, and knowledge forms, and promoting the construction of third-culture perspectives as common ground (Patel et al., 2014). Third-culture perspectives recognise the rights of both local and global communities to utilise their language, history, and culture within the education system (Patel, 2020). Ethnicity and cultural background should not be used against individuals or prevent them from accessing education.

WSU (2020) intends to assess how its teaching and learning, research and innovation, and community engagement contribute to sustainable and equitable development by considering specific frameworks. At the local level, it will adhere to the Eastern Cape Vision 2030 Provincial Development Plan. Nationally, it aligns with the National Development Plan, which aims to eradicate poverty and reduce inequality by 2030 through fostering sustainable growth and development. At the continental level, it will adhere to the African Union (AU) Agenda 2063, which outlines the vision for the desired future of Africa. Additionally, it will incorporate the Sustainable Development Goals, which highlight 17 critical areas requiring urgent global action to steer the world towards a new developmental trajectory.

Dwesini (2015) argues that WSU is committed to transforming the curriculum, epistemology, and metaphysical approaches to knowledge creation. This transformation is crucial for developing students' metacognitive abilities in response to the evolving world of technology (Patel, 2020). Therefore, universities such as WSU, CPUT, and CUT should train a cohort of students who have acquired scientific knowledge and skills across various disciplinary and professional contexts. This will enable students to effectively address glocal challenges such as unemployment, sexual violence, and crime (Hicks & Holden, 2007).

Similarly, the CUT introduced Vision 2030, shifting to a hybrid model of learning to align with the needs of the 21st century and embrace technology-enhanced learning (Nhamo, 2020). Vision 2030 is not unique to South Africa; it is a global phenomenon seen in other countries, such as Saudi Arabia, with initiatives like Vision 2023 aimed at education system reform. However, despite efforts to create smart institutions using technology, disparities persist, creating challenges for students from disadvantaged backgrounds (Simamora et al., 2020). Issues such as poor connectivity, lack of data, and inadequate devices hindered access to the curriculum for students from disadvantaged backgrounds. Such inequities hinder the promotion of a quality and equitable education system that responds to students' strengths and cultural wealth (Patel & Lynch, 2013).

According to the CUT's (2020) vision statement, by 2030, the university will become a leading African university of technology. This will be achieved by shaping the future through innovation. In addition, the vision statement states that the concept of a top African university is to recognise the university's geographical location and remember its location in the matrix of social and economic challenges facing Africa. In addition, it emphasised the importance of recognising IK and the urgent need to decolonise the curriculum to solve African problems, speak to Africans, and express African values such as Ubuntu. The university's vision talks about shaping the future through innovation, meaning that the university wants to be an active force of change where innovative solutions to South Africa's problems and the world can be discovered (CUT, 2019).

From the literature mentioned above, it appears that these higher learning institutions have inclusive policies that address the diverse needs of their students. However, Dwesini (2015) points out that academics and administrators should play a significant role in implementing university policies, such as graduate attributes and strategic plans for 2030. In other words, having progressive policies without effective implementation would be futile, as it would perpetuate the marginalisation of certain groups within society. Academics are tasked with reinforcing these policies and ensuring that glocalisation occurs by integrating the theory taught in lecture halls into WIL experiences (Madadzhe, 2019; Patel, 2020). Therefore, the curriculum and assessment should incorporate the perspectives of both students and lecturers to cultivate proficient individuals in both theory and practice (Dwesini, 2015).

## Lessons Learned from the Review

Even though the apartheid system was abolished in South Africa, literature reveals that South African higher education still faces challenges in achieving inclusion and adoption of inclusive curriculum that accommodates the diverse need of all students in the country (Madadzhe, 2019; Mdepa & Tshiwula, 2012).

To this day, some HEIs continue to struggle with the inclusion of IK and the adoption of a fully decolonised approach to education. According to Saurombe (2018) and Mheta et al. (2018), the curriculum in HEIs remains Eurocentric. This Eurocentric approach hinders the development of a curriculum that reflects the realities of African students. In this chapter, the analysis focussed on the role of graduate attributes in shaping inclusive education in higher education. Bester et al. (2018) emphasise that graduate attributes are crucial for providing students with the necessary skills and values to navigate the world of work. However, while the importance of graduate attributes is recognised, implementing these attributes across institutions remains a significant challenge (Fataar, 2018b).

Furthermore, the review highlighted the importance of WIL, which serves as a bridge between the theoretical knowledge that student–teachers receive at their institutions and the practical skills required in the workforce. Dlamini (2018) notes that WIL is a vital element in higher education as it ensures that graduates are academically prepared and equipped with the necessary experience to meet workforce demands. However, a challenge in higher education is the inconsistent implementation of the WIL component in programmes like the Bachelor of Education (BEd) (Awung et al., 2024). Lastly, the review of graduate attributes from institutions like CPUT, CUT, and WUS reveals that inclusivity remains a challenge due to existing language policies. For instance, students from diverse backgrounds and with different languages are often only acknowledged or supported in two or three languages. Foley (2004) argues that the linguistic diversity within African languages poses challenges for institutions of higher learning in creating inclusive learning spaces. As a result, some languages or dialects are promoted while others are marginalised, leading to ongoing inequalities in the higher education system (Foley, 2004). These lessons from the review form the foundation for the recommendations that follow.

## Recommendations

In this chapter, we recommend that the Department of Higher Education develop an education system with an inclusive curriculum aligned with the GEF dimensions. Institutions of higher learning should ensure their curriculum includes WIL, which will be meaningful in achieving Vision 2030 statements and ensuring that graduates in the 21st century meet societal demands. WIL should foster practical skills acquisition and problem-solving through experiential learning (Dlamini et al., 2023). Furthermore, the chapter recommends that lecturers and administrators find ways to decolonise curriculum content to embrace diversity and acknowledge marginalised groups in society. The curriculum should include more African/IK and perspectives in the taught content (Patel, 2020). The curriculum content should be designed to be responsive to the diverse student population and flexible enough to accommodate the needs of all students enrolled in higher education. However, Mpu and Adu (2021) argue that making the curriculum flexible is not always feasible due to the diverse nature of higher education. Another recommendation is that institutions of higher learning should strengthen language policies to ensure that multilingualism in higher education is observed. The chapter calls for comprehensive curriculum transformation to realise the constitutional vision of accessible and equitable higher education in South Africa.

## Conclusion

In conclusion, decolonisation in higher education is critical, especially in South Africa, especially by looking at past injustices that segregated education. In this chapter, we argue that glocalisation can be a solution to the challenges of South African higher education because it will assist in placing people at the centre of a shared identity, where students from different backgrounds learn to live together and embrace the diversity that exists.

Placing people at the centre of a shared identity, where students from different backgrounds learn to live together and embrace diversity. This chapter examines how inclusive curricula can be developed in HEIs to accommodate students from different backgrounds with different learning needs. How can students be accommodated to prepare them for the future? As mentioned in this chapter, the complex history of apartheid in South Africa still affects the country's education system.

This chapter provides a comprehensive analysis of curriculum inclusivity in South African higher education through the lens of university vision and mission statements. South African higher education is progressive in terms of curriculum inclusivity. The sampled university's vision 2030 statements show that universities are willing to transform the curriculum to make it inclusive. Evidence from the Vision 2030s of the sampled universities shows that the universities want to address the needs of the country, especially a diverse and complex country like South Africa, and respond to the needs of the world as well.

CPUT Vision 2030 is based on Ubuntu philosophy, which is an African philosophy that says *umntu ngumntu ngabantu* (I am, because you are), and that is where the oneness dimension comes from. Irrespective of our different backgrounds, religions, learning styles, or sexual orientations, we are still one, and we can work together. The university's oneness means that no student will be left behind because of a different learning ability, language, religion, and other differences. According to the graduates identified by CPUT, CUT, and WSU, the offered curriculum will be inclusive and current to ensure that the institutions produce graduates who are ready to solve the world's challenges.

After analysing the three universities' Vision 2030 statements, it can be argued that the university's visions are clear in developing a curriculum suitable for the needs of the country and the world. However, with all these visions, the 2030s and inclusive curriculum are universities producing what the country needs. With the higher unemployment rate in South Africa, a question should be asked if these visions and progressive curricula are only good on paper as there are not enough entrepreneurs in the country to solve the unemployment problem. Is the curriculum inclusive enough when university students still protest for funding and residences every year?

## References

Ainscow, M. (2020). Promoting inclusion and equity in education: Lessons from international experiences. *Nordic Journal of Studies in Educational Policy*, 6(1), 7–16.

Awung, F., Felix, A., Botes, W., Fru, R., Wepener, T., & Moloele, R. (2024). Induction-phase challenges faced by South African higher education students: A case study of Sol Plaatje University. *African Journal of Inter/Multidisciplinary Studies*, 6(1), 1–12.

Barrie, S. C. (2004). A research-based approach to generic graduate attributes policy. *Higher Education Research & Development*, 23(3), 261–275.

Beale, M. A. (1998). *Apartheid and university education, 1948–1970*. [Doctoral dissertation, Wits University].

Bester, M., Sebolao, R., Machika, P., Scholtz, D., Makua, M., Staak, A., & Ronald, N. (2018). In search of graduate attributes: A survey of six flagship programmes. *South African Journal of Higher Education*, 32(1), 233–251.

Booysen, S. (2016). Edging out the African national congress in the city of Johannesburg: A case of collective punishment. *Journal of Public Administration*, 51(si1), 532–548.

Bowden, J., Hart, G., King, B., Trigwell, H., & Watts, O. (2000). *Generic capabilities of ATN University graduates*. Australian Government Department of Education, Training and Youth Affairs. http:/www.clt.uts.edu.au/atn.grad.cap.project.index.html

Bunting, I. (2006). The higher education landscape under apartheid. *Transformation in Cape Peninsula University of Technology. 2020. Vision 2030*. Retrieved July 2, 2024, from https://www.cut.ac.za/mission-statement.

Central University of Technology. (2020). Graduate attributes: Shaping the future through education and innovation. Central University of Technology. https://www.cut.ac.za/graduateattributes

Cini, L. (2019). Disrupting the neoliberal university in South Africa: The# FeesMustFall movement in 2015. *Current Sociology*, 67(7), 942–959.

Cloete, N., Maassen, P., Fehnel, R., Moja, T., & Perold, H. (Eds.), (2006). *Higher education: Global pressures and local realities* (pp. 35–52). Springer Netherlands.

Cook, P.S. (2018). Examining the graduate attribute agenda in Australian universities: A review of (continuing) problems and pitfalls. *Learning and Teaching*, 11(3), 49–62.

Costandius, E., Nell, I., Alexander, N., McKay, M., Blackie, M., Malgas, R., & Setati, E. (2018). # FeesMustFall and decolonising the curriculum: Stellenbosch University students' and lecturers' reactions. *South African Journal of Higher Education*, 32(2), 65–85.

Council on Higher Education (CHE). (2013). *A framework for qualification standards in higher education*. Council on Higher Education. http://www.che.ac.za/documents/d000248/

Council on Higher Education and Training. (2016). *South African higher education reviewed—two decades of democracy*. CHE. https://www.che.ac.za/sites/default/files/inline-files/CHE%20MONITOR%2016_DIGITAL%20COPY_HI%20RES.pdf

Cronin, P., Ryan, F., & Coughlan, M. (2008). Undertaking a literature review: a step-by-step approach. *British Journal of Nursing*, 17(1), 38–43.

Dlamini, M. E. (2018). Preparing student teachers for teaching in rural schools using work integrated learning. *The Independent Journal of Teaching and Learning*, 13(1), 86–96.

Dlamini, N. Z., Mpofu, K., Ramatsetse, B., & Makinde, O. (2023). Immersive virtual work integrated learning: A scoping review. *Procedia CIRP*, 118, 1044–1049.

Dwesini, N. F. (2015). Assessing learners' preparedness for work-integrated learning (WIL) at Walter Sisulu University, South Africa. *African Journal of Hospitality, Tourism and Leisure*, 4(2), 1–12.

Faller, F., Burton, S., Kaniki, A., Leitch, A., & Ntshoe, I. (2023). Achieving doctorateness: Is South African higher education succeeding with graduate attributes?' *South African Journal of Higher Education*, 37(2), 93–108.

Fataar, A. (2018a). Decolonising education in South Africa: Perspectives and debates. *Educational Research for Social Change, 7*(SPE), vi–ix.
Fataar, A. (2018b). Placing students at the centre of the decolonizing education imperative: Engaging the (mis) recognition struggles of students at the post-apartheid university. *Educational Studies, 54*(6), 595–608.
Florian, L. (2014). Preparing teachers to work with students with disabilities: An international perspective. In *Handbook of research on special education teacher preparation* (pp. 47–64). Routledge.
Foley, A. (2004). Language policy in higher education in South Africa: Implications and complications: perspectives on higher education. *South African Journal of Higher Education, 18*(1), 57–71.
Greeff, M., Mostert, K., Kahl, C., & Jonker, C. (2021). The# FeesMustFall protests in South Africa: Exploring first-year students' experiences at a peri-urban university campus. *South African Journal of Higher Education, 35*(4), 78–103.
Hicks, D., & Holden, C. (2007). *Teaching the global dimension: Key principles and effective practice*. Routledge.
Hill, J., Walkington, H., & France, D. (2016). Graduate attributes: Implications for higher education practice and policy: Introduction. *Journal of Geography in Higher Education, 40*(2), 155–163.
Human Rights Law in Africa. (1999) The African charter on the rights and welfare of the child. *Human Rights Law in Africa Online, 3*(1), 127–127.
Le Grange, L. (2020). Decolonising the university curriculum: The what, why and how. In N. Gough & J. Chi-Kim (Eds.), *Transnational education and curriculum studies* (pp. 216–233). Routledge.
Lloyd, A. (2002). A theoretical analysis of the reality of children's rights in Africa: An introduction to the African Charter on the Rights and Welfare of the Child. *African Human Rights Law Journal, 2*(11), 11–42.
Madadzhe, R. N. (2019). Using African languages at universities in South Africa: The struggle continues. *Stellenbosch Papers in Linguistics Plus, 58*(1), 205–218.
Magopeni, N., & Tshiwula, L. (2010, July). The realities of dealing with South Africa's past: A diversity in higher education. Paper presented at the Tenth International Conference on Diversity in Organizations, Communities & Nations, 19–21 July, Queen's University Belfast, Northern Ireland.
McGrath, S. (2004). Reviewing the development of the South African further education and training college sector ten years after the end of apartheid. *Journal of Vocational Education and Training, 56*(1), 137–160.
Mdepa, W., & Tshiwula, L. (2012). Student diversity in South African higher education. *Widening Participation and Lifelong Learning, 13*(1), 19–33.
Mheta, G., Lungu, B. N., & Govender, T. (2018). Decolonisation of the curriculum: A case study of the Durban University of Technology in South Africa. *South African Journal of Education, 38*(4), 1–7.
Mpu, Y., & Adu, E. O. (2021). The challenges of inclusive education and its implementation in schools: The South African perspective. *Perspectives in Education, 39*(2), 225–238.
Mugambi, M. M. (2017). Approaches to inclusive education and implications for curriculum theory and practice. *International Journal of Humanities Social Sciences and Education, 10*(4), 92–106.
Muswede, T. (2017). Colonial legacies and the decolonisation discourse in post-apartheid South Africa – A reflective analysis of student activism in Higher Education. *African Journal of Public Affairs, 9*(5), 200–210.
Nhamo, G. (2020). Higher education and the energy sustainable development goal: Policies and projects from University of South Africa. In G. Nhamo & V. Mjimba (Eds.), *Sustainable development goals and institutions of higher education* (pp. 31–48). Springer.

Ntshoe, I. (2017). Resegregation and recreation of racism in education in a post-apartheid setting. *Southern African Review of Education with Education with Production, 23*(1), 70–90.

Ogude, N., Nel, H., & Oosthuizen, M. (2005). *The challenge of curriculum responsiveness in South African higher education.* Council on Higher Education.

Okoli, C., & Schabram, K. (2010). *A guide to conducting a systematic literature review of information systems research.* Sprouts.

Patel, S. (2017). Colonial modernity and methodological nationalism: The structuring of sociological traditions of India. *Sociological Bulletin, 66*(2), 125–144.

Patel, F. (2020). Glocal development for sustainable social change. In J. Servaes (Eds.), *Handbook of communication for development and social change* (pp. 501–517). https://doi.org/10.1007/978-981-10-7035-8_77-1

Patel, F., Li, M., & Piscioneri, M. (2014). Cross-institutional and interdisciplinary dialogue on curriculum for global engagement: Emerging perspectives and concerns. *Journal of International and Global Studies, 5*(2), 40–43.

Patel, F., & Lynch, H. (2013). Glocalization as an alternative to internationalization in higher education: Embedding positive glocal learning perspectives. *International Journal of Teaching and Learning in Higher Education, 25*(2), 223–230.

Ramdhani, A., Ramdhani, M. A., & Amin, A. S. (2014). Writing a literature review research paper: A step-by-step approach. *International Journal of Basic and Applied Science, 3*(1), 47–56.

Saurombe, A. (2018). The teaching of indigenous knowledge as a tool for curriculum transformation and Africanisation. *Journal of Education, 138*(1), 30–39.

Sharma, S., Devi, R., & Kumari, J. (2018). Pragmatism in education. *International Journal of Engineering Technology Science and Research, 5*(1), 1549–1554.

Simamora, R. M., De Fretes, D., Purba, E. D., & Pasaribu, D. (2020). Practices, challenges, and prospects of online learning during COVID-19 pandemic in higher education: Lecturer perspectives. *Studies in Learning and Teaching, 1*(3), 185–208.

Stentiford, L., & Koutsouris, G. (2022). Critically considering the 'inclusive curriculum' in higher education. *British Journal of Sociology of Education, 43*(8), 1250–1272.

The United Nations Educational, Scientific and Cultural Organization (UNESCO). (1990). *World declaration on education for all and framework for action to meet basic learning needs.* Inter-Agency Commission.

The United Nations Educational, Scientific and Cultural Organization (UNESCO). (1994). *The Salamanca Statement and framework for action on special needs education.*

Thomas, B., Tachble, A., Peiris, D., Malhi, R., Godlovitch, G., & Lin, Y. (2015). Making literature reviews more ethical: A researcher and health sciences librarian collaborative process. *Future Science OA, 1*(4), 1–6.

United Nations. General Assembly. (1948). *Universal declaration of human rights* (Vol. 3381). Department of State, United States of America.

United Nations. (1989). *UN convention on the right of the child.* Author.

Van der Berg, S. (2007). Apartheid's enduring legacy: Inequalities in education. *Journal of African Economies, 16*(5), 849–880.

Walter Sisulu University (WSU). (2020). *Vision and strategic 2030.* Retrieved February 10, 2024, from https://www.wsu.ac.za/index.php/home/organisational-strategy/2030-strategic-plan

Winberg, C., Bester, M., Machika, P., Makua, M., Monnapula-Mapesela, M., Ronald, N., Sabata, S., Sebelao, R., Scholtz, D., Snyman, J., & Staak, A. (2018). In search of graduate attributes: A survey of six flagship programmes. *South African Journal of Higher Education, 32*(1), 233–251.

Chapter 5

# Strategies of Support for Inclusive Teaching and Learning in Higher Education

*Thabo Makhalemele and Appolonia Masunungure*

North-West University, South Africa

## Abstract

Inclusive teaching strategies are fully employed in institutions of further and higher learning to ensure access to teaching and learning. Strategies such as the Universal Design for Learning (UDL) and Open Education Resources (OER) emerged as the most effective types of inclusive learning and teaching in further and higher education institutions (HEIs) worldwide. This chapter presents a systematic literature review of reflections on equity, access, and inclusion in the implementation of inclusive education in South African institutions of higher learning, with specific reference to the UDL and OER. A systematic search of databases was conducted to select articles related to UDL and OER in HEIs for this review. The objective is to explore the use of UDL and OER in higher education (HE). The findings of this literature review allow HEIs to explore the efficient use of UDL and OER strategies to enhance equity, access, and inclusion in supporting diverse students in South African HE.

*Keywords*: Access; equity; higher education institutes; inclusive education; open education resources; universal design for learning

## Introduction

This chapter reports on a study that investigated strategies used for enhancing equity and inclusion to support diverse students in South African HE. Different approaches towards inclusive teaching and learning in institutions of higher learning have been implemented and regarded as predictors of success to ensure accessibility to the general education curriculum for students with disabilities and reducing learning barriers or unnecessary learning obstacles.

Since the World Declaration on Education for All (UNESCO, 1990), the Salamanca Statement (UNESCO, 1994), the Dakar Framework for Action (UNESCO, 2000), and Policy Guidelines on Inclusion in Education (UNESCO, 2009), inclusive education has been at the centre stage of education (Dalton et al., 2019). The core issues of inclusive education include 'the (1) recognised need for access to education for all persons around the world, (2) recognised need for equity in educational rights and opportunities, and (3) recognised right to receive adequate and appropriate accommodation and support for all students' (Dalton et al., 2019, p. 2). This is emphasised in the Salamanca statement which mentioned that:

> Regular schools with [an] inclusive orientation are the most effective means of combating discriminatory attitudes, creating welcoming communities, building an inclusive society and achieving education for all; moreover, they provide an effective education to the majority of children and improve the efficiency and ultimately the cost-effectiveness of the entire education system.

Based on the Salamanca Statement, inclusive education is therefore an equitable, human right, and social justice agenda that benefits all students and contributes to a more enriching educational experience. The aim is to create an equitable and supportive learning environment for all students, regardless of their background or identity. The HEI lecturer/experts are required to take cognisance of racial and socio-economic factors that impact student engagement and to provide support to all the students to enhance equity, access, and inclusion.

In institutions of further and higher learning, inclusive teaching strategies should be fully employed to ensure access to teaching and learning. The strategies such as the UDL and OER emerged as the most effective types of inclusive learning and teaching in further and HEIs worldwide (Kurelovic, 2016). The strategies are the most preferred as they help to make teaching and learning more accessible to all students. These strategies assist lecturers in their planning and delivery of their modules in inclusive learning environments. The effective use of UDL and OER gives students an opportunity to access course materials and access learning environments. However, in South African HEIs the implementation of UDL and OER still poses challenges that hampers the effective use of these strategies. Therefore, this study aims to explore the use of UDL and OER in HEIs. In view of the above, the following objectives were formulated:

- to identify the benefits of using UDL and OER in HEIs;
- to examine the challenges of implementing UDL and OER in HIEs; and
- to recommend the effective use of UDL and OER in HEIs.

To achieve the above objectives, this literature review study follows the following methodology.

## Methodology

A systematic review methodology was used to explore how the OER and UDL in HEIs were used as strategies that can enhance equity, access, and inclusion HEIs. The authors sought to identify the benefits of both UDL and OER as well as their challenges on implementation thereof. Peer-reviewed journal articles and books from Google Scholar published in English were considered for inclusion in the systematic literature review (Uman, 2011). Moreover, inclusive education policies were also reviewed to gain an in-depth understanding of the use of OER and UDL in South African HEIs. The systematic review methodology suggested by Materla et al. (2017) was employed to include papers published up to January 2023. Although the literature search was not confined to a specific starting time frame, all papers included in the literature review were published after 2006. The review methodology is illustrated in Fig. 5.1.

The papers included in the systematic literature review describe policy frameworks, concepts, and the use of UDL and OER in the implementation of inclusive education. The systematic review began by evaluating each of the A–Z databases

---

Planning the review

Step 1: Identify the objectives of the systematic literature review.

Step 2: Select keywords and databases.

---

Conducting the review

Step 3: Search the databases such as EBSCO, ERIC, Google Scholar as well as journal tables of contents and citations in previous reviews.
Results 360 search results

Step 4: Review the title and abstract to eliminate papers for duplication, foreign languages, and non-educational application.

Step 5: Detailed review of papers to eliminate papers that were not applied in higher educational contexts.
59 papers selected for full review

---

Reporting and dissemination

Step 6: Group the selected literature based on common themes.

Step 7: Report the key findings.

---

Fig. 5.1. Systematic Review Methodology.

relevant to the research area, with the preliminary search of keywords 'inclusive education', 'UDL', 'OER', and 'Higher Education' in the 'All Text' field of the advanced search for each database and limiting the search to include only peer-reviewed journal articles. These databases were significantly chosen as they systematically enclose the extensive base of application areas of equity, access, and inclusion. In some instances, other databases did not yield any satisfactory results.

Furthermore, grey literature, repeated search results, and papers that did not contain full text in English were excluded. A detailed review of the title and abstract of the remaining papers was conducted to eliminate those that did not meet the inclusion criteria for this study/systematic review (Subhash & Cudney, 2018). Fifty-nine papers remained after this step. Only papers found in the databases through the authors' institutional library were included.

## South African Policies on Inclusive Education

In South Africa, the National Plan for Higher Education commits our HEIs to increasing the access of students with special education needs. The purpose as stated clearly by DoE (2001) is to ensure access to all institutions of higher learning for disabled students and others who experience barriers to learning and this can be achieved through properly coordinated student support services. According to Chiwandire (2019), the South African government implemented policies that were aimed at radical transformation of the HE curriculum. The Higher Education Transformation-White Paper 3 was aimed at facilitating access to HE for the historically disadvantaged students (DoE, 1997). In the EWP3, lecturers were encouraged to use 'flexible models of learning and teaching, including modes of delivery, to accommodate a larger and more diverse student population (DoE, 1997, p. 7). However, Lange (2014) argued that debates on curriculum and transformation within the South African HE mainly focus of racial issues. In addition, the 2001 Education White Paper 6: Special needs education, building an inclusive education and training system (EWP6), states that 'new curriculum and assessment initiatives will be required to focus on the inclusion of the full range of diverse learning needs' (DoE, 2001, pp. 31–32). According to Ntombela (2022), having the UDL framework in HEI in South Africa would provide all students continued access to materials and resources.

## The Universal Design for Learning

South Africa has undertaken the implementation of inclusive education as a vehicle for achieving enhanced educational outcomes and equity. The UDL acknowledges that students with and without disabilities struggle to learn 'due to elements of course design, teaching, or assessment' (Temple University, 2021). Olaussen et al. (2019) acknowledge that the UDL thus challenges the traditional academic thinking about how education can be designed to accommodate all students including students with disabilities. The UDL was seen in South Africa as an instructional design framework that considers the wide range of variations in skills and abilities that exist across all students and provides a research-based set of principles and guidelines for inclusive curriculum development and delivery (McKenzie & Dalton, 2020). According to Kumar and Wideman (2014) and Smith (2012), evidence has continued to emerge that UDL has considerable potential for developing inclusive curricula. Moriña et al. (2015) is of the opinion that one of the principles of UDL emphasises the value of presenting information in multiple ways and offering multiple means of engagement. As an inclusive education strategy, the UDL embraces principles of equity, flexibility, simple and intuitive, perceptible information, and tolerance (Center for Universal Design, 1997). Capp (2017) also argues that the UDL, as an inclusive framework, is aimed at creating and implementing adaptable teaching and learning strategies that consider the diversity of students in the classroom. Students in inclusive settings would have increased understanding and appreciation of diversity (Van Mieghem et al., 2018) when lectures use the UDL. In addition, using UDL as an instructional and assessment strategy, the 'why', 'how', and 'what' of learning are addressed and this ensures that all students have access to appropriate instruction and could learn the course content (Boothe et al., 2018). Table 5.1 shows the UDL principles and their examples.

Table 5.1. Examples of Universal Design for Learning (UDL) Principles.

| UDL Principle | Examples of UDL Principle |
| --- | --- |
| Multiple means of representation<br>1. Options for perception<br>2. Options for language<br>3. Options for comprehension | • Visual information<br>  ○ Enlarged text or highlighted text<br>  ○ Lighted or different colour background<br>  ○ Use of charts, tables, and graphs<br>• Auditory information<br>  ○ Sign language, transcripts for auditory clips, closed captioning<br>  ○ Amplify sound, change rate or tone of speech<br>• Tactile information<br>  ○ Tactile graphics and models<br>  ○ Use of manipulatives: number or letter tiles, counters<br>  ○ Story box with objects<br>  ○ Books with embedded textures<br>• Other suggestions<br>  ○ Picture cards<br>  ○ Picture dictionary<br>  ○ System of prompts |

(*Continued*)

Table 5.1. (*Continued*)

| UDL Principle | Examples of UDL Principle |
| --- | --- |
| Multiple means of engagement<br>1. Options for gaining interest | • Small-group, large-group, and individual activities |
| 2. Options for sustaining interest | • Active tasks that include exploration |
|  | • Activities drawing out imagination and complex problem-solving skills |
| 3. Options for self-regulation | Use of technology: Computers, iPads, videos, cameras |
|  | • Cooperative learning groups or peer tutors |
|  | • Display of goals and schedules (lists, pictures, objects) |
|  | • Visual behaviour supports |
|  | Use of timers to regulate time sense |
| Multiple means of expression<br>1. Options for physical action | • Alternative pencils (size, colour) or pencil grips |
| 2. Options for communication | • Raised lines on paper or increased width of spacing for writing |
|  | • Large or colour paper |
|  | • Paper and pencil, computer and printer, oral composition |
|  | • Use of social media and web tools: Web design, animation, storyboards, PowerPoint, blogs, Skype, Twitter, YouTube, Instagram, Pinterest, or online journal |
|  | • Writing a play or poem, acting out a scene, creating a diagram, or developing a project |
|  | • Assistive technology: Voice-output device, single switches, iPad, scanning program, or answers (pictures) in a field of two or three |

*Source*: Adapted from materials developed by Anderson (2022, p. 260).

## *Benefits of UDL to Students*

According to Hills et al. (2022), UDL assumes that the more inclusive the course design, delivery, assessment, and engagement, the more accessible the course will be to the greatest number of students. The UDL approach calls for the course to be altered, not the student and this eliminates a one size-fits all in teaching a learning (Al-Azawei et al., 2016; Kumar & Wideman, 2014). For example, during the HEI examinations, students may opt for a take-home assignment instead of a sit-down examination (Hills et al., 2022). In this case, students are empowered to become experts who can command their own learning which gives them more control of their lives, and ways in which they do things (Novak, 2016). In addition, the use of UDL principles in HEI is vital as it accommodates all students including students with disabilities and even mental health issues who may not be able to come in the open to express their challenges (Black et al., 2014; Raue & Lewis, 2011) for fear of stigmatisation by their colleagues or their lecturers. Furthermore, using UDL as an instructional and assessment strategy, the 'why', 'how', and 'what' of learning are addressed and this ensures that all students have access to appropriate instruction and could learn the course content (Boothe et al., 2018).

### *Benefits of UDL to Lectures*

Using UDL as an inclusive strategy is also beneficial to subject experts. According to Novak (2016), lecturers who use UDL empower students to become experts who can command their own learning which gives them more control of their lives and ways in which they do things. This enhances inclusivity in teaching and learning of content. Centre for Applied Special Technology (CAST, 2018) Professional Learning argues that in a class that uses UDL, lecturers become facilitators of teaching and learning, and students become in charge of their own learning. The move from the traditional ways of teaching and learning is valuable, as this helps in promoting student engagement and collaboration. The teaching strategies include, among others offering content in various formats, videos, texts, and audios to accommodate different learning styles among students (Posey, 2021). This concurs with the DoE (2001), which asserts that the most important way of addressing barriers is to enable the process of learning and teaching to be flexible enough to accommodate different learning needs and styles, irrespective of their learning needs.

## The Implementation of UDL in South African HEI

The implementation of the UDL in South African HEIs remains a challenge as most South African HEIs still have an inflexible and inaccessible curriculum (Chiwandire & Vincent, 2019). This includes the use of Afrikaans in some universities and the use of English only as the mode of delivery in other universities. In addition, although there have been frantic efforts to decolonise and transform HEIs, issues of unwillingness and ignorance of lectures to meet the diverse needs of students have been reported (Ndlovu, 2021a). This implies that the South African education system has not been fully transformed and decolonised.

Ndlovu (2021b) also argued that although efforts have been made to provide multiple means of presentation within the UDL framework in South African HEIs, the current debates in SA are still addressing inadequacies of relevant assistive technologies and devices to accommodate students with disabilities. The following section presents the OER in HEIs.

## Open Education Resources

Many students in institution of higher learning were disadvantaged to access teaching and learning resources, depending on the nature and context of the institutions. Teaching and learning resources in these institutions of further and HE were often considered as key intellectual property accessible exclusively to privileged groups of students (Kurelovic, 2016). However, recently institutions and students share such digital resources via the Internet free of any legal, financial, or technical barriers. Torres (2013) is of the opinion that with OER education can become accessible to everyone who want to learn, while teachers can enrich their teaching practice. The open access in education was initiated by the OpenCourseWare from Massachusetts Institute of Technology, which uploaded most of their course materials on the Web in 2001, thus making them accessible worldwide and free of charge (Butcher, 2011). This was followed by other universities including those in South Africa, which extended their influence both within the academic community and among those who wish to learn.

Butcher (2011) describe OER as encompassing any educational and research resources including curriculum maps, course materials, entire and parts of e-courses, lessons plans, learning materials, textbooks, audio and video records, simulations, experiments, multimedia content, applications and games, and any other materials that have been designed for use in teaching, learning, and researching that are openly available for use without an accompanying need to pay fees. The definition of OER currently most often used is 'digitised materials offered freely and openly for educators, students and self-learners to use and reuse for teaching, learning and research' (OECD, 2007). Wiley et al. (2014) provide the following definition of OER: 'Educational materials which use a Creative Commons license, or which exist in the public domain and are free of copyright restrictions are OER.'

## Advantages of OER

According to the literature, OER has advantages for various stakeholders to ensure inclusivity in institutions of higher learning. For the benefit of this chapter reference is made to stakeholders such as government, institutions, lecturers, and students.

### *Government*

In South Africa, access to information and knowledge is the fundamental right of every human being as enshrined in the constitution. Moreover, South Africa passed the Promotion of Access to Information Act (PAIA), 2000 (Act No. 2 of 2000) to enable citizens to access information to actively promote a society in which the people have effective access to information to enable them to more fully exercise and protect all their rights. In this respect, the OER fulfil this through advancement of knowledge by unlocking information for the benefit of all (Hodgkinson-Williams, 2010). Letsoalo et al. (2022) added that OER has a potential to promote access to information to transform the teaching and learning and provides a choice to access education information in the language of their choice. Furthermore, widening participation in further and HE is high on the South African Government's policy agenda. Inclusive education policies such as Education White Paper 6 (DoE, 2001) and screening, identification, assessment, and support policy (DBE, 2014) advocate maximising the participation of all students in the culture and the curriculum of educational institutions and uncovering and minimising barriers to learning. In accordance with maximal participation, d'Antoni (2009) argues that OER has a potential to widening participation in further and HE by expanding access to non-traditional students. Archer et al. (2003) declared that widening participation is aimed to encourage more students to 'stay on' in education. The idea is to bring potential students and universities together, overcoming real and imagined barriers.

Promoting lifelong learning is regarded as one of the priorities in the South African government to enhance equity, access, and inclusion in education. Within the institution of further and HE, the Green Paper, which facilitate the transformation process, was introduced. This paper declared that the institution of higher learning shall fulfil its role in promoting lifelong learning, personal development, economic growth, nation-building, and the creation of a just and equitable society (DoE, 1998). Relating to this, Kim et al. (2015), Wiley and Hilton (2018), and Hodgkinson-Williams (2010) emphasise the significance of OER as focusing on lifelong learning. In a study conducted by van den Berg and du Toit-Brits (2023), it was declared that OERs have been used and can be used to aid lifelong learners', address the demands of knowledge, economy, and society, by examining the concept of OER, need for OER, its limitations, and promotion of OER-oriented learning.

### *Institutions*

HEIs also benefitted from OER in different ways including sharing of knowledge. Inclusivity can be defined as equitable opportunities, where no person is excluded regardless of their identities or beliefs. An inclusive learning environment goes beyond equitable opportunities and accessible design. Inclusive learning should generate a sense of belonging and mattering through meaningful contributions in an area of interest. This is affirmed by Cesar and Santos (2006) when stating that the practice of knowledge sharing has the potential to create an inclusive space. According to Hodgkinson-Williams (2010), sharing knowledge is congruent with the academic tradition. Knowledge sharing is an important aspect in HEIs as it is associated with executive support to motivate the employees (Liu, 2016; Ramjeawon & Rowley, 2017). Knowledge sharing allows workers to innovate and allow institutions of HE to exploit knowledge-based assets (Lievre & Tang, 2015). In this way, knowledge sharing is prioritised in the South African further and HEIs to preserve knowledge of experienced academics. Some of the factors that contribute to knowledge sharing in HEIs include rewards, recognition, promotion, and bonuses (Mazorodze & Mkhize, 2022). Mabaso and Dlamini (2018) mentioned that rewards are real forms of motivation to attract and keep the best talent in institutions of HE. Likewise, Suliman (2019) maintained that recognition contributes to employee retention and engagement. Moreover, according to the opinion of Rosyidah and Rosyidi (2019), promotion motivates employees to share knowledge in academic institutions. Bonuses are also old forms of motivation that could contribute to nurturing a knowledge sharing culture change in HEIs of developing countries (Mazorodze & Mkhize, 2022).

Bali et al. (2020) argued that using the OER optimally enhances the public image of the institution of further and higher learning, and the new students are further attracted. Parisky and Boulary (2013) argued that when strengthening the OER in institutions, its public image may be enhanced, and new students attracted and gaining publicity or reaching the market more quickly and thus result in an economic advantage. Furthermore, Gerber (2022) believes that OER provides a resource for students and faculty that support learning and collaboration. Griffiths et al. (2022) highlighted that OER invites collaboration among faculty, students, library staff, and institutions. In this instance, Smith et al. (2023) demonstrated that faculty and librarian collaboration can bridge together ideas and resources to benefit students. Last, the institution of further and higher learning also benefitted from the OER through attracting alumni as lifelong learners (Hodgkinson-Williams, 2010). OERs provide an excellent way for alumni to stay connected to the institution and continue with a programme of lifelong learning (Feldstein et al., 2012). Most importantly, OER give alumni the opportunity to continue to access resources as their careers and current thinking in their field of study change and develop (Sarnow & Vuorikari, 2007).

### *Lecturers*

The advantage of OER to lecturers is to access a broad range of learning resources that in many cases are peer-reviewed, which they can use for their own personal learning, incorporate into their existing units, and adapt and include in new units (Parisky & Boulary, 2013). Literature affirmed that learning resources keep lecturers updated with relevant information and helps in their professional development. According to Bušljeta (2013) lecturers use the resources to know how they can improve themselves and contribute to the learning process of their students. Urip and Kurniawati (2019) argue that the OER contribute to lecturers' personal gain through increased reputation. Reputation enables individuals to get rewards, such as autonomy and opportunity, especially for individuals who have a powerful reputation in the institution. Furthermore, Hodgkinson-Williams (2010) mentions that through OER lecturers are gaining publicity or reaching the market more quickly, which may result in an economic advantage. Publicity is important because it helps increase awareness and visibility of lecturers, which is perceived as more promotional.

### *Students*

OER can promote informal learning, where a credential is not needed (Parisky & Boulary, 2013). The literature suggests that one advantage of the informal curriculum is that it has a more flexible structure than more formal curricula. Informal curricula may be capable of adapting to the needs and interests of students, for which time is not a pre-established factor but is contingent upon the student's work place and certainly does not correspond to those comprised by formal education (Melnic & Botez, 2014). Furthermore, through OER an independent student who has access to the Internet can access material from some of the best universities in the world (Hodgkinson-Williams, 2010). In this respect, accessible materials provide students with equal access to course materials and learning opportunities. Accessibility practices help remove barriers to the student learning and lower the extra cognitive load of understanding poorly formatted materials or instructions. Moreover, OER increases student engagement and motivation by providing a wide range of experiences and learning materials online. In a study conducted by Rajiv (2017), it was found that OER helps students to access institutions by looking at their materials made available by other institutions. The subsequent section presents the recommendations for the study.

## Recommendations

To ensure equity, access, and inclusion through the effective implementation of UDL and OER in South African HEIs, the following recommendations may serve as a guide:

- Although the UDL and OER are effective inclusive strategies, most HEIs focus on improving the units of disabilities at the expense of other diverse needs of students. It is recommended that HEIs should also consider the diverse needs of all students.
- Some lecturers are not well-versed in the use of multiple means of presentation as recommended by the UDL to accommodate students who are deaf and dumb. It is thus recommended that HEIs should invest in training staff in the use of sign language so they can accommodate these students.
- The UDL relies more on multiple means of assessments that includes a take-home assignment and a sit-down examination. However, in most of South African HEIs the summative assessments are still examination oriented. It is recommended that HEIs should consider adopting multiple means of assessment including the continuous assessments to determine students' progression.
- In South Africa, we have 12 official languages while the teaching and learning including the learning resources in HEIs is mainly in English and Africans. To accommodate the diverse needs of all students, it is recommended that teaching, learning, and some study materials be printed in other languages.
- One of the successes of OER in HEIs is through collaboration of different stakeholders which seems invisible in South African. To enhance equity, access, and inclusion, it is recommended that there should be effective collaboration among faculty, students, library staff, and institutions.

The following section presents the conclusion of the study.

## Conclusion

This chapter further discussed inclusive education in South Africa and HE, and the focus was on inclusive teaching strategies. While these teaching strategies are important for the success of inclusion in further and HE, in this chapter, we argue that they both enhance equity and access since they embrace change, which is a fundamental aspect of achieving inclusion. In South Africa, there has been a growing trend towards the use of inclusive teaching strategies such as UDL and OER in HE. Both the UDL and OER promote equality by challenging the commercialisation of educational resources and hold transformational benefits for an unequal country like South Africa. However, there are numerous challenges that hinder the effective implementation of UDL, OER, and HEIs.

## References

Al-Azawei, A., Serenelli, F. & Lundqvist, K. (2016). Universal Design for Learning (UDL): A content analysis of peer-reviewed journal papers from 2012 to 2015. *Journal of the Scholarship of Teaching and Learning, 16*, 39–56.

Anderson, L. K. (2022). Using UDL to plan a book study lesson for students with intellectual disabilities in inclusive classrooms. *Teaching Exceptional Children, 54*(4), 258–267.

Archer, L., Hutchins, M., Ross, A., Leathwood, C., Gilchrist, R., & Phillips, D. (2003). *Higher education and social class: Issues of exclusion and inclusion*. Routledge Falmer.

Bali, M., Cronin, C., & Jhangiani, R. S. (2020). Framing open educational practices from a social justice perspective. *Journal of Interactive Media in Education, 1*, Article 10. http://doi.org/10.5334/jime.565

Black, R. D., Weinberg, L. A., & Brodwin, M. G. (2014). Universal design for instruction and learning: A pilot study of faculty instructional methods and attitudes related to students with disabilities in higher education. *Exceptionality Education International, 24*(1), 48–64.

Boothe, K. A., Lohmann, M. J., Donnell, K. A., & Hall, D. D. (2018). Applying the principles of universal design for learning (UDL) in the college classroom. *Journal of Special Education Apprenticeship, 7*(3), 3.

Bušljeta, R. (2013). Effective use of teaching and learning resources. *Czech-Polish Historical and Pedagogical Journal, 5*(2), 55–70.

Butcher, N. (2011). *A basic guide to open educational resources (OER)*. Commonwealth of Learning & UNESCO. http://www.col.org/resources/basic-guide-open-educational-resources-oer

Capp, M. J. (2017). The effectiveness of universal design for learning: A meta-analysis of literature between 2013 and 2016. *International Journal of Inclusive Education, 21*(8), 791–807.

Centre for Applied Special Technology (CAST). (2018). *UDL questions and answers. Universal Design for Learning Guidelines version 2.2*. http://udlguidelines.cast.org

Center for Universal Design. (1997). *The Principles of Universal Design*. https://www.ncsu.edu/ncsu/design/cud/about_ud/udprinciples.htm

Cesar, M., & Santos, N. (2006). From exclusion to inclusion: Collaborative work contributions to more inclusive learning settings. *European Journal of Psychology of Education, 21*(3), 333–346.

Chiwandire, D. (2019). Universal design for learning and disability inclusion in South African higher education curriculum. *Alternation Interdisciplinary Journal for the Study of the Arts and Humanities in Southern Africa, 27*, 6–36.

Chiwandire, D., & Vincent, L. (2019). Funding mechanisms to foster inclusion in higher education institutions for students with disabilities. *African Journal of Disability*, *8*, 1–12.

D'Antoni, S. (2009). Open educational resources: Reviewing initiatives and issues, open learning. *Journal of Open and Distance Learning*, *24*(1), 3–10.

Dalton, E. M., Lyner-Cleophas, M., Ferguson, B. T., & McKenzie, J. (2019). Inclusion, universal design and universal design for learning in higher education: South Africa and the United States. *African Journal of Disability*, *8*, 519.

Department of Basic Education (DBE). (2014). *Policy on screening, identification, assessment and support (SIAS)*. Government Printers.

Department of Education (DoE). (1997). Education White Paper 3: A programme for higher education transformation. *Government Gazette*, *390*, 18515.

Department of Education (DoE). (1998). *Green paper on further education and training (Pretoria)*. Department of Education.

Department of Education (DoE). (2001). *White Paper 6 on special needs education: Building an inclusive education and training system*. Government Printers.

Feldstein, A., Martin, M., Hudson, A., Warren, K., Hilton, J., & Wiley, D. (2012). Open textbooks and increased student access and outcomes. *European Journal of Open, Distance and E-Learning*, *1*, 1–9.

Gerber, A. (2022). OA and OER at academic libraries survey. *Library Journal*, *147*(8), 14–16.

Griffiths, R., Mislevy, J., & Wang, S. (2022). Encouraging impacts of an open education resource degree initiative on college students' progress to degree. *Higher Education (00181560)*, *84*(5), 1089–1106. https://doi.org/10.1007/s10734-022-00817-9

Hills, M., Overend, A., & Hildebrandt, S. (2022). Faculty perspectives on UDL: Exploring bridges and barriers for broader adoption in higher education. *Canadian Journal for the Scholarship of Teaching and Learning*, *13*(1), 1–18.

Hodgkinson-Williams, C. (2010). *Benefits and challenges of OER for higher education institutions*. https://www.researchgate.net/publication/242551671_Benefits_and_Challenges_of_OER_for_Higher_Education_Institutions

Kim, B. W., Lee, W. G., Lee, B. R., & Shon, J. G. (2015). Influencing factors in OER usage of adult learners in Korea. http://www.irrodl.org/index.php/irrodl/article/view/2051/3325

Kumar, K. L., & Wideman, M. (2014). Accessible by design: Applying UDL principles in a first-year undergraduate course. *Canadian Journal of Higher Education*, *44*(1), 125–147. https://doi.org/10.47678/cjhe.v44i1.183704

Kurelovic, K. E. (2016). Advantages and limitations of usage of open educational resources in small countries. *International Journal of Research in Education and Science*, *2*(1), 136–142.

Lange, L. (2014). Rethinking transformation and its knowledge(s): The case of South African higher education. *Critical Studies in Teaching and Learning*, *2*(1), 1–24.

Letsoalo, N., Mabaso, D., & Gouws, P. (2022). Access to information through translation: A case of multilingual OER robotics project at a South African university. *South African Journal of Libraries and Information Science*, *88*(1), 1–10.

Lievre, P., & Tang, J. (2015). SECI and inter-organisational and intercultural knowledge transfer: A case-study of controversies around a project of co-operation between France and China in the health sector. *Journal of Knowledge Management*, *19*(5), 1069–1086. https://doi.org/10.1108/JKM-02-2015-0054

Liu, S. (2016). *Introduction to knowledge management*. Retrieved February 22, 2024, from http://web.archive.org/web/20160319233812/Introduction_to_Knowledge_Management.htm

Mabaso, M. M., & Dlamini, B. I. (2018). Total rewards and its effects on organisational commitment in higher education institutions. *South African Journal of Human Resource Management*, *16*, a913. https://doi.org/10.4102/sajhrm.v16i0.913

Materla, T., Cudney, E. A., & Antony, J. (2017). The application of kano model in the healthcare industry: A systematic literature review. *Total Quality Management and Business Excellence*, *28*(7), 1–22.

Mazorodze, A. H., & Mkhize, P. (2022). Factors and variables to promote a knowledge-sharing culture change in higher education institutions of developing countries. *South African Journal of Information Management*, *24*(1), a1491. https://doi.org/10.4102/sajim.v24i1.1491

McKenzie, J. A., & Dalton, E. M. (2020). Universal design for learning in inclusive education policy in South Africa. *African Journal of Disability*, *9*, a776. https://doi.org/10.4102/ajod.v9i0.776

Melnic, A. S., & Botez, N. (2014). Formal, non-formal and informal interdependence in education. *Economy Transdisciplinarity Cognition*, *17*(1), 113–118.

Moriña Díez, A., López Gavira, R., & Molina, V. M. (2015). Students with disabilities in higher education: A biographical-narrative approach to the role of lecturers. *Higher Education Research & Development*, *34*(1), 147–159.

Ndlovu, S. (2021a). Challenges of the universal design of learning in South African higher education. In S. Ndlovu (Ed.), *Mediating learning in higher education in Africa* (pp. 98–117). Brill.

Ndlovu, S. (2021b). Provision of assistive technology for students with disabilities in South African higher education. *International Journal of Environmental Research and Public Health*, *18*(8), 3892.

Novak, K. (2016). *UDL now! A teacher's guide to applying universal design for learning in today's classroom*. CAST Professional Publishing.

Ntombela, S. (2022). Reimagining South African higher education in response to COVID-19 and ongoing exclusion of students with disabilities. *Disability & Society*, *37*(3), 534–539.

Olaussen, E. J., Heelan, A., & Knarlag, K. A. (2019). Universal design for learning–License to learn: A process for mapping a universal design for learning process on to campus learning. In S. Bracken, & K. Novak, (Eds.),*Transforming higher education through Universal Design for Learning* (pp. 11–32). Routledge.

Organisation for Economic Co-operation and Development (OECD). (2007). *Giving knowledge for free: The emergence of open educational resources*. https://www.oecd.org/education/ceri/givingknowledgeforfreetheemergenceofopeneducationalresources.htm

Parisky, A., & Boulary, R. (2013). Designing and developing open education resources in higher education: A molecular biology project. *International Journal of Technology, Knowledge and Social Sciences*, *9*(2), 145–155.

Posey, A. (2021). *Universal design for learning (UDL): A teacher's guide*. https://www.understood.org/articles/en/understanding-universal0design-for-learning

Rajiv, J. (2017). Pragmatism vs idealism and the identity crisis of OER advocacy. *Open Praxis*, *9*(2), 141–150.

Ramjeawon, P., & Rowley, J. (2017). Knowledge management in higher education institutions: Enablers and barriers in Mauritius. *The Learning Organisation*, *24*(5), 1–24. https://doi.org/10.1108/TLO-03-2017-0030

Raue, K. & Lewis, L. (2011). *Students with disabilities at degree-granting postsecondary institutions (NCES), U.S. Department of Education, National Center for Education Statistics*. Washington, DC: U.S. Government Printing Office.

Rosyidah, N., & Rosyidi, U. (2019). Internationalisation in higher education: University's effective promotion strategies in building international trust. *European Journal of Educational Research*, *9*(1), 351–361. https://doi.org/10.12973/eu-jer.9.1.351

Sarnow, K., & Vuorikari, R. (2007). European national educational school authorities' actions regarding open content and open-source software. In R. Vuorikari, & K. Sarnow, (Eds.), *Open Source for Knowledge and Learning Management* (pp. 18–35). Irvine.

Smith, A., Workman, J., Hartsell, T., & Hill, D. (2023). Open educational resources: Collaboration between community college librarians and faculty. *Journal of Open Educational Resources in Higher Education, 2*(1), 160–175. https://doi.org/10.13001/joerhe.v2i1.7723

Smith, F. G. (2012). Analysing a college course that adheres to the universal design for learning (UDL) framework. *Journal of the Scholarship of Teaching and Learning, 12*(3), 31–61.

Subhash, G., & Cudney, E. A. (2018). Gamified learning in higher education: A systematic review of the literature. *Computers in Human Behavior, 87,* 1–15

Suliman, A. (2019). Talent management, employee recognition and performance in the research institutions. *Studies in Business and Economics, 14*(1), 127–140. https://doi.org/10.2478/sbe-2019-0010

Temple University. (2021). *Disability resources and services.* https://disabilityresources.temple.edu/universal-design-learning-udl

Torres N. P. M. (2013). Embracing openness: The challenges of OER in Latin American education. *Open Praxis, 5*(1), 81–89. https://doi.org/10.5944/openpraxis.5.1.33

Uman, L. S. (2011). Systematic reviews and meta-analyses. *Journal of the Canadian Academy of Child and Adolescent Psychiatry, 20*(1), 57–59.

UNESCO, United Nations Educational, Scientific and Cultural Organisation. (1990). *World Declaration on Education for All.* http://www.unesco.org/education/pdf/JOMTIE_E.PDF

UNESCO, United Nations Educational, Scientific and Cultural Organisation. (1994). *The Salamanca Statement and Framework for Action on Special Needs Education.* UNESCO and Ministry of Education and Science.

UNESCO, United Nations Educational, Scientific and Cultural Organisation. (2000). *Inclusive Education and education for all: A challenge and a vision (Draft).* UNESCO.

UNESCO, United Nations Educational, Scientific and Cultural Organisation. (2009). *World Conference on Higher Education.* http://www.unesco.org/en/higher-education

Urip, S. R., & Kurniawati, N. (2019). The concept of maintaining personal reputation in educational institutions. *KnE Social Sciences, 11,* 522–530.

van den Berg, G., & du Toit-Brits, C. (2023). Adoption and development of OERs and practices for self-directed learning: A South African perspective. *Teacher Education through Flexible Learning in Africa (TETFLE), 4,* 3–29.

Van Mieghem, A., Verschueren, K., Petry, K. & Struyf, E. (2018). An analysis of research on inclusive education: a systematic search and meta review. *International Journal of Inclusive Education, 24*(4), 1–15.

Wiley, D., Bliss, T. J., & McEwen, M. (2014). Open educational resources: A review of the literature. In D. Wiley, (Ed.), *Handbook of research on educational communications and technology* (pp. 781–789). Utah State University: COSL Press.

Wiley, D., & Hilton, J. (2018). Defining OER-enabled pedagogy. *International Review of Research in Open and Distributed Learning, 19*(4). http://www.irrodl.org/index.php/irrodl/article/view/3601/4769

Chapter 6

# Inclusive Assessment in Higher Education

*Heloise Sathorar and Deidre Geduld*

*Nelson Mandela University, South Africa*

## Abstract

This chapter explores inclusive assessment in the context of South African higher education. Through the literature review, the notion of inclusive assessment is conceptualised in this chapter, reflections on assessment practices within the South African higher education context are discussed, and the extent to which inclusive assessment has been integrated into the assessment practices is evaluated. The chapter further identifies challenges associated with inclusive assessment, presents some opportunities, and recommends measures to enable the implementation of inclusive assessment in institutions of higher learning.

*Keywords*: Assessment; inclusive education; inclusive assessment practices; higher education; humanising pedagogy

## Introduction

The widening participation agenda in higher education institutions (HEIs) in South Africa has facilitated the enrolment of more students with diverse abilities, many of whom come from low socioeconomic backgrounds. South Africa's political and legal landscape has changed significantly since the first democratic elections in 1994; however, many South Africans are still disadvantaged and struggle to obtain a proper education. Efforts to increase access to HEIs in South Africa have led to a rise in enrolments nationwide, and this has contributed to the growth of the post-schooling education sector. It is crucial to acknowledge that HEIs have a responsibility to provide access, retention, and successful completion of studies for all students, reducing the potential for ableism within the university environment and eliminating discrimination against people with disabilities.

The South African government has consistently failed to adequately facilitate access to higher education for all despite the availability of developed inclusion legislation, policies on transition, and financial resources. This failure to provide an enabling environment for disabled or differently abled students to succeed at university is a significant challenge. The government also struggles to create ample economic opportunities for independent living for people who are disabled or differently abled. The lack of economic opportunities further hinders the goal of inclusion (Bam & Ronnie, 2020). The Higher Education Act 101 of 1997 strongly advocates for and upholds the quality of higher education through the Higher Education Quality Committee. It also emphasises providing adequate and quality support to all students across gender, race, class, and even international border enrolled in HEIs. Additionally, the 2013 White Paper for Post-School Education and Training outlines the government's vision for the post-schooling education system in South Africa and elaborates on requirements for providing practical and quality support to all students (DHET, 2013). The 2013 White Paper is aligned with the National Development Plan of 2030, which advocates for equal and quality education for all (South African Government, 2013).

The Education for All initiative advocates for all students to participate in mainstream education. Consequently, there is a need to adapt the curriculum, including assessment methods, to cater to the varied needs of this diverse student population. Bain (2023, p. 1) 'defines inclusive assessment as the provision of assessments that allow all students to do well without receiving alternative or adapted assessments'. Bain (2023) further argues that assessment should be considered as part of a more comprehensive aspect of pedagogy and should not be treated in isolation from learning and teaching. This chapter, therefore, conceptualises the notion of inclusive assessment and illuminates how it is operationalised, enacted, and practiced within the South African higher education context, particularly for previously disadvantaged students.

Progress with regard to the issue of inclusive assessment has been slow, and most of the time, students are expected to engage in the same activities and under the same conditions as fully abled students often leading to frustration and dropout. Underrepresented groups in HEIs denote groups previously marginalised in the HE space, particularly from access to the HE environment (Trudgett et al., 2022). This chapter delves into the development of inclusive assessment that acknowledges the diversity in students' learning and strives to ensure that no student faces discrimination based on factors unrelated to their ability to meet appropriate standards. We aim to initiate discussions on how assessment practitioners and HEIs can accomplish this objective. First, we will define what assessment for inclusion entails. We propose some steps to be followed when considering applying inclusive assessment practices. Subsequently, we explore how inclusive assessment has been implemented in South African HEIs. We reflect on success stories experienced by lecturers and students applying assessment practices and look at persisting challenges that create barriers to student success. Fig. 6.1 illustrates the

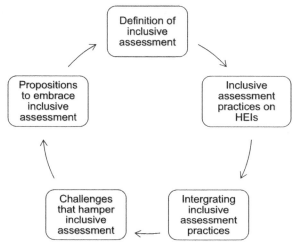

Fig. 6.1. Main Aspects That Contribute to Inclusive Assessment Practices in Higher Education.

key ideas focussed on in this chapter. In this chapter, we advocate for these ideas to be carefully considered in redesigning inclusive assessment in higher education.

## Clarification of Terms

- Inclusion is a multifaceted and context-dependent concept beyond mere presence and access. The Salamanca Statement strives to define inclusion as providing equal opportunities and access for a wide range of learners, encompassing differences in race, skin colour, gender, sexual orientation, trauma, learning styles, or disability (UNESCO, 1994, p. 6; Valente & Danforth, 2016).
- Inclusive education: The UNCRPD (2016, p. 3) identifies inclusive education as a process of:

> strengthening the capacity of the education system to reach out to all learners. It focuses on the full and effective participation, accessibility, attendance, and achievement of all children, especially those who, for different reasons, are excluded or at risk of being marginalized. Inclusion involves access to and progress in high-quality formal and informal education without discrimination.

Throughout our exploration, we draw upon pertinent literature spanning disability and social inclusion to broaden the discourse beyond merely accommodating specified equity groups, aiming instead to outline comprehensive directions for assessment design. Thus, this chapter aims to enhance the understanding of what inclusive assessment entails and how it should be practised. The chapter also highlights some opportunities to enhance the practice of inclusive education as well as some challenges that hamper the implementation of inclusive assessment.

## Methodology

The research was conducted through a literature review. The literature review process was guided by the following objective:

- to conceptualise an inclusive assessment within the South African higher education context;
- to identify different assessment practices in the South African higher education context;
- identify challenges and opportunities of inclusive assessment in the South African context and recommend how inclusive assessment could be enhanced.

The literature with empirical evidence was prioritised in the choice of literature that was reviewed. We avoided the literature that was not evidence-based. While the literature was reviewed for a study focussed on inclusive assessment in higher education, some of the reviewed work was inclined towards secondary school education.

We consulted several databases, such as the Web of Science, Scopus, and Google Scholar. Internationally accredited journals, including the *International Journal of Inclusive Education*, were further sources of relevant information. We also consulted the Nelson Mandela University (NMU) library and perused books, articles, theses, and electronic sources for relevant, up-to-date literature on the topic. Key phrases that guided the search for relevant literature included inclusive education in higher education, assessment practices in higher education, inclusive assessment practices, success stories regarding the implementation of inclusive assessment and some challenges experienced when implementing inclusive assessment. The findings of the literature review will be discussed next.

## What Does Inclusive Assessment Entail in the Higher Education Context?

In the realm of higher education literature, the term 'inclusion' encompasses both disability inclusion and social inclusion. Stentiford and Koutsouris (2021) highlight that 'inclusion is an elusive concept, entangled with tensions that are hard to resolve' (p. 2245). Inclusion can encompass various equity groups typically associated with disability access, such as physical disabilities, learning disabilities, mental and physical health conditions, as well as initiatives aimed at broadening participation, including students from low socio-economic backgrounds, Indigenous peoples, and mature age students. Therefore, we embrace the term 'inclusion' with all its connotations as mentioned above.

The question of whether assessment in HEIs can be avoided has been posed at various levels and by different researchers. Quite frankly, the answer is no. It is inevitable within higher education. You could ask, why? Because it validates proficiency, stimulates learning, and encourages the development of new knowledge. Lambert et al. (2022) explicate that assessment significantly influences students' learning. It focusses on what is essential and functions as a motivation for studying. Furthermore, it has an influential impact on what students do and how they do it. Even though students might manage to avoid certain aspects of the higher education journey, they cannot avoid assessment (Lambert et al., 2022). Nonetheless, while all students are mandated to partake in assessment, their encounters with it may vary significantly (Tai et al., Ajjawi, Bearman, Dargusch et al., 2022). According to the Council for Higher Education (CHE), assessment refers to the systematic evaluation of students' abilities to demonstrate their having achieved the learning goals set for a curriculum (CHE, 2016, p. 2). This can include a variety of tasks, the development of products, outputs, or competencies used to gather evidence and compare the students' performance against the set assessment criteria and outcomes. Similarly, assessment is described in the Curriculum and Assessment Policy Statement (2015) as a process that measures individual learners' attainment of knowledge (content, concepts, and skills) in a subject and collects, analyses, and interprets the data and information obtained from this process to inform students about their strengths, weaknesses, and progress as well as to assist teachers, parents, and other stakeholders in making decisions about the learning process and the progress of students. Assessment should be mapped against the content and intended objectives of a subject. Furthermore, assessment can be both informal and formal, and in both cases, regular feedback should be provided to learners to enhance the learning experience (CAPS, 2015).

Inclusive assessments encompass various assessment tasks, such as essays, problem sets, and dissertations, completed under different conditions, including invigilated and non-invigilated settings. Moreover, these assessments are scheduled for undergraduate and postgraduate programmes across the years of study. Inclusive assessment stems from recognising the fact that certain student groups may underperform or require accommodations within current assessment practices. Inclusive assessments aim to address disparities. These adjustments, such as extra time or a quiet exam environment, are provided to students who have disclosed and substantiated their needs (Tai et al., 2021). Nieminen (2022) suggests that in higher education, students might require accommodation rather than enriching academic aspects to facilitate full inclusion. Sharp and Earle (2000) critique such adaptations as exclusionary and problematic, noting that they are based on a compensatory principle. Instead, they argue for alternative assessment methods that will ensure every student can participate fully and equally, becoming valued members of the learning community (Sharp & Earle, 2000).

According to Tai, Ajjawi, Bearman, Boud et al. (2022), inclusive assessment recognises that:

- Diversity has many dimensions, including intersectional qualities.
- Assessment practices and decisions are always made within specific contexts, which impacts generalisability.
- There will always be new frontiers to make inclusive advances (i.e., in the future, we will not only accept the present reductive categorisations when considering something to be inclusive or not).

Inclusive assessment should cater to and be accessible to all students. 'Inclusive assessment methods should accommodate the needs of every student while also addressing the requirements of specific groups' (Morris et al., 2019, p. 437). Inclusion here entails offering assessments that enable all students to perform successfully without alternative or modified conditions. This is further emphasised by Hanesworth (2019), who highlights that inclusive assessment design is increasingly recognised as an excellent educational practice and benefits all students. We agree with the University of Plymouth (2019), which stipulates that inclusive assessment does not compromise academic or professional standards but improves the opportunities for all students to demonstrate their acquisition of the learning outcomes under the same conditions.

## Reflecting on Inclusive Assessment Practices at HEIs in South Africa

Following 1994, the development of university assessment policies emphasised pedagogies tailored to individual students' needs. In 2016, the CHE took a definitive step towards devolving management and control of assessment to HEIs. The Council issued Policies on the Recognition of Prior Learning (RPL), Credit Accumulation and Transfer (CAT), and Assessment in Higher Education to these institutions. These policies give HEIs clear directives and procedures for formulating, implementing, and evaluating the effectiveness of their internal mechanisms concerning RPL, CAT, and assessment. The Assessment in Higher Education policy (2016) outlines specific directives and procedures for developing, applying, and evaluating the effectiveness of internal assessment mechanisms. The Council mandates that all HEIs formulate assessment policies (CHE, 2016).

South African HEIs operate autonomously (Zaahedah et al., 2020). HEIs assessment policy documents illustrate their understanding of the purpose and suitability of assessment (Boughey & McKenna, 2021). This chapter reflects on how South African universities have interpreted inclusive assessment. This section highlights the recent shifts to embrace inclusive assessment practices at three South African universities under the pseudonyms Winnie Mandela University, Adelaide Tambo University, and the University of Nomalizo Leah Tutu.

The revised 2022 assessment policy at Winnie Mandela University refrains from prescribing specific assessment strategies. For this university, assessment serves multiple purposes, including diagnostic assessment, formative assessment (assessment for learning), summative assessment (assessment of learning), and assessment for quality promotion. While the policy suggests providing adequate formative assessment opportunities for students to gauge their progress, it does not explicitly address assessment as a tool for learning. The policy empowers lecturers to make informed choices regarding assessment methods tailored to their respective contexts (Sims et al., 2023, p. 157). This policy promotes a flexible approach to assessment, encouraging faculties and assessment centres to incorporate diverse assessment methods throughout the modules. Sims et al. (2023, p. 158) further aver that these policy changes align with the University's Teaching and Learning Policy, emphasising 'quality teaching and learning that embraces the needs of the diverse student body and the importance of producing graduates capable of contributing to a complex society'.

According to Adelaide Tambo University's assessment policy, fairness means ensuring that all students are treated impartially, without bias, and receive the support needed to address any limitations or disadvantages. Assessment tasks are designed to be comprehensible and interpretable by students from diverse backgrounds and abilities. This policy enriches the learning experience by enabling students to cultivate their discipline's valued knowledge, skills, and attitudes through constructive feedback and chances to revise and enhance their assessments. This approach promotes a diverse assessment methodology, safeguarding students from being disadvantaged by overreliance on specific assessment formats. It empowers students to assume accountability for their learning. Adelaide Tambo University's policy also advocates for opportunities for students to assess their work and that of their peers, including evaluations of both team and individual efforts. The policy fosters a sense of ownership over their learning journey by allowing students to craft their assessment tasks and evaluate their own work as well as that of their peers.

The assessment policy at the University of Nomalizo Leah Tutu emphasises the importance of validity, ensuring that assessments are aligned with predetermined outcomes and employ suitable methods relevant to the context, including consideration of language and cultural factors which might influence the students' learning. The policy also outlines various types of validity, such as face validity, which ensures that assessments are perceived as fair and provide students with a reasonable opportunity to demonstrate their knowledge and mastery. For instance, any indication of bias, such as gender or ethnic bias, which may disadvantage students, would diminish the face validity of assessments. Additionally, the policy emphasises equity in assessment, which entails considering the instructional context and students' backgrounds, including prior knowledge, cultural experiences, language proficiency, cognitive styles, and interests. Construct validity pertains to how effectively an assessment measures and evaluates the theoretical or practical constructs associated with students' abilities that it aims to assess. The assessment practices to ascertain construct validity must be culturally sensitive, contextually relevant, and aligned with the intended constructs. Rather than adopting a 'one-size-fits-all' approach, the policy advocates for employing alternative assessment opportunities.

In formulating and implementing the three assessment policies, attention was given to language and cultural diversity considerations. At the core of fostering inclusive assessment environments, the policies perceive assessment as a social endeavour. In conclusion, these policies focus on inclusive assessments, emphasising the importance of ensuring equal opportunities and access for all learners, regardless of their diverse backgrounds and characteristics. This approach aligns with the principles outlined in the Salamanca Statement, which advocates for inclusive education practices that accommodate various student needs and differences.

## Developments Regarding Inclusive Assessment Practices at South African Universities

Inclusive assessment, especially when integrated into an inclusive curriculum, promises to offer all students relevant graduate outcomes compared to assessments rooted solely in regurgitation. The ideal scenario is that all students should complete their education with diverse knowledge and be better equipped to navigate various worldviews and cultures in their future endeavours.

Ahmad (2015) reports that students at the University of Kwazulu-Natal revealed positive experiences after the learning material and exam content had been modified to suit the diverse needs of the students. Moreover, students reported that many of their lecturers allowed them to audio record lectures, which supported auditory learning and provided them with something to refer to when preparing for assessments. Students also mentioned that lecturers were supportive and flexible, allowing extra time for those who needed it, to complete tests and assignments (Ahmad, 2015).

Similarly, the University of Johannesburg established guidelines to shift assessment practices away from being teacher-centred towards empowering students with the skills necessary to thrive as lifelong, competent professionals in the future (Mutanga, 2017). Consistent with this change in assessment policy, the university provides training for lecturers to support the adoption and integration of alternative assessment methods to support inclusive assessment.

At NMU, assessment practices are underpinned by a humanising approach emphasising dialogue in the learning situation. It is proposed that instead of imposing rubrics and other evaluation tools on students, the latter could be positioned as active participants in the assessment process. It is not suggested that by applying a humanising approach tests and examinations must be replaced as forms of assessment – but rather that lecturers should identify strategies to administer tests and examinations that encourage broader student participation and enhance student success (Mdzanga et al., 2023). At this university, the view is held that assessment activities are opportunities for students to exhibit their skills and apply what they have learned to their realities. For example, linking assessment activities to problem-based community activities will enhance deep learning (Mdzanga et al., 2023). Such activities will enable students to interact with each other, make judgments about the topics under discussion, ponder on issues that emerge, and provide sustainable solutions. NMU also embraces a multilingual approach to assessment, enabling students to respond to assessment activities and discuss ideas in a language they understand best. To facilitate this, students are used as resources to support translation and interpretation (Mdzanga et al., 2023). Bilingual tutors are trained to facilitate the assessment of written texts.

While significant strides have been achieved and are ongoing in South Africa's efforts to mainstream disability and facilitate inclusion since 1994, there appears to be a necessity to guarantee and regulate inclusive education within the higher education sector as some persisting challenges continue to prevail (Mutanga, 2017).

## Challenges That Hamper Inclusive Assessment at South African HEIs

The aspiration to inclusive education and assessment has yet to become fully supported. Despite high-level supporting policy changes being made at a national level, implementing these policies has been delayed due to a lack of understanding by lecturers at an institutional level of the policies and how they should be implemented. This is further hindered by the lack of training, persisting biases, and lack of resources, resulting in universities defaulting to what they are used to, a one-size fits-all approach (Lambrechts, 2020). Thus, universities often apply a deficit approach and make special arrangements for students with disabilities or diverse needs rather than creating assessment activities that can be done by all students similarly (Vincent & Chiwandire, 2019).

Furthermore, higher education perpetuates stereotypical perceptions and biases, often labelling students from non-white, non-English-speaking, and working-class backgrounds as 'disadvantaged'. This view portrays these students as less capable individuals who lack the 'cultural capital' needed to navigate university terminology and procedures (Sims et al., 2023, p. 160). Indigenous students are particularly affected, facing additional challenges as they study in second or third languages without adequate support for content translation.

Also, outdated, and unaccommodating assessment practices like sit-down exams and monolingual activities are still the norm at most universities, as performance evaluation remains the only determinant of student success and progress (Brown, 2022). The current design of assessments at most universities fails to result in fair assessment processes, experiences, and outcomes for all (Lambrechts, 2020). Thus, ensuring 'fairness' in assessment is often interpreted as all students need to encounter identical conditions rather than designing assessment activities that cater to the diverse needs of the students (O'Neill, 2017, p. 228).

Current inclusive assessment practices often emphasise individual, unassisted performance, offering limited chances for collaboration and creating an artificial divide between students with diverse learning needs (Lipnevich et al., 2021). Additionally, such assessments isolate students from the usual resources, such as internet access and peers' advice, that professionals commonly utilise in real-world scenarios. These unaddressed constraints disproportionately affect the success of individuals who benefit most from a more inclusive assessment approach.

Additionally, perceptions play a significant role in determining fairness, with students sometimes expressing concerns that accommodations or adjustments may provide an 'unfair' advantage to students with disabilities or other conditions. The primary reason is that those responsible for facilitating special arrangements often lack a thorough understanding of what is necessary to support inclusive assessment (O'Neill, 2017). This is further perpetuated by universities not openly addressing the topic of inclusive assessment with all students so that everybody understands what is required.

Prioritising inclusive assessment strategies could be crucial in mitigating disparities in academic achievement. However, in the absence of an understanding of what inclusive assessment entails, students who lack confidence and suffer from low self-esteem (usually those from a low socioeconomic background) exhibit a greater hesitancy in seeking academic assistance than their more advantaged counterparts (Devlin & McKay, 2017).

## Opportunities to Address Some of the Persistent Challenges That Hamper Inclusive Assessment

It is important to note that inclusive assessment is not confined to a single approach but is a comprehensive concept covering institution-wide adjustments that should be integrated across all levels (Hanesworth, 2019). It is valuable to realise that in the realm of assessment for inclusion, a persistent challenge across various domains is the distinction between the 'work as imagined' and the 'work as done' (Hollnagel, 2015, p. 255). While envisioning ideal assessment methodologies is straightforward, executing them in complex as real-world settings are fraught with budgetary limitations, time constraints, and organisational dynamics presents a considerable challenge (Bearman et al., 2017).

To enhance inclusive assessment, we support four practical principles in striving for Assessment for Inclusion (AfI) (Nieminen, 2022). First, accommodations represent a widespread global approach in higher education, primarily intended to afford all students equal opportunities to engage in assessments. The practice and research surrounding accommodations strive to promote inclusion in assessments provided to students, yet they generally need to assess the assessments' effectiveness, relevance, or authenticity (Nieminen, 2022). While accommodations can be offered for various assessments or any student, they are commonly implemented in higher education contexts as 'testing accommodations', often utilised by students with disabilities. In essence, accommodations are crafted to grant access to an assessment without altering its fundamental constructs, mainly when the conventional presentation or response conditions present a hindrance (Thurlow & Bolt, 2001).

Second, Ketterlin-Geller and Crawford (2011) postulate that the term 'accessibility' in assessments pertains to students' capacity to interact with the test in a manner that enables them to effectively showcase their knowledge, skills, and abilities concerning the content being tested. Accessibility is shaped by the dynamic relationship between students' traits and test design features. Inclusive assessment is accessible when students engage meaningfully with the tested content and produce responses that accurately demonstrate their proficiency in the intended learning outcomes. Therefore, ensuring the creation of accessible assessments that yield reliable data for decision-making should become a primary concern for all HEI lecturing staff when designing assessments.

Third, flexibility and choice are often advocated as an inclusive approach to assessment, allowing students to avoid tasks that could potentially put them at a disadvantage (Lawrie et al., 2017). Keating et al. (2012) advocate for assessment choice by allowing students to select from existing options or suggest alternative formats. A study by Ragpot (2011) did not offer a choice in task selection but instead adapted task types based on Universal Design for Learning principles.

These tasks included class discussions, group poster projects, dramatic enactments, and end-of-term essays. Students participating in these tasks reported that it encouraged deeper learning and increased engagement with the subject matter.

Finally, encouraging student agency has been identified as the key objective of contemporary learning and assessment environments designed to cultivate essential skills (Charteris & Smardon, 2018). As per the Organisation for Economic Co-operation and Development (2022, p. 1), student agency is characterised as the 'ability to establish objectives, contemplate, and respond responsibly to initiate change'. This suggests that students can take responsibility for their learning and actively participate in discussions regarding assessment.

In addition to the above, Schuwirth and Van der Vleuten (2011) also propose a programmatic approach to inclusive assessment, as it is beneficial when utilised explicitly to establish a shared understanding of the timing and methods of assessing learning outcomes across various assessments. Teams responsible for designing programmatic inclusive assessments should include individuals' knowledge about the exclusionary impacts of various assessment methods to ensure that the needs of all relevant stakeholders are addressed. Appropriately supported inclusive assessment, such as tasks scaffolded with increasing complexity or difficulty instead of sit-down tests or exams, can also alleviate the anxiety, stress, and pressure which many students reportedly experience during exams (Craddock & Mathias, 2009).

## Lessons Learnt from the Literature Reviewed

Despite rigorous policy changes to encourage inclusive education and assessment practices at HEIs, changes in the classroom are slow and hampered by persistent challenges. It is clear from the literature review that universities are making a concerted effort to embrace inclusion and to provide access, retention and support to all students to successfully complete the qualifications they enrol for. However, the literature also revealed that there is a lack of understanding of inclusive education policies and how they should be implemented. Thus, there is a need to provide one-size-fits-all information to help them understand the policies and support them in implementing the policies.

The literature also emphasised the importance of lecturers getting to know their students and understanding their diverse needs. This will allow them to steer clear from a one size fits all approach to learning and assessment. The application of a humanising pedagogy will allow lecturers to utilise the realities of students as an integral part of educational practice and cast them as critically engaged, active participants in the learning process (Sathorar, 2018). Humanising pedagogy is a dialogic approach to education that allows lecturers to develop critical consciousness regarding diversity and embrace inclusive practices rather than see it as a barrier (Sathorar, 2018). It encourages lecturers to engage their students in dialogue regarding their diverse needs and contexts. It is only when lecturers understand the diverse needs of their students and their learning context that they can design and develop inclusive assessment activities.

The ultimate aim of inclusive assessment is that all students have equal access to the same assessment activity (Hanesworth, 2019; Morris et al., 2019). By default, HEIs make accommodations and provide concessions to differently abled students to complete an assessment activity (Lambrechts, 2020). Instead, what is required is a change of mindset regarding assessment that allows for setting assessment activities with a choice of tasks, allowing students to choose to do the tasks in the assessment activity where they can draw on their individual strengths to complete the task. There is also a strong argument made for a variety of assessment activities to be offered (including oral presentations, projects, assignments, etc.), allowing students to choose which activities they would like to complete instead of having one sit-down test or exam. What is clear from the literature is that there is still a lot that needs to happen at HEIs in South Africa to completely embrace inclusive assessment practices, but the journey continues.

## Conclusion

In conclusion, this chapter has highlighted several key points regarding inclusive assessment in higher education institutes. We have explored ways HEIs can guarantee access, retention, and successful completion of studies for all students, reducing the potential for ableism within the university environment and eliminating discrimination against people with disabilities. Future considerations should focus on inclusive assessment practices and strategies. To achieve our goals effectively, we are recommending the implementation of the following actionable recommendations: accommodation, accessibility, flexibility and choice, and promoting student agency. Assessments need to be adaptable to accommodate the unique requirements of each student, which could include offering tasks with varying difficulty levels, extended time allowances, or alternative assessment styles. Inclusive assessment seeks to uphold standards while ensuring equitable conditions for all students to demonstrate their learning and understanding of the content. It recognises that learning can be expressed in various ways, going beyond the limitations of a single testing format. By doing so, we can move closer to achieving inclusive assessment in HEIs.

## References

Ahmad, F. K. (2015). Use of assistive technology in inclusive education: Making room for diverse learning needs. *Transcience*, 6(2), 62–77.

Bain, K. (2023) Inclusive assessment in higher education: What does the literature tell us on how to define and design inclusive assessments? *Journal of Learning Development in Higher Education*, 27. https://doi.org/10.47408/jldhe.vi27.1014

Bam, A., & Ronnie, L., (2020). Inclusion at the workplace: An exploratory study of people with disabilities in South Africa. *International Journal of Disability Management*, 15(6), 1–9.

Bearman, M., Dawson, P., Bennett, S., Hall, M., Molloy, E., Boud, D., & Joughin, G. (2017). How university teachers design assessments: A cross-disciplinary study. *Higher Education, 74*(1), 49–64. https://doi.org/10.1007/s10734-016-0027-7

Boughey, C., & McKenna, S. (2021). *Understanding higher education: Alternative perspectives.* African Minds.

Brown, G. (2022). The past, present and future of educational assessment: A transdisciplinary perspective. *Frontier Education, 7,* 1060633. https://doi.org/10.3389/feduc.2022.1060633

Charteris, J., & Smardon, D. (2018). "Professional learning on steroids": Implications for teacher learning through spatialised practice in new generation learning environments. *Australian Journal of Teacher Education, 43*(12). https://doi.org/10.14221/ajte.2018v43n12.2

Council for Higher Education (CHE). (2016). *Policies on the recognition of prior learning, credit accumulation and transfer, and assessment in higher education.* Council on Higher Education.

Craddock, D., & Mathias, H. (2009). Assessment options in higher education. *Assessment and Evaluation in Higher Education, 34*(2), 127–140. https://doi.org/10.1080/02602930801956026.

Curriculum and Assessment Policy Statement. (2015). Grades 10-12: FET Grade 10-12 CAPS amendments. Government Printing Works.

Devlin, M., & McKay, J. (2017). *Facilitating success for students from low socioeconomic status backgrounds at regional universities.* Federation University Australia. https://www.ncsehe.edu.au/wp-content/uploads/2018/05/55_Federation_MarciaDevlin_Accessible_PDF.pdf.

DHET. (2013). *White paper for post-school education and training: Building an expanded, effective and integrated education and training system.* Department of Higher Education and Training.

Hanesworth, P. (2019). Inclusive assessment: Where next? *Advance HE.* https://www.advance-he.ac.uk/news-and-views/inclusive-assessment-where-next

Higher Education Act, (1997). *Government Gazette, 390*(18515), 1–24.

Hollnagel, E. (2015). Why is work-as-imagined different from work-as-done? In R. L. Wears, E. Hollnagel, & J. Braithwaite (Eds.), *Resilient health care: The resilience of everyday clinical work* (pp. 249–264). CRC Press. https://doi.org/10.1201/9781315605739

Keating, N., Tanya, Z., & Karl, R. (2012). Inclusive assessment at point-of-design. *Innovations in Education and Teaching International, 49*(3), 249–256. https://doi.org/10.1080/14703297.2012.703022

Ketterlin-Geller, L. R., & Crawford, L. (2011). Improving accommodations assignment: Re-conceptualizing professional development to support accommodations decision-making. In M. Russell (Ed.), *Assessing students in the margins* (pp. 105–126). Information Age Publishing.

Lambert, S., Funk, J., & Adam, T. (2022). What can decolonisation of curriculum tell us about inclusive assessment? In R. Ajjawi, J. Tai, D. Boud, & T. Jorre de St (Eds.), *Assessment for inclusion in higher education: Promoting equity and social justice in assessment* (1st ed., pp. 52–62). Routledge.

Lambrechts, A. A. (2020). The super-disadvantaged in higher education: Barriers to access for refugee background students in England. *Higher Education, 80*(1), 803–822. https://doi.org/10.1007/s10734-020-00515-4

Lawrie, G., Marquis, E., Fuller, E., Newman, T., Qiu, M., Nomikoudis, M., Roelofs, F., & Van Dam, L. (2017). Moving towards inclusive learning and teaching: A synthesis of recent literature. *Teaching and Learning Inquiry, 5*(6), 1–20. https://doi.org/10.20343/teachlearninqu.5.1.3

Lipnevich, A., Panadero, E., Gjicali, K., & Fraile, J. (2021). What's on the syllabus? An analysis of assessment criteria in first year courses across US and Spanish universities. *Educational Assessment, Evaluation and Accountability, 33*(4), 675–699. https://doi.org/10.1007/s11092-021-09357-9

Mdzanga, N., Sathorar, H., Geduld, D., & Moeng, M. (2023). Rethinking assessment practices in teacher education programmes: A Nelson Mandela case. In C. E. M. Tabane, B. M. Diale, A. S. Mawela, & T. V. Zengele (Eds.), *Fostering diversity and inclusion through curriculum transformation* (pp. 156–173). IGI Global.

Morris, C., Milton, E., & Goldstone, R. (2019). Case study: Suggesting choice inclusive assessment processes. *Higher Education Pedagogies, 4*(1), 435–447. https://doi.org/10.1080/23752696.2019.1669479

Mutanga, O. (2017). *Policy brief: Inclusive policy for students with disabilities. A capabilities approach.* Routledge Taylor and Francis Group.

Nieminen, J. H. (2022). Assessment for inclusion: Rethinking inclusive assessment in higher education. *Teaching in Higher Education, 32*(1), 1–19. https://doi.org/10.1080/13562517.2021.2021395

O'Neill, G. (2017). It's not fair! Students and staff views on the equity of the procedures and outcomes of students' choice of assessment methods. *Irish Educational Studies, 36*(2), 221–236. https://doi.org/10.1080/03323315.2017.1324805

Organisation for Economic Co-operation and Development. (2022). *Student agency for 2030.* https://www.oecd.org/education/2030-project/teaching-and-learning/learning/student-agency/Student_Agency_for_2030_concept_note.pdf

Ragpot, L. (2011). Assessing student learning by way of drama and visual art: A semiotic mix in a course on cognitive development. *Education as Change, 15*(SUPPL. 1), 63–79. https://doi.org/10.1080/16823206.2011.643625

Sathorar, H. (2018). *Exploring lecturer preparedness on applying a critical approach to curriculum implementation: A case study.* [Thesis, Nelson Mandela University].

Sharp, K., & Earle, S. (2000) Assessment, disability and the problem of compensation. *Assessment & Evaluation in Higher Education, 25*(2), 191–199. https://doi.org/10.1080/713611423

Sims, D., Lundie, S., Titus, S., & Govender, R. (2023). Shifting assessment paradigms in South African higher education: Evolving towards transformative approaches to policy development. *SOTL in the South, 7*(3), 137–170.

South African Government. (2013). *National Development Plan 2030.* Retrieved February 1, 2024, from https://www.gov.za/issues/national-development-plan-2030.

Stentiford, L., & Koutsouris, G. (2021). What are inclusive pedagogies in higher education? A systematic scoping review. *Studies in Higher Education, 46*(11), 2245–2261. https://doi.org/10.1080/03075079.2020.1716322

Schuwirth, L. W., Van der Vleuten, C. P. (2011). Programmatic assessment: From assessment of learning to assessment for learning. *Med Teach, 33*(2), 478–485.

Tai, J., Ajjawi, R., Bearman, M., Boud, D., Dawson, P., & Jorre de St Jorre, T. (2022). Assessment for inclusion: Rethinking contemporary strategies in assessment design. *Higher Education Research and Development.* https://doi.org/10.1080/07294360.2022.2057451

Tai, J., Ajjawi, R., Bearman, M., Dargusch, J., Dracup, M., Harris, L., & Mahoney, P. (2022). *Re-imagining exams: How do assessment adjustments impact on inclusion?* National Centre for Student Equity in Higher Education. https://www.ncsehe.edu.au/publications/exams-assessment-adjustments-inclusion/

Tai, J., Ajjawi, R., & Umarova, A. (2021). How do students experience inclusive assessment? A critical review of contemporary literature. *International Journal of Inclusive Education*, 1–18. https://doi.org/10.1080/13603116.2021.2011441

Thurlow, M., & Bolt, S. (2001). *Empirical support for accommodations most often allowed in state policy* [Synthesis Report (p. 41)]. University of Minnesota, National Center on Educational Outcomes.

Trudgett, M., Page, S., & Coates, S. K. (2022). Peak bodies: Indigenous representation in the Australian higher education sector. *Australian Journal of Education, 66*(1), 40–56.

UNESCO. (1994). *The Salamanca Statement and framework for action on special needs education.* UNESCO.

United Nations Committee on the Rights of Persons with Disabilities (UNCRPD). (2016). *General comment No. 4, Article 24: Right to inclusive education.* https://www.refworld.org/docid/57c977e34.html

University of Plymouth. (2019). *Inclusive assessment.* Retrieved February 10, 2024, from www.plymouth.ac.uk/about-us/teaching-and-learning/inclusivity/inclusive-assessment

Valente, J. M., & Danforth, S. (Eds.). (2016). *Life in inclusive classrooms: Storytelling with disability studies in education.* Bank Street Occasional Papers #36. https://educate.bankstreet.edu/occasional-paper-series/vol2016/iss36/

Vincent, L., & Chiwandire, D. (2019). Funding and inclusion in higher education institutions for students with disabilities. *African Journal of Disability, 8*(1), 1–12. https://doi.org/10.4102/ajod.v5i1.563

Zaahedah, V., Matlala, R., Sibiya, T., & Makhoabenyane, T. (2020). *Country report working paper: South Africa.* https://acqf.africa/resources/mapping-study/south-africa-country-report/@@display-file/file/South%20Africa%20EN_ACQF%20Country%20Report_WEB*.pdf

Chapter 7

# Decolonisation of Higher Education, Indigenous Knowledge, and Inclusion

*Xolani Khalo and Benjamin Damoah*

University of Fort Hare, South Africa

## Abstract

The chapter explored the process of decolonisation and Indigenous knowledge towards ensuring access, equity, and inclusion within the South African higher education context. Through a literature review, the chapter conceptualises the notions of decolonisation, Indigenous knowledge in relation to inclusive education, and inclusive and exclusive practices within the South African higher education context. The chapter also demonstrates how decolonisation can accelerate the implementation of inclusion, ensure teaching and learning that respects the diversity of students, and also enable an inclusive Indigenous pedagogy. Furthermore, the attribution of Indigenous knowledge without acknowledgement is not acceptable in the context of educational reforms and reconciliation. The reformation of higher education should encourage the integration of African philosophies and Indigenous knowledge into teaching and learning curricula that support the growth of society and the fulfilment of a sustainable, dignified existence for everyone.

*Keywords*: Decolonisation; higher education; inclusion; Indigenous knowledge; Indigenous pedagogy

## Introduction

This chapter seeks to unload decolonisation and Indigenous knowledge in ensuring inclusion in the higher education sector. It is sub-divided into three interwoven subsections, the decolonisation of higher education to intensify inclusion, inclusion, and diversity in higher education and the valuing of Indigenous knowledge.

Decolonisation in the South African education system involves bringing back and highlighting historically and presently marginalised narratives and acknowledging Indigenous knowledge systems that were previously suppressed. It also means critically examining the impact of race, class, gender, sexuality, culture, and other identity and disadvantage categories within disciplines. By prioritising social transformation and considering how disciplines can contribute to society's development, the goal is to realise a dignified and sustainable life for all South Africans. Curriculum transformation is a worldwide challenge that higher education institutions must address (Franco et al., 2019).

The South African higher education transformation promotes the inclusion of Indigenous knowledge and African philosophies in teaching and learning curricula that contribute to society's development and the realisation of a dignified, sustainable life for all (Damoah et al., 2023). This disposition defines a nose-dive from the colonial education system which includes imposing the colonisers' education and language on the local population.

The United Nations Sustainable Development Goals (2015) identify equitable and inclusive quality education as vital to overcoming poverty and reducing inequalities (UNESCO, 2016). This sparked a paradigm shift and revised focus for post-schooling institutions to become more inclusive, guided by best practices in equity, diversity, and inclusion (Damoah et al., 2024).

Calls to 'Africanise' curricula, which eliminate the embodied reality of alleged Eurocentric, racist, and colonial effects, are widely expressed by South Africans. Therefore, according to Moosavi (2020), the best way to decolonise education is not through undifferentiated curricula that encourage one-size-fits-all teaching and learning methodologies and practices while ignoring the concept of driving inclusive or intercultural education. This necessitates a new strategy for teaching and learning that adapts student differentiation to meet their various needs. The three ideas that need to be carefully considered to redesign higher education are depicted in Fig. 7.1.

## Conceptual Map

The chapter further discusses in detail the three components in Fig 7.1:

- *Indigenous knowledge* is defined by Zidny et al. (2020) as an accumulated body of knowledge, practice, and belief about the interactions between living things – including humans – that has developed through adaptive processes and been passed down through cultural transmission through the generations.

*Decolonisation of Higher Education, Indigenous Knowledge, and Inclusion* **103**

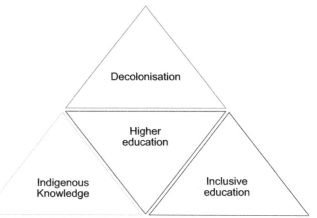

Fig. 7.1. Main Factors That Contribute to the Transformation of the Higher Education System.

- *Decolonisation*, as per Adefila et al. (2022) definition is the process of recognising the significance of Indigenous knowledge and wisdom and uniting both Indigenous and non-Indigenous individuals to acquire and honour Indigenous knowledge.
- *Inclusive education* refers to a broad range of tactics, initiatives, and procedures aimed at realising everyone's right to a good, suitable, and relevant education. By doing this, it hopes to empower communities, institutions, and structures to fight prejudice, embrace diversity, encourage involvement, and remove obstacles to learning and engagement for all students (Haug, 2017).
- *Inclusion* as described by Bešić (2020) is the intersection of three factors: the physical, which refers to location; the social, which refers to participation; and the psychological, which deals with the individual experiences of students being included in the higher education system. Their methodology does not include academic benefits or other significant results, nor does it pertain to the goals they would set for inclusive education.
- *Social exclusion* might be characterised as the incapacity to engage with society and gain acceptance from it. According to Slee (2019), social exclusion is a continuum that ranges from total absence of integration at one end of the spectrum to full integration into society at the other.

Therefore, this chapter aims to conceptualise the notions of decolonisation, Indigenous knowledge concerning inclusive education, and inclusive and exclusive practices within the South African higher education context. It assesses how decolonisation can accelerate the implementation of inclusion, ensure teaching and learning that respects students' diversity, and enable an inclusive Indigenous pedagogy. As a result, the chapter contributes a conceptual understanding of inclusion with the decolonisation of higher education.

## Methodology

The research was conducted through a literature review, and the following objectives guided the literature review process:

- description of Indigenous knowledge, decolonisation, inclusion, and inclusive education and social exclusion in higher education;
- the decolonisation of higher education to intensify inclusion;
- to explore inclusive education as an approach towards decolonisation;
- to investigate the role of all stakeholders towards inclusion and diversity in higher education;
- to determine how cultural diversity in higher education is valued through Indigenous inclusive pedagogy.

The literature with empirical evidence was prioritised in the choice. We avoided the literature that needed to be more evidence-based. While the literature was reviewed for a study focussed on decolonisation in higher education, some of the reviewed work was inclined towards studies in equity studies and social justice education.

We consulted several databases, such as the Web of Science, Scopus, and Google Scholar. Internationally accredited journals, including the *International Journal of Inclusive Education*, were further relevant information sources. We consulted the Nelson Mandela University library and perused books, articles, theses, and electronic sources for relevant, up-to-date literature.

## Decolonisation of Higher Education to Intensify Inclusion

Higher education institutions have seen significant changes throughout the years, which have been credited to the persistent counter-hegemonic activities of academics, community activists, and students (Damoah and Khalo, 2024). Many have questioned whether higher education can truly be 'decolonised', nevertheless, and to what extent these changes have succeeded in doing so (Battiste, 2017; Stein, 2019). More precisely, interrelated trajectories have sparked discussions about decolonising the curriculum in academia during the past 20 years.

With highly ambiguous relationships with the government during the apartheid years, the predominantly white English-medium colleges saw themselves as 'liberal' establishments. According to the Department of Education (2008), the epistemological shift that took place after 1994 was meant to involve a 'reorientation away from the [colonial and] apartheid knowledge system, in which curriculum was used as a tool of exclusion, to a democratic curriculum that value diversity'. The multidimensional decolonial project in academia aimed to reverse the marginalisation of academics, scholarship, and students who are marginalised in academia because of colonial aftereffects, which has led to ongoing stigmatisation and exclusion based on nationality, ethnicity, and/or language (Moosavi, 2020).

According to Heleta (2016), we must consider Garuba's two methods when discussing and working towards the reconceptualisation and decolonisation of the curriculum in South Africa. 'Adding new items to an existing curriculum' is the first strategy. Rethinking how the object of study is produced and reconstructing it to bring about fundamental change is the second approach (Garuba, 2003). The first strategy is used by individuals who favour keeping things as they are. To bring South Africa, Southern Africa, and Africa together through a collaborative approach to teaching, learning, and research, universities must entirely rethink, reframe, and reconstruct the curriculum.

## The Origin of Inclusive Education and a Move Towards Decolonisation

The Constitution of the Republic of South Africa (Republic of South Africa, 1996) marked the beginning of the inclusive educational approach education institutions. By eliminating unfair discrimination and fostering tolerance, the act pledged to defend the rights of all students. The Department of Basic Education (2014) established and approved the Natural Strategy on SIAS and the White Paper 6 (DoE, 2001) as the legal guidelines for creating an inclusive education and training system. Apprehensions have been raised over the fact that inclusive education, as recommended by White Paper 6 (DoE, 2001), is a Western ideology that has been embraced without question in South Africa and is dominated by Western researchers. Thus, creating inclusive curricula ought to be viewed as an ongoing process intimately linked to social inclusion which need to be adopted in the higher education sector as well.

According to Shurr and Bouck (2013), a unified national education policy and curriculum vision should support the diversification of teaching modalities and learning resources. On the other side, reflecting curriculum arguments occurring in other nations, the debate over the curriculum is perceived to be between academic content, general curriculum, mainstream and functional skills, distinct curriculum, in higher education institutions. Examining procedures, tactics, policies, and activities can help to guarantee the success in all learning environments. According to Moriña (2017), to move towards a more inclusive university, several changes could be taken into consideration in higher education, both at the institutional level and in the practices of the classroom.

The 2006 Convention on the Rights of Persons with Disabilities (CRPD) is the first international agreement to explicitly support inclusive education as a right, setting a new precedent. It builds on earlier texts such as the Standard Rules on Equalisation of Opportunities for Persons with Disabilities (1993), the World Programme of Action (UN Enable, 1982), and the Salamanca Statement and Framework for Action (UNESCO, 1994). Below are a few programmes and conventions that support inclusion in the education sector:

(i) The World Programme of Action (UN Enable, 1982): The World Programme of Action on Disability aims to promote effective strategies for disability prevention, rehabilitation, and full inclusion in society. This involves ensuring equal opportunities and access to improved living conditions resulting from social and economic progress, regardless of a nation's level of development.

(ii) The Standard Rules on Equalisation of Opportunities for Persons with Disabilities (1993): The Rules are designed to guarantee that men, women, and girls with disabilities can participate in their societies and have the same rights and responsibilities as other members. It is still challenging for people with disabilities to fully engage in their societies' activities and to exercise their rights and freedoms in all countries across the world. States must take the necessary steps to remove these barriers. In this process, people with disabilities and the organisations that support them ought to be active participants. Ensuring that individuals with disabilities have equal opportunity is a crucial aspect of the global endeavour to mobilise human resources. Certain populations may require extra care, including women, children, the elderly, the impoverished, migrant workers, those with multiple disabilities, Indigenous people, and ethnic minorities. Furthermore, many disabled refugees have unique needs that need for care.

(iii) The Salamanca Statement and Framework: The idea that all students should be accommodated in higher learning institutions, irrespective of their linguistic, intellectual, social, emotional, or physical disabilities, serves as the foundation for the Framework. It conveys a few specific fundamental inclusion notions, such as that students differ greatly in their requirements and traits. To enjoy human dignity and all of one's rights, inclusion is necessary, and all students gain knowledge and insight from inclusive institutions and will contribute to the development of an inclusive society.

(iv) The Convention on the Rights of Persons with Disabilities: The process of drafting the CRPD was difficult yet inspiring, with the involvement of the disability community and civil society. It sparked passionate and diametrically opposed opinions in the special vs inclusive education debate, emphasising that no person with a disability can be excluded from the general education system on the grounds of their disability, and children with disabilities can receive inclusive, high-quality, and free primary and secondary education on an equal basis with others in their community. Effective individualised support measures are given in environments that maximise academic and social development, consistent with the goal of full inclusion. People with disabilities should receive the assistance they require within the general system, which should offer 'reasonable accommodation' of the individual's requirements. Equal access to lifelong learning, including postsecondary and vocational education, should be granted to all students with disabilities.

(v) The World Education Forum, Dakar, Senegal: The World Education Forum focussed on six goals for meeting the learning needs of all children, youth, and adults by 2015. Some of the goals looked at ensuring that the learning needs of all young people and adults are met through equitable access to appropriate learning and life skills programmes, achieving a 50% improvement in levels of adult literacy by 2015, especially for women, and equitable access to basic and continuing education for all adults, eliminating gender disparities in education by 2005, and achieving gender equality in education by 2015, with a focus on ensuring girls' full and equal access to and achievement in basic education of good quality and improving every aspect of the quality of education and focussing on addressing the educational needs of all children, youth, and adults by 2015 were six goals set forth by the World Education Forum. The objectives, as stated in the following, were examined. Ensuring their excellence so that recognised and measurable learning outcomes are achieved by all, especially in literacy, numeracy, and essential life skills.

Within the discourse on decolonisation, inclusive education has, very rightly, received a lot of attention. More people are embracing it, particularly in the higher education sector, where it has been instrumental in maintaining colonialism and establishing systems of knowledge production (disciplines, institutions, and professional development within each discipline) (Alvares & Faruqi, 2014). Stabilising, validating, and/or excluding systems of knowledge formation are critically dependent on inclusive education's curriculum and pedagogy. The inclusion notion is essential to ensuring that people learn the social skills required for everyday living. Knowledge creation, verification, and marginalisation processes are strongly linked to curriculum, pedagogy, and these processes.

## Inclusion and Africanisation of Higher Education

The concept of decolonisation as Africanisation highlights the strong interaction between the offending and harmed parties. To be relevant and appropriate to Africans' needs and ideals, education must be extensively reconstructed in order to 'Africanise' it (Kinuthia, 2022). The core tenets of African values, community, and education will be restored via scholarly efforts towards creating an inclusive education with an African focus, ensuring more inclusive approaches to education. Numerous academics have determined that inclusive education and Africanising/decolonising education in general are necessary (Elder, 2020; Muthukrishna & Engelbrecht, 2018; Muzata et al., 2021; Walton, 2018). Fomunyam and Teffera (2017) assert that because Africa has gained political independence, it is imperative to abandon colonial structures and consider African culture or traditional wisdom. To avoid being overwhelmed in meeting world standards, Africa must take advantage of its abundant cultural riches while also recognising its social and economic disparities. Africanisation is necessary because, according to Heleta (2016), colonial education obliterated nearly all the linkages that black students may have with the prescribed texts, propagated narratives, debates, and learning on the one side and their history, lived experiences, and dreams on the other side.

The fundamental focus of this argument is that efforts to promote inclusive education in the African context should emphasise the wealth of information found in the Indigenous knowledge and culture of African societies, much of which is compatible with inclusive education. According to Kinuthia (2022), curriculum reform is necessary to incorporate the Indigenous knowledge systems of African people and achieve Africanisation of inclusion. Africanising inclusive education means redefining diversity to consider the needs of students in an African context, investigating the state of higher learning institutions and devising plans to make them accommodate, creating a curriculum that is learner-centred and community-oriented, utilising a variety of approaches, including community-based participatory education, preparing teachers and classrooms for diversity, and enlisting the support of all relevant parties.

The curriculum must be designed in a way that ensures that no student is excluded or marginalised and that all student groups are respected and taken into consideration by addressing a variety of histories and identities. Additionally, the values and norms of society must be linked to the lessons acquired in the classroom. Phasha (2016), referenced in Walton (2018), argues that the Ubuntu philosophy is based on humanness, interdependence, and communalism, and that it is compatible with the goals of inclusive education through collectivism.

It's easier to follow the history of inclusive education and its evolution than to define it. It is more difficult to define inclusive education and define its parameters than it is to trace its historical origins and development. The discursive community shifts between nuances and emphases, giving rise to contested interpretations (Walton, 2018). The following questions must be addressed to Africanise the inclusive education curriculum:

(a) Does the Curriculum reflect the African Way?

Some scholars argue that the curricula constructed on Indigenous African epistemologies can contribute to addressing the problem of viewing knowledge as something divorced from the learner and thus removed from the responsibility, as well as the opportunity to be actively involved in one's own learning. African curriculum theories should consider the social and political contexts within which such an educational system is rooted (Themane, 2020; Van Wyk & Higgs, 2011).

(b) Does it suggest social issues such as Humanisation?

We require a broad definition of the purpose of higher education which according to Gracia-Calandín and Tamarit-López (2021) as cited in Walker (2024), the humanisation of people, rather than profit and market values, is the goal of higher education, which is based on the fundamental idea of the pursuit of understanding through open-ended (decolonised) critical inquiry. An African ethic can also serve as the cornerstone for the principles upheld by the university and its operations. Institutions of higher learning should foster critical thinking, epistemic fairness, a diversity of social practices, and the generous exchange of epistemic engagements in a truly inclusive environment.

(c) Is it culture-sensitive and responsive?

The goal of decolonising education is to challenge and transform the overbearing legacy of European ideas and culture in the classroom. According to Kumalo (2021), pedagogies ought to harness the epistemic agency of all students in a context where the agency of some has been marginalised and arrested.

(d) Is it liberatory?

By fostering an environment that allows students to actively engage in their own learning, inclusive education fosters liberatory educational praxis. According to Freire (1985), liberatory education facilitates an understanding of social systems of oppressions for students and equips them with an understanding of how to challenge and change those systems.

(e) Does it redress the laws and infringements of the past?

Anti-discrimination laws and regulations in nation states, as well as several international agreements that are overseen by United Nations committees form the basic principles of Inclusive education. It should be implemented in such a way that it safeguards every child and young person's right to an inclusive and high-quality education as enshrined in SDG 4.

(f) Is it Inclusive?

Inclusive practices can be created, especially if we mean that inclusion encompasses every student. We need to be explicit about what is meant by inclusion and the stand should be taken that inclusion involves every student and, in some instances at least, the creation of communities in the higher learning environment.

Slee (2011), cited in Walton (2018), claims that inclusive education can be used to gain support for the decolonial endeavour by framing it as a strategy for lessening exclusion by identifying systemic injustice and disadvantage and reallocating resources. The first emphasis, as previously mentioned, is its tradition of recognising the contextual variety in its representation. This improves accessibility, significance, and effectiveness of education. By admitting systematic injustice and disadvantage and allocating resources, inclusive education can be viewed as an approach for reducing exclusion. It can also be enlisted as a partner in the decolonisation process. According to Akena (2012), those who seek to reveal oppression and organise for freedom should be the ones who provide information for emancipator value. Alternative knowledge systems, ideas, and views can be included in the current educational structures thanks to the decolonisation process.

## Valuing Cultural Diversity and Indigenous Pedagogy in the Education Arena

In culturally varied societies, everyone has the right to create their cultural identity and self-identification and each other's difference. But this process is influenced by other factors, including how everyone understands origin versus religion, how they connect with people from different ethnic groups and cultures, and how they are raised in their home nation. Multicultural education is based on the idea that all cultures are valuable and should be respected in educational settings. According to Vandeyar (2003), certain South African schools have an inclusive philosophy that celebrates the diversity of their student body. The definition of multicultural education, according to critics, is respect for other cultures, but it ignores the nuanced ways in which people form opinions about one another (Kirova, 2008; Le Roux, 2000). They argue that an antiracist strategy should be used instead to represent African culture and way of life, considering the background and current state of South African education. Teachers who practice inclusive education should make sure that cues and instructions are brief, clear, consistent, and culturally appropriate for the continent of South Africa. Curriculum development is required to meet the needs of students and foster a diverse learning environment in the classroom. According to Magos et al. (2013), the context of intercultural education should go beyond a cursory discussion of similarities and contrasts with classmates from different cultural backgrounds.

Considering inclusion and interculturalism from a sustainability standpoint, our suggested paradigm's ontological and epistemological foundation is built (Kinuthia, 2022). When considering the suggested paradigm from a sustainability standpoint, this implies that its ontological and epistemological basis is based on inclusivity and interculturalism. According to Sorkos and Hajisoteriou (2021), both inclusive and intercultural education prioritise offering all students a fair and high-quality education, so they may both effectively help achieve the goal of sustainable development. Sustainability is concerned with meeting demands both within and between generations, emphasising quality above quantity as a crucial consideration. The creation of the cultural conditions required for the sustainability of this right will not occur if the current generations fail to guarantee intergenerational equality. Therefore, in the pursuit of sustainability, equal chances for access to and participation in social and educational settings shouldn't be seen as a given.

The 1960s saw the emergence of Indigenous higher education with the introduction of Indigenous knowledge in public universities (Battiste & Barman, 1995). Pidgeon (2016) defines indigenisation of education as the meaningful integration of Indigenous knowledge(s) into the institution's routine operations, from policies to practices across all levels, not simply in the curriculum.

The definition of Indigenous knowledge is 'a complex accumulation of local context-relevant knowledge that embraces the essence of ancestral knowing as well as legacies of diverse histories and cultures' (Akena, 2012, p. 601). Decolonisation is seen by some scholars (Fomunyam & Teffera, 2017; Kaya & Seleti, 2013) as a corrective discourse to centre African Indigenous systems within the academic mainstream. Indigenous wisdom provides an opportunity to introduce an inclusive educational approach (Ronoh, 2018).

African academics and intellectuals are very concerned about the importance of the school curriculum to the sociocultural worldview of the African student, both in terms of substance and orientation (Shizha, 2013). To embrace indigenisation as a strategy for social inclusion, it is important to recognise the effort and dedication made to affect systemic and broader societal change, from the lower echelons of a firm to the top executive leadership.

According to Pidgeon (2016), Indigenisation of the academy refers to the meaningful inclusion of Indigenous knowledge(s), in the everyday fabric of the institution from policies to practices across all levels, not just in curriculum. Indigenous wisdom presents the Afrocentric ideas that provide a reasonable strategy for inclusive education. They must be sufficiently thorough to answer inquiries about the organisation and application of information by educators and students (Van Wyk, 2014). Using an Afrocentric paradigm requires that learners be at the centre of the discourse and that the curriculum define our experiences, historical or modern. It accomplishes this by focussing on Indigenous knowledge. 'The knowledge and skills constructed by Indigenous people to advance their identity, culture, and history or the next generation' is how Akena (2012) defines the idea. Furthermore, according to Mahlo (2017, p. 107), 'inclusive schooling cannot be detached from the African way of living'.

There is a limit to how much inclusive education can permeate African philosophy and culture. Thus, these constraints also restrict the ability of Africanising inclusive education to decolonise inclusive education. First, research indicates that certain traditional African societies have positive attitudes about people and children with disabilities, but it also shows that disability is not always fully accepted in these groups. Stereotypes and myths have the potential to hinder inclusive education principles. For instance, in many African nations, individuals with disabilities believe that pregnant promiscuity, ancestral disfavour, or witchcraft are the root causes of their affliction.

Parenting a disabled child is viewed as embarrassing, and there is a misconception that disability is contagious (Chataika, 2012). The focus of inclusive education has also been drawn to the educational marginalisation of children and young people who have additional identity markers that are devalued in different situations. Curricula in different countries seem to reflect debates about curriculum, with the primary ones centred around academic content, general curriculum, mainstream and functional skills, separate curriculum, and special school curriculum. Examining various practices, procedures, methods, and regulations can help guarantee the achievement of the student. To advance towards a more inclusive university, we think that several changes should be taken into consideration in higher education, both at the institutional level and in the classroom practices (Moriña, 2017).

Le Grange (2016) as cited in Khalo and Mpu (2023) proposes a four-pillar humanistic approach central to the emergent Indigenous paradigm such as:

(i) *Relational accountability*: This is associated with the notion that every curriculum element is linked and accountable for interactions with humans and other living things.
(ii) *Respectful representation*: This has to do with how the curriculum acknowledges Indigenous people and their voices and creates opportunities for understanding them.
(iii) *Reciprocal appropriation*: This suggests that the advantages of information creation and dissemination are shared by communities and universities.
(iv) *Rights and regulation*: This is the observance of ethical norms that, when applicable, grant copyright to knowledge to Indigenous peoples worldwide.

## Lessons Learnt from the Review

Reconciliation and educational and systemic change must be carried out concurrently to topple hierarchical practices and structures that impose a concealed curriculum of privilege and racism. The higher education institutions cannot continue to use attrition and retention as a justification for stepping up their efforts to integrate students from different cultural backgrounds. These methods haven't changed much on their own and frequently exacerbated the estrangement. Rather, we need to reevaluate the basic nature and goal of higher education, and when we do, we'll discover that the institution's overall goal is to improve society and benefit all people (Barkaskas & Gladwin, 2021; Kirkness & Barnhardt, 1991; Reitsma, 2015).

The creation and dissemination of information regarding Indigenous knowledge by institutions can be advantageous to the communities. As a result, there will be a chance for Indigenous knowledge to generate truly novel and original information that can advance mutual healing. Because human rights and intellectual property have developed independently, access to Indigenous knowledge has decreased. The effects of Intellectual Property Rights have led to a change in understanding of Indigenous knowledge. According to Martin and Vermeylen (2005), rights and regulations are becoming more widely acknowledged in the conflict between Indigenous knowledge, intellectual property, and human rights are a significant factor in the creation of new international legal norms.

The reformation of higher education in South Africa encourages the integration of African philosophies and Indigenous knowledge into teaching and learning curricula that support the growth of society and the fulfilment of a sustainable, dignified existence for everyone.

## Conclusions

Despite having diverse origins and a basis in many discourses, inclusive education is recognised as a worldwide social issue and its goals may be misunderstood, it might be inferred. As part of inclusion, the curriculum modifications include academic material, general curriculum, mainstream and functional skills, separate curriculum, and special school. The inclusion notion is essential in the higher education institutions to warrant the idea allowing people to learn social skills required for everyday living. To decolonise higher education institutions, curriculum reforms should promote the educational Afrocentric value of Indigenous pedagogy in multicultural education. Society should also embrace diversity by embracing differences. Indigenous knowledge systems, ideas, and views should be incorporated into the current educational structures as suggested by the decolonisation progression. African nations should take the lead in decolonising education since their curricula should be Afrocentric. The intended curriculum should be designed by Africans, embracing African ideals. The current curriculum for teacher education, education policy, and curricular reforms should be modified to reflect the principles of decolonisation that are evident in the practices of the teachers. Together, we need to work towards creating an inclusive education system that is decolonised.

# References

Adefila, A., Teixeira, R. V., Morini, L., Garcia, M. L. T., Delboni, T. M. Z. G. F., Spolander, G., & Khalil-Babatunde, M., (2022). Higher education decolonisation: Whose voices and their geographical locations?. *Globalisation, Societies and Education, 20*(3), 262–276.

Akena, F. A. (2012). Critical analysis of the production of Western knowledge and its implications for Indigenous knowledge and decolonization. *Journal of Black Studies, 43*(6), 599–619.

Alvares, C., & Faruqi, S. S. (Eds.). (2014). *Decolonising the university: The emerging quest for non-Eurocentric paradigms (Penerbit USM)*. Penerbit USM.

Barkaskas, P., & Gladwin, D. (2021). Pedagogical talking circles: Decolonizing education through relational indigenous frameworks. *Journal of Teaching and Learning, 15*(1), 20–38.

Battiste, M. (2017). *Decolonial ways of knowing and doing at Banglar Gann O Katha at CFCR 90.5 Saskatoon Radio Program*. Retrieved March 11, 2023, from https://drive.google.com/file/d/0B68It2SOL0p5U0NRVGpCMlU3SlE/viewhttps://drive.google.com/file/d/0B68It2SOL0p5U0NRVGpCMlU3SlE/view

Battiste, M., & Barman, J. (Eds.). (1995). *First Nations education in Canada: Circle unfolds*. University of British Columbia.

Bešić, E. (2020). Intersectionality: A pathway towards inclusive education? *Prospects, 49*(3), 111–122.

Chataika, T. (2012). Disability, development and postcolonialism. In D. Goodley, B. Hughes, & L. Davis (Eds.), *Disability and social theory: New developments and directions* (pp. 252–269). Palgrave-MacMillan.

Department of Basic Education. (2014, December 19). *Policy on screening, identification, assessment and support*. No. 1044.

Department of Education (DoE). (2001). *Education White Paper 6: Special needs education – Building an inclusive education and training system*.

Department of Education. (2008). *Report of the Ministerial Committee on Transformation and Social Cohesion and the Elimination of Discrimination in Public Higher Education Institutions* [Final report]. Department of Education, Pretoria.

Damoah, B., Khalo, X., & Omodan, B. (2023). Disparities in rural universities transformation: A review from a South African perspective. *Prizren Social Science Journal, 7*(3), 1–10.

Damoah, B., & Khalo, X. (2024). Constructivist mentor: Influence of mentor teachers on mentees. *JETT, 15*(1), 62–71.

Damoah, B., Owusu, S., Yeboah, C., Acquah, A., & Paintsil, D. (2024). Deciphering The Complexities And Uncertainties in Public Schools in the United States. *Social Sciences and Education Research Review, 11*(1), 7–16.

Elder, B. (2020). Decolonizing inclusive education: A collection of practical inclusive CDS-and DisCrit-informed teaching practices. *Disability and the Global South, 7*(1), 1852–1872.

Fomunyam, K. G., & Teferra, D. (2017). Curriculum responsibilities within the context of decolonization in South African higher education. *Perspectives in Education, 35*(2), 196–207.

Franco, I., Saito, O., Vaughter, P., Whereat, J., Kanie, N., & Takemoto, K. (2019). Higher education for sustainable development: Actioning the global goals in policy, curriculum and practice. *Sustainability Science, 14*(6), 1621–1642.

Freire, P. (1985).Reading the world and reading the word: An interview with Paulo Freire. *Language arts, 62*(1), 15–21.

Garuba, A. (2003). Inclusive education in the 21st century: Challenges and opportunities for Nigeria. *Asia Pacific Disability Rehabilitation Journal, 14*(2), 191–200.

Haug, P. (2017). Understanding inclusive education: Ideals and reality. *Scandinavian Journal of Disability Research, 19*(3), 206–217.

Heleta, S. (2016). Decolonisation: Academics must change what they teach, and how. *The Conversation.* Retrieved February 24, 2024, from https://theconversation.com/decolonisation-academics-must-change-what-they-teach-and-how-68080

Hungwe, J. P., & Ndofirepi, A. P. (2022). A critical interrogation of paradigms in discourse on the decolonisation of higher education in Africa. *South African Journal of Higher Education, 36*(3), 54–71.

Kaya, H. O., & Seleti, Y. N. (2013). African indigenous knowledge systems and relevance of higher education in South Africa. *International Education Journal: Comparative Perspective, 12*(1), 30–44.

Khalo, X., & Mpu, Y. (2023). Inclusive education a vehicle towards decolonization of the South African curriculum. *Journal for Educators, Teachers and Trainers, 14*(6), 55–62.

Kinuthia, C. N. (2022). Africanizing inclusive education: Why, how, who, where and what to be included. *East African Journal of Education Studies, 5*(1), 204–216.

Kirkness, V. J., & Barnhardt, R. (1991). First Nations and higher education: The four R's—Respect, relevance, reciprocity, responsibility. *Journal of American Indian Education, 30*(3), 1–15.

Kirova, A. (2008). Critical and emerging discourses in multicultural education literature: A review. *Canadian Ethnic Studies, 40*(1), 101–124.

Kumalo, S. H. (2021) Justice through higher education: Revisiting White Paper 3 of 1997. *Higher Education Quarterly, 75,* 175–188.

Kunene, A. (2009). CHAPTER NINE: Learner-centeredness in practice: Reflections from a curriculum education specialist. *Counterpoints, 357,* 139–152.

Le Roux, J. (2000). Multicultural education: A new approach for a new South African dispensation. *Intercultural Education, 11*(1), 19–29.

Magos, K., Tsilimeni, T., & Spanopoulou, K. (2013). Good morning Alex-Kalimera Maria: Digital communities and intercultural dimension in early childhood education. *Intercultural Education, 24*(4), 366–373.

Mahlo, D. (2017). Teaching learners with diverse needs in the Foundation Phase in Gauteng Province, South Africa. *SAGE Open, 7*(1), 2158244017697162.

Martin, G., & Vermeylen, S. (2005). Intellectual property, indigenous knowledge, and biodiversity. *Capitalism Nature Socialism, 16*(3), 27–48.

Moosavi, L. (2020). Can East Asian students think? Orientalism, critical thinking, and the decolonial project. *Education Sciences, 10*(10), 286.

Moriña, A. (2017). Inclusive education in higher education: Challenges and opportunities. *European Journal of Special Needs Education, 32*(1), 3–17.

Muthukrishna, N., & Engelbrecht, P. (2018). Decolonising inclusive education in lower income, Southern African educational contexts. *South African Journal of Education, 38*(4), 1–11.

Muzata, K. K., Simui, F., Mahlo, D., & Ng'uni, P. (2021). Inclusive education status through the lenses of teachers in Zambia. *African Journal of Teacher Education, 10*(1), 1–20.

Pidgeon, M. (2016). More than a checklist: Meaningful indigenous inclusion in higher education. *Social Inclusion, 4*(1), 77–91. https://doi.org/10.17645/si.v4i1.436

Reitsma, E. S. (2015). *Dynamics of respectful design in co-creative and co-reflective encounters with indigenous communities.* University of Northumbria at Newcastle.

Republic of South Africa. (1996). *The Constitution of the Republic of South Africa (Act 108 of 1996).* Government Printer.

Ronoh, J. C. (2018). *Indigenous knowledge in the school curriculum: Teacher educator perceptions of place and position* [Doctoral dissertation, Nelson Mandela University].

Shizha, E. (2013). Reclaiming our indigenous voices: The problem with postcolonial Sub-Saharan African school curriculum. *Journal of Indigenous Social Development, 2*(1), 1–18.

Shurr, J., & Bouck, E. C. (2013). Research on curriculum for students with moderate and severe intellectual disability: A systematic review. *Education and Training in Autism and Developmental Disabilities, 48*(1), 76–87.

Slee, R. (2019). Belonging in an age of exclusion. *International Journal of Inclusive Education, 23*(9), 909–922.

Sorkos, G., & Hajisoteriou, C. (2021). Sustainable intercultural and inclusive education: Teachers' efforts on promoting a combining paradigm. *Pedagogy, Culture & Society, 29*(4), 517–536.

Stein, S. (2019). Beyond higher education as we know it: Gesturing towards decolonial horizons of possibility. *Studies in Philosophy and Education, 38*, 143–161.

Themane, M. (2020). Rethinking curriculum theory that can deliver a decolonised African curriculum. In K. G. Fomunyam & S. B. Khoza (Eds.), *Curriculum theory, curriculum theorising, and the theoriser* (pp. 38–52). Brill.

UN Enable. (1982). World programme of action concerning disabled persons. Adopted by the General Assembly on, 3.

UNESCO's Salamanca Statement (UNESCO). (1994). Beyond Salamanca: A citation analysis of the CRPD/GC4 relative to the Salamanca Statement in inclusive and special education research. *International Journal of Inclusive Education, 27*(2), 123–145.

United Nations. (1993, December 20). *Standard rules on the equalization of opportunities for persons with disabilities* [Universal Instrument, General Assembly]. https://www.ohchr.org/en/instruments-mechanisms/instruments/standard-rules-equalization-opportunities-persons-disabilities

United Nations. (1994). *Department of Public Information. The standard rules on the equalization of opportunities for persons with disabilities*. UN.

United Nations Sustainable Development Goals. (2015). *United Nations sustainable Development Goals 2015*. UN.

United Nations Educational, Scientific, & Cultural Organization (UNESCO). (2016). Reviews of *national policies for education education* in Thailand: *An OECD–UNESCO perspective*. OECD Publishing.

Van Wyk, B., & Higgs, P. (2011). The curriculum in an African context. *Indilinga African Journal of Indigenous Knowledge Systems, 10*(2), 171–181.

Van Wyk, M. (2014). Conceptualizing an Afrocentric-indigenous pedagogy for an inclusive classroom environment. *Mediterranean Journal of Social Sciences, 5*(4). https://doi.org/10.5901/miss.2014.y5n4p292

Vandeyar, S. (2003). The jagged paths to multicultural education: International experiences and South Africa's response in the new dispensation. *South African Journal of Education, 23*(3), 193–198.

Walker, M. (2024). A capabilitarian approach to decolonising curriculum. *Education, Citizenship and Social Justice, 19*(1), 110–123.

Walton, E. (2018). Decolonising (through) inclusive education? *Educational Research for Social Change, 7*(SPE), 31–45.

Zidny, R., Sjöström, J., & Eilks, I. (2020). A multi-perspective reflection on how indigenous knowledge and related ideas can improve science education for sustainability. *Science & Education, 29*(1), 145–185.

Chapter 8

# A Critical Review of Pre-service Teacher Education and Inclusion in the South African Higher Education Context

Cina P. Mosito[a] and Lulama Mdodana-Zide[b]

[a]Nelson Mandela University, South Africa
[b]University of Free State, South Africa

### Abstract

There is consensus in the literature that pre-service teacher preparation is important for ensuring that teachers are ready for inclusive teaching. There have been efforts in South African higher education (HE) to incorporate inclusive education (IE) content into the teacher education programmes. This chapter entails a systematic review of literature that analyses teacher education and its impact on teacher preparation for inclusive pedagogy. The chapter also highlights some challenges this process has encountered, what has been achieved so far, and some suggestions for going forward.

*Keywords*: Inclusive education; pre-service teacher education; higher education; inclusive teaching; teacher preparation

## Introduction

UNESCO's call for education for all (EFA) has been at the forefront of the IE agenda worldwide (UNESCO, 1994, 2015, 2019, 2020, 2021). The most instrumental of UNESCO's calls was the 1994 Salamanca statement and framework on special needs education. The statement provided an initial conceptualisation of inclusivity as a philosophy that embraces all learners and people experiencing a variety of barriers to learning. While the seminal concern of special education had been on creating pedagogies for learners with disabilities, IE emphasises that even in the absence of disabilities, learners experience barriers to learning. The task thereon has been for member states to develop policies and programmes on how their education systems would realise the objectives of quality, access, and equity for all the learners including those living with disabilities. In South Africa, the 1994 UNESCO call for action for IE systems coincided with the country's introduction to a democratic dispensation after many years of apartheid rule. The drive for inclusivity therefore became part of the agenda of transformation to end racially motivated educational provisioning that had resulted in disparities between different racial categories. As Education White Paper 6 points out, racialised provisioning in education had also affected special needs education, with the ensuing position being that by the turn of democracy there was a great divide in resourcing between special schools for whites and other racial groups (Department of Education (DoE), 2001).

Transformation in education involved the development of policies that envisaged equal and equitable EFA, underpinned by social justice (Sayed & Kanjee, 2013). Expressed in the White Paper on Education and Training, and many education policies that followed since the democratic rule, has been a need to bring change in the wider education landscape (Pendlebury, 1998; Sayed & Ahmed, 2015; Sayed & Kanjee, 2013). Teacher education is placed at the centre of the transformation agenda because 'world class education systems get the right people to be teachers and develop them into effective instructors to ensure that the system delivers the best possible instruction for every child' (Sayed & Ahmed, 2015, p. 336). This, by extension, suggests teacher education as a crucial area for promoting inclusivity and EFA. The position further finds expression in the latest UNESCO publication proposing a 10-point tool to support countries in moving towards IE (UNESCO, 2021). Within this tool, to deliver quality content that is inclusive, member states should finance training for teaching staff that will equip them on what it means to be inclusive. The Department of Basic Education in South Africa concurs with a view that knowledgeable and skilful teachers play a role that 'has strategic importance for the intellectual, moral, and cultural preparation of our young people' (DoE, 2006, p. 6).

We embark on this chapter with the goal of answering the question: how does pre-service teacher education contribute to IE in post-apartheid South Africa? Towards this end, we employed a systematic literature review method to provide answers to the question. A literature review is a systematic collection and synthesis of previous research, which qualifies as a research method that creates 'a firm foundation for advancing knowledge and facilitating theory' (Snyder, 2019, p. 333). Accordingly, we integrated perspectives from many sources of literature to arrive at an answer to the question by first examining the literature that describes and analyses the overall landscape of education in South Africa. Next, we clarify how initial teacher education (ITE) programmes have interpreted policy calls for teachers who graduate with attributes and skills for engendering inclusive pedagogy. The chapter concludes by identifying the challenges and opportunities that the literature review has illuminated. As stated by Snyder (2019), a systematic literature review has the potential to contribute to knowledge and facilitate theory.

The chapter, therefore, is not guided by a specific theory but seeks to critically review literature that clarifies the role of ITE in contributing to social justice by clarifying related concepts like critical literacy and cognitive justice. The underlying aim of the chapter is to understand key developments in teacher education, challenges, and current gaps.

## Systematic Literature Review Approach

In conducting the systematic literature review, we stated our research question: how does pre-service teacher education contribute to IE in post-apartheid South Africa? We then carried out a systematic search for all sources that were relevant and evidently related to pre-service teachers and IE. We consulted several databases, such as the Web of Science, Scopus, and Google Scholar. Internationally accredited journals, including the *International Journal of Inclusive Education*, were further relevant information sources. We consulted the Nelson Mandela University library and perused books, policy documents, articles, theses, and electronic sources for relevant, up-to-date literature.

Our search was directed by key concepts of pre-service teachers such as pre-service teachers' preparation, development and training for inclusive teaching, inclusive pedagogy, inclusive learning facilitation, inclusive assessment, etc. We also searched the words 'challenges and opportunities' for pre-service teacher education for inclusion. Sources which did not help us answer the research question and were deliberately avoided. Once the relevant sources were collected, we developed a protocol to go through the sources. The protocol was based on the concepts we used for the search. We then synthesised our analysis by harvesting themes emerging from the sources to formulate our conclusions and arguments.

## Overall Education Landscape in SA

South Africa is a country on a healing journey as it carries a legacy of past inequalities, inequities, injustices and non-inclusive practices that were entrenched in various spheres of life, including the education system. The apartheid government ensured that, among all the other systems of its state, segregation and repression were essential components of the schooling system and therefore ensuring a crippled education system and life for all Black South Africans (Bantu Education Act of 1953) and people of colour (1963 Coloured Person's Education Act and 1965 Indian Education Act) within the country (Serrurier-Zucker, 2023). As Serrurier-Zucker (2023, p. 406) directly puts it, during those 'turbulent times' of the apartheid government, 'obtaining an education as a black person became a Herculean task'.

When the country was liberated from the claws of the Apartheid government in 1994, an African National Congress ANC-led democratic government took over. This was a government system that promised freedom for all, a government of hope for all races, with an ANC Freedom Charter, that stated 'free, compulsory, universal and equal' EFA children and a new South African Constitution constructed on a lens that made access to education a basic right for everyone

(The Freedom Charter, 1954; South African Constitution of 1996, Bill of Rights, Section 29 (1)). In a race against time, and to align itself globally, the South African democratic government made strides to ensure an education system that is inclusive of all its citizens regardless of race, skin colour, gender, demographic sphere, socioeconomic background, ethnicity, to mention a few, etc. For both the Department of Basic Education (DBE-Gr. R-12) and the Department of Higher Education and Training (DHET – Universities, TVET, colleges, etc.), as the education system is currently categorised, additional to the laws, acts, plans and guidelines already in place, various policies towards a push to promote inclusivity such as (i) Education White Paper 6, (ii) Language in Education Policy, (iii) 2014 Policy on Screening, Identification, Assessment and Support (SIAS), (iv) 2015 White Paper on the Rights of Persons with Disabilities (WPRPD), and (v) The Council for Higher Education's (CHE) 2014 policy on Massification of HE and many more, have been developed to ensure change, and an effective, efficient education system inclusive of all (CHE, 2014; DBE, 2014; DoE, 1997, 2001; DSD, 2015).

Fulfilling the South African people's desires of an education system that is accessible and equal for all deemed to be a conundrum. The South African democratic government inherited a highly fragmented education structure, and its attempt to evolve from the historically rooted disparities and injustices has proven to be complex. The echoes of the country's past apartheid systems in the education landscape are still heard and deafening beyond the 30 years of the era of democracy and reconciliation. The South African Education system is faced with glaring challenges that continue to perpetuate disproportions in its schooling setting.

Looking at some of the challenges plaguing the DBE level, one stark divide exists between urban and rural schools, where the quality of education often varies substantially. Urban schools, especially the former Model C and Private schools, have better infrastructure, resources, and access to the best educators as compared to their rural school counterparts who are struggling with basic teaching and learning resources, let alone computers, libraries, and internet access, yet it is where majority of the learner population is situated (Gardiner, 2008; National Education Infrastructure Management System [NEIMS], 2020; Shikalepo, 2020). Another prominent divide is in the lower and higher quintile funding system with schools in lower quintiles (1–3) located in economically disadvantaged areas, such as rural schools, faced with resource shortages, overcrowded classrooms, and a lack of essential facilities. With these challenges facing the DBE proving to be the norm of the day, learner performance in various literacies such as Language, Mathematics, and Science is a pressing concern is a pressing concern. This is evidenced by international assessments such as the Progress in International Reading Literacy Study (PIRLS) showing SA high learner reading inabilities and Trends in International Mathematics and Science Study showing SA performance below the average score in Mathematics and Science compared globally (DBE, 2023a; Reddy et al., 2022). The National Senior Certificate examination results, though there is a show of improvement in the quantity pass rate in 2023, however, the concern remains on poor quality and implications for access to Higher Education Institutions (HEIs) (DBE, 2023a).

To address the inequalities of the past, the DHET drafted a HE White Paper to convert a racially segregated HE system into one that meets the demands of an inclusive society in a new global period (Agumba et al., 2023; DoE, 1997). The #FeesMustFall movement added to pressuring the SA government to declare free education and therefore giving more access to HE. However, efforts to eradicate imbalances of the past in the HE sector seem to be an uphill task. The DHET inherits some of its inequalities outside of the HE segment, such as, DBE and other sectors and complements the inherited challenges with its own disparities of 'unfair admission processes, unequal funding arrangements, and financial constraints, especially students[1] from socioeconomically disadvantaged backgrounds (especially those from poor-rural areas)' (Agumba et al., 2023, p. 24). Low-income students still struggle with money to cover basic needs such as housing, food, transport, books, etc. (Agumba et al., 2023; Martinez-Vargas et al., 2020). Additionally, both old and extant literature portrays a picture of more concern on student's unpreparedness to succeed at university level, especially students coming from rural schools (Agumba et al., 2023; Ajani & Gamede, 2020; Lea & Street, 2006; Pineteh, 2014)

This overview of South Africa's journey towards educational equity reflects a nation striving to overcome the deep-rooted inequalities inherited from its apartheid past. The post-apartheid era, marked by promises of inclusivity and equal access to education, has witnessed commendable policy efforts, including the development of various acts and plans. Nevertheless, comprehensive changes and persistent work towards an inclusive, accessible, and high-quality education system are still critical as South Africa struggles with these issues with implications to teaching and teacher knowledge, as outlined in the following section.

## Teaching, Teacher Knowledge, and IE

Teaching and teacher knowledge are multifaceted and complex concepts that are defined varyingly by literature. In the various conceptualisations of the term teaching, the definition comes down to establishing common trends that shape the concept such as an artistic and scientific process, imparting knowledge, classroom interactions, and learning stimulus to mention a few (Rajagopalan, 2019). Definitions of teacher knowledge revolve around the three components Shulman (1987) term as content knowledge (CK), pedagogical knowledge (PC), and pedagogical content knowledge (PCK), which in simple terms means understanding how to teach the content of the subjects in a way that is accessible and meaningful and productive to learners. Whichever way one would explain or define the concepts of teaching and teacher knowledge, most important is the significance of both concepts to ensure effective education for an improved student achievement.

Inclusion in education encompasses practices of ensuring that all learners, regardless of their abilities or backgrounds, receive equitable opportunities to learn and actively participate in the classroom community. Teaching and teacher

---

[1] Student or students is used to refer to those studying in higher education such as at a university or college. Learners refers to those in basic education (grades R-12).

knowledge form an integral part in IE (Tirri & Laine, 2017). The integration of inclusive practices into subject-specific teaching requires teachers to possess certain knowledge and abilities that capacitates them to respond to individual learners among learners in a manner that avoids marginalisation. This is commonly known as inclusive pedagogy (Florian & Beaton, 2018). It integrates subject knowledge (what to teach) with pedagogical knowledge (how to teach), as well as a comprehension of how to modify these approaches to accommodate the various requirements of all learners, including those with special needs or impairments. In order to establish a learning environment that is both accessible and helpful for all students, regardless of their various needs and abilities, educators must possess a range of skills, attitudes, and practices related to inclusion (Suleymanov, 2015). Teacher comprehension of the diversity of learners and the barriers learners face in the educational process together with grasping the content of the various subjects, is a core element of teaching and teacher knowledge in inclusive classroom settings. Thus, teachers need to understand and appreciate diversity, put inclusive practices into practice, modify lessons and resources, and create a welcoming and inclusive classroom atmosphere as all essential components of successful teaching and teacher expertise in inclusion (Sanger, 2020).

In South Africa, the legacy of past inequalities, injustices, and non-inclusive practices in the education system has left an indelible mark and several profound implications for the effective teaching and teacher knowledge in inclusion. Despite the advancements in IE, the various barriers experienced in the education sphere hinder its successful implementation (Adewumi & Mosito, 2019; Mpu & Adu, 2021). The diverse socio-economic backgrounds of learners in schools require teachers who adopt varied teaching strategies to accommodate different learning needs. As such, this necessitates a meticulous understanding of the contextual factors influencing students' educational experiences. Teachers serve as the cornerstone in realising the objective of IE, and as such, should possess the capability to cater to the educational requirements of all their students, including those facing obstacles to learning, within their classroom (Engelbrecht et al., 2015; Skae et al., 2020; White Paper 6 DoE, 2001). Acknowledging and addressing the diverse needs of learners contribute to a more inclusive and effective educational system.

The realities on the ground on the pedagogical practices (teaching) and the mastering of content (teacher knowledge) teachers should possess to ensure effective inclusive learning and improved learner achievement in schools have portrayed a concerning picture. Literature attests that teachers in South African schools have strived for years to implement IE since the inception of Education White Paper 6; yet they experience various challenges constraining the implementation (Mpu & Adu, 2021; Skae et al., 2020). These challenges include, but are not limited to, inadequate support from the department, lack of resources, overcrowded classrooms (multi grading), lack of time, lack of teacher professional development, etc. (Adewumi & Mosito, 2019; Mpu & Adu, 2021).

Comprehensive measures addressing IE issues in South African classrooms and promoting an atmosphere where teachers may improve their teaching techniques and develop their knowledge to suit the different requirements of all learners are urgently needed. These measures are essential if an inclusive and successful educational system is to be genuinely achieved. For example, teacher education institutions play a critical role in shaping the attitudes and competencies of future educators. Embedding inclusive strategies within the curriculum for student teachers and providing practical experiences in inclusive classrooms can better prepare them for the complexities of diverse learning environments. Such embedding would empower future educators to overcome challenges, implement inclusive strategies, and create a learning environment that accommodates the diverse needs of all students, fostering a truly inclusive and supportive educational system for the benefit of society as a whole.

## IE in South Africa

### Historical Developments

IE has undergone many shifts and developments in South Africa (Dalton et al., 2012). Prior to the 1994 democratic elections, the education system was characterised by duality of provisioning in the form of special schools and mainstream schools (Naicker, 2019). Furthermore, the pre-1994 apartheid's policy of racialised fiscal allocation resulted in white schools being allocated a bigger slice of the budget which gave way to inequalities in the quantity and quality of infrastructure that are prevalent to date (Makoelle, 2012; Naicker, 2000). Following these apartheid realities, 'the broad transformation of the South African society towards equality coincided with the initiation of inclusion as promulgated in international documents such as the Salamanca Statement (1994) and Dakar World Education Forum' (Makoelle, 2012, p. 94). The implication therefore is that IE in South Africa is a combination of factors which take into account 'the context of the country's broader political, social, and cultural developments since 1994' (Engelbrecht, 2020, p. 219). These are: (i) the development of policies that speak to the ideals of an IE system, (ii) that all learners of school going age are in schools, (iii) graduating teachers who have knowledge and the competence to teach diverse learners through responsive pedagogical practices, and (iv) ensuring that different levels of the education system are receptive and open to promoting quality and equitable EFA. It is these four issues that the next section of the chapter examines.

### IE Policies

South Africa has one of the most impressive policies, emanating from an equally impressive constitution and bill of rights. Underpinning the general education policy framework is the basic intent to position education as a basic right to all and as a social justice tool through which the wrongs of the past should be righted. The list of these policies follows in Table 8.1.

While all the above policies are relevant in promoting IE, of interest is how the DHET policies take up the inclusion agenda through teacher education. Equally important would be how faculties and schools of education engage with IE in teacher education curriculum to graduate teachers that are capacitated to deliver what Makoelle (2014) calls cognitive justice. The concept of cognitive justice refers to education that enables learner participation through their existing forms of Indigenous knowledge (Makoelle, 2014).

Table 8.1. Inclusive Education Policy Development in South Africa.

| Year | IE Policy Document | Focus and Intended Impact |
| --- | --- | --- |
| 2001 | Education White Paper 6 | Outlines a national strategy for systematically addressing and removing barriers to learning 'so that all learners, with or without disabilities, pursue their learning potential to the fullest' (DOE, 2001, p. 11) |
| 2005 | The South African Children's Act | Protects the rights of children so they are able to grow up safely and develop well |
| 2011 | DBE: Guidelines for Responding to Learner Diversity in the Classroom | It provides strategies for differentiated teaching and learning to meet the diversity of learners' needs |
| 2011 | DBE: Policy on Screening Identification, Assessment and Support (SIAS) | Framework of procedures to identify, assess, and provide programmes for all learners who need additional support to boost their participation and inclusion in school |
| 2011 | South African Council for Educators (SACE): Draft Professional Teacher Standards | Details 10 principles for professional teaching |
| 2012 | The South African National Development Plan 2030 | Promotes nation building as a key element within social cohesion schemes. Identifies 31 actions that will help to achieve this based on values, equal opportunities, inclusion, cohesion, citizenship, and leadership |
| 2013 | African Union: Agenda 2063—Africa's Agenda for Children | Strategic plan for the socio-economic transformation of the continent. Emphasises the importance of education and children's civil and political rights as the foundations of sustainable, rights-based development |
| 2014 | Southern African Development Community (SADC): Care and Support for Teaching and Learning (CSTL) framework | Aims to realise the educational rights of all children, including those who are most vulnerable, by addressing barriers to learning and participation. Supports schools through nine programmes to become inclusive centres of teaching, learning, care and support |

Table 8.1. (*Continued*)

| Year | IE Policy Document | Focus and Intended Impact |
| --- | --- | --- |
| 2015 | DHET Revised Policy on Minimum Requirements for Teacher Education Qualifications | All teachers need to be familiar with what is needed to implement inclusive education practices |
| 2018 | DBE: Draft Norms and Standards for Funding | Addresses how an inclusive education system will be funded and resourced |
| 2018 | DHET: Standards for Inclusive Teaching | Identifies standards for the development of inclusive teachers in five key areas: valuing and understanding learner diversity; agency for social justice and inclusion; collaborating to enable inclusive teaching and learning; developing professionally as an inclusive teacher; employing classroom practices that promote learning for all |

*Source*: Adapted from British Council (2019, pp. 17–18) Unit 1: Inclusive Education.

## *IE in Pre-service Education Programmes*

The Minimum Requirements for Teacher Education Qualifications (MRTEQ) is described as 'a policy that provides the basis for the construction of core curricula for ITE, as well as for Continuing Professional Development (CPD) Programmes' (DHET, 2015, p. 8). The policy makes three important statements about IE in teacher education programmes:

1. All BEd (including PGCE) graduates must be knowledgeable about IE and skilled in identifying and addressing barriers to learning, as well as in curriculum differentiation to address the needs of individual learners within a grade (pp. 23, 29).
2. Newly qualified teachers
   a. must know who their learners are and how they learn;
   b. they must understand their individual needs and tailor their teaching accordingly;
   c. must understand diversity in the South African context in order to teach in a manner that includes all learners;
   d. must also be able to identify learning or social problems and work in partnership with professional service providers to address these; and
   e. must be able to manage classrooms effectively across diverse contexts in order to ensure a conducive learning environment (p. 62).

In 2017 British Council, MIET Africa, DBE, DHET, and UNISA embarked on a project called *Teaching for All*. Teaching for All aimed to provide teachers (pre- and in-service) with the skills, attitudes and knowledge to teach inclusively in diverse classrooms in diverse communities through a research-informed curriculum (British Council, 2024). Later, 10 more South African universities joined the project and are integrating the Teaching for All curriculum in their programmes. In the 2018 project report, *The state of inclusive education in South Africa and implications for teacher training programmes* (Majoko, Phasha, et al., 2018), it was found that of the 21 HEIs offering pre-service teacher education, only 17 of those had IE as a standalone module or embedded in either education studies of educational psychology. Another critical finding from the same study was that pre-service teacher educators (lecturers) had multiple understandings with no commonality of what IE is, with the dominant understanding of inclusion as education about and for learners with disabilities. On this point, it was not surprising because the long-standing duality of educational provision from the days of apartheid, had been driven by the medical model which categorised learners between those who could be in special or mainstream schools. Under the medical model, the crux of the matter was that learners who struggled in school tasks did so because of some underlying problem which mainstream teachers had no skills and knowledge about. The study further revealed a lower take up of policy recommendations such as a need for new teachers to graduate with diversity management skills (DoE, 2006) and IE-related skills stipulated by MRTEQ (DHET, 2015).

Following these illuminating findings by Majoko, Phasha et al. (2018), a recommendation for the development of a curriculum and material that would lead to the mainstreaming of IE in pre-service teacher programmes was instituted through the Teaching for All project. Subsequent reports have demonstrated different ways in which interaction with the Teaching for All curriculum has shifted knowledge, attitudes and to some extent skills of student teachers and their educators in HEIs on IE. The first impact report by Sayed et al. (2020) indicated that these two key stakeholders in HEIs experienced a variety of positive shifts related to exposure to the new curriculum. For students these were enhanced knowledge about IE, change in attitudes and beliefs, and some acquisition of new skills. Lecturers reported to have found the material beneficial as it either enhanced what they were already teaching or brought in new content, which had been overlooked. They also found the networking opportunities and a community of practice they have become part of since working from the same curriculum beneficial.

In 2022, a follow-up evaluation into how Teaching for All is impacting pre-service teacher education was conducted by the Centre of International Teacher Education at Cape Peninsula University of Technology. In this impact evaluation phase of the programme, only 8 of the 17 universities that had participated in the Majoko, Phasha, et al. (2018) state of IE study reported on how they had continued to use the material. Sayed, Singh, Williams & Sadeck (2022) report that while the Teaching for All programme brought to the universities similar content, there were many differences in how each university institutionalised it. We believe that there could be other noteworthy individual university initiatives, which have not have not been disseminated to the public in a manner Teaching for All has been. This therefore suggests and offers opportunities for a large-scale study that could examine how all the 17 universities that had participated in the 2017/2018 study on the state of IE in South Africa are currently engaging with IE in their ITE programmes.

## Challenges and Opportunities

IE in pre-service teacher education is a field that is undergoing constant scrutiny and changes. As the foregoing sections have demonstrated, being an offshoot of special and specialised education has contributed to a lack of shared understanding of what the concept and its practices mean. The impact of the history of separate development on education in South Africa necessitates a nuanced understanding and definition of what it means to teach inclusively. For example, one cannot ignore the tensions that are embedded in identity markers such as gender, race, language, culture, ability, ethnicity, socio-economic status, and many more. This therefore means IE in pre-service teacher curriculum should expose students to critical literacy(ies) learning approaches that promote student teachers access into talking and teaching about the intersections of power, access, and diversity (Janks & McKinney, 2021) in a manner that promotes cognitive justice so that the Indigenous knowledges of diverse learners in South African classrooms are not oppressed by Western hegemony (Makoelle, 2014). It therefore means pre-service education should be at the forefront of graduating new teachers with knowledge, values, beliefs, and skills that take into account multiplicity of what IE is in a system that (i) was dominated by duality of teachers who saw themselves as either special education or mainstream education ready, and (ii) teachers who see themselves and their learners through gendered, classed, and ableist lenses. The danger of the continuing dual approach are teachers who graduate with low beliefs about designing responsive pedagogies for diverse learners. The binary approach to classroom realities is equally debilitating to teachers as it does not allow them to see possibilities beyond, e.g. the realities they might have always believed in around gender, languages, religion and culture, and many other identity markers.

Teaching practice (TP) is another component of teacher education that offers opportunities for promoting IE. TP undisputedly plays a critical role in socialising student teachers into the profession (Mangope et al., 2018) and should as such offer authentic experiences that are representative of what students will experience when they enter the field. Within this context, mentor teachers are considered a critical bridging element between students' university acquired theory and diverse school realities (Kimmel et al., 2021). A potential problem that could undermine this scaffolding possibility is when mentor teachers themselves have multiple interpretations of what it means to be an inclusive teacher. Here lies another opportunity for CPD opportunities that align the acquisition of inclusion knowledge, skills and dispositions for both in-service and pre-service teachers.

## Conclusion

In conclusion, the chapter has highlighted various developments and tensions related to IE, earmarked significantly by UNESCO's call for Education for All (EFA), in South African teacher education. As such, South Africa has developed a coherent policy framework since its re-entry into the United Nations. While the country has made significant policy advancements towards IE, the practical realisation of these policies requires sustained effort, particularly in teacher education. The lingering legacy of apartheid has demanded that faculties and schools of education develop IE curriculum that raises students' consciousness on barriers to teaching and learning that they need to address once they enter the field of teaching. Therefore, addressing the historical inequities and contemporary challenges through well-supported, cohesive, and contextually relevant teacher training is crucial for fostering an inclusive and equitable education system for all learners in the South African context.

# References

Adewumi, T. M., & Mosito, C. (2019). Experiences of teachers in implementing inclusion of learners with special education needs in selected Fort Beaufort District primary schools, South Africa. *Cogent Education*, 6(1), 1703446.

African National Congress. (1954). The freedom charter. The Peoples' Congress.

Agumba, H., Simpson, Z., & Ndofirepi, A. (2023). Towards understanding the influence of rurality on students' access to and participation in higher education. *Critical Studies in Teaching and Learning (CriSTaL)*, 11(1), 22–42.

Ajani, O. A., & Gamede, B. T. (2020). Challenges of high school learners' transition into universities: A case of a South African rural university. *Gender & Behaviour*, 18(2), 15803–15812. Retrieved from https://www.researchgate.net/publication/342889551

British Council. (2019). *Teaching for all Unit 1*. British Council.

British Council. (2024). *Teaching for All*. https://www.britishcouncil.org.za/programmes/education/teaching-all

Council on Higher Education (CHE). (2014). *Annual report 2013/2014*. https://mail.google.com/mail/u/0/#inbox/QgrcJHsNhNbrXTfnRDPjTNZmWnJpGLbZzZV?projector=1&messagePartId=0.2

Dalton, E. M., Mckenzie, J. A., Kahonde, C., (2012). The implementation of inclusive education in South Africa: Reflections arising from a workshop for teachers and therapists to introduce Universal Design for Learning, *African Journal of Disability*, 1(1), 13.

Department of Basic Education (DBE). (2014). *Policy on screening, identification, assessment and support (SIAS)*. Government Printer.

Department of Basic Education (DBE). (2023a). *National Senior Certificate (NSC) exam results technical report*. Government Printer.

Department of Basic Education (DBE). (2023b). *PIRLS 2021: South African preliminary highlights report*. Department of Basic Education.

Department of Education (DoE). (Republic of South Africa). (1997). *Language in education policy*. Department of Education.

Department of Education (DoE). (1997). *Quality Education for All: Report of the National Commission for Special Needs in Education and Training (NCSNET) and the National Commission on Education Support Services (NCESS)*. Government Printer.

Department of Education (DoE). (2001), *Education White Paper 6. Special needs education: Building an inclusive education and training system*. Government Printer.

Department of Education (DoE). (2006). *The national policy framework for teacher education and development in South Africa*. More teachers; Better teachers.

Department of Higher Education and Training (DHET). (2015). 2nd National Higher Education Summit 15–17 October 2015, Annexure 3, Are we making progress with systemic structural transformation of resourcing, access, success, staffing and researching in higher education: What do the data say? Department of Higher Education and Training. Retrieved from http://www.dhet.gov.za/summit/Docs/2015Docs/Annex%203_DHET_Progress%20with%20transformation%20_What%20do%20the%20data%20say.pdf.

Department of Social Development (DSD). (2015). *White Paper on the Rights of Persons with Disabilities (WPRPD)*. Government Printer.
Engelbrecht, P. (2020). Inclusive education: Developments and challenges in South Africa. *Prospects, 49*(3), 219–232.
Engelbrecht, P., Nel, M., Nel, N., & Tlale, D. (2015). Enacting understanding of inclusion in complex contexts: Classroom practices of South African teachers. *South African Journal of Education, 35*(3), 1–10. https://doi.org/10.15700/saje.v35n3a1074
Florian, L., & Beaton, M. (2018). Inclusive pedagogy in action: Getting it right for every child. *International Journal of Inclusive Education, 22*(8), 870–884. https://doi.org/10.1080/13603116.2017.1412513
Gardiner, M. (2008). Education in rural areas. *Issues in Education Policy, 4*, 1–33.
Janks, H., & McKinney, C. (2021). Critical literacies in post-apartheid South Africa. In Z. C. Pandya, R. A. Mora, J. H. Alford, N. A. Golden, & R. S. deRoock (Eds.), *The handbook of critical literacies* (pp. 227–236). Retrieved February 20, 2024, from https://www.researchgate.net/publication/367894489_Critical_Literacies_in_Post-Apartheid_South_Africa#fullTextFileContent
Kimmel, L., Lachlan, L., & Guiden, A. (Center on Great Teachers & Leaders). (2021). *The power of teacher diversity: Fostering inclusive conversations through mentoring*. American Institutes for Research. Retrieved February 20, 2024, from https://files.eric.ed.gov/fulltext/ED615359.pdf.
Lea, M. R., & Street, B. V. (2006). The "academic literacies" model: Theory and applications. *Theory into Practice, 45*(4), 368–377. https://doi.org/10.1207/s15430421tip4504_11
Majoko, T., Phasha, N.D., Brown, A., Brown, A., Trishana Devi Soni, T. V., Duku, N., Febana, Z., Maharajh, L. R., Mkra, P., Mngomezulu, S., Moodley, S., Mosito, C. P., & Ndlovu, S. (2018). *The state of inclusive education in South Africa and the implications for teacher training programmes*. British Council.
Makoelle, T. (2012). The state of inclusive pedagogy in South Africa: A literature review. *Journal of Sociology and Social Anthropology, 3*(2), 93–102.
Makoelle, T. (2014). Cognitive justice: A road map for equitable inclusive learning environments. *International Journal of Education and Research, 2*(7), 505–518. Retrieved February, 26, 2024 from http://www.ijern.com/journal/July-2014/39.pdf
Mangope, B., Otukile-Mongwaketse, M., Dinama, B., & Kuyini, A. B. (2018). Teaching practice experiences in inclusive classrooms: The voices of University of Botswana special education student teachers. *International Journal of Whole Schooling, 14*(1), 57–92.
Martinez-Vargas, C., Walker, M., & Mkwananzi, F. (2020). Access to higher education in South Africa: Expanding capabilities in and through an undergraduate photovoice project. *Educational Action Research, 28*(3), 427–442.
Mpu, Y., & Adu, E. O. (2021). The challenges of inclusive education and its implementation in schools: The South African perspective. *Perspectives in Education, 39*(2), 225–238.
Naicker, S. M. (2000). *From apartheid education to inclusive education: The challenges of transformation*. International Education Summit for a Democratic Society. Retrieved February 27, 2024, from http://www.wholeschooling.net/WS/WSPress/From%20Aparthied%20to%20Incl%20Educ.pdf
Naicker, S. M. (2019). History of special education in South Africa and the challenges of inclusive education. In *Oxford Research Encyclopedia of Education*.
Pendlebury, S. (1998). Transforming Teacher education in South Africa: A space-time perspective. *Cambridge Journal of Education, 28*(3), 333–349.
Pineteh, E. A. (2014). The academic writing challenges of undergraduate students: A South African case study. *International Journal of Higher Education, 3*(1), 12–22. http://dx.doi.org/10.5430/ijhe.v3n1p12
Rajagopalan, I. (2019). Concept of teaching. *Shanlax International Journal of Education, 7*(2), 5–8.

Reddy, V., Winnaar, L., Arends, F., Juan, A., Harvey, J., Hannan, S., & Isdale, K. (2022). *The South African TIMSS 2019 grade 9 results: Building achievement and bridging achievement gaps*. HSRC Press. http://hdl.handle.net/20.500.11910/19286

Sanger, C. S. (2020). Inclusive pedagogy and universal design approaches for diverse learning environments. In C. Sanger & N. Gleason (Eds.), *Diversity and inclusion in global higher education: Lessons from across Asia* (pp. 31–71). Palgrave Macmillan. https://doi.org/10.1007/978-981-15-1628-3_2

Sayed, Y., & Ahmed, R. (2015). Education quality, and teaching and learning in the post-2015 education agenda. *International Journal of Educational Development, 40*, 330–338.

Sayed, Y., & Kanjee, A. (2013). An overview of education policy change in post-apartheid South Africa. In Y. Sayed, A. Kanjee, & M. Nkomo (Eds.), *The search for quality education in post-apartheid South Africa* (pp. 5–38). Human Sciences Research Council.

Sayed, Y., Salmon, T., & Balie, L. (2020). *Embedding inclusive education in teacher professional development in South Africa: Impact evaluation report on the Teaching for All project*. British Council.

Sayed, Y., Singh, M., Williams, T., & Sadeck, M. (2022). *Academics and student-teachers champion inclusive education in initial teacher education programmes in South Africa: Experiences, challenges and opportunities*. British Council.

Serrurier-Zucker, C. (2023). Healing through education: A South African perspective. In G. Teulié & M. Joseph-Vilain (Eds.), Healing South African Wounds (pp. 403–425). Presses universitaires de la Méditerranée.*Healing South African Wounds*, 403–425.

Shikalepo, E. E. (2020). Challenges facing teaching at rural schools: A review of related literature. *International Journal of Research and Innovation in Social Science (IJRISS), 4*(5), 211–218.

Shulman, L. (1987). Knowledge and teaching: Foundations of the new reform. *Harvard Educational Review, 57*(1), 1–23.

Skae, V. A., Brown, B. J., & Wilmot, P. D. (2020). Teachers' engagement with learners in inclusive foundation phase classrooms. *South African Journal of Childhood Education, 10*(1), 1–11.

Snyder, H. (2019). Literature review as a research methodology: An overview and guidelines. *Journal of Business Research, 104*, 333–339.

South African Constitution. (1996). Bill of Rights, Section 29 (1) www.info.gov.za/documents/constitution/index.htm

Suleymanov, F. (2015). Issues of inclusive education: Some aspects to be considered. *Electronic Journal for Inclusive Education, 3*(4), 8.

Tirri, K., & Laine, S. (2017). Teacher education in inclusive education. In D. J. Clandinin & J. Husu (Eds.), *The SAGE handbook of research on teacher education* (Vol. 2, pp. 761–776).

UNESCO. (1994). *Final report - World conference on special needs education: Access and quality*. UNESCO.

UNESCO. (2015). *Incheon declaration and framework for action for the implementation of Sustainable Development Goal 4*. UNESCO. https://unesdoc.unesco.org/ark:/48223/pf0000245656.

UNESCO. (2019). *Leading SDG 4 – Education 2030: Coordinating the work to reach the ten targets of the Sustainable Development Goal for education*. Retrieved January 12, 2024, from https://en.unesco.org/themes/education2030-sdg4

UNESCO. (2020). *Inclusion and education: All means all*. Retrieved February 26, 2024, from https://apa.sdg4education2030.org/sites/apa.sdg4education2030.org/files/2020-06/373718eng%20%281%29-compressed-1.pdf

UNESCO. (2021). *Welcoming learners with disabilities in quality learning environments: A tool to support countries in moving towards inclusive education*. Retrieved February 26, 2024, from https://unesdoc.unesco.org/ark:/48223/pf0000380256

# Chapter 9

# Mentoring Pre-service Teachers for Inclusive Pedagogies

*Tsediso Michael Makoelle*

Nazarbayev University, Kazakhstan

## Abstract

Mentoring has been used as one of the training methods for pre-service teachers (Hobson et al., 2012). During the pre-service teacher practicum, teacher mentors are appointed to mentor the pre-service teacher in teaching and learning. This chapter is devoted to analysing the extent to which mentoring during the practicum prepares pre-service teachers for inclusive teaching. This chapter analyses the partnership of teacher training institutions of higher learning and schools, identifies practices that promote inclusion, and makes recommendations about how institutions of higher learning may enhance this process.

*Keywords*: Mentoring; pre-service teacher; practicum; inclusive teaching; inclusive pedagogy

## Introduction

The foundations of a good teacher education in South Africa were always based on the practical component of initial teacher education (ITE) called *Teaching Practice (TP)*. The colleges of education were historically famously known to devote most of their teacher preparation to this practical component, but also through other forms of practical experience such as 'micro-teaching', which was a technologically simulated TP by pre-service teachers to enhance their teaching skills and competencies. The current teacher education reviews aimed at improving pre-service teacher education have made this practical component a subject of research and debate.

The adoption of the White Paper 6 (2001) proposed that schools and teacher education institutions integrate inclusive education as part of the teaching. Lately, efforts have been made to update the curriculum content of teacher education institutions to prepare pre-service teachers for inclusive teaching in schools. Both teacher education institutions and mentor teachers have the mandate to produce teachers who can respond sufficiently to students with special educational needs and disabilities but also include students with diverse needs leading to a teaching that can deal with diversity in inclusive classrooms.

This review chapter aims to provide an understanding of the aim, role, benefits, opportunities, and challenges of pre-service teacher mentoring during practice teaching, particularly with inclusive teaching. Therefore, the following questions guided the enquiry process during the review:

- What is the current state of pre-service teacher mentoring in South Africa?
- How does pre-service teacher mentoring within the practicum prepare pre-service teachers for inclusive teaching?

To answer these research questions, the chapter conceptualises the notion of 'practicum' or 'practice teaching' as it is called in South African teacher education institutions of higher learning. The notion of inclusive education is defined in the international and South African context. The theory of mentoring is presented as a theoretical framework for pre-service teacher education mentoring.

The policy context regarding pre-service teacher placement is discussed. The literature concerning the models, goals, benefits, challenges, and opportunities for pre-service teacher mentoring is discussed.

## Review Methodology

This review was aimed at exploring the mentoring of pre-service teachers during the practicum. The review was mapped to achieving the following objectives:

- to explore the current state of pre-service teacher mentoring in South Africa; and
- to investigate how pre-service teacher mentoring within the practicum prepares pre-service teachers for inclusive teaching, and (if necessary) make some recommendations for future practice.

The criteria used to select the literature were guided by the availability of supportive empirical evidence. Speculative literatures were deliberately excluded. While the literature was reviewed for a study focussed on inclusion, some of the reviewed work had inclined towards general educational student support and interventions as closely related disciplines such as psychology and sociology of education were considered.

I consulted several databases such as Eric, Scopus, and Google Scholar. Further sources of relevant information were internationally accredited journals among others the *International Journal of Inclusive Education*. The Nazarbayev University library was consulted and books, articles, theses, and electronic sources were perused for relevant, up-to-date literature on the topic.

## Conceptualising the Notion of 'Practicum' or 'Practice Teaching'

Pratiwi (2020) defines teaching practicum as a placement of students in a real school situation to acquire teaching skills and improve their professional practice under the supervision of a teacher mentor. It is called in many ways depending on the context. For instance, in some cases, it is referred to as practicum, TP, teaching placement, field experience, apprenticeships, teaching internship, or practical experience. Lawson et al. (2015) indicate that practicum is a process through which pre-service teachers are exposed to the challenges of teaching and prepare them to develop the mechanisms of generating solutions to such challenges. Makoelle and Mosito (2023) postulate that practicum is a vehicle through which pre-service teachers may learn different pedagogical practices to support students in their classroom including those who are experiencing barriers to learning. Nkambule and Mukeredzi (2017), on the other hand, state that the practicum enables professional thinking, learning, and meaning, particularly in the South African context. While practicum could be useful for pre-service teacher feedback on their teaching Malikebu et al. (2024) caution that the assessment of pre-service teachers during the practicum tends to be more summative than formative as a result most pre-service teachers in the study conducted in the Western Province of South Africa, pre-service teachers thought although it was providing insightful feedback, it lacked the developmental aspect to enhance their teaching skills.

## Teachers and Inclusive Education: International and South African Perspectives

Scholars in the field of inclusive education have not agreed on the definition of the concept of inclusive education (Graham, 2020). The understanding of inclusive education depends on the model that each country adopts in the quest to support diverse students including those with special educational needs, disability, and other barriers that may impede student participation in the process of learning. Two dominant models of student support continue to influence debates and discussions about inclusive education, i.e. the medical model and the social model. In South Africa, while the medically oriented approach has not been eradicated, a social model of inclusion has been lately foregrounded. Nevertheless, inclusive education is regarded as a kind of education that seeks to minimise the effect of barriers such as disability, language, socio-economic status, race, gender, ethnicity, and other barriers that may affect student learning negatively (Hlalele & Makoelle, 2024).

Teachers are regarded as the implementers of inclusive education in schools. According to Li and Ruppar (2021), teachers through their agencies are the main role players in changing the teaching and learning environment to that which is inclusive. Therefore, the success of inclusive education is dependent on credible, skilful but also competent teachers who can deliver inclusive teaching that facilitates inclusive learning among all diverse students. It is therefore important that the attitudes of teachers towards inclusive education and student diversity in general are positive (Boyle et al., 2020).

The preparation of pre-service teachers as credible teachers who can respond to the needs of diverse students is important. For instance, Vandervieren and Struyf (2021) believe that in the context of inclusion, mentoring may enable pre-service teachers to learn more about practices related to support, needs-based assessment model, universal design for learning, and this gain practical experience on how to apply than in real classroom situation, but also enable them to collaborate at all levels with fellow students, teachers, teacher educators, and school counsellors.

According to Friesen and Cunning (2020), building strong pre-service teachers' skills, beliefs, and knowledge about inclusive education was very crucial for their confidence in teaching inclusively. Therefore, internationally and in South Africa preparation of pre-service teachers to teach inclusive has become critical.

The current review of ITE programmes found that universities' approaches towards teacher preparation for inclusive teaching were different and varied (Walton & Rusznyak, 2019). The Department of Higher Education, the European Union Teaching and Learning Development Capacity Improvement Project, and the British Council were involved in the development of standards for inclusive teaching. While the discussion about developing standards was needed, Walton and Rusznyak (2019) referred to dilemmas that emerged as a result of the process of developing standards for inclusive teaching. There were contestations on whether standards for inclusive teaching should be separate or embedded into the general teaching and learning process, whether the definition of inclusive education should be disability focus or broadened beyond disability, and whether standards were to relate to context.

The standards developed were framed on the following: agency for social justice and inclusion; valuing and understanding learner diversity; classroom practices that support collaboration and individual learning; collaboration to enable inclusive teaching and learning; and developing professionally as an inclusive teacher.

While these standards are a promising endeavour to see inclusive teaching thrive in schools, it would be important to see how pre-service teachers would be familiarised with the standards and how well the standards would inform curriculum delivery at pre-service teacher institutions of higher learning. It is also important to observe how such standards will be part of the mentoring of pre-service teachers during the practicum. It will also be important that the school mentors are familiar with standards and how such could be applied in the classroom.

## The Policy Context Regarding Pre-service Teacher Placement

According to the qualification framework, teacher education qualifications are regulated in the policy 'Revised Policy on the Minimum Requirements for Teacher Education Qualifications' offered only at the university, i.e. Bachelor of Education (BEd) for four years and Postgraduate Certificate in Education for a year. According to Robinson (2016), the qualifications are based on skills and knowledge which are embedded in these programs based on disciplinary, pedagogical, practical, fundamental, and situational learning. The school-based component is 8–12 weeks per year of structured, supervised, and integrated learning, which is formally assessed, although mentoring by schools is not contractual or funded, with no joint planning by schools and universities.

Following the teacher development summit in 2009 attended by many teacher education stakeholders a need to develop a new, strengthened, and integrated national plan for teacher education an Integrated Strategic Planning Framework for Teacher Education and Development in South Africa 2011–2025 emerged.

According to Robinson (2013), the placement of pre-service teachers has always presented a challenge and there was a need to explore alternative ways of making placement work more efficiently and effectively. As a result, the problematic nature of pre-service teacher placement led to the proposed model of Professional Practice Schools (PPS). According to Robinson (2016), these schools, regardless of resourcefulness, would provide quality support to pre-service teachers and be used as hubs for professional learning communities. They would be close to teacher education institutions. They would be used as observation and practice sites or incubators for pre-service teachers. In analysing the significance and impact these schools would have on pre-service teacher education by Robinson's (2016) study, several lessons stand as important:

There is a need for good school–university partnerships, effective mentor education, university–community collaboration, school improvement in general, strong inter-sectoral communication, clear school mentor–university supervisor expectations, dealing with historical inequalities, attending to school resourcefulness, considering the teachers' workload and teacher–student ratios.

The discussion shows that pre-service teacher mentoring through the practicum is an important aspect of teacher preparation for teaching. Therefore, it is important to conceptualise what mentoring is and how it is operationalised in the pre-service teacher learning process.

## The Theory of Mentoring for Pre-service Teacher Development

The notion of mentoring refers to the process of facilitating another person's development. It encapsulates role modelling by the mentor teacher over a long period. With mentoring, there could be short-term focussed coaching aimed at a particular skill (Kamarudin et al., 2020). According to Ambrosetti et al. (2017), there is a move away from the single mentor–mentee model to other forms. Ambrosetti and Dekkers (2010) also indicate that mentoring practices are also changing in terms of hierarchy, as mentoring can now happen between peers rather than from the person of authority to the subordinate. Various mentoring and coaching models exist and some have been used to develop pre-service teachers. In this chapter, some mentoring models that were used to facilitate professional development for pre-service teachers are discussed.

First, Kamarudin et al. (2020) highlight the three mentoring approaches, i.e. Zone of Proximal Development by Vygotsky (1978), Biggs's (1993) Presage-Process-Product (3Ps), and Grow model of mentoring. The zone of proximal development assumes that the mentee may be able to achieve more success in learning when given support by mentors within the proximal environment. The process of interaction and scaffolding are pivotal for learning between the knowledgeable and the less knowledgeable other during the mentoring process. On the other hand, Biggs's (1993) 3Ps model departs from the premise that during the presage the mentee has past experiences, knowledge, and cultural capital that may influence how he/she deals with the process stage which entails how the mentee deals with the mentoring tasks, acquires new knowledge, declares motives and intentions and makes decisions. This will consequently impact the product which means understanding and reflecting on the outcome to chart the way forward. Biggs's model encourages collaborative learning. The Grow model, on the other hand, is a solution based base on the analysis of reality, exploring the options, choosing the best option, and charting the way forward.

Orland-Barak and Wang (2021) extend the discussion on pre-service teacher mentoring to two other models, i.e. the Core-Practice model, which assumes the behaviour-cognitive approach which emphasises the significance of learning adaptation according to context, i.e. enabling the mentee to be able to apply core practices to a different context. The critical transformative mentoring model is based on the fact that mentoring is a political act intended to transform an unjust and inequitable situation into that which is fair and just. It is inspired by critical pedagogy which aims to empower and emancipate both the mentor and the mentee.

On the other hand, Ndebele and Legg-Jack (2022) postulate that the Five-Factor mentoring approach by Hudson (2004) seems effective in the South African pre-service teacher education context. The five factors, i.e. personal attributes of the mentor could inspire confidence in the mentee; the systems requirement which the mentor embodies, e.g. school policies, curriculum, and school aims could enable the mentee to operate effectively, pedagogical knowledge of the mentor holds from long experience may be fruitful to the mentee as she/he navigates teaching. Modelling is based on the sharing of teaching expertise with the mentor, and lastly, the feedback the mentor would provide to the mentee may provide much-needed reflection, guidance, and advice.

According to Langdon and Ward (2015), the notion of educative mentoring has become crucial in pre-service teacher mentoring. They define educative mentoring as a non-transmissive model where the mentee's learning is facilitated rather than knowledge transfer. It is based on the philosophy of constructivism.

The mentee constructs their knowledge. Rather than focus on *knowledge for practice*, the focus is on *knowledge of practice*. This means the mentee is empowered with skills to research, critique, and reflect on their practice to improve it. This process occurs within the collaborative atmosphere with the professional learning community. This view is echoed by Islam (2012) who advocates for community of practice as a framework for pre-service teacher learning.

Stanulis et al. (2019) postulate that educative mentoring should be based on concrete practices engaged with professional learning. Langeveldt et al. (2023) posit that pre-service teacher learning must enable their agency that would empower them as agents of change rather than maintain the status quo. Mukeredzi (2017) suggests that enabling pre-service teacher agency exposure to different mentoring approaches could enrich their knowledge and thus enable them to act as agents of change. Regarding mentoring aimed at enabling pre-service teacher agency, Makoelle (2016) postulates that pre-service teachers have to be empowered with self-action research skills to investigate their teaching. Makoelle (2016) states that inclusion requires teachers who can think outside of the box and can take risks by trying new approaches in the classroom rather than rigidly adopting practices from textbooks, peers, or mentors.

## The Pre-service Teacher Mentoring and the Practicum

Although mentoring is thought to be helpful in pre-service teachers' professional growth, Cohen et al. (2013) believe that the practicum for pre-service teachers is focussed on developing the pre-service teacher competencies and familiarity with student diversity. However, they mention that this relationship between the mentor and the pre-service teacher is often characterised by tensions as a result of different interests and educational philosophies. It is also understood that the different expectations for the practicum by school leadership, mentors, and pre-service teachers may defeat the ideal purpose of mentoring.

The mentoring relationships in schools are also compounded by a lack of involvement by school principals towards pre-service teachers during the practicum period. Li et al. (2023) postulate that although the practicum is an orderly experiential process by pre-service teachers, the process through which pre-service teachers learn is dynamic and complex thus influenced by several contextual factors. Pre-service teachers' learning is influenced by interactions between individuals, schools, and social discourses. Hence Ambrosetti (2014) emphasises the preparation of pre-service teachers and mentors before the mentoring process. As Jita and Munje (2022) state, the process of mentoring can also be influenced negatively if the mentor is not sufficiently prepared or experienced. Ntshangase and Nkosi (2022) lament the fact that in South Africa, rural schools, mentoring may be affected by factors associated with underprivileged schools, so the prospect of effective mentoring may be very low.

According to Nel et al. (2021), to overcome disruptions to mentoring such as that happened during the pandemic, various mentoring approaches, such as backup plans, need to be in place all the time, i.e. the placement that can supplement and harness the authenticity of school-based experience.

## Lessons from the Review

From this review, one can conclude that the mentoring of pre-service teachers for inclusive teaching should be based on the five key strategic pillars. Fig. 9.1 shows the relationship between the five strategic pillars and pre-service teacher mentoring.

### *Policy*

First, it is clear from the review that pre-service teacher mentoring for inclusive teaching will require a clear and well-articulated policy. The development of inclusive standards was a critical step in the development of policy that embed inclusive teaching within the practicum or practice teaching arrangement. In the process, it would be prudent to ensure that the policy on placement and the mentoring procedure are outlined in the policy and advocated to all concerned stakeholders.

### *University School Partnerships*

Second, the proposal to have PPS designated for the practicum sounds good. However, one of the critical lessons from the review is that such schools should not perpetuate inequalities. It would be important that in the choice of schools, cognisance that schools are not homogeneous in terms of resources and status, i.e. rural–urban, previously advantaged schools, previously advantaged schools, full-service schools, mainstream schools, special schools, and reformatory schools. It would be interesting to see the representation of designated schools as PPS.

### *Pedagogy and Practice*

It is evident from the review that standards for inclusive teaching would have to be embedded into the curriculum for pre-service teachers and the school

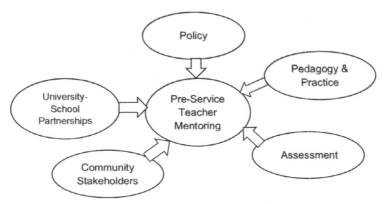

Fig. 9.1. Mentoring Framework for Pre-service Teacher Practicum.

curriculum. It would be prudent for teacher educators and mentors in schools to have a common understanding, and interpretation of standards and thus have a similar approach to their implementation. While there are different models of mentoring, it is evident from the review that collaborative forms of mentoring are preferred over the single mentor–mentee models. Because developing inclusive practices requires a concerted effort to develop local theories of practice, the transformative model which promotes collaborative learning on the part of the mentors and mentees is crucial. In this review collaborative models of mentoring such as the educative mentoring model and communities of practice model are encouraged as they promote knowledge of practice rather than knowledge for practice. What this means is that pre-service teacher has to be taught how to research, critique, and reflect on their teaching to improve it. It will be important that pre-service teachers are empowered with self-action research skills, rather than rely on their mentors, they should be able to try innovative methods in their classroom and conversations with their mentors develop local inclusive pedagogical practices.

### *Community Stakeholders*

While the mentoring of pre-service teachers may involve the school's mentors and university supervisors, it is evident from this review that the mentoring arrangements should go beyond these two and incorporate other school stakeholders responsible for the inclusion and support of diverse students including those with special educational needs and disability. The pre-service teachers could, for example, be part of school-based support teams and engage with educational, psychologists, speech therapists, school health representatives, socio-pedagogues, and support tutors. The involvement of school leadership in discussions about pre-service teacher mentoring could influence the school processes of school development planning and thus mentoring of pre-service teachers will not be viewed as an external activity but embedded into the goals of placement schools.

### *Assessment*

While the assessment purpose of university supervisors is to give feedback to pre-service teachers about their teaching, such assessment seems not to prioritise the assessment of inclusive pedagogical skills. Evidence from this review indicates that observing how pre-service teachers embed the inclusive teaching standard would be interesting. For instance, how pre-service teachers develop their teaching and learning strategy for inclusion, how they arrive at inclusive pedagogical choices, and how such are executed during the curriculum delivery process. There is a piece of strong evidence that preparing pre-service teachers for inclusion should be a developmental rather than a once-off judgmental process. The mentors and university supervisors could adopt a continuous assessment approach built on the incremental development of skills and competencies for teaching in a diverse inclusive classroom.

## Conclusion

This chapter explored pre-service teacher mentoring for inclusive teaching during the practicum. The review focussed on policy developments and research conducted in this area. Mentoring as part of the practicum or the TP is a subject of ongoing discussions in South Africa. While this review contributes to the discussion regarding this topic, the author is aware that propositions in this chapter may not be conclusive as this topic is currently a matter of policy debates and research. However, the chapter makes a valuable contribution to the discussion and could be used as one of the sources for research and policy discussions.

## References

Ambrosetti, A., & Dekkers, J. (2010). The interconnectedness of the roles of mentors and mentees in preservice teacher education mentoring relationships. *Australian Journal of Teacher Education, 35*(6). https://doi.org/10.14221/ajte.2010v35n6.3

Ambrosetti, A. (2014). Are you ready to be a mentor?: Preparing teachers for mentoring pre-service teachers. *Australian Journal of Teacher Education, 39*(6), 30–42.

Ambrosetti, A., Dekkers, J., & Knight, B. A. (2017). Mentoring triad: An alternative mentoring model for preservice teacher education?. *Mentoring & Tutoring: Partnership in Learning, 25*(1), 42–60. https://doi.org/10.1080/13611267.2017.1308093

Biggs, J. (1993). What do inventories of students' learning processes really measure? A theoretical review and clarification. *British Journal of Educational Psychology, 63*(1), 3–19.

Boyle, C., Anderson, J., & Allen, K.A. (2020). The importance of teacher attitudes to inclusive education. In C. Boyle, J. Anderson, A. Page & S. Mavropouluo (Eds.), *Inclusive education: Global issues and controversies* (Chap. 8, pp. 127–146). Brill. https://doi.org/10.1163/9789004431171_008

Cohen, E., Hoz, R., & Kaplan, H. (2013). The practicum in preservice teacher education: A review of empirical studies. *Teaching Education, 24*(4), 345–380. https://doi.org/10.1080/10476210.2012.711815

Friesen, D. C., & Cunning, D. (2020). Making explicit pre-service teachers' implicit beliefs about inclusive education. *International Journal of Inclusive Education, 24*(14), 1494–1508. https://doi.org/10.1080/13603116.2018.1543730

Graham, L. J. (2020). Inclusive education in the 21st century. In L. J. Graham (Ed.), *Inclusive education for the 21st century* (pp. 3–26). Routledge.

Hlalele, D., & Makoelle, T. (2024). Inclusion in Southern African education, understanding, challenges and enablement. Springer Publishers.

Hobson, L. D., Harris, D., Buckner-Manley, K., & Smith, P. (2012). The importance of mentoring novice and pre-service teachers: Findings from a HBCU student teaching program. *Educational Foundations, 26*, 67–80.

Hudson, P. (2004). Specific mentoring: A theory and model for developing primary science teaching practices. *European Journal of Teacher Education, 27*(2), 139–146.

Islam, F. (2012). Understanding pre-service teacher education discourses in communities of practice: A reflection from an intervention in rural South Africa. *Perspectives in Education, 30*(1), 19–29.

Jita, T., & Munje, P. N. (2022). Preservice teachers mentorship experiences during teaching practice in a South African teacher preparation program. *International Journal of Higher Education, 11*(1), 140–150. https://doi.org/10.5430/ijhe.v11n1p140

Kamarudin, M., Kamarudin, A. Y., Darmi, R., & Saad, N. S. M. (2020). A review of coaching and mentoring theories and models. *International Journal of Academic Research in Progressive Education and Development, 9*(2), 289–298.

Langdon, F., & Ward, L. (2015). Educative mentoring: A way forward. *International Journal of Mentoring and Coaching in Education, 4*(4), 240–254. https://doi.org/10.1108/IJMCE-03-2015-0006

Langeveldt, D. C., Pietersen, D., & Van Wyk, A. (2023). South African legal framework to prepare pre-service teacher education programmes: A Freirean approach. *Research in Educational Policy and Management, 5*(3), 95–107. https://doi.org/10.46303/repam.2023.24

Lawson, T., Çakmak, M., Gündüz, M., & Busher, H. (2015). Research on teaching practicum – A systematic review. *European Journal of Teacher Education, 38*(3), 392–407. https://doi.org/10.1080/02619768.2014.994060

Li, L., & Ruppar, A. (2021). Conceptualizing teacher agency for inclusive education: A systematic and international review. *Teacher Education and Special Education, 44*(1), 42–59. https://doi.org/10.1177/0888406420926976

Li, M., Kuang, F., & Dan, W. (2023). Exploring the characteristics of pre-service EFL teachers' practicum experiences: A complexity theory-based case study in China, Li et al. *Asian-Pacific Journal of Second and Foreign Language Education, 8*(13). https://doi.org/10.1186/s40862-023-00187-4

Makoelle, T. M. (2016). *Inclusive teaching in South Africa*. Sun Media Publishers.

Makoelle, T. M., & Mosito, C. P. (2023). Pre-service teacher preparation for inclusive teaching in South Africa. In G. Boadu, G. Odhiambo, & P. Marandi (Eds.), *Practices and perspectives of teaching and teacher education in Africa* (pp. 1–23). IGI Global. https://doi.org/10.4018/978-1-6684-7722-9.ch001

Malikebu, F. N. A., McDonald, Z., & Jordaan, A. (2024). Student teacher experiences of the teaching practicum in an initial teacher education programme in the Western Cape. Education Annual Volume 2023. IntechOpen.

Mukeredzi, T. G. (2017). Mentoring in a cohort model of practicum: Mentors and pre-service teachers' experiences in a rural South African school. *Sage Open, 7*(2), 2158244017709863.

Ndebele, C., & Legg-Jack, D. W. (2022). The impact of mentoring in the development of pre-service teachers from a university in South Africa. *International Journal of Learning, Teaching and Educational Research, 21*(3), 88–105.

Nel, C., Botha, C., & Marais, E. (2021). A COVID-19 re-envisioned teaching practicum curriculum. *Research in Social Sciences and Technology, 6*(2), 249–266. https://doi.org/10.46303/ressat.2021.29

Nkambule, T., & Mukeredzi, T. G. (2017). Pre-service teachers' professional learning experiences during rural teaching practice in Acornhoek, Mpumalanga Province. *South African Journal of Education, 37*(3). https://doi.org/10.15700/saje.v37n3a1371

Ntshangase, Z., & Nkosi, Z. (2022). Effective mentoring: Understanding factors affecting the holistic development of preservice teachers during teaching practice. *South African Journal of Education, 42*(4). https://doi.org/10.15700/saje.v42n4a2062

Orland-Barak, L., & Wang, J. (2021). Teacher mentoring in service of preservice teachers' learning to teach: Conceptual bases, characteristics, and challenges for teacher education reform. *Journal of Teacher Education, 72*(1), 86–99.

Pratiwi, D. (2020). Teaching practicum in pre-service teacher education. *Journal of English Language Education, 1*(1), 31–24.

Robinson, M. (2013). Selecting teaching practice schools across social contexts: Conceptual and policy challenges from South Africa. *Journal of Education for Teaching, 40*(2), 114–127. https://doi.org/10.1080/02607476.2013.869970

Robinson, M. (2016). Professional practice schools as a form of school-university partnership in teacher education: Towards a social justice agenda. *Education as Change, 20*(2), 11–26.

Stanulis, R. N., Wexler, L. J., Pylman, S., Guenther, A., Farver, S., Ward, A., Croel-Perrien, A., & White, K. (2019). Mentoring as more than "Cheerleading": Looking at educative mentoring practices through mentors' eyes. *Journal of Teacher Education, 70*(5), 567–580.

Vandervieren, E., & Struyf, E. (2021). Facing social reality together: Investigating a preservice teacher preparation programme on inclusive education. *International Journal of Inclusive Education, 25*(13), 1524–1539. https://doi.org/10.1080/13603116.2019.1625451

Vygotsky, L. S. (1978). *Mind in society: The development of higher psychological processes.* Harvard University Press.

Walton, E., & Rusznyak, L. (2019). Developing standards for inclusive teaching in South Africa: A dilemma analysis. *Southern African Review of Education, 25*(1), 89–106.

Chapter 10

# Exploring the Value of Critical Disability Theory in Public Technical and Vocational and Training Colleges in South Africa

Lucky Maluleke and Anelisa Pezisa

*Nelson Mandela University, South Africa*

### Abstract

The implementation of inclusive education in technical and vocational education and training (TVET) colleges has become critical in the South African TVET college context. This chapter, through a review of literature using a Critical Disability Theory (CDT) as a lens, investigates inclusive education in the South African TVET colleges, especially with regard to the inclusion and quality education provision for students with disabilities. Among the main findings from the review is that TVET colleges continue to face challenges such as a lack of suitable and user-friendly infrastructure for students with disabilities, poor policy adoption, adaptation and implementation, shortage of staff and units that focus on disability, and lack of pedagogical practices that foster and promote inclusivity. Therefore, in this chapter, we recommend that the issue of disability be looked at from a critical perspective, such as the CDT, to ensure that the historical legacies of apartheid and colonialism that continue to perpetuate inequality be addressed. This critical perspective will help us to move beyond instrumental approaches to focus on the broader issues that surround disability in TVET colleges. We also recommend that TVET college lecturers must be trained in inclusive education and pedagogy, resources be provided, and infrastructure be improved to accommodate various forms of disability.

*Keywords*: Inclusive education; disability; technical and vocational education; model of disability; critical disability theory

## Introduction

Approximately 15% of the world's population are people living with disabilities (World Bank Group, 2023). This 15% translates into about one billion people worldwide. Of these one billion people, at least 785 million are of working age. The African continent has a share of approximately 80 million people living with disabilities. Often, people with disabilities are generally excluded from formal education and employment. As a result of this exclusion, they are more likely to live in poverty than their non-disabled counterparts. The problem with disability is that it increases the risk of poverty, and poverty increases the risk of getting a disability (Boat & Wu, 2015; Department for International Development, 2000; MyRight, 2023; Owens, 2013). In developing countries, poor healthcare and constrained healthcare provision fail to prevent some health conditions from escalating or evolving into disability (Owens, 2013).

The effects of disability are felt in every stage of life. In some cases, children with disabilities are prevented from going to school due to stigmatisation in their communities (Owens, 2013; Watermeyer et al., 2011). In developing countries of Africa, factors such as a lack of adapted facilities for persons with disabilities and poor economic prospects for these persons hampers their opportunity to study like their non-disabled counterparts (Mji et al., 2011; Owens, 2013). Among African countries, South Africa also grapples with the challenge of disability in education, including TVET colleges (Delubom & Marongwe, 2022; Ndlovu, 2019; Sedibe & Buthelezi, 2014).

In this chapter, we explore the issue of disability and how it is handled in public TVET colleges in South Africa. Through this exploration, we seek to establish the extent to which TVET colleges make provision for students with disabilities. We further aim to identify the challenges the colleges may face with the inclusion of students with disabilities. Moreover, we make suggestions to promote inclusion in public TVET colleges. To achieve the objectives stated above, we follow several steps. We start the chapter by alerting the readers to our connection with disability and why it matters to society and us. We then outline some international and national policy interventions and recommendations concerning persons with disability. We also explore some weaknesses of these policy imperatives. We further explore literature, usually journal articles and dissertations on disability in public TVET colleges in South Africa (Delubom & Marongwe, 2022; Ndlovu, 2019).

This literature usually focusses on the challenges TVET colleges face regarding inclusivity. The findings typically revolve around poor infrastructure, poor funding, lack of training, and lack of awareness, in teaching students with a visual disability (Ndlovu, 2019), the experiences of TVET college lecturers (Ntombela, 2020), the experiences of students with physical impairments (Siwela, 2017). In contemporary discourse, understanding disability goes beyond simply recognising physical or mental disabilities. It aims to address the complex interplay of cultural, historical, and political factors that shape the experiences of people with disabilities. CDT provides a differentiated perspective for analysing and deconstructing common ideas about disability. In this chapter, we explore the basic principles of CDT, its departure from traditional models of disability, and its implications for research and social understanding (Delvin & Pothier, 2006; Hosking, 2008; Meekosha & Shuttleworth, 2009). In this regard, we explore how the CDT can contribute to a more inclusive public TVET college sector in South Africa (Meekosha, 2008; Tremain, 2005).

## Why Disability Matters

We need not cite any expert to claim that disability matters. It matters to people living with various forms of disabilities. It also matters to their families, communities, and society at large. It matters to governments and states. It is also important to us as university-based academics. We relate to disability in different ways, and our motivations to write about disability are different. Despite our differences, our point of convergence is that persons with disabilities cannot be discriminated against and that investments must be made to ensure that they also participate in cultural, economic, political, and social life like any other person. Below, we share why disability matters to each of us.

Lucky Maluleke is a lecturer at the Faculty of Education at Nelson Mandela University in South Africa. His work is mainly about the professional development of public TVET college lecturers. Consequently, he spends some of his time in different TVET colleges nationwide. Some TVET colleges invite him to attend their events, including the graduation ceremony. Over the years, he has noted that the graduation halls at some colleges do not have ramps for someone who uses a wheelchair. After many years of grappling with this idea, he discovered that the student support services and disability units are not fully developed in all public TVET colleges in South Africa. However, he also noted that some colleges have well-established disability support systems, including hardware and software for students with different disabilities.

Anelisa Pezisa is a social worker and currently works as an assistant lecturer at Nelson Mandela University in the Faculty of Health Science in the Social Development Professions. As a social worker, she believes in equality, dignity, and empowerment for all individuals, including those with disabilities. Our mandate is to improve the 'clients' social functioning, addressing individual needs and systemic factors that influence 'clients' well-being. While she may not have direct experience with TVET colleges, she recognises the importance of advocating for inclusive practices that ensure access and support for people with disabilities within educational settings. As a social worker, she emphasises the importance of recognising and nurturing the full potential of individuals with disabilities rather than defining them by their limitations.

We believe that people with disabilities must be treated as individuals with unique abilities, talents, and aspirations. Despite societal misconceptions and stereotypes surrounding disability, individuals with disabilities possess the capability to achieve and contribute meaningfully to society. Access to education is a fundamental human right that should be upheld for all individuals, regardless of ability or disability. TVET colleges are crucial in providing vocational education and skills training to diverse populations, including people with disabilities. However, limited resources and accessibility barriers often pose significant challenges for individuals with disabilities in accessing educational opportunities. TVET colleges must prioritise efforts to enhance accessibility, remove physical and attitudinal barriers, and provide necessary resources, infrastructure, and support services to ensure equal access for all students (Department of Higher Education and Training, 2020b; Fourie, 2012; Sedibe & Buthelezi, 2014; Siwela, 2017; Van Wyk & Hodgkinson-Williams, 2022).

Education is a powerful tool for empowerment and social inclusion but can also be a source of exclusion. By providing people with disabilities with access to quality education and vocational training, TVET colleges can empower them to achieve their goals, pursue meaningful careers, and participate actively in society (International Labour Organisation, 2017). Promoting equality and access for people with disabilities in TVET colleges requires a collaborative and critical approach, such as CDT (Tremain, 2005). Not only that but to address the exclusion, inequity and injustice of people with disabilities will mean the TVET colleges must focus on systems that hinder access to this group and implement effective strategies for promoting accessibility and inclusion within educational settings (Makgetla, 2020; Van der Berg & Hofmeyr, 2020).

South Africa takes the issue of disability seriously, but this has yet to manifest in every space, including public TVET colleges. Over the years, the number of students with disabilities has increased and attitudes towards them have improved. Nonetheless, As we explore later in the chapter, TVET colleges continue to handle the issue of disability with variance, and at times with slowness and passivity. The slow and passive handling of the issue of disability-related problems manifests in the continuation of a lack of adequate accessible buildings and learning resources for students living with disabilities (Buthelezi, 2014). In some cases, students with disabilities are expected to learn under the same conditions as their able-bodied counterparts (Siwela, 2017). While the country has inclusion policies, some colleges seem to lag in developing and implementing institutional and contextually relevant policies (Ndlovu, 2019; Siwela, 2017). The following section explores the policy landscape on inclusive education and practices.

## Policy Landscape

Concerning children with disabilities in South Africa, the then Minister of Education, Kader Asmal, stated that:

> the place of these children is not one of isolation in dark backrooms and sheds. It is with their peers, in schools, on the playgrounds, on the streets, and in places of worship that they can become part of the local community and cultural life, as well as part of the reconstruction and development of our country. Only when these among us are a natural and ordinary part of us can we indeed lay claim to the status of cherishing all our children equally. (Republic of South Africa, 2001, p. 4)

The above quotation is a point of departure when planning to cater education to all without discrimination. Non-discrimination is also emphasised in the Constitution of the Republic of South Africa [hereafter referred to as 'the Constitution'] (Republic of South Africa, 1996). The Constitution states that the state may not discriminate against any person based on, among other things, disability, be it directly or indirectly (Republic of South Africa, 1996). In section 22, the Constitution adds that every citizen must choose their career path freely. Section 29(1)(b) states that every citizen 'has the right to further education, which the state, through reasonable means, must make progressively available' (Republic of South Africa, 1996). The issue of disability is neither new nor only a South African concern.

Organisations such as the International Labour Organisation (ILO) (International Labour Organisation, 1983; International Labour Office, 2010) and the United Nations (UN) (1948, 2006) are equally concerned about disability and inclusion. According to the International Labour Office (2010), four out of five people with disabilities live in poverty, mainly below the poverty line. The poverty line is determined by household or individual income. Those who live below the poverty line do so primarily because they are not economically active or their economic activities are not viable (International Labour Office, 2010). They are not financially active because they cannot work alongside their non-disabled counterparts in various sectors. This is usually the case because industries are not necessarily adapted to accommodate people with different forms of disability. According to the International Labour Office (2010), this is a significant loss for countries.

Despite this perceived loss (International Labour Office, 2010), the UN is concerned that persons with disabilities continue to face various barriers and their human rights continue to be violated (UN, 1948, 2006). Countries have not been able to accommodate everyone, including non-disabled persons. For example, unemployment is high, poverty is vast, and many young people are not in employment, education, or training, whether they are disabled or not. So, when countries like South Africa spend their budgets on essential services such as military, education, health, and social grants, a gap is left, such as developing facilities for people with disabilities. Thus, the challenge of disability is confronted with other social, cultural, economic, legal, and political difficulties. Given that people with disabilities are a minority, their inclusion is often to non-governmental organisations (NGOs) and pressure groups. Moreover, the provision of social grants for disabled persons seems to be considered a primary solution to the inclusion of persons with disabilities.

The international and national policy landscape has its limitations regarding inclusivity. The *R99 Vocational Rehabilitation (Disabled) Recommendation*, 1955 (International Labour Organisation, 2006) fails to address broader societal issues around the inclusion of persons with disabilities. Also, the fact that it is merely a recommendation renders it powerless as it cannot be e enforced. In South Africa, the *Strategic Policy Framework on Disability for the Post-School Education and Training System* (Republic of South Africa, 2018) faces some implementation challenges. Implementing guidelines requires standardisation and awareness. Unfortunately, this is not always the case for various reasons, such as a lack of staff training in some institutions, poor infrastructure, and limited financial resources.

The shortcomings are also evident in the Constitution; for example, Chapter 2 (Bill of Rights) guarantees several human rights, but this does not mean that all citizens will fully understand their rights (Republic of South Africa, 1996). Also, having rights does not mean automatic exercise of these rights. For example, marginalised and poor citizens struggle to access legal aid to protect their rights. In addition, differing literacy levels also affect what people from different backgrounds know and can do to protect their rights. Despite various shortcomings, South Africa boasts a wide range of policies that seek to address the issue of disability (Department of Higher Education and Training, 2020a, 2020b; Republic of South Africa, 2009, 2016, 2018).

Although human rights are enshrined in the *United National Declaration of Human Rights* (UN, 1948) and special rights for persons with disabilities are tabled in the *Convention on the Rights of Persons with Disabilities and Optional Protocol* (UN, 2006), this does not mean that all is good and well in the world. As Owens (2013) indicated, African states have neglected the rights of people living with disabilities. So, having a convention and its recommendations does not translate into action and implementation. An international recommendation tends to need more binding force. Also, recommendations do not provide funds, but it is expected that countries must finance their inclusion initiatives. Unfortunately, countries do not always comply or have ready budgets to implement recommendations and policies.

Political frameworks and laws play an essential role in shaping the implementation of inclusive education in developing countries (Republic of South Africa, 2009, 2018). A robust legal framework explicitly supporting inclusive education is essential to ensure equal access, reasonable accommodation, and non-discrimination. However, translating policy into practice remains a significant challenge (Delubom and Marongwe, 2022). Although college management recognises the importance of inclusivity, they face obstacles such as inadequate infrastructure, lack of support structures, and delays in providing services to students with disabilities (Delubom & Marongwe, 2022).

## Some Barriers to Inclusive Education

There is increasing awareness of inclusive education in South Africa in educational institutions (Sedibe & Buthelezi, 2014). This recognition was sparked by the White *Paper on Inclusive Education* publication, commonly known as White Paper 6 (Republic of South Africa, 2001). White Paper 6, on the other hand, is progressive in its approach to inclusive education and promoting access for all, regardless of disability. Despite the growing awareness, the inclusion of people living with disabilities remains a considerable challenge. One issue affecting inclusive education implementation is resource constraints in South African public vocational schools (Delubom & Marongwe, 2022; Sedibe & Buthelezi, 2014).

Lack of resources is one of the biggest challenges for inclusive education in developing countries (Delubom & Marongwe, 2022). Limited financial resources, inadequate infrastructure, and a lack of trained educators are common barriers in many low- and middle-income countries. As highlighted in the study by Sedibe and Buthelezi (2014), these resource constraints limit the number of students with disabilities accessing education. Consequently, people living with disabilities are left out of education and training, thereby increasing inequality between non-disabled people and those living with various forms of disability. Thus, education and training institutions need adequate funding and support to provide the necessary facilities and services to students with diverse needs (Ntombela, 2020).

Infrastructure issues exacerbate the challenges faced by students living with disabilities (Ntombela, 2020). Although TVET college leadership recognises the importance of inclusivity, they face obstacles such as inadequate infrastructure, funding constraints, and staff shortages in supporting students with disabilities (Sedibe & Buthelezi, 2014). Infrastructure and accessibility are fundamental aspects of inclusive education, but many schools and educational institutions in developing countries lack accessible infrastructure. Without reasonable accommodations, students with disabilities may experience barriers to accessing educational resources and fully participating in classroom activities. Many education and training institutions lack accessible infrastructure, such as ramps, elevators, and adaptive classrooms, making it difficult for students with physical disabilities to participate in educational activities fully. Addressing these infrastructure challenges is critical to creating an inclusive learning environment where all students can thrive (Ngubane-Mokiwa & Khoza, 2021; Ntombela, 2020). Providing ramps, elevators, accessible restrooms, and sensory-friendly classrooms is essential to creating an inclusive learning environment where all students can thrive (Sedibe & Buthelezi, 2014).

In addition to resource constraints and infrastructure challenges, changing attitudes and social prejudice are significant barriers to inclusive education in developing countries. However, society's attitudes towards disability can influence students' self-esteem, confidence, and sense of belonging in educational settings. Ndlovu (2019) highlights the importance of addressing attitudinal barriers to inclusive education. Cultural norms and beliefs influence perceptions of disability and inclusion within the community. In some cultures, disability can be seen as a curse or punishment, leading to prejudice and exclusion. Raising awareness of inclusive education among communities, religious leaders, and elders is essential to foster acceptance and create an inclusive ethos. However, culture change takes time and requires ongoing education and advocacy efforts (Republic of South Africa, 2001).

Negative attitudes and misconceptions about disabilities can lead to prejudice, discrimination, and exclusion and prevent students with disabilities from fully participating in educational opportunities. Changing these attitudes requires a concerted effort to raise awareness, challenge stereotypes, and promote acceptance and inclusion (Ndlovu, 2019). Despite challenges such as inadequate infrastructure and funding, students with learning disabilities demonstrate resilience and positive attitudes to learning. Building a culture of inclusion requires ongoing education and advocacy to challenge stereotypes and promote a more inclusive society (Department of Higher Education and Training, 2020b; Republic of South Africa, 2009, 2018).

## Some Solutions

Teacher preparation is another crucial element for successful inclusive education initiatives. Educators are critical in creating inclusive learning environments, adapting curriculum materials, and responding to diverse learning needs. However, many teachers lack the training and support they need to meet the needs of students with disabilities effectively. Providing teachers with ongoing professional development opportunities is essential to building their capacity to support diverse learners and create inclusive classrooms. Delubom and Marongwe (2022) highlight the importance of prioritising teacher training and the needs of students with disabilities in educational institutions. Investing in teacher training programmes and professional development initiatives can help address these challenges and help educators create more inclusive learning environments (Delubom & Marongwe, 2022).

Curriculum adaptation and differentiated instruction are essential elements of inclusive education, allowing educators to meet the diverse learning needs of students with disabilities (Department of Higher Education and Training, 2020b). Designing a flexible curriculum that accommodates diverse learning styles, speeds, and abilities is essential to foster meaningful participation and engagement. However, adapting textbooks and teaching materials can be resource-intensive, especially in resource-limited settings (Department of Higher Education and Training, 2020b).

Collaboration and partnership are essential to the success of inclusive education initiatives. Government agencies, NGOs, civil society organisations, and international donors all have a role to play in supporting inclusive education efforts. By sharing resources, sharing best practices, and coordinating efforts, stakeholders can increase their impact and drive systemic change. However, fostering sustainable partnerships requires ongoing communication, trust-building, and mutual respect between all parties (Delubom & Marongwe, 2022).

Monitoring and evaluation are essential to assess the effectiveness of inclusive education programs and identify areas for improvement. To ensure continuous improvement, students' progress must be evaluated regularly, gaps in service delivery identified, and strategies adopted. However, limited data collection capacity and evaluation mechanisms can hinder effective monitoring and evaluation efforts, making it difficult to assess the impact of inclusive education initiatives accurately (Sedibe & Buthelezi, 2014).

## Competing Models of Disability

At the heart of disability discourse are competing models that seek to explain the nature and origins of disability. Medical models based on biomedical paradigms envision disability as a deviation from the norm and emphasise individual deficiencies and impairments. In contrast, the social model places disability within the broader context of social structures and institutions and shows how institutional barriers and discrimination contribute to the marginalisation of disabled people (Meekosha, 2008; Tremain, 2005). The social model of disability used by early scholars asserts that disability is not an inherent characteristic of individuals but rather a product of social constructs and barriers. According to this model, if society removes these barriers and ensures universal access to all aspects of life, disability would no longer be a significant factor in people's lives. Although both models have contributed significantly to our understanding of disability, they are not without limitations. For example, medical models tend to pathologise disability and reinforce prejudicial attitudes towards disabled people. Conversely, although the social model emphasises the role of social barriers, it may ignore the personal experiences and behavioural options of people with disabilities (Tremain, 2005).

## Critical Disability Theory

CDT originates from Critical Theory, introduced by Max Horkheimer in 1937, which aims to enhance human freedom and eliminate domination rooted in social constructs like class, power, and race (Hosking, 2008). CDT similarly seeks to address disability by explaining social realities, identifying change agents, and setting norms for societal transformation. Hosking (2008) emphasises that comprehensive critical theory must be explanatory, practical, and normative, highlighting societal flaws, identifying change agents, and setting practical goals for transformation.

Building on this foundation, Delvin and Pothier (2006) introduce the concept of 'dis-citizens' to describe individuals with disabilities who are denied full citizenship. Drawing from Hammar's (1990) idea of denizens, they argue that disabled individuals often experience 'citizenship minus' or disabling citizenship. To address this, they call for reimagining disability and citizenship through new policies and legal frameworks that genuinely meet the needs of disabled individuals. Delvin and Pothier (2006) contend that disability is fundamentally about politics and power dynamics, not merely a matter of health or compassion. They argue that CDT uniquely challenges the core assumptions of liberalism by focussing on the specific needs of disabled individuals.

CDT advocates for an anti-necessitarian understanding of disability, promoting authentic inclusivity over theoretical rights. By rethinking disability and citizenship, CDT aims to empower disabled individuals and transform societal structures perpetuating their marginalisation (Delvin & Pothier, 2006). The concepts of 'dis-citizens' and 'citizenship minus' can be applied to TVET college students in South Africa, especially when we consider the issue of stereotyping and exclusion. For example, the lack of seriousness to develop inclusion policies (Ndlovu, 2019) demonstrates a lack of seriousness to fully include students with disabilities. Ndlovu (2019) also shows that career pathways for students with disabilities are limited as colleges are not ready to offer all programmes to all students equally. Also, lecturers remain untrained in inclusive pedagogy and assistive device utilisation further demonstrates how students with disabilities continue to experience little attention (Ndlovu, 2019).

CDT stems from Critical Theory, which originated in 1937 by Max Horkheimer in his presentation of the 'critical theory of society' in the essay *Traditional and Critical Theory* (Hosking, 2008). It encompasses various approaches to enhance human freedom and eliminate domination based on class, power, race, or other social constructs. Its purpose is to explain oppression and transform society to achieve human emancipation. According to Hosking (2008), comprehensive critical theory must simultaneously be explanatory, practical, and normative. This means it must identify and explain the flaws in current social realities, pinpoint the agents of change, and offer clear standards for critique and practical goals for societal transformation.

As part of the critical theory tradition, CDT similarly aims to be explanatory, practical, and normative in addressing disability. It seeks to explain the social realities of disability, identify who can effect change, and set norms and goals for transforming society to be more inclusive of disabled individuals (Hosking, 2008). This is crucial for TVET colleges that remain marginalised in the broader educational landscape in South Africa. According to Ntombela (2020), TVET college infrastructure is inferior and not user-friendly for students with disabilities. Some colleges continue to operate without disability units or offices, thereby further neglecting the needs of students with disabilities (Ntombela, 2020). Such omissions further reinforce the status of students with disabilities as 'dis-citizens'.

Delvin and Pothier (2006) explain CDT by building on Hammar's (1990) concept of denizens, guest workers who have some social rights but lack political rights in countries like Germany – by introducing the notion of 'dis-citizens'. This term refers to individuals with disabilities who are frequently denied complete citizenship, both in formal and substantive terms, leading to what can be described as 'citizenship minus' or disabling citizenship (Delvin & Pothier, 2006; Hammar, 1990). The authors argue that to address this dis-citizenship, we must reimagine how we conceptualise disability and citizenship. The call for new policies that genuinely meet the needs of disabled individuals and a revised legal framework that clearly outlines their entitlements are some of the measures that can be considered when reimagining disability and citizenship. According to Delvin and Pothier (2006), the goal of CDT is to move beyond merely granting abstract rights to ensuring true inclusiveness.

This approach advocates for an anti-necessitarian understanding of disability that focusses on authentic inclusivity rather than just theoretical rights (Delvin & Pothier, 2006). These authors' central argument is that disability is not primarily an issue of medicine or health, nor is it merely a matter of sensitivity and compassion. Instead, it is fundamentally about politics and power dynamics, encompassing powerlessness and empowerment. Despite liberalism facing numerous critiques over the past few decades from various perspectives – such as feminist, communitarian, critical race, and queer theories – they assert that CDT presents unique challenges to the core assumptions of liberalism due to the specific needs of disabled individuals (Delvin & Pothier, 2006).

Furthermore, CDT may pose more profound challenges to liberalism than other critical theories (Hosking, 2008; Meekosha & Shuttleworth, 2009; Tremain, 2005). Liberalism, as a dominant ideology and social organising principle, struggles particularly with addressing disability. It inherently views disability as a misfortune and prioritises normalcy over abnormality. This perspective leads to societal structures based on able-bodied norms being seen as inevitable and equates productivity with personhood (Meekosha, 2011). The objective of CDT is to contest these deeply embedded assumptions, aiming to create a society where persons with disabilities can fully participate. The theory provides a comprehensive framework for understanding and addressing the unique challenges faced by individuals with disabilities. It encompasses five central tenets: social constructivism, intersectionality, ableism, disability as diversity, and inclusive politics (Campbell, 2008, 2019; Delvin & Pothier, 2006; Whitehead et al., 2024).

## Social Constructivism

Social constructivism posits that disability is not merely a biological or medical condition but is significantly shaped by societal attitudes and structures. Delvin and Pothier (2006) argue that the experiences of disabled individuals are primarily influenced by social, cultural, and environmental factors that define and often constrain their participation in society. This perspective shifts the focus from the individual's impairments to the societal barriers that create disabling conditions. Thus, understanding disability through a social constructivist lens allows for a critical examination of how societal norms and practices contribute to the marginalisation of disabled persons.

When addressing the issue of inclusivity, social structures must recognise that it is not only about lack of infrastructure that makes students with disability feel excluded, but the environment also must be supportive. In the South African TVET college context, the social constructivist approach of CDT is relevant due to the historical legacies of colonialism and apartheid, which have profoundly influenced societal attitudes towards disability. Meekosha (2011) argues that understanding disability in Africa requires critically examining how colonial histories and traditional beliefs about disability intersect to shape contemporary experiences. This perspective allows for a deeper analysis of how societal norms and lack of infrastructure continue to marginalise disabled individuals (Watermeyer et al., 2011).

## Intersectionality

Intersectionality highlights how various social identities, such as race, gender, and class, intersect with disability to create unique experiences of oppression and discrimination. McKinney and Amosun (2020) explain CDT focusses on understanding and improving the real-life experiences of disabled people. It uses critical and intersectional analysis, which means looking at how different forms of discrimination (like racism, sexism, and ableism) overlap and impact disabled individuals. The authors underline the importance of considering these intersecting identities to understand the diverse and complex experiences of disabled individuals fully (McKinney & Amosun, 2020).

This approach reveals that the challenges faced by disabled individuals cannot be understood in isolation from other social categories. For instance, Delvin and Pothier (2006) argue that an intersectional analysis can uncover the compounded disadvantages experienced by disabled women or disabled people of colour, thus necessitating a more comprehensive approach to addressing disability rights and advocacy. Therefore, it is not only about infrastructure access in TVET colleges but also about how the institution, with its policies, aims to improve the experiences of people with disabilities.

As we have argued before, the education system often fails to effectively address the needs of people with disabilities, perpetuating systemic inequalities. Lorenzo (2024) examines how the curriculum does not adequately respond to these needs, highlighting the systemic structures that contribute to their marginalisation. By applying Paulo Freire's principle of conscious awareness (Freire, 1970), Lorenzo (2024) emphasises the importance of recognising and disrupting the various forms of power that continue to oppress individuals with disabilities. This approach aligns with Goodley (2016), who argues that educational frameworks often overlook the unique challenges faced by students with disabilities, further entrenching their exclusion. Both authors advocate for a critical examination of existing policies and practices to empower individuals with disabilities and promote their rights (Goodley, 2016). Lorenzo's use of CDT underscores the potential for academics, policymakers, and society to act as change agents, challenging oppressive systems and fostering social change.

Addressing the educational needs of people with disabilities requires a concerted effort to dismantle systemic barriers and promote inclusive practices. The CDT provides a pathway for meaningful social change (Lorenzo, 2024). Through intersectionality, we can better understand the challenges created by different identities. In so doing, we will be able to establish a more nuanced approach to inclusion. This is important for TVET colleges in South Africa that continue to struggle with the idea of inclusivity.

## Ableism

Ableism refers to the pervasive discrimination and prejudice against disabled individuals, rooted in the belief that *able-bodiedness* is the norm (Campbell, 2008, 2019; Chataika, 2009; Whitehead et al., 2024). Campbell (2008) discusses how ableism manifests in various forms, from overt discrimination to more subtle, systemic biases that privilege non-disabled individuals. This tenet of CDT calls for a critical examination of how societal institutions and practices reinforce ableist assumptions and exclude disabled individuals. Challenging ableism requires fundamentally rethinking societal values and norms, prioritising *able-bodiedness* and marginalising those who do not fit this ideal (Chataika et al., 2012). While ableism in African contexts often intertwines with other forms of discrimination, making it a pervasive issue that CDT seeks to address. Scholars such as Chataika et al. (2012) have explored how deeply ingrained ableist attitudes in African societies contribute to the exclusion of disabled individuals from education, employment, and social life.

Nevertheless, viewing disability as a form of diversity recognises the value and contributions of disabled individuals to society (Babik & Gardner, 2021). Babik and Gardner (2021) advocate for a shift from perceiving disability as a deficit to appreciating it as an integral aspect of human diversity. This perspective aligns with broader diversity and inclusion efforts, emphasising that disabled individuals bring unique perspectives and skills that can enrich communities and workplaces (Babik & Gardner, 2021). By framing disability as diversity, CDT promotes a more inclusive and equitable society that values all human variation. Viewing disability as diversity within the African context emphasises the need to recognise and value the contributions of disabled individuals. This perspective is vital for shifting public attitudes and policies from seeing disability as a burden to appreciating it as an integral aspect of human diversity.

In South Africa, initiatives such as inclusive education programs and disability rights movements have embraced this tenet, promoting a more positive and inclusive view of disability (Delubom & Marongwe, 2022; Republic of South Africa, 2001; Van Wyk & Hodgkinson-Williams, 2022). However, this is still insufficient, considering that some people are still experiencing exclusion. Thus, the CDT perspective can guide TVET colleges in how to challenge ableist assumptions, thereby promoting an inclusive culture that values everyone equally.

## Inclusive Politics

Inclusive politics involves creating political and social systems that actively include and empower disabled individuals (Charlton, 2000; Mji et al., 2011). Delvin and Pothier (2006) argue that true inclusion requires legal rights and substantive measures that ensure disabled individuals can fully participate in all aspects of society. This includes accessible environments, equitable education and employment opportunities, and meaningful representation in political decision-making processes. Inclusive politics in African studies involves advocating for policies and practices that ensure the full participation of disabled individuals in all aspects of society. This advocacy is important in African countries, where disabled people often face significant barriers to political participation and representation. Scholars like Mji et al. (2011) argue that achieving inclusive politics in Africa requires legislative measures and grassroots activism to address systemic barriers and promote the rights of disabled individuals.

CDT has gained traction in South African and broader African studies as scholars and activists seek to address the unique challenges faced by disabled individuals on the continent. The tenets of the theory align with the complex socio-political landscapes of African countries, where historical, cultural, and economic factors interplay to shape the experiences of disabled people. While CDT offers a robust framework for addressing disability in African contexts, its applicability faces several challenges. These challenges include limited resources in public institutions, cultural attitudes that may resist change and political instability. However, the theory's emphasis on social justice and equity provides a strong foundation for advocating for the rights and inclusion of disabled individuals across the continent.

## Towards CDT in TVET Colleges

CDT encompasses a variety of approaches that share the common goal of examining disability in the broader context of culture, history, relativity, social structure, and politics. In contrast to traditional models that often attribute disability to individual disabilities or structural barriers, this theory offers a more holistic perspective that considers the complex interplay of sociocultural forces in shaping disability experiences (Meekosha, 2008; Meekosha & Shuttleworth, 2009). It draws attention to the social norms and structures that define characteristics as disorders.

Furthermore, it emphasises the intersection of disability with other axes of identity, such as race, gender, sexuality, and class (Tremain, 2005). Recognising the complex interplay of various forms of oppression, CDT emphasises the need for nuanced analyses considering the intersecting manifestations of marginalisation and privilege. It challenges the dichotomy between medical and social models of disability. CDT advocates a more nuanced approach considering the interplay between individual experiences and structural factors. CDT provides a framework for understanding disability beyond simple classification by examining the underlying power relations and social structures that shape it (Meekosha & Shuttleworth, 2009).

The CDT offers a comprehensive framework for analysing and addressing the systemic issues that contribute to the exclusion of people with disabilities. Rooted in the broader tradition of Critical Theory, it interrogates power dynamics, social structures, and cultural norms that perpetuate inequality and marginalisation. It challenges prevailing attitudes about disability and advocates for transformative change within educational institutions. This theory critiques traditional views on disability, which have often oppressed individuals with disabilities and violated their rights. CDT challenges the legitimisation of paternalistic treatment and oppression of disabled individuals by those without disabilities. It questions the societal restrictions that limit disabled 'people's access to economic and social opportunities, which are often imposed by the non-disabled population.

CDT predicts that systems designed without considering the needs and experiences of people with disabilities will inherently perpetuate exclusionary practices. Therefore, CDT has the power to explain the marginalisation of individuals with disabilities within TVET colleges because of deeply entrenched societal prejudices and institutionalised discrimination. From inaccessible facilities to negative perceptions, these barriers reflect broader inequities within the educational system. Moreover, using this theory necessitates proactive advocacy and concrete actions to promote inclusivity and accessibility at TVET colleges. This includes reviewing policy reforms, infrastructure enhancement, awareness sensitisation and support services. This will help address intervention methods that TVET colleges can pursue to ensure student success for all.

## Lessons from the Review

This chapter explored the literature on disability and inclusivity in public TVET Colleges in South Africa. Our point of departure was that inclusivity is an undeniable need in public TVET Colleges. We are concerned by the slow pace at which this sector is moving in terms of accommodating students with disabilities. We acknowledge that as a developing country, South Africa faces various competing budgetary priorities, and students with disabilities are usually left out. For example, public TVET Colleges struggle with financial aid, transport, and accommodation. As colleges try to address these issues, matters of disability get ignored. Literature shows that some TVET colleges have limited infrastructure and resources such as student support services and disability units (Ntombela, 2020). The literature further shows that some TVET colleges are characterised by inaccessible buildings for students with disabilities, inadequate support, and several barriers to success (Buthelezi, 2014).

Poor infrastructure forces students with disabilities to learn under unfavourable conditions, that is, learning conditions meant for able-bodied students (Siwela, 2017). This challenge is orchestrated by the slow pace at which colleges move to adopt national policies and tailor them for their internal use. Such poor policy adoption leads to non-training of lecturers to meet the needs of students with disabilities, be it pedagogically, technologically and socially (Siwela, 2017). From the literature, we also found that there is less effort to ensure that TVET colleges are fully accommodative to students with disabilities (Delubom & Marongwe, 2022).

In light of the above, we argue that the issue of disability be looked at from a critical theory perspective. Through the CDT, we argue that colleges are more likely to address disability issues more radically. We acknowledge that disability is a matter of perception and interaction, and if these institutions can eliminate negative perceptions and attitudes, they can work hard to accommodate students with disabilities. Our point of view is that availability or unavailability of resources emanate from the ability of management to think. Therefore, the CDT can help to drive managers to take constructive action. For example, various industries fund disability initiatives, and critical thinking and a desire to address social inequality can prompt managers to act with determination. Through CDT application, activists and researchers can work towards creating more inclusive environments that accommodate and celebrate diversity.

The introduction of CDT has significant implications for both research and 'society's understanding of disability. CDT allows researchers to uncover how disability is constructed and experienced by different individuals (Meekosha, 2008; Tremain, 2005). This approach enriches academic research and influences advocacy efforts to combat anti-disability and promote the rights of people with disabilities. Furthermore, CDT emphasises the importance of centring the voices and experiences of people with disabilities in all aspects of research and policymaking.

By prioritising the perspectives of those directly affected by disability, it challenges dominant discourses and amplifies marginalised voices. In doing so, we promote more inclusive and just societies that recognise all people's inherent dignity and worth, regardless of their abilities (Meekosha, 2008; Tremain, 2005).

## Conclusion

In this chapter, we explored the concept of disability and how it is handled in public TVET colleges in South Africa. This exploration highlighted the extent to which TVET colleges make provision for students with disabilities. We further identified the challenges the colleges face with the inclusion of students with disabilities. We also made recommendations on how to promote inclusion in public TVET colleges. The chapter conceptualised the notion of disability and explained why it matters. We then outlined some international and national policy interventions and recommendations concerning persons with disability. We also explored some weaknesses of these policy imperatives. We did not conduct an empirical study, we are aware that some of our assertions may form the basis for empirical investigations.

## References

Babik, I., & Gardner, E. S. (2021). Factors affecting the perception of disability: A developmental perspective. *Frontiers in Psychology, 12*, 1–25. https://doi.org/10.3389/fpsyg.2021.702166

Boat, T. F., & Wu, J. T. (2015). *Mental disorders and disabilities among low-income children.* National Academies Press.

Buthelezi, M. M. (2014). *Exploring challenges experienced by physically challenged students at a Further Education and Training College in KwaZulu-Natal Province* [Master's thesis, University of South Africa].

Campbell, F. K. (2008). Refusing able(ness): A preliminary conversation about ableism. *M/C Journal, 11*(3). https://doi.org/10.5204/mcj.46

Campbell, F. K. (2019). Precision ableism: Studies in ableism approach to developing histories of disability and abledment. *Rethinking History: The Journal of Theory and Practice, 23*(2), 138–156. https://doi.org/10.1080/13642529.2019.1607475

Charlton, J. I. (2000). *Nothing about us without us: Disability oppression and empowerment.* University of California.

Chataika, T. (2009). Inclusion of disabled students in higher education in Zimbabwe. In J. Lavia & M. Moore (Eds.), *Cross-cultural perspectives on policy and practice: Decolonising community context* (pp. 116–131). Routledge.

Chataika, T., McKenzie, J., Swart, E., & Lyner-Cleophas, M. (2012). Access to education in Africa: Responding to the United Nations Convention on the Rights of Persons with Disabilities. *Disability & Society, 27*(3), 385–398.

Delubom, N. E., & Marongwe, N. (2022). Managers' strategies for inclusive implementation in technical vocational and training colleges in South Africa. *International Journal of Education and New Learning Technologies, 14*(7), 44–48. https://doi.org/10.36315/2022v2end010

Delvin, R., & Pothier, D. (2006). *Critical disability theory: Essays in philosophy, politics and law.* UBC Press.

Department of Higher Education and Training. (2020a). *A report on the investigation of services offered to students with disabilities in TVET colleges.* [Online]. Retrieved

August 27, 2024, from https://www.dhet.gov.za/siteassets/a%20report%20on%20the%20investigation%20of%20services%20offered%20to%20students%20with%20disabilities%20in%20tvet%20colleges.pdf

Department of Higher Education and Training. (2020b). *Technical and vocational education and training colleges: 2020 student support services annual plan.* [Online]. Retrieved August 24, 2024, from https://www.dhet.gov.za/SiteAssets/Technical%20and%20Vocational%20Education%20and%20Training%20Colleges%202020%20Student%20Support%20Services%20Annual%20Plan.pdf

Department for International Development. (2000). Disability, poverty and development. www.dfid.gov.uk

Fourie, L. (2012). *Experiences of adult learners with learning disabilities in cosmetology as a TVET college.* Master of Technology Degree in Somatology, University of Johannesburg.

Freire, P. (1970). *Pedagogy of the oppressed.* Continuum.

Goodley, D. (2016). *Disability studies: An interdisciplinary introduction* (2nd ed.). Sage Publications.

Hammar, T. (1990). *Democracy and the Nation State: Aliens, denizens, and citizens in a world of international migration.* Routledge.

Hosking, D. L. (2008). Critical disability theory. *Disability Studies, 2*(4), 7.

International Labour Office. (2010). *A skilled workforce for strong, sustainable and balanced growth: A G20 training strategy.* International Labour Organisation. https://doi.org/10.1042/bj1250104Pb

International Labour Organisation. (1983). C159 Vocational rehabilitation and employment (disabled persons) convention. *New York, 1983*(168), 6–11.

International Labour Organisation. (2006). R99 Vocational rehabilitation (disabled) recommendation, 1955. *International Labor Organization, 99,* 1–12. Retrieved August 27, 2024, from https://www.ilo.org/dyn/normlex/en/f?p=NORMLEXPUB:12100:0::NO::P12100_INSTRUM ENT_I D:312437

Internation Labour Organization. (2017). *Making TVET and skills system inclusive of person with disabilities.* [Online]. Retrieved August 16, 2024, from https://www.google.com/url?sa=t&source=web&rct=j&opi=89978449&url=https://www.ilo.org/media/421351/download&ved=2ahUKEwi5jJ2C15WLAxVbZ0EAHeMsKDAQFnoECCsQAQ&usg=AOvVaw02W4yyHSSOWcdmR81GRL_G

Lorenzo, T. (2024). Political reasoning for disability inclusion: Making policies practical. In M. B. Cole & J. Creek (Eds.), *Global perspectives in professional reasoning* (pp. 77–98). Routledge.

Makgetla, N. (2020). *Inequality in South Africa: An overview.* TIPS working paper. www.tips.org.za

McKinney, V., & Amosun, S. L. (2020). Impact of lived experiences of people with disabilities in the built environment in South Africa. *African Journal of Disability, 9,* 1–11.

Meekosha, H. (2008). *Contextualizing disability: Developing southern/global theory.* Lancaster.

Meekosha, H. (2011). Decolonising disability: Thinking and acting globally. *Disability & Society, 26*(6), 667–682. https://doi.org/10.1080/09687599.2011.602860

Meekosha, H., & Shuttleworth, R. (2009). What's so "critical" about critical disability studies? *Australian Journal of Human Rights, 15*(1), 47–76.

Mji, G., Gcaza, S., Swartz, L., MacLachlan, M., & Hutton, B. (2011). An African way of networking around disability. *Disability & Society, 23*(6), 365–368.

MyRight. (2023). *Poverty and disability.* Retrieved June 25, 2024, from https://myright.se/en/vart-arbete/fattigdom-och-funktionsnedsattning

Ndlovu, L. M. (2019). *Access with success: A case of students with learning disabilities at a technical and vocational education and training college.* University of KwaZulu-Natal.

Ngubane-Mokiwa, S. A., & Khoza, S. B. (2021). Using community of inquiry (COI) to facilitate the design of a holistic e-learning experience for students with visual impairments. *Education Sciences, 11*(4). https://doi.org/10.3390/educsci11040152

Ntombela, B. P. (2020). *Exploring the experiences of students with physical impairments studying at a technical vocational education and training (TVET) college in Kwazulu-Natal.* University of KwaZulu-Natal.

Owens, T. (2013, September 16). Disabled people in Africa have been marginalised for too long. *The Conversation.* https://theconversation.com/disabled-people-in-africa-have-been-marginalised-for-too-long-18207

Republic of South Africa. (1996). *Constitution of the Republic of South Africa (Act 108 of 1996), South African Government Gazette.* Republic of South Africa. http://housingfinanceafrica.org/app/uploads/Constitution-of-the-Republic-of-South-Africa-Act-108-of-1996.pdf

Republic of South Africa. (2001). *Education White Paper 6: Special needs education – Building an inclusive education and training system.* Government Printers. http://www.education.gov.za/LinkClick.aspx?fileticket=gVFccZLi/tI=&tabid=191&mid=484

Republic of South Africa. (2009). *Student support services framework: Further education and training colleges.* Department of Education.

Republic of South Africa. (2016). *White paper on the rights of persons with disabilities.* Government Gazette.

Republic of South Africa. (2018). *Strategic policy framework on disability for the post-school education and training system.* Department of Higher Education and Training.

Sedibe, M., & Buthelezi, M. M. (2014). Exploring challenges experienced by physically challenged students at a further education and training college in Kwazulu-Natal Province. *Journal of Educational and Social Research, 4*(3), 421–428. https://doi.org/10.5901/jesr.2014.v4n3p421

Siwela, S. (2017). *An exploratory case study of the experiences of students with disabilities at a TVET college. Factors that facilitate or impede their access and success* [Master's thesis, University of KwaZulu-Natal].

Tremain, S. (2005). Foucault, governmentality, and critical disability theory: An introduction. In S. Tremain (Ed.), *Foucault and the government of disability* (pp. 1–24). University of Michigan Press.

United Nations. (1948). *The international bill of human rights: Universal Declaration of Human Rights.* General Assembly of the United Nations. https://doi.org/10.1093/he/9780199672813.003.0004

United Nations. (2006). *Convention on the rights of persons with disabilities and optional protocol.* United Nations. https://doi.org/10.1177/0924051917722294

Van der Berg, S., & Hofmeyr, H. (2020). *An incomplete transition: Overcoming the legacy of exclusion in South Africa.* https://openknowledge.worldbank.org/handle/10986/30029

Van Wyk, G., & Hodgkinson-Williams, C. A. (2022). *Disability access: Opening TVET education in South Africa through an inclusive approach to students with disabilities.* Case #8. African Minds.

Watermeyer, B., Swartz, L., Lorenzo, T., Schneider, M., & Priestley, M. (2011). *Disability and social change: A South African agenda.* University of Cape Town, Faculty of Health Sciences, Division of Occupational Therapy. http://hdl.handle.net/11427/4145.

Whitehead, S. N., Kathard, H., Lorenzo, T., & Amosun, S. L. (2024). Is ableism still entrenched in the medical profession in South Africa? *South African Medical Journal, 114*(2), e1766. https://doi.org/10.7196/.

World Bank Group. (2023). *Disability inclusion.* [Online]. Retrieved July 20, 2024, from https://www.worldbank.org/en/topic/disability#:~:text=One%20billion%20people%2C%20or%2015,outcomes%20than%20persons%20without%20disabilities

Chapter 11

# African Women Leaders in Universities: Using Memory in the Establishment of Leadership Practices

*Siphokazi Tau and Dikeledi A. Mokoena*

*University of Johannesburg, South Africa*

## Abstract

The higher education landscape in South Africa is framed by a multiplicity of tension and contestations and rooted in gender and racial tensions – amongst others. Fundamental to these tensions is how institutional cultures were established to exclude and create bodies that do not belong. African women, in particular, join the university space against this history of exclusion through *the analysis of literature and narratives obtained through one-on-one interviews with five African women leaders.* This chapter considers how history curates our collective memory and, in so doing, creates mistrust of what is not documented as part of history. In other words, history by Western epistemology places African women as bodies without (pre-existing) knowledge in the idea of the university, which is contradictory to how African epistemology places women as central to the knowledge-making system.

*Keywords*: Women leadership; exclusion; memory; narratives; universities; higher education

## Introduction

African cosmology awards respect and legitimises power based on seniority because of the role and contribution one makes in society. Age, wisdom, humanity, and role in community legitimises one's power through responsibility over time. African[1] and Black[2] women who lead within the South African academy have affirmed that, indeed, the university was not created with African women in mind (Tau, 2022). The university and its disciplinary canons have historically excluded Africans, women's narratives and realities from their curriculum and institutional cultures. The shift towards transformation has led to opening up space for women to assume leadership roles within the university. Seven universities in South Africa have appointed female and women leaders en masse, many of them being the firsts of their gender and race in various positions. Thus, these women are classified as uMafungashe,[3] the first daughters of those academic institutions. Although other ethnicities have first-born daughters within their family structures, we intentionally use the linguistic and cultural reference of uMafungashe of the AmaXhosa language. As the linguistic meaning, ukufunga – to swear by someone, is equally important to the cultural meaning of being a leader amongst your siblings. The analogy of the familial concept is useful here because the same African women leaders are the 'products' of the academy and form part of this cultural understanding. uMafungashe is an isiXhosa word denoting the first-born daughter of a family or a senior female-bodied being (Magoqwana, 2021). The role of uMafungashe and any first-born child is to hold the institutional knowledge, dignity and memory of the family and home, as taught by the elders in the family. Importantly, because oMafungashe are the first girl children in the household, they become the blueprint for how the other children will be parented. They are expected to become embodiments of their homes and institutions. This concept, academically transposed by Magoqwana (2021), is applicable in the current discourses around the expectation of African women leaders in the higher education landscape and what they are expected to do in terms of transforming institutional cultures. Their leadership can be understood as the yardstick for determining future opportunities for other black women academics to assume leadership roles in the academy. Their experiences ought to be grasped in light of the nature of the university, which has been a site for the reproduction of various struggles, particularly for historically excluded groups such as African women.

The contradiction of the university as a space that produces knowledge is in how it produces patriarchal and colonial relations, as well as feminist and postcolonial critiques within itself, and sometimes engagement in self-critique (Blackmore, 2002; Odhiambo, 2011). uMafungashe, as the first-born daughters of the family (in this case, the academy), play a role in producing or reproducing the institutional cultures and ways of being, socialised from their family institution, which is a site characterised by the embodiment and performance of memories passed through ancestral lineages. In this chapter, we draw on recollections

---

[1]Referring to people of African descent, former colonised groups of people, geographically from the global south. In the context of South Africa includes, blacks, coloureds, Indians.
[2]Referring to black people of African descent and is used interchangeably with African.
[3]Also spelt as uMafungwashe.

from interviewing five African women leaders in South African universities to draw out memories and stories of self which contribute to the ways in which they lead in the university. We argue that the university is a site of memory, infusion and construction. Additionally, the memory-making process of the university, which we use in establishing institutional cultures, does not factor in memory collections from the lived realities of the African women leading them.

## Methodology

In this study, we reviewed literature on women's leadership in the South African higher education context. We collected narratives from five African women leaders, recollecting their experiences in the university and how they used those to influence their leadership decisions. In this study, we made use of phenomenology as a methodology to guide the collection of data. We intentionally use phenomenology, as theorised by Bibi Bakare-Yusuf (2008) and Nthabiseng Motsemme (2011), on phenomenology as a framework to best understand the experiences of African women.

In their articulation of phenomenology, Motsemme (2011) reminds us that the body remembers and holds memory and consciousness. What that means in relation to how we draw out these narratives is that we make the argument that the African women's body has unique experiences at university when they enter the university and as they ascend to leading in the university. That is because the university, as an institution of colonialism, was imagined to be a Eurocentric, white and male space. Even in the articulation of the university in Africa through African bodies occupying these very institutions, African men entered the university before African women did.

The criteria for selecting African women leaders was based on four factors. First, they had to have been in the university as a leader for at least five years. Second, we selected participants in middle- to high-level leadership positions ranging from directorship to vice-chancellor/principal. Third, the selection was based on race, and Africans were used as markers. This meant that the identity had to represent someone who was historically colonised. In the context of South Africa, our participants included the Black, Coloured, and Indian categories as developed by the colonial-apartheid regime.

Last, in the context of participants who were not South African citizens, participants were required to have been born of African ancestry and historically racially reporting through a non-white identity. Race-related complexities and categories are unique to each African country, even in their postcolonial state formation and post-independent afterlives. Once we had collected the narratives, we analysed them. We employed thematic analysis as an analytical tool to see the points of convergence, variance, and diversity in experiences. We then connected the analysed narratives to the existing literature.

We used purposive sampling to identify our participants; through a Google search, we identified African women leaders across different types of higher education institutions, noting their backgrounds as well as the institutions they come from, as these would have distinct experiences. In our selection, we ensured that

Table 11.1  Summary of Participants.

| Participants | Name | Leadership Position | Years in Leadership Positions |
|---|---|---|---|
| 1 | Matshepo | Vice Chancellor | 15 |
| 2 | Chantel | Director Transformation office | 6 |
| 3 | Lesego | Deputy Vice-Chancellor | 8 |
| 4 | Ntombi | Deputy Dean | 9 |
| 5 | Kubu | Executive Dean | 12 |

historically black and historically white institutions were represented in terms of their current and past affiliations.

Table 11.1 summarises the participants of our study. (The narratives include various points of view from people in leadership positions and are not only reflective of their current leadership position.)

We used pseudonyms instead of participant names and removed any other possible identifiers. These include, but are not limited to, the institutions they were employed in and specific information about their experiences that would make their identities known to others. We did this to protect their anonymity and safety from any emotional distress that the narratives shared in this study could expose them to.

## Memory as Theory

As a theory, this paper locates itself within memory and collective memory studies as theories relevant to how we analyse the experiences of African women leaders. More so, we consider the ways in which universities as institutions carry memory, which we see and witness as reflected within the institutional cultures of these spaces. Memory institutions, according to Byrne (2015), are spaces that

> transmit experience and creativity across the borders of time, space, language and custom, tribe and individuality. As institutions, they have their own memories, enshrined in their collections and buildings, and are as mutable as human memory. Those memories echo through the institutions, shaping expectations and possibilities. (Byrne, 2015, p. 259)

Both Bakare-Yusuf (2008) and Motsemme (2011) have argued that being in the world is more than just being a physical entity because it is the body that grounds our experiences of meaning-making. In thinking about memory, this chapter (which centres on African women's bodies as carriers of memory, history, and futures) makes the argument that the past, present, and future are embodied within the new and transformed universities that they lead. The ways in which institutions as spaces carry the materiality of pasts, which then become institutionalised and authorised cultures – institutional cultures. What Byrne (2015) argues is the process of making institutionalised versions of the past, 'anchoring official memory [of which this process], involves both remembering and forgetting, inclusion and exclusion' (p. 146).

In the discipline of history, the concept of collective memory as a point of theory is found in the works of French sociologist Maurice Halbwachs (1925, 1941), who argues that memory is social and passed from one generation to the next. Scholars of the concept of memory, such as Halbwachs, have argued that memory is relational; thus, it encompasses a collective or community of people. Furthermore, Garde-Hansen (2011) too suggests that memory and remembering are fundamental to one's existence and the process of becoming and belonging for an individual because memory 'destabilises grand narratives of history and power' (Bosch, 2016, p. 2).

Be that as it may, Wang (2008) reminds us that despite power and belonging being individual experiences, 'there is agreement that such memory is shareable among members of a social group or community, be it a nation, an institution, a religious group, or a family' (p. 305). Scholars Dudai (2002) as well as Wertsch and Roediger (2008) argue that along with memory is the process of remembering, which then shows that memory is not static but rather a process. The immeasurable scholarship and literature remind us that collective memory ought to be understood in line with how the past carries political and social representations, which can be contentious.

Memory thus can be understood to be in motion, fluid and moving along with the various contestations brought by remembering the past or the memory, 'a space in which local groups engage in an ongoing struggle against elites and state authorities to control the understanding of the past' (Wertsch & Roediger, 2008, p. 319). This understanding is thus relevant for African women leaders in the current higher education space. Space that has, in line with transformation imperatives, allowed African women to lead institutions they would not have been a part of, particularly in the idea and curation of the university.

## Memory in Institutions

The work of African women leaders also mediates how to make the invisible visible in complex and productive ways when colonialism and apartheid have particularly 'used these women's hypervisibility as a way to violate them' (Gqola, 2007, p. 84). Gabeba Baderoon's (2011) work specifically challenges us to consider the ways in which we look at bodies, where the ways in which those bodies are understood and viewed are a consequence of history.

So then, how do we work with memory or draw from memory to bring black women leaders' beings and experiences into an exclusionary space? When is the university, in its day-to-day, also grappling with maintaining itself as a university and the new imaginations of what it could be? What does that mean for the future when the space constantly tries to ensure that it does not become something else, other than an exclusive space, despite the contemporary attempts to present itself as open to other beings and pieces of knowledge?

The notion and idea of collective memory have been applied in various disciplines, from psychology, history, and sociology, amongst others. Of which the general understanding of the concept is that as a form of memory, collective memory 'transcends individuals and is shared by a group' (Wertsch & Roediger, 2008, p. 318). Halbwachs (1925) rejection of the individual approach to memory argued that it is the collective memory of a society that establishes 'centrality in individuals' lives' (Bosch, 2016, p. 3).

Halbwachs (1925) argued that history functions as dead memory and preserves pasts in ways that may not sustain an organic relation. This suggests that history's 'epistemological claim is devalued in favour of memory's meaningfulness' (Olick & Robbins, 1998, p. 110). In the context of this chapter, we challenge the idea that history is a dead memory because the history of the university as an exclusive space continues to be the experience of African women leaders in today's context. In this rejection, we insist that against this elitist and masculinist history are the memories of African women leaders who carry histories of inclusion but find meaning in transforming university spaces and thus making them spaces of belonging and inclusive. This then demonstrates that through the shifting of the body (physical) and body of knowledge (which contains memories), one can imagine different cultures of belonging in the university.

This further indicates that one's ideological epistemic position (in the ways in which it embodies ethics based on history), collective memory, and remembering are also embodied in one's identity and, therefore, an understanding of how identities navigate spaces such as the university.

In other words, African cosmology and its relationship with the past in the present helps us understand the value of memory in establishing new institutional cultures in today's universities. Fundamentally, collective memory is not to be understood to be history, but it carries traces of history. Thus, it should be understood in the ways in which, in its manifestations, 'it often privileges the interests of the contemporary' (Kansteiner, 2002, p. 180).

According to Roediger et al. (2000), memories of our past experiences or moments are shared with a collective of people of which 'in many circumstances in society, remembering is a social event' (p. 129). Memory or the act of remembering in South Africa is typically situated or contained in time, making it stationary and expressed through commemorative events. This is because memory is often stored in institutions like museums, schools, and libraries and is reflected through the naming of streets, schools, buildings, and statues. We are in motion, either through going to the memory place or emotion through the attachment of memory to these institutions or landmarks. Therefore, because of the contrast in emotions that we have as people and the different directions from which we are in motion, these memories are often diverse and can be in conflict with each other.

This chapter uses memory as the practice of remembering to 'pay attention to the size and nature of different groups with different histories, aims, and structures, and to the different cultural or institutional roles that group members play' (Barnier & Sutton, 2008, p. 178). Importantly, we focus on the memories of these African women leaders in terms of them being excluded or navigating belonging in the university, to specifically draw out these memories. These are memories which speak to how 'decision-making and other executive roles are distributed, and by which particular methods, the group tracks its own past actions and decisions over time' (Barnier & Sutton, 2008, p. 178), as influential to the type of leadership or institutional culture they create. Since memories are part of a more extensive process of cultural negotiation, this defines memories as narratives, as fluid, mediated cultural and personal traces of the past (Sturken, 2008). Consequently, collective 'memory rests upon the assumption that every social group develops a memory of its past, which allows it to preserve and pass along its self-image' (Bosch, 2016, p. 3). This identity of self is negotiated in relation to the changing socio-political power contexts (Bosch, 2016; Neiger et al., 2011). We draw on African women leaders' journeys across various times in the university, from entering the university to being a junior and eventually building their scholarships and earning experience and authority over time. We recognise the distinction between the exclusion of African women from the university as a consequence of history. Moreover, now, there is a transformation of the university to have African women as leaders in the present and future because history places us in time-specific understandings, which are beneficial. However, memory and remembering recognise the ways in which 'the past is tied interpretatively to the present, and [how because of knowledge institutions such as the university], part of an account of the past may be deleted or distorted in the service of present needs' (Wertsch & Roediger, 2008, p. 320).

## Remembering and Memory in the Experiences of African Women Leaders

This section captures narratives from African women leaders where they tap into memories of self in their journey in the academy as well as memories that relate to their identities. These are analysed through an African feminist lens, which Bakare-Yusuf (2003) argues gives us a theoretical account of the embodied gendered experiences of African women's lived experiences. According to Bakare-Yusuf (2005), this accounts for historical accounts and exclusions that 'intersect with a plurality of power formations' (p. 1) experienced by African women leaders in the university space across time. Furthermore, as a theory, it engages the changing ways in which African women encounter the university, as excluded, included and as leaders, and the imagination of what other future possibilities may emerge.

We start these narratives with a reflection from Prof. Matshepo[4] who, as a Vice-Chancellor, shared her reflection of navigating bureaucracies that are created by institutional cultures. Prof. Matshepo says,

> One time a dean came up to me following something I had done and they said, 'No, you can't talk to people in my portfolio directly. You can't give instructions to people who report to me without

---
[4]Pseudonym.

coming via me.' So, I (Prof Matshepo) said, Where do you get that from? No, I will talk to everyone anytime I want to talk to at this institution.

Prof. Matshepo further explained how she models her leadership based on her upbringing and how people interact with each other within society or at home. In how we draw from the home as an institution and the concept of *uMafungashe* as a body with institutional memory of the principles of home and also the leader. More so, what Prof. Matshepo shows us is how she, as head of the institution, can bypass various structures when needed, especially in a way of ensuring that there is quality in how the institution is being run. We see from this that Prof. Matshepo's model of leading challenges bureaucracy and is linked to the one she remembers: every home has a head; the head is responsible for the vision of the home and, as such, can bypass various structures if the intention is to achieve a shared vision of effectiveness.

The Vice-Chancellor highlights this tension that oftentimes visions are individualised and people within the structure want to be custodians of visions at specific points. This is contrary to how homes as institutions are framed, where everyone is responsible for the upkeep of the home and ensuring that the home functions. From a more ideological perspective, the perception of the family outside of the home is the responsibility of everyone to protect its dignity. Prof. Matshepo also demonstrates how leadership and asserting one's authority are acts of resistance against the undermining of her position as she is knowledgeable about her position at the university.

In another context, Professor Chantel,[5] a director of the transformation office in her university, has been in that role for about 6 years, and shares how they want to ensure that the next generation of African women academics are able to navigate the space better:

> I think it's difficult to change anything as an individual … and we need to build, you know, networks and communities that create space for us and create space for others and particularly the people who are going to come after us. We need to create those spaces. But I do some very individual things like I mentor young African women, especially at PhD level or just post their PhD.

This reflection of this shows how community is important in achieving transformation in the university space. She also shows how individuality is not a strength and nor does it help in the sustainability of the work that African women leaders do, particularly ensuring that the next generation of African women entering the university space, find the environment different. Therefore, the experience of the university should not be navigated alone, and networks help create safer spaces to navigate potential exclusions.

---

[5]Pseudonym.

In another case, the African women leaders speak about how authority is never guaranteed for them even when they are actually in senior decision-making positions. Dr Lesego, in a reflection on her time as Deputy Vice-Chancellor, speaks about how, after doing a presentation, a colleague said to them:

> You know, Lesego, if anyone thought you were an affirmative action candidate, you silenced them today. So, I started thinking and then I said he is the one who thought that. You cannot come to say, 'If anyone thought you were an affirmative action candidate, you have silenced them today.' You know, that just made me start thinking that, you know, when you are a woman and an African woman for that matter, you are in a certain position. People automatically think that it's not affirmative action. You are there because of quotas. They never think that you are there because you are the best candidate for that position.

This further speaks to the psychological effects one could have on one's worth and abilities if one were to buy into thinking one was an equity candidate. Furthermore, Dr Lesego further shares another experience of being made to question their merits in the university space; she says:

> And so, I found support there, but I also found othering, and I also found people who felt ... who made me feel that I did not belong. Immediately when I arrived, somebody said to me, 'You know you got this position because of affirmative action, right?' So that already put me on my guard, and the fighter in me then came to the fore, and I said to her, 'Right, I know I got this position because of affirmative action; we need these policies because if we do not have these policies, we would not be in these spaces. You would continue to be in these spaces,' I said to her. I told her, 'But let me tell you, I am just as capable as you.'

These statements about affirmative action hires reflect the colonially constructed memories of black women's exclusion and beliefs about their non-belonging in the academy. These comments further perpetuate these colonial positions. Besides those memories, there is an embeddedness of gendered racist colonial history about black women in society in general. The statements also remove agency from the women leaders and further seek to re-inscribe notions of powerlessness. However, the responses, especially from Dr Lesego,[6] are a signal of resistance to such. The existence of African women academics serves as memory reconfiguration and a challenge to existing memories embedded in the consciousness and judgements of those operating in the academy about African women leaders. What these raise is how even though people know

---

[6]Pseudonym.

you are the Deputy Vice-Chancellor, their senior, they still show a challenge to the merits of one being in such a position, insinuating that there was no trust in the merit to begin with. This is also typical of questioning the authority of women leaders as well as resisting the presence of African women in the academy as racialised others (Grahame, 2004). This becomes the case in how belonging is established and negotiated because there is a history of one's identity not being part of the culture of a space; once one is in that space – you have to negotiate to be trusted.

This, one would argue shows how the politics of belonging continue to carry textures of exclusion in the sense that even though the inclusion of African women in the space, it 'excludes the bestowing of rights on those at the margins of the institutionalised citizenry' (Belluigi, 2023, p. 18). What is important to remember is that African women were not excluded in the university based on any prior actions, but based on patriarchy and racism. Therefore, the trust that one has to negotiate is not based on any prior action but simply on ensuring that there is regulation of bodies in the university space, and to further exclude those who do not suit the culture of the space.

In another reflection by Prof. Ntombi, who is a Deputy Dean, she speaks to how authority is perceived through a singular lens, which closes other ways of defining authority in the university. Prof. Ntombi shares:

> I remember that, as deputy dean and working with male deans, they were not scrutinised the way I'm scrutinised for my decisions. I think you know there ... that men come with this authority. But, yeah, and also, I think often there's a stereotype of women leaders being too emotional or whatever. I think that hasn't come to me. The one stereotype I've been characterised with is that I'm too nice. The subtext of being too nice is that I can't make tough decisions. And it's an interesting one because yeah, I guess it's that image of, you know, a woman not having authority not being able to make tough decisions, yeah. So, it's very interesting. I think I've thought about it a lot I mean, I understand that it is a stereotype, so I'm rational about it, but I often wonder what it is ... that they are actually saying, and sometimes, in my approach to things I don't shout, I don't argue, I'm very diplomatic, I try and be disarming, and so maybe that comes across as being too nice but ultimately what is important is the result. And I have found that there are a lot fewer fights now, you know, we have these meetings where it's all academics in the faculties. They happen once a quarter and, in [my faculty], we've got this reputation that that meeting is the worst thing [laughter], so tense and people shouting at each other and things. It hasn't happened in the year and a half I've been there. So, I think people also respond to a particular style of leadership differently. So, if I adopted a more kind of authoritarian leadership, I think it wouldn't help in terms of that response.

Goniwe and Gqola (2005) argues that engaging memory requires us to 'process the historical consciousness of institutions and the pitfalls of memory making' (p. 14) in the national imaginary of South Africa. And in the ways in which African women work on creating institutional cultures, they have to navigate the tension of being these othered bodies in the space, and creating new histories of what the university can be. A key role of institutional cultures is in place-making and making new meanings. The making of spaces, or place-making, which is commonly used in the fields of architecture and town planning, seeks to make meaning of a process of establishing spaces that should be useful and appealing for people to exist in, to live in, and to work in Lennon (2020).

According to Pellegrino and Jeanneret (2009), space in the architectural discipline enables us access to know what our external reality is. Space, thus, influences the ways in which 'our own body moves and objects are placed… the movement of one's own body' (Pellegrino & Jeanneret, 2009, p. 269). Üngür (2011) and de Certeau (1984) suggest that there is a distinction between place and space. Place 'is the positioning of objects to each other; space is the experience of them' (Üngür, 2011, p. 6); in other words, space becomes the embodiment of the place; space-making or the meaning of space carries the culture of the place.

In the reflection by Prof. Ntombi above, she remembers the early days of leadership and how stereotypes are used and placed on African women leaders, and in responding to this, one can respond to these in changing the culture of leading. Considering how universities have been 'sites of exclusion and elitism' (Odhiambo, 2011, p. 669), this approach to leading challenges the traditional practices that do not serve the transformation trajectory of the postcolonial university in Africa.

Prof. Kubu[7] reflects on how the work of African women leaders is to change the character of the spaces that they lead; she says:

> […] and so what we really need to do is to be conscious that these spaces were not established for the kind of thinking you have around leadership and two things you need to do there is a process and I know we can be impatient sometimes rightfully so because we have been marginalised for a long time but there is one thing you should do is to see yourself in your role as a person who must … if you cannot influence outside of your space but you must influence change where you are. So, in terms … An example here is that the issues of gender equity are really important in terms of staffing firstly. So, all our appointments with a resignation or a vacancy, we fill it with a woman or a black person, but it's been easy for people to say let's get a woman, you know, and they say not just any woman now I think we've filled our quota for women. So, I think we consciously do that and understand how uncomfortable it is because we do these things. It's uncomfortable even to

---

[7]Pseudonym.

> articulate them, but with the determination that these things need to happen. So, there's a small shift that we can make in the spaces because we determine our own rules within the faculty structures, but then outside of this, it is very difficult. I've been in this space, like I said, for a very long time. It is very difficult to influence the dismantling of the systems and the procedures, the processes that have been in place, but I think bit by bit, we need to do that.

Prof. Kubu's reflection highlights how decision-making processes by African women leaders need to reflect transformation and the future of the university. In this she remembers the tensions that would exists in being direct about the ways in which appointments ought to look like as we transform the university culture. Institutional organisations enable change to be effected but the autonomy within departments or faculties have enabled bureaucratic processes that open space for women. However, at the higher echelons of the academy, transformation is difficult, because the university is modelled like elite theory. But the difference is that in elite theory the power is only concentrated with the elite group and not others below the top of the hierarchy. Fundamentally, this also shows how progress in dismantling exclusionary systems and traditions requires time and commitment.

The politics of recognition (Mabokela & Magubane, 2005) can play a fundamental role in the lives of emerging African women in the academy, especially because the 'presence of black women in the academy brings discomfort to those who have crafted them out of the bio-politics of knowledge' (Khunou et al., 2019, p. 2). The challenge with adopting an institution with a particular ideology, such as the European university, is that you adopt a way of thinking that 'disregards other epistemic traditions' (Mbembe, 2016, p. 32). Particularly because, the university is political and through this, establishes a stratification of powers which places and reduces value on minds and bodies of people (Visvanathan, 1997). Because the university through the knowledge produced, bodies that lead and belong, and institutional cultures, standardises knowledge. Hoppers (2002) warns that if you

> standardise the mind, you destroy the fecundity of citizenship. In other words, the citizen should not be posited as a layperson before scientists. Every person is a scientist, and every village is a science academy. Citizens must have institutionalised access to institutions. (p. viii)

## A Brief Discussion of the Findings

In analysing the narratives, we found some insights on the ways in which African women leaders make meaning of their experiences and translate this into their leadership cultures. First, universities are still largely institutions of hierarchical and cultural practices. It is evident that even when women are in positions of power, efforts are made to undermine their authority, as institutional practices have not transformed.

It also became evident that institutions of higher learning could be a constraining ecology for women leaders. In some cases, they are not able to apply their agency in leadership, which requires institutional change rather than changing individuals (see Hlatshwayo et al., 2022). Revealing how the culture of the spaces has not caught up with the change envisioned in the transformative imperatives of these spaces.

Whilst universities are viewed as institutions whose decisions are based on merit, the appointment of women leaders is often linked to affirmative action appointees which is associated with demerit and, as such, has implications for their functioning and the exercise of their role as leaders. This too affects their sense of belonging in the space as well and impacts their leadership practices and style.

Whilst women leaders are supposed to gain recognition in their positions, their leadership positions become the embodiment of a perpetual struggle against the ills of patriarchy and racism (Butcher, 2022). The narrative demonstrates that because women leaders sometimes find it hard to enforce their authority, persuasive leadership has worked better than coercive leadership. This is complicated as this often means that African women leaders then have to revert to the same traditional leadership styles, which have been synonymous with masculinity and Eurocentric. Thus leaving very little space for the inclusion and exploration of African women-centred ways of leading and creating institutional cultures.

## Conclusion

In this chapter, we use the process of remembering, relying on memory to map the ways in which African women leaders remember their past experiences of exclusion in the university to establish transformative ways of being. These African women use their memories as standpoints to not maintain the same exclusionary traditions that have become the character and culture of the university. From these, one is able to see how African women leaders understand that the university is a 'major site of cultural practice, identity formation and symbolic control' (Odhiambo, 2011, p. 669). African women, as bodies and as knowledge producers, have not been considered significant in the culture of the space. These reflections, coupled with transformative action through decision-making, show how African women change these spaces to make them symbolise belonging and inclusion – particularly for future generations entering the space.

## References

Baderoon, G. (2011). 'This is our speech': Voice, body and poetic form in recent South African writing. *Social Dynamics*, *37*(2), 213–227. https://doi.org/10.1080/02533952.2011.600822

Bakare-Yusuf, B. (2003). Beyond determinism: The phenomenology of African female existence. *Feminist Africa*, *2*. https://www.jstor.org/stable/48724973

Bakare-Yusuf, B. (2005). I love myself when I am dancing and carrying on: Refiguring the agency of black women's creative expression in Jamaican Dancehall culture. *International Journal of Media & Cultural Politics*.

Bakare-Yusuf, B. (2008). Rethinking diasporicity: Embodiment, emotion, and the displaced origin. *African and Black Diaspora: An International Journal*, *1*(2), 147–158

Barnier, A. J., & Sutton, J. (2008). From individual to collective memory: Theoretical and empirical perspectives. *Memory*, *16*(3), 177–182

Belluigi, D. (2023). De-idealising the problem of academic freedom and academic autonomy: Exploring alternative readings for scholarship of South African higher education. *Southern African Review of Education*, *28*(1), 10–31.

Blackmore, J. (2002). Leadership for socially just schooling: more substance and less style in high risk low trust times? *Journal of School Leadership*, *12*, 198–219.

Bosch, T. E. (2016). *Memory studies, a brief concept paper* [Unpublished Working Paper]. MeCoDEM. ISSN 2057-4002.

Butcher, J. T. (Ed.). (2022). *Black female leaders in academia: Eliminating the glass ceiling with efficacy, exuberance, and excellence*. IGI Global. https://doi.org/10.4018/978-1-7998-9774-3

Byrne, A. (2015). Institutional memory and memory institutions. *The Australian Library Journal*, *64*(4), 259–269. https://doi.org/10.1080/00049670.2015.1073657

De Certeau, M. (1984). *The practice of everyday life*. University of California Press.

Dudai, Y. (2002). *Memory from A to Z: Keywords, concepts and beyond*. Oxford University Press.

Garde-Hansen, J. (2011). *Media and memory*. Edinburgh University Press.

Goniwe, T., & Gqola, P. D. (2005). A neglected heritage: the aesthetics of complex Black masculinities. *Agenda*, *19*(63), 80–94. https://doi.org/10.1080/10130950.2005.9674572

Gqola, P. D. (2007). How the 'cult of femininity' and violent masculinities support endemic gender-based violence in contemporary South Africa. *African Identities*, *5*(1), 111–124. https://doi.org/10.1080/14725840701253894

Grahame, K. M. (2004). Contesting diversity in the academy: Resistance to women of colour teaching race, class and gender. *Race, Gender & Class*, *11*, 54–73.

Halbwachs, M. (1925). *Les Cadres sociaux de la memoire*. Alcan.

Halbwachs, M. (1941). *La Topgraphie legendaire des Evangiles en Terre Sainte: Etude de memoire collective*. Presses universitaire de France.

Hlatshwayo, M. N., Adendorff, H., Blackie, M., Fataar, A., & Maluleka, P. (2022). *Introduction in decolonising knowledge and knowers: Struggles for university transformation in South Africa*. Routledge.

Hoppers, O. C. (2002). *Indigenous knowledge and the integration of knowledge systems towards a philosophy of articulation*. New Africa Books.

Kansteiner, W. (2002). Finding meaning in memory: A methodological critique of collective memory studies. *History and Theory*, *41*(2), 179–197.

Khunou, G., Phaswana, E. D., Khoza-Shangase, K., & Canham, H. (Eds.). (2019). *Black academic voices: The South African experience*. HSRC Press.

Lennon, M. (2020). The art of inclusion: phenomenology, place making and the role of the arts. *Journal of Urban Design*, *25*(4), 449–466. https://doi.org/10.1080/13574809.2020.1717331

Mabokela, R. O., & Magubane, Z. (Eds.). (2005). Hear our voices: Race, gender and the status of black south african women in the academy, *Imagined South Africa* (vol. 8). Brill.

Magoqwana, B. (2021). Gendering social science: Ukubuyiswa of maternal legacies of knowledge for balanced social science studies in South Africa. In B. Muthien & J. Bam (Eds.), *Rethinking Africa: Indigenous women re-interpret Southern Africa's pasts*, (pp. 87–102). Jacana Media.

Mbembe, A. (2016). Decolonizing the university: New directions. *Arts and Humanities in Higher Education*, *15*(1), 29–45.

Motsemme, N. (2011). *Lived and embodied suffering and healing amongst mothers and daughters in Chesterville Township, KwaZulu-Natal* [Unpublished PhD dissertation]. University of KwaZulu Natal, Durban.

Neiger, M., Meyers, O., & Zandberg, E. (2011). *On media memory: Collective memory in a new media age*. Palgrave Macmillan.

Odhiambo, G. (2011). Women and higher education leadership in Kenya: A critical analysis. *Journal of Higher Education Policy and Management*, *33*(6), 667–678. https://doi.org/10.1080/1360080X.2011.621192

Olick, J. K., & Robbins, J. (1998). Social memory studies: From "collective memory" to the historical sociology of mnemonic practices. *Annual Review of Sociology*, *24*, 105–140. https://doi.org/10.1146/annurev.soc.24.1.105

Pellegrino, P., & Jeanneret, E. (2009). Meaning of space and architecture of place. *Semiotica*, *2009*(175), 269–296. https://doi.org/10.1515/semi.2009.049

Roediger, H. L., Bergman, E. T., & Meade, M. L. (2000). Repeated reproduction from memory. In A. Saito (Ed.), *Bartlett, culture, & cognition* (pp. 115–134). Psychology Press.

Sturken, M. (2008). Memory, consumerism and media: Reflections on the emergence of the field. *Memory Studies*, *1*(1), 73–78. https://doi.org/10.1177/1750698007083890

Tau, S. (2022). *African feminism(s) as it informs the experiences of African women leaders at universities in South Africa*. Master's thesis, Nelson Mandela University.

Üngür, ET. (2011). Thinking by design: Design as a tool for idea development. In *Proceedings of the theory of architecture conference: Theory for the sake of theory* (pp. 460–475). Archtheo'11.

Visvanathan, S. (1997). *A carnival for science: Essays on science, Technology, and Development*. Oxford University Press.

Wang, Q. (2008). On the cultural constitution of collective memory. *Memory*, *16*(3), 305–317. https://doi.org/10.1080/09658210701801467

Wertsch, J. V., & Roediger, H. L., III. (2008). Collective memory: Conceptual foundations and theoretical approaches. *Memory*, *16*(3), 318–326.

Chapter 12

# Embracing the Melting Pot in Teacher Training: Language and Inclusion in Education

*Erasmos Charamba[a] and Shalom Ndhlovana[b]*

[a]*University of Limerick, Ireland*
[b]*University of Witwatersrand, South Africa*

## Abstract

The study, through desk research, aims to explore some of the challenges and opportunities of teaching in multilingual and multicultural teacher education contexts. Guided by a sociolinguistic lens on the funds of knowledge (FoK) and Vygotsky's sociocultural theories, findings reveal that pre-service teachers and in-service teachers acquire pedagogical skills in addition to what they have been taught mostly in a monolingual pedagogy and this does not only affect their teaching but also influences the way they think about multilingual learners. This poses both constraints and opportunities for learners, some of whom fail to understand the epistemology of concepts while others get to be advantaged due to the diverse home languages. Some of the challenges include communication, cultural sensitivity and equity, while opportunities include fostering inclusive learning environments, promoting intercultural understanding and preparing students for a globalised world. It is concluded that by embracing the diversity within these contexts, teachers can create enriching educational experiences that empower students to thrive academically and personally as their teacher identity develops through practice. It is recommended that translanguaging in South African higher education (HE) be upgraded to allow lecturers, teachers and students to use their home languages, in addition to English, to broaden their understanding and help in their training to be linguistically competent and relevant teachers in the rainbow nation.

*Keywords*: Higher education; home language; monolingualism; multiculturalism; multilingualism; teacher training; translanguaging

## Introduction

In the field of teacher education in South Africa, the issue of languages has been highly emotive and controversial, extremely contentious and deeply political (Seethal, 2023). This has resulted in both challenges and opportunities when it comes to teaching in multilingual and multicultural contexts. On the one hand, it poses obstacles to effective communication (Kim, 2020) and understanding, while on the other hand, it provides opportunities to learn from different perspectives (Ngubane & Makua, 2022), fostering a rich and inclusive learning environment (Hibbert, 2023). This has demanded teachers to be flexible, adaptable and culturally sensitive, while also promoting equity and inclusion (Musa, 2023).

Over the years, South African schools have become increasingly multilingual, with students needing targeted support to develop their academic language skills (Ndhlovana & Charamba, 2023a). Like other universities across the globe, South African universities are seeing a surge in the enrolment of a linguistically diverse student body for teacher education (Lumadi, 2021), which implies that higher academic demands are placed on these establishments. This subject has been of great significance to scholars and policymakers who have recognised the critical role of identifying and describing the language and literacy demands, highlighting an essential role for pre-service teacher training (see, for example: Cele, 2021; Ngubane & Makua, 2022; Ramnarain & Mavuru, 2020).

Though multilingualism has always been the norm within the country monolingual pedagogies have prevailed since the colonial era (Gobodwana, 2023), the transformation in South African HE as far as language is concerned however, has been slow paced (Ngubane & Makua, 2022). This has resulted in conflict over the language use which provided the spark that precipitated the Soweto 1976 uprising and ushered in the push that led to the collapse of the apartheid state and the transition in April 1994 to a democratic state. It then provides an unquestionable argument in favour of using multilingual teaching strategies that obfuscate linguistic distinctions.

Cognisant of the fact that South Africa recognises 12 official languages namely: Ndebele, Pedi, Sotho, South African Sign Language, Swazi, Tsonga, Tswana, Venda, Xhosa, Zulu, Afrikaans, and English, these languages are used in selected schools as mediums of instruction in the first three grades only (Carrim & Nkomo, 2023). Thereafter education is offered solely in English in most institutions. This has been pointed out by most scholars (see, for example: Lumadi, 2021; Ndhlovana & Charamba, 2023b; Ndhlovu & Makalela, 2021) as the stumbling block to multilingual student's epistemological access which inevitably affects their pass rate in both national and international assessments.

Though South African matric pass rate has seemingly improved from approximately 76.2% in 2020 to 76.4% in 2021 to 80.1% in 2022 and the latest 82.9% in 2023 most learners as highlighted by Charamba (2022a) perform inadequately with a majority of them getting marks that are below 50%. It should be noted that the country's education cycle takes 12 years and involves a four-phase model, namely foundation phase (Gr R-3), intermediate phase (Gr 4-6), Senior phase (Gr 7-9) and the Further Education and Training phase (Gr 10-12). Grade 12 learners are approximately 16 years old, and they sit for national school leaving examination where they need to get a minimum of 30% in all their subjects in order to pass matric (Zondo et al., 2021). However, to qualify for the limited university entrance a learner needs to get a minimum of 50% in most of their subjects (Mabizela & George, 2020) which makes it reasonable to assume that the minority who enrol for HE have ambitions to further their education and should be helped to achieve even more through conceptualising content.

Nevertheless, there have been various reasons for students to continue struggling in HE and some include things like the cumulative effect of learning losses given the COVID-19 – an infectious disease that is passed from person to person by the SARS-CoV-2 virus-pandemic that undoubtedly exerted a lot of pressure on the education system globally (Maja, 2023), insufficient psycho-social support, difficulty in navigating the linguistic barriers and even loadshedding (Mabena et al., 2021). Chief among these according to many scholars and educationists is the misalignment between the learners' home language and the language of instruction (Charamba, 2022c; Mavuru & Ramnarain, 2020).

Few (if any) studies have focussed on the Bachelor of Education degree specialising in science education particularly in South Africa. Therefore, this paper will focus on some opportunities and challenges of teaching in multilingual and multicultural science HE context. The study reviews studies conducted in HE of teacher education science students regarding multilingual pedagogy as well as the latter's efficacy as taught in South African universities. The term 'melting pot' refers to the idea of diverse cultures and languages coming together. It emphasises the importance of embracing this diversity which can lead to enhanced learning outcomes and the development of global citizenship skills as argued by Ndhlovu and Makalela (2021). This implies that by recognising and harnessing the power of multilingualism we can create a more inclusive and enriching educational experience for both teachers and students. The current study, guided by a sociolinguistic lens, sought to explore some of the challenges and opportunities of teaching in multilingual and multicultural teacher education contexts.

## Methodology

The study adopted a desktop methodology. Desk research is the term used to describe secondary data, or data that can be gathered outside of fieldwork. Since desk research mostly entails gathering data from already-existing resources – executives' time, phone bills, and directories – it is frequently regarded as a less expensive method than field research. The study therefore drew upon nine previously published research, reports, and statistics of international assessments such as **PIRLS** and **TIMSS** between the years 2020 and 2023. The online journals and library provided easy access to this secondary data. We used the Google search engine, ResearchGate, and Academia to get the article we wanted. Using translanguaging, multiculturalism, multilingualism, and decolonial education, we sought articles that were published in Scopus and Web of Science indexed journals as these journals subject all articles to a double-blind peer review. We were only interested in articles published between 2020 and 2023, focussing on translanguaging, multiculturalism, multilingualism, and decolonial education and published in Scopus and Web of Science indexed journals.

We then analysed the data through Braun and Clarke's (2006) thematic analysis, opting to analyse the data inductively. We started off by reading and re-reading the data so we could become familiar with what the data entailed, paying specific attention to patterns that emerged. We then went on to generate the initial codes by documenting where and how patterns occurred. The next step was for us to combine codes into overarching themes that accurately depicted the data. The next step was for us to looks at how the themes supported our data and the overarching theoretical perspective. Next, we decided which themes made meaningful contributions to our understanding of what was going on within the data. This led us to coming up with six themes from the data analysed.

## Theoretical Framework

In the present study, the challenges and opportunities of teaching in multilingual and multicultural teacher education context has been appraised through a sociolinguistic lens on the FoK and Vygotsky's sociocultural theories. These theories acknowledge and celebrates the diverse cultural and linguistic backgrounds of both teachers and students (Li et al., 2021) and involve creating an inclusive learning environment that values the various languages and cultures present in the classroom.

FoK are a diverse range of knowledge and skills that individuals acquire from their cultural, social, and familial backgrounds. They are collections of information rooted in various cultural customs that are a part of everyday activities or internal culture (Herrera Porter & Barko-Alva, 2020). It is the understanding knowledge that students and their family members possess as a result of their positions in their communities. The information that these students actively participate in multicultural, multilingual, and multigenerational households and/or community activities has potential, which is acknowledged by the theory of FoK (González, 2005). Thus, students do not enter the classroom as blank slates, regardless of their gender, colour, language, or socioeconomic status (Marshall, 2023). Accordingly, the FoK theory contends that academic education needs to be connected to students' real-world experiences and that the specifics of a successful pedagogy ought to be connected to the language, culture, and socialisation contexts of the local past and community (González, 2005).

The foundation of this theory is Vygotsky's Social Development Theory, which is based on three ideas: the Zone of Proximal Development, the More Knowledgeable Other, and Social Interaction. Together, these ideas, according to Vygotsky, support a social learning strategy that entails a form of academic apprenticeship.

With the latter, students can investigate and expand on their own experiences in a way that recognises them as unique persons with unique knowledge bases (González et al., 2006).

Making learning 'real' is the focus of the FoK hypothesis (Charamba, 2022a). By focussing on the academic journey rather than only comparing the student's weaknesses to the desired outcome, FoK aims to break free from the current deficit model. In order to generate new ways of knowing, it explores various discourses connecting the home and school environments and integrates academic learning with everyday knowledge (González, 2005). Students' linguistic repertoire ingrained in their knowledge, is therefore also utilised in the classroom. Regardless of the subject matter being studied, these theories view language and learning as action-situated within a historical, cultural, and social context (Ramnarain & Mavuru, 2020).

Vygotsky's views centre on the idea that language is essential to the formation of concepts and the mind, concentrating on how individuals interacted with one another and their sociocultural environment through shared experiences (Nardo, 2021). It has been demonstrated that using various languages in the classroom helps students understand scientific concepts more thoroughly, quickly, and simply (Ndhlovana & Charamba, 2023a). It also provides a more seamless bridge between home and school knowledge (Chisango & Marongwe, 2021). Garcia (2009) defines translanguaging as the simultaneous use of multiple languages.

## Literature Review

Over the past decade, scholars have increasingly recognised the power of translanguaging in the South African English first additional language (EFAL) classroom. Using students' native language alongside English to enhance language learning has been pointed out to be of much benefit to learners (De Wilde et al., 2020). Rapid linguistic developments have provided innovative language learning opportunities, particularly in turbulent times such as the COVID-19 pandemic (Maja, 2023). Through translanguaging pedagogy, teaching and learning has managed to occur freely, learners can express themselves and teachers can transfer more information to a larger number of learners. The assessment regime for university students has also been adjusting to account for multilingual students, considering the different languages that are found in their communities where students spend most of their time.

## Language Acquisition, Communication, and Translanguaging in HE

Language is a fundamental aspect of human existence, serving as a vehicle for expression, connection and understanding. From birth, we embark on a remarkable journey of language acquisition, gradually mastering the intricacies of communication (Nasrollahi Shahri, 2019). There is indeed a fascinating realm of language acquisition and its profound impact on our ability to communicate effectively. According to Gass et al. (2020), language acquisition refers to the process of learning a language, either as first language or as second language. It involves the development of linguistic skills, including vocabulary, grammar, phonetics, and pragmatics.

Onishchuk et al. (2020) highlighted the important theories, processes and factors that shape language acquisition. Through systematising theoretical issues and generalising the experience of developing foreign language education for future teachers at pedagogical universities of Ukraine, they managed to identify some of the most effective methods of foreign language education which include grammar-translation method, audio-lingual method, and cognitive-code methodologies. These, they argue, necessitates a deeper understanding of how language is acquired and the role it plays in our daily lives. If they are implemented in South African HEs they can help improve the foreign language education of future teachers and will contribute to successful integration of national education into the world educational space.

Furthermore, Kohnke (2023) explored a different dimension where he looked at the introduction of a chatbot as an independent language learning tool at a HE in Hong Kong. In his two-phase study, a chatbot was developed and a questionnaire ($N = 128$) was employed followed by semi-structured interviews ($N = 12$). It was found that the participants enjoyed interacting with the chatbot as it was interactive, flexible and provided individualised learning and perceived that it improved their English skills. This insinuates that independent language learning is paramount for those wishing to develop proficiency in a second or foreign language. Additionally, as concurred by Maja (2023), the chatbot or online platforms provides students with the opportunity to interact actively in their target language which can also be adopted in our South African institutions and can even help the lecturers to learn the students' languages.

The notion that immersing multilingual EFAL students in English content courses alone is insufficient to support language, literacy, or academic development has gained widespread recognition on a global scale. Even though most EFAL learners pick up conversational English fairly quickly, mastering academic language – which contains many low-frequency and technical words unique to various subject areas – takes at least five years, and frequently much longer (Schmitt & Schmitt, 2020). In Ollerhead's (2020) study in Australia where he presented various components of teacher learning to 11 Australian science pre-service teachers enrolled in a Master of Education in language and literacy course, he analysed the ways in which the training contributed to their development of scientific pedagogical language knowledge. Through interviews and assessments, the findings demonstrated that the students enhanced their professional identities as teachers and their awareness of the variety of language and literacy strengths and challenges faced by their multilingual learners.

Similarly, Moshtari and Safarpour (2024) unravel the mysteries of language acquisition and delve into the art of communication. In their qualitative study they aimed to shed light on the challenges of internationalisation of HE in low-income countries in East Africa. After reviewing their literature and interviewing academics, the data that they obtained were thematically analysed. Among the many challenges they found, their results point out the inefficiency of the language use mong HEs and that for effective communication to occur certain factors should be considered such as encoding and decoding messages, understanding context and considering cultural factors. They emphasise the development of national policies and laws based on contextual and environmental conditions, as well as participation in international meetings to expand communication. This signifies that to fully cater for multilingual students, multilingual systems should be put in place and be followed closely so as to not disadvantage other students lest they become irrelevant for the global market by embracing their indigenous language.

Interestingly, Musa (2023) investigated factors influencing students' attitudes towards learning English as a foreign language in HE in Zanzibar. Through a desktop methodology he discovered students' level of interest, confidence, vocabulary knowledge, anxiety, readiness to take risks, curiosity, and understanding of the function of English were among the factors that affected their learning. In line with these findings, it is important to note that translanguaging does away with the language hierarchies and return the power to the speaker. Wei and García (2022) argue that when our languages are internal, we do not know when one ends and the other begins. This means that the speaker's idiolect shapes their own language repertoire (García, 2022) and this idiolect is surrounded by the communicative repertoire that is gestures, context and other ways of meaning making (Tyler, 2023).

Translanguaging therefore is the act that allows people to deploy the features of their repertoire and there is a transaction between the interlocuters. This means that a translanguaging classroom takes into account the unitary linguistic system and gives learners the opportunity to deploy their full linguistic repertoire and not only the particular named languages as highlighted in Charamba's (2022b) study in Zimbabwe. He advocates for the use of multilingual technology in modify learning by instituting a new model of intertwined instruction. In his study he explored the role language played in e-learning and how educators could use multilingualism as a teaching/learning resource in HE. The study presented results from a mixed methods approach in which 42 purposively sampled distance teacher education undergraduate students were taught through English and Shona. Data were collected through focus group interviews and a written assessment activity. From the study it is clear that the use of multilingual approaches in today's linguistically diverse e-learning HE classrooms can be beneficial and by acknowledging multilingualism we promote academic excellence especially to multilingual students who have been previously disadvantaged.

Subsequently, Wunseh and Charamba (2023) examined the multifaceted nature of communication, exploring the various channels and elements that facilitate meaningful interaction. This encompassed how individuals exchange information, ideas and emotions through verbal and non-verbal means. They however mainly focussed on language brokering and code-switching which form part of the everyday teaching and learning tools used in South African multilingual classroom. Through observation and semi-structured interviews, while using snowball sampling to select Francophone immigrant learners and using the sociocultural theories and the FoK, their study rejected a deficit model, where linguistically and culturally diverse institutions of learning are reputed to be incapable of offering rich learning experiences and resources. This therefore assures that all forms of communication should be incorporated into the classroom to enhance learner's understanding.

In like manner, Seethal (2023) argues that in South Africa, hegemony and power has become meshed with language. In his study, he discusses the politics and linguistic disputes in South Africa as well as the state's deceit in igniting societal unrest over language use and then seeking to diffuse it. He looks at how South Africa's indigenous languages have been marginalised and regionalised, how English and Afrikaans have become the dominant languages in the country creating social contradictions. Undoubtedly, though some policies have been adopted their implementation in some institution still lag behind hence there is need for a more radical approach to language given the ever-expanding linguistic dynamics in our classrooms.

## Findings

When it comes to teaching in multilingual and multicultural teacher education context, there are both exciting opportunities and unique challenges to consider. On one hand this setting allows for the celebration and integration of diverse languages, cultures, and perspectives, fostering a rich learning environment. On the other hand, it poses extreme pressure to teacher educators and even students who have to not only teach scientific concepts but decipher language to students whose home language is different from the language of instruction. Following are some of the challenges and opportunities that either students or teacher educators face in multilingual classrooms.

## Challenges: Effective Communication

One of the main challenges when teaching or learning in a multicultural environment is ensuring effective communication. Facilitating effective communication as pointed out in most of the reviewed studies (see, for example, Blignaut, 2021; Cele, 2021; Charamba, 2022a; Ngubane & Makua, 2022; Ramnarain & Mavuru, 2020) has been a challenge especially when students have varying levels of proficiency in the language of instruction. As a result, teachers often experience pedagogical difficulties when invoking learners' home languages in science instruction.

De Wilde et al. (2020) asserted that language is essential to education because it is the main method for disseminating information. This means that effective communication is at the core of effective education, and teachers must possess great communication abilities. It is important to note that learners get to select from their unitary repertoire therefore teachers must find ways to bridge language gaps and facilitate understanding among students who may have varying levels of proficiency in the language of instruction (Gobodwana, 2023). They should employ strategies such as scaffolding, visual aids, gestures and other non-verbal cues to support language acquisition and comprehension. Additionally, teachers can encourage peer collaboration and cooperative learning, which can help students learn from each other and build their language skills through interaction.

## Teacher Unpreparedness

Most scholars argue that the success of language training in the classroom depends on the pedagogical toolkits of the teachers. However, often times teachers are unequipped with the adequate pedagogical skills they truly need in a multilingual environment. Cele (2021) in his study claims that due to a lack of thorough monitoring and methodical implementation, the creation of language policies for social inclusion and transformation has fallen well short of the ideal state of affairs. He explores the prevalent and reinforcement of the supremacy of English as opposed to enhancing the development of African languages and argues that if pre-service teachers continue to be immersed in such policies it makes it hard for transformation to occur in schools as teachers do not have the skills to implements in their classroom.

This is in line with Charamba's (2022a) study which explored perceptions of masters students towards multilingualism and investigated how their respective students language in their classrooms. By adopting a qualitative ethnographic research design in which seven master's students were purposively sampled for data collection purposes, the results revealed a shift of lenses from monolingual and parochial biases to a full embrace of multilingualism and translanguaging as a 'normal' practice they encounter in their daily teaching experiences. This shows that most pre-service teachers lack exposure to multilingual pedagogies and fail to use it to cater for the needs of learners and by role modelling it in HE this can help them implement it in their classrooms. Ramnarain and Mavuru (2020) go on to suggest using various instructional strategies to support language development and comprehension and argue that teachers/lectures need to adopt translanguaging which implicitly make use of collaborative learning and students get to learn from each other to enhance their understanding.

## Cultural Differences

Another challenge is addressing cultural differences and fostering cultural sensitivity. Cultural differences as argued by Ngubane and Makua (2022) may impact student's learning styles and expectations. Blignaut (2021) concurs that teachers must recognise and respect the diverse cultural backgrounds of their students, as well as their unique perspective and experiences. This requires creating a safe and inclusive classroom environment where students feel valued and respected, regardless of their cultural identity.

It is without a doubt that with multiple cultures students, students may have varying communication styles and may struggle to understand one another at times. This also entails varying values and beliefs which can lead to misunderstandings or conflicts. Thus, Makalela (2021) advocates for ubuntu translanguaging which promotes unity and togetherness amongst students as well as teachers where teachers can incorporate culturally relevant materials and examples into their lessons and encourage students to share their own experiences. This means that teachers need to be culturally responsive and adaptable in their teaching approaches so that they can help students thrive academically.

Blignaut (2021) holds the view that education is a great leveller of opportunities and can change people's lives around almost overnight. In other words, educators' work is located somewhere in the nexus between struggling to make ends meet as a result of multiple cultures and varying levels of language proficiency of learners which has undoubtedly affected the pass rate in international assessments in the past and being agencies of change by embracing multilinguals.

## Opportunities: Equity and Access

Despite these challenges, teaching in multilingual and multicultural contexts also offers numerous opportunities. Multilingual and multicultural contexts often highlight disparities in educational opportunities and resources and teachers are encouraged to provide equitable access to quality education for all students, regardless of their linguistic or cultural background. This includes addressing systemic barriers and implementing inclusive teaching practices.

Ngubane and Makua (2022) in their study highlight the fact that by adopting multilingual pedagogies, HE institutions stand a chance of mitigating the imbalances caused by the Western philosophies and world views. It is clear that a majority of students in HE are from African cultures and as declared by Ndlovu-Gatsheni (2018); the continuous oppression and neglect of belief systems and values that they bring to HE is undoubtedly 'epistemic violence'. Thus, translingual pedagogies as concurred by other scholars (Blignaut, 2021; Maistry, 2021) are an agent for 'epistemic freedom' as they are decolonial and transformative.

### *Collaboration and Community Engagement*

Exposure to different languages and cultures can broaden student's horizons (Ndhlovana & Charamba, 2023a), enhance their intercultural competence and promote global citizenship (Maseko & Mkhize, 2021). It allows students to develop a deeper understanding and appreciation for diversity, fostering empathy and respect for others. Teachers can leverage this diversity to create engaging and meaningful learning experiences that draw on students' linguistic and cultural backgrounds. This can include incorporating multicultural literature, music, art and other forms of cultural expression into the curriculum.

Drawing from the theory of Vygotsky, building strong relationships with students, families and community members is vital in multilingual and multicultural contexts. Teachers therefore can facilitate collaboration among diverse stakeholders to create a supportive learning environment and promote cultural exchange. Charamba (2022a) argues that sociocultural perspectives have allowed us to approach language, gestures, and physical artifacts as mediating means, with affordances and constraints for multilingual students. This means that before explicating the purpose of education, it is important to consider what education can do and what it cannot do in multilingual contexts.

### *Intercultural Competence and Global Citizenship*

Teaching in multicultural contexts offers opportunities to develop students' intercultural competence and fosters global citizenship. By exposing students to different languages, cultures and perspectives, teachers can help them develop empathy, respect and a broader understanding of the world. Drawing from Ngubane and Makua's (2022) study that brings to the fore the notion of Ubuntu pedagogy, it is clear that classroom practices should be designed to respond to students' cultural competencies, embracing all linguistic repertoires that students bring to the classroom for learning and treating them equally, with dignity and respect regardless of their social backgrounds. Thus, embracing the diversity and allowing students to teach others about their culture while also learning about other people's validates the bilingual community practices.

## Discussion

This study intended to address opportunities and challenges created by the ever-increasing diverse nature of our 21st century classrooms as institutions worldwide continue to enrol large numbers of diverse students. It looked on how teacher trainers prepare teachers to meet these challenges and it was found that by embracing the melting pot that is incorporating multicultural and multilingual perspectives into the curriculum, providing professional development opportunities for teachers to enhance their cultural competence, and promoting open dialogue and collaboration among students from different backgrounds, teacher training can equip educators with the knowledge and skills needed to effectively support and empower learners in diverse educational settings.

According to Musa (2023), tertiary institutions are recognised for their crucial role in fulfilling societal demands for human resources. It is therefore imperative for all instructors to acknowledge their impact on their students' perspectives regarding the acquisition of language and their academic achievements putting into perspective the student's internal wiring as far as language acquisition is concerned. This is to say language has a unitary meaning making system of speakers that is always within and translanguaging flexes the entanglement of worlds (García, 2022), cultural practices and words linguistic practices in which all multilinguals are always immersed. Charamba (2021) emphasises the need to integrate culture into the foreign language teaching process; organisation of specialised centres and associations to raise the level of awareness of the conducted studies in the field of multilingual education.

## Conclusion

To sum up, when translanguaging is not considered, injustices prevail in higher institutions. Teaching in multilingual and multicultural teacher education contexts thus requires educators to navigate various challenges related to communication, cultural sensitivity, and equity. However, it also offers opportunities for fostering inclusive learning environments, promoting intercultural understanding, and preparing students for a globalised world. By embracing the diversity within these contexts, teachers can create enriching educational experiences that empower students to thrive academically and personally. Pre-service teachers need to be trained to embrace the melting pot and adapt instructional strategies to meet the diverse needs of learners. It is important to note that these themes are not exhaustive but provide insight in some of the challenges and opportunities of teaching in multicultural and multilingual teacher education contexts.

## Recommendations

This research endeavour holds potential benefits for a multitude of stake holders, and it is recommended that individuals refrain from engaging in disruptive behaviours both within and outside of multilingual instructional settings. Such behaviours may include monolingual instructions, the use of humour that is deemed inappropriate and looking down upon other cultures. In addition, it is imperative that individuals cultivate their passion, amiability, pedagogical expertise and aptitude, communicative tactics, dispositions towards learners and the field, conduct, and instructional obligations in multilingual spaces.

## References

Blignaut, S. (2021). Transforming the curriculum for the unique challenges faced by South Africa. *Curriculum Perspectives, 41*, 27–34.

Braun, V., & Clarke, V. (2006). Using thematic analysis in psychology. *Qualitative Research in Psychology, 3*(2), 77–101. https://doi.org/10.1191/1478088706qp063oa

Carrim, A., & Nkomo, S. A. (2023). A systematic literature review of the feasibility of a translanguaging pedagogy in the foundation phase. *Journal of Languages and Language Teaching, 11*(2), 195–210.

Cele, N. (2021). Understanding language policy as a tool for access and social inclusion in South African higher education: A critical policy analysis perspective. *South African Journal of Higher Education, 35*(6), 25–46.

Charamba, E. (2022a). Bridging discourses in science education through translanguaging amongst sixth-grade students in the free state province. *Journal of Educational Studies, 21*(3), 26–46.

Charamba, E. (2022b). Emerging pedagogies in higher education: Cutting through 'either-or' binaries with a heteroglossic plurilingual lens. *Teacher Education through Flexible Learning in Africa (TETFLE), 3*(1), 3–23. https://doi.org/10.35293/tetfle.v3i1.4171

Charamba, E. (2022c). Translanguaging as a disruptive pedagogy in education: Analysis of metacognitive reflections and self-efficacious stances of Masters students. *African Journal of Development Studies, 12*(1), 229.

Chisango, G., & Marongwe, N. (2021). The digital divide at three disadvantaged secondary schools in Gauteng, South Africa. *Journal of Education (University of KwaZulu-Natal), 82*, 149–165.

De Wilde, V., Brysbaert, M., & Eyckmans, J. (2020). Learning English through out-of-school exposure. Which levels of language proficiency are attained and which types of input are important? *Bilingualism: Language and Cognition, 23*(1), 171–185.

García, O. (2009). Education, multilingualism and translanguaging in the 21st century. In T. Skutnabb-Kangas, R. Phillipson, A. K. Mohanty, & M. Panda (Eds.), *Social Justice through Multilingual Education* (pp. 140–158). Multilingual Matters.

García, O. (2022). 18 A Sociolinguistic biography and understandings of bilingualism. *Multilingualism and Education: Researchers' Pathways and Perspectives*, 150.

Gass, S. M., Behney, J., & Plonsky, L. (2020). *Second language acquisition: An introductory course*. Routledge.

Gobodwana, A. (2023). *The use of translanguaging in assisting educators to teach African languages: A case study of Tshwane South Education District, Pretoria*. Faculty of Humanities, School of Languages and Literatures. http://hdl.handle.net/11427/38479

González, N. (2005). Beyond culture: The hybridity of funds of knowledge. In N. González, L. C. Moll, & C. Amanti (Eds.), *Theorizing practices in households, communities, and classrooms* (pp. 29–46). Lawrence Erlbaum.

González, N., Moll, L. C., & Amanti, C. (Eds.). (2006). *Funds of knowledge: Theorizing practices in households, communities, and classrooms*. Routledge.

Herrera, S. G., Porter, L., & Barko-Alva, K. (2020). *Equity in school–parent partnerships: Cultivating community and family trust in culturally diverse classrooms*. Teachers College Press.

Hibbert, L. (Ed.). (2023). *English as a language of learning, teaching and inclusivity: Examining South Africa's higher education crisis*. Taylor & Francis.

Kim, D. (2020). Learning language, learning culture: Teaching language to the whole student. *ECNU Review of Education*, 3(3), 519–541.

Kohnke, L. (2023). L2 learners' perceptions of a chatbot as a potential independent language learning tool. *International Journal of Mobile Learning and Organisation*, 17(1–2), 214–226.

Li, G., Anderson, J., Hare, J., & McTavish, M. (Eds.). (2021). *Superdiversity and teacher education: Supporting teachers in working with culturally, linguistically, and racially diverse students, families, and communities*. Routledge.

Lumadi, M. W. (2021). Decolonising the curriculum to reinvigorate equity in higher education: A linguistic transformation. *South African Journal of Higher Education*, 35(1), 37–53.

Mabena, N., Mokgosi, P. N., & Ramapela, S. S. (2021). Factors contributing to poor learner performance in mathematics: A case of selected schools in Mpumalanga province, South Africa. *Problems of Education in the 21st Century*, 79(3), 451.

Mabizela, S. E., & George, A. Z. (2020). Predictive validity of the National Benchmark Test and National Senior Certificate for the academic success of first-year medical students at one South African university. *BMC Medical Education*, 20(1), 1–10.

Maistry, S. (2021). South Africa's comorbidity: A chronic affliction of intersecting education, economic and health inequalities. *Education as Change*, 25(1), 1–21. https://doi.org/10.25159/1947-9417/8677

Maja, M. (2023). Using ICT-based pedagogy to teach English first additional language during the COVID-19 pandemic: A rural case study. *Teacher Education through Flexible Learning in Africa (TETFLE)*, 4, 3–27. https://doi.org/10.35293/tetfle.v4i1.4185

Nasrollahi Shahri, M. N. (2019). Second language user identities in stories of intercultural communication: A case study. *Language and Intercultural Communication*, 19(4), 342–356. https://doi.org/10.1080/14708477.2018.1544253

Makalela, L. (2021). Multilingual literacies and technology in Africa: Towards ubuntu digital translanguaging. *Rethinking Language Use in Digital Africa: Technology and Communication in Sub-Saharan Africa* (pp. 3–18). Multilingual Matters.

Marshall, T. R. (2023). *Understanding your instructional power: Curriculum and language decisions to support each student*. ASCD.

Maseko, K., & Mkhize, D. N. (2021). Translanguaging mediating reading in a multilingual South African township primary classroom. *International Journal of Multilingualism*, 18(3), 455–474.

Mavuru, L., & Ramnarain, U. (2020). Learners' socio-cultural backgrounds and science teaching and learning: A case study of township schools in South Africa. *Cultural Studies of Science Education*, 15, 1067–1095.

Moshtari, M., & Safarpour, A. (2024). Challenges and strategies for the internationalization of higher education in low-income East African countries. *Higher Education, 87*(1), 89–109. https://doi.org/10.1007/s10734-023-00994-1

Musa, M. (2023). Factors influencing students attitudes towards learning English as a foreign language in tertiary institutions in Zanzibar, Tanzania. *International Journal of Linguistics, 4*(1), 14–26.

Nardo, A. (2021). Exploring a Vygotskian theory of education and its evolutionary foundations. *Educational Theory, 71*(3), 331–352.

Ndhlovana, S. N., & Charamba, E. (2023a). Sink or swim? Choosing to swim through translanguaging pedagogies in a culturally diverse natural sciences classroom. *Cross-Cultural Studies: Education and Science, 8*(2), 65–73.

Ndhlovana, S. N., & Charamba, E. (2023b). The efficacy of translanguaging in selected South African mathematics and science intermediate phase classrooms. *Journal of Languages and Language Teaching, 11*(3), 373–389.

Ndlovu-Gatsheni, S. (2018). The dynamics of epistemological decolonisation in the 21st century: Towards epistemic freedom. *The Strategic Review for Southern Africa, 40*(1).

Ndhlovu, F., & Makalela, L. (2021). *Decolonising Multilingualism in Africa: Recentering Silenced Voices from the Global South*. Multilingual Matters.

Ngubane, N. I., & Makua, M. (2022). *Intersection of Ubuntu pedagogy and social justice: Transforming South African higher education*. Mangosuthu University of Technology (MUT).

Ollerhead, S. (2020). 'The pre-service teacher tango': pairing literacy and science in multilingual Australian classrooms. *International Journal of Science Education, 42*(14), 2493–2512.

Onishchuk, I., Ikonnikova, M., Antonenko, T., Kharchenko, I., Shestakova, S., Kuzmenko, N., & Maksymchuk, B. (2020). Characteristics of foreign language education in foreign countries and ways of applying foreign experience in pedagogical universities of Ukraine. *Revista Romaneasca Pentru Educatie Multidimensionala, 12*(3), 44–65.

Ramnarain, U., & Mavuru, L. (2020). Fostering a multicultural science curriculum in South Africa. In M. M. Atwater (Ed.), *International Handbook of Research on Multicultural Science Education* (pp. 1–32). Springer International Publishing.

Schmitt, N., & Schmitt, D. (2020). *Vocabulary in language teaching*. Cambridge University Press.

Seethal, C. (2023). The state of languages in South Africa. In S. D. Brunn, & R. Kehrein (Eds.), *Language, Society and the State in a Changing World* (pp. 169–185). Springer International Publishing.

Tyler, R. (2023). *Translanguaging, coloniality and decolonial cracks: Bilingual science learning in South Africa* (Vol. 4). Channel View Publications.

Wei, L., & Garcia, O. (2022). Not a first language but one repertoire: Translanguaging as a decolonizing project. *RELC Journal, 53*(2), 313–324.

Zondo, N., Zewotir, T., & North, D. E. (2021). The level of difficulty and discrimination power of the items of the National Senior Certificate Mathematics Examination. *South African Journal of Education, 41*(4), 1–13. https://www.ajol.info/index.php/saje/article/view/224429

Chapter 13

# Beyond Rhetoric: Reimagining Inclusive Education for Sexual and Gender Diversity in South African Higher Learning Institutions

*Obakeng Kagola[a] and Anthony Brown[b]*

[a]*Sol Plaatje University, South Africa*
[b]*UNISA, South Africa*

## Abstract

This book chapter provides a comprehensive exploration of the complexities surrounding the inclusion of sexual and gender diversity within South African higher education. Drawing upon a literature review of existing research, the chapter illuminates the lived experiences of Lesbian, Gay, Bisexual, and Transgender (LGBT) students and staff in universities, highlighting the pervasive challenges of homophobia, transphobia, heteronormativity, and compulsory heterosexuality that shape the academic landscape and hinder authentic inclusion and belonging. The chapter troubles the dominant discourses of inclusion, social inclusion, and social justice education, arguing for the need to move beyond narrow conceptions of accessibility and representation towards a more intersectional and transformative approach. Through a critical analysis of the accounts of early-career academics, researchers, and students, the chapter exposes the risks and challenges associated with advocating for LGBT inclusion within heteronormative and homophobic institutional cultures. The chapter examines the structural and symbolic manifestations of heteronormativity within university policies, practices, and spaces, revealing the multiple, intersecting forms of oppression and marginalisation faced by LGBT individuals. Drawing upon the insights of queer theory, the chapter proposes a range of strategies for widening inclusion and strengthening meaningful responses to sexual and gender diversity in higher education, encompassing policy reform, curriculum transformation, capacity building, support services, inclusive residence life, collaborative research, accountability, institutional culture change, and leadership and advocacy. Ultimately, the chapter argues that the journey towards authentic inclusion and social justice for LGBT individuals in South African higher education requires sustained commitment, critical reflexivity, and collective action to dismantle oppression, challenge heteronormativity, and foster belonging and agency for all.

*Keywords*: Sexual and gender diversity; LGBT inclusion; South African higher education; heteronormativity; gender identity

## Introduction

Three decades since the dawn of democracy in South Africa, the complex tapestry of the higher education landscape, dedicated to addressing historical inequities through inclusion, has been centred primarily around themes such as disability, race and to some extent issues around gender (Koenane, 2013; Msibi, 2013; Sithole, 2015; Vincent & Chiwandire, 2019). For example, there has been much focus on inclusion in higher education for individuals with disabilities, which is centred on ensuring equitable access to learning opportunities (Sithole, 2015; Vincent & Chiwandire, 2019). Institutions have implemented reasonable accommodations, encompassing physical accessibility, assistive technologies, alternative formats for materials, and support services like sign language interpreters or notetakers, facilitating the full participation of students with disabilities in academic activities (Badat, 2015). In terms of aspects of race in higher education institutions of South Africa, policies such as affirmative action and equity initiatives are aimed at addressing and ensuring equal access and representation for individuals from all racial backgrounds. This was done through actively promoting the inclusion of underrepresented racial groups in higher education spaces. Despite strides made, challenges persist in realising complete inclusion in higher education. Recognising the intersectionality of identities is paramount. LGBT individuals may encounter issues related to race, class, disability, and more. Scholars like Fourie (1999) underscore the importance of widened systemic transformation, for the realisation of fully inclusive higher education institutions. This results in reshaping policies, curricula, and institutional practices to rectify historical imbalances and foster a more diverse and equitable academic environments, therefore, inclusive practices must account for the diverse intersections of identity to prevent any group from being marginalised. Nevertheless, as our comprehension of equality and diversity evolves, it becomes important to broaden our perspective through which inclusion is examined reflected up on. Moreover, to possibly monitor the work done to bridge the gap between minority groups such as LGBT's experiences in higher education in South Africa a perceived liberatory context for the realisation of the democratic ideals as enshrined in the republic's progressive constitution. This review of literature chapter delves into the realm of inclusion for people of sexual and gender diversity, particularly LGBT individuals, in South African higher education. It explores the challenges and opportunities that define this critical facet of academic life. Attempting to reflect on the question: How do higher education institutions in South Africa create and response to the inclusion for LGBT students?

This chapter's introduction provided a rationale for the review of the research done so far on the inclusion of sexual and gender identities in South African higher education. In the next section we trouble the silence of social inclusion, towards social justice for marginalised sexual and gender identities. We then explore reviewed research within the South African higher education, in response to the inclusion of diverse sexual and gender identities. Lastly, we provide possible suggestions on how we can widen inclusion in higher education for sexual and gender diverse identities.

## Defining Inclusion in Higher Education

Before we unravel the complexities of LGBT inclusion in South African higher education, we must grasp the broader concept of inclusion in this context. Inclusion, in the academic realm, extends beyond mere representation to encapsulate a commitment to dismantling barriers that hinder the full participation of all individuals in the educational experience. It involves creating an environment where diversity is not only acknowledged but celebrated, fostering a sense of belonging for every student, academics, and support staff member. The notion of inclusion in higher education signifies an institutional commitment to acknowledging and rectifying historical injustices. As Walker (2018) notes, universities and colleges have, to a large extent, grappled with insidious forms of identity discrimination targeting minority groups within society. While the transformation scholarship in higher education has historically focussed on race and gender, the imperative now is to broaden the discourse to encompass the experiences of LGBT individuals.

## Troubling the Silence of Social Inclusion; Towards Social Justice for Marginalised Sexual and Gender Identities

Inclusive education has gained traction globally as moral imperative, human right and vehicle for social justice (United Nations, 2016). It is lauded for potential to dismantle exclusionary barriers and inequities permeating educational systems and spaces. However, as scholarship interrogates the concept and its application, critical tensions and limitations surface. What constitutes meaningful, transformative inclusion remains contested, particularly within higher education contexts grappling with complex diversity across racial, gender, sexual, religious, ability, and other axes of difference (Tienda, 2013). This discussion troubles notions of inclusion dominating policies and rhetoric to consider how substantive, socially just framings might re-orient efforts within South African universities still struggling with historical legacies of discrimination and marginalisation.

Nearly three decades since mandating inclusive education, progress remains slow within the South African higher education landscape (Walton & Rusznyak, 2020). Policy primarily and predominantly tackles physical accessibility and support services for students with sensory/mobility/learning disabilities. Important gains materialise through infrastructure adaptations, assistive technologies, alternative teaching procedures and flexible assessment accommodating functional diversity in classrooms (Republic of South Africa, 2018). However, a medicalised approach targeting fixed bodily states dominates, with less advancement around recognising situational, fluid barriers facing those experiencing socioeconomic, epistemic, linguistic or cultural alienation within university contexts. While technological aids, ramps or extra time allow for 'integration' of students living with disabilities into existing systems little efforts exist to change or value marginalised positions (Howell & Lazarus, 2003). True inclusion involves celebrating diversity, nurturing belonging and enabling equitable participation beyond baseline access (Donohue & Bornman, 2014). From this lens, contemporary practice remains limited. Discourses emphasise helping vulnerable, disadvantaged individuals fit particular environments rather than committing institutional transformation or consciousness raising addressing roots of exclusion (Walton & Lloyd, 2011).

Additionally concerning is the lack of comprehensive data on disabled students' experiences and support provision across South African higher education institutions more broadly (Bam et al., 2023). Monitoring and reporting remain patchy, signalling needs for strengthened accountability mechanisms (Nakidien et al., 2021). Where statistics exist, they highlight low participation rates for disabled youth in universities – well below broader population, suggesting persisting obstacles (StatsSA, 2019). Overall, assessments reveal ad hoc, inconsistent approaches to inclusion thus far rooted in compliance logics prioritising basic access, rather than nuanced understandings of environments required to nourish success for marginalised groups (Lourens, 2015). Cursory policy adoption fails to catalyse wholesale culture change. This prompt reiterating necessity of grounding efforts in social justice.

## Embracing a Social Justice Imperative

Conceptually, inclusion traces back to principles of equal rights, enacting democratic values of non-discrimination to address historic and systemic injustice (Martin et al., 2020). It envisions moving beyond assimilationist directives seeking to 'fix' non-conforming individuals. Instead, belonging, participation and achievement are framed as relational – demanding adaptations within environments, systems and mentalities upholding certain norms that disadvantage those outside dominant paradigms (Artiles & Dyson, 2005). This aligns to Fraser's (2001) definition emphasising inclusion as a matter of social justice – tackling institutionalised obstacles that prevent equitable access and outcomes across lines of difference. She problematises limited diversity efforts failing to engage power, focussing only on celebratory recognition of multiculturalism devoid of redistribution. Without confronting the underlying roots perpetuating marginalisation, 'addition' of different groups becomes tokenistic, leaving culture unchanged rather than leading to authentic integration and valuing (Ahmed, 2022).

South African scholarship affirms these imperatives, outlining necessary movement beyond technicist support for disabled students towards what Walton and Lloyd (2011) term full recognition, acceptance and embrace of diverse identities and realities. Leibowitz (2016) and Mafumo (2010) situate inclusion within wider transformation agenda to redress past race-based discrimination through curricula, language policy, and academic staff profiles. However, both argue issues of poverty, gender inequities, sexual violence, homophobia, transphobia, and beyond signal ongoing exclusionary environments threatening students' participation, necessitating intersectional social justice praxis engaging multiple, concurrent systems preserving advantage/disadvantage. Without overt analytical attention to power and privilege dynamics permeating higher education spaces, diversity initiatives slide into superficial messaging rather than action (Tobbell et al., 2021). Well-meaning rhetoric risks covering over ongoing marginalisation of minority groups. Embracing substantive inclusion founded upon redistributing access, resources and status to foster belonging and capabilities for those historically excluded remains imperative (Gidley et al., 2010).

Examining what meaningful inclusion constitutes through a social justice orientation spotlights the necessity of moving beyond current disability centeredness to embrace multiplicative experiences of disadvantage. Of particular note is addressing ongoing 'othering' of gender and sexual diversity within higher education spaces reflecting cis/heteronormative traditions (Buthelezi & Brown, 2023). Rich scholarship documents assumptions and behaviours rooted in gender essentialism and compulsory heterosexuality that alienate, delegitimise and impose distress for queer students and staff (DePalma & Francis, 2014; Msibi, 2012). Concerns like inclusive student residences, mentoring gaps, risks of harassment, stereotyping impose unique barriers. Yet language framing inclusion as 'adding' minority groups without disrupting normalcy renders such issues invisible (Falconer & Taylor, 2017).

Queer theory offers vital tools to denaturalise environments and practices reifying binary notions of gender and sexuality that profoundly shape access and participation (Bacchi & Eveline, 2010). It rejects presenting some groups as inherently outside norms needing 'accommodation'. Instead, diversity becomes understood through troubling environments and knowledge constructs that impose particular identity performances while sanctioning non-conformity (Byron, 2017). Inclusion then moves from tolerance of deviance towards valuing multiplicity and enabling same legitimacy for diverse modes of gender/sexual being (Wolbring & Lillywhite, 2021). These demands confronting bias within curriculum, resources, events, facilities and procedures that alienates queer communities. Without this interrogation of norms, cultures stay oblivious to marginalisation (Lythreatis et al., 2022). Truly inclusive universities require purposeful consciousness raising around advantage and barriers driven by sexual and gender diversity so issues, needs and experiences of LGBTQ+ students and staff shift from margins to centre in guiding policy and practice. In essence, centring social justice and queer perspectives compels fundamentally reimagining inclusion – moving beyond technicist support or celebratory diversity notions towards purposeful empowerment of minorities through systemic redistribution and consciousness raising. This necessitates confronting complex questions of privilege, disadvantage and power differentials permeating higher education spaces to enable transformative action – not just helping individuals 'fit' but proactively adapting systems and nurturing humanised cultures that fully embrace, value and facilitate belonging, capabilities and success for those facing situational barriers.

Assessments of inclusion within South African higher education reveal narrow application dominated by disability considerations of physical adjustments and learning support thus far failing to catalyse wholesale culture change. Persisting experiences of alienation and discrimination facing wider marginalised groups signals urgent need to widen social justice imperatives addressing multiplicative disadvantage. Queer theory spotlights necessity of interrogating environments through lens foregrounding gender and sexual diversity to progress authentic inclusion. Overall, this compels reimagining the purpose and reach of efforts from basic compliance to fostering empowered participation through systemic redistribution of resources alongside accumulating cultural consciousness raising that values and responds to situated barriers diverse groups face. Rethinking inclusion this way propels possibility of universities moving beyond espoused rhetoric to become sites enacting equity and social change.

## Methodological Considerations for Reviewing Literature on Sexuality and Gender Diversity in South African Universities

This systemic methodology outlines the process of conducting a comprehensive review of literature that informed the reflections on sexuality and gender diversity in universities in South Africa. The purpose of this review is to systematically identify, analyse, and synthesise the existing literature on this topic, providing a solid foundation for understanding the current state of knowledge and informing future research and policy recommendations (Booth et al., 2016). The methodology employed in this review follows the guidelines for conducting systematic reviews in the social sciences, as outlined by Petticrew and Roberts (2006) and adapted for the specific context of higher education research by Bearman et al. (2012).

The first step in conducting a literature review is to clearly define the research question that guides the entire process (Booth et al., 2016). In this case, the research question is: What is the current state of knowledge regarding sexuality and gender diversity in South African universities, and how can this knowledge inform efforts to create more inclusive and equitable higher education environments? To ensure that the review captures the most relevant and appropriate literature, it is necessary to establish clear inclusion and exclusion criteria (Gough et al., 2017). These criteria are based on the research question and the specific parameters of the review, such as the time frame, geographic scope, and types of publications considered.

For this review, the inclusion criteria are as follows:

1. Studies that focus on sexuality and gender diversity in the context of South African universities, including the experiences of LGBT students, staff, and other stakeholders.
2. Studies published in peer-reviewed journals, academic books, or conference proceedings.
3. Studies that employ qualitative, quantitative, or mixed-methods research designs.
4. Studies published in English between 2000 and 2024, to capture the most recent and relevant literature.

The exclusion criteria are:

1. Studies that do not focus specifically on sexuality and gender diversity in South African universities, such as those that examine these issues in other educational contexts or geographic regions.
2. Non-academic publications, such as newspaper articles, blog posts, or opinion pieces.
3. Studies that do not employ a clear research methodology or do not provide sufficient information about their data collection and analysis procedures.

For this review, the following electronic databases were searched:

1. Google Scholar.
2. EBSCOhost (including Academic Search Complete, Education Source, and ERIC).
3. ProQuest (including Education Database and Social Science Database).
4. Web of Science.
5. Scopus.

The search terms used included combinations of keywords related to sexuality and gender diversity (e.g., LGBT, queer, gay, lesbian, bisexual, transgender, non-binary), higher education (e.g., university, college, tertiary education), and South Africa (e.g., South African, SA). Boolean operators (AND, OR) and truncation symbols (*) were used to refine the search results and capture variations in terminology (Bearman et al., 2012). After conducting the initial search, the next step is to screen the retrieved literature to determine which studies meet the inclusion criteria and are relevant to the research question (Gough et al., 2017). This process involves several stages, beginning with a review of titles and abstracts to identify potentially relevant studies, followed by a full-text review of those studies to assess their eligibility for inclusion. Once the final set of studies has been identified, the next stage is to extract and analyse the relevant data from each study (Booth et al., 2016). This process involves a systematic and standardised approach to recording key information about each study, including the research questions, methodology, sample characteristics, main findings, and conclusions.

For this review, a data extraction form was developed to ensure consistency and thoroughness in the data collection process (Bearman et al., 2012). The form included the following categories:

1. Study identification (author, year, title).
2. Research question(s) and objectives.
3. Methodology (research design, data collection methods, sample characteristics).
4. Main findings related to sexuality and gender diversity in South African universities.
5. Conclusions and implications for policy and practice.
6. Limitations and quality assessment.

For this review, a thematic analysis approach was employed, following the guidelines outlined by Braun and Clarke (2022). This involved a systematic process of coding the data, identifying and refining themes, and producing a coherent and meaningful synthesis of the findings. For this review, the synthesis was structured around the key themes that emerged from the analysis, with a focus on the experiences, challenges, and opportunities related to sexuality and gender diversity in South African universities. The synthesis also considered the broader context of higher education in South Africa, including the historical legacies of apartheid and the ongoing efforts to promote transformation and social justice (Msibi, 2013).

By following the guidelines for conducting systematic reviews in the social sciences, and adapting them to the specific context of higher education research, this review aims to contribute to a deeper understanding of the current state of knowledge and inform efforts to create more inclusive and equitable higher education environments.

## Lived Realities and Responses to the Inclusion of Diverse Sexual and Gender Identities in South African Higher Education

The primary objective of education in South Africa is to work towards correcting the injustice of the past and promote social justice values and practices, this is embedded in the country's progressive constitution. That positions South Africa to be one of the world's leading countries in how gender and sexual orientation are constitutionally and legislatively reflected. Therefore, institutions of learning such as the higher education sector play a critical role in engaging with diversity and inclusion in its curriculum. Francis (2021a) postulate that even though worldwide and in South Africa higher education institution are perceived as contexts where many young people (early career academics and students) start to discover and explore aspects of their gender and sexual identities and possible enact them openly. Moreover, the space serves as a platform for scholarship on issues of diversity, human rights, inclusion and possibly social justice studies. However, these institutions remain less researched and silent how **LGBT** minority groups experiences of inclusion are accounted for in South Africa. There are many underlaying factors to such claims. According to Sutherland et al. (2016), Francis (2021a), and Louw (2024) there are dominant factors that persist in higher education sector that centres around the discourses of homophobia and compulsive heterosexist which mirrors the South African sociocultural norms and values. For instance, Msibi (2013) in his reflection being an early career teacher educator at one of the institutions of higher learning located in the Kwa-Zulu Natal province of South Africa experienced forms of homophobia and prevalence of heteronormativity. Msibi (2013, p. 69) states in his reflective accounts that

> A colleague I trusted and respected called me to her office to 'guide' me before I left. In the meeting, I was warned to be careful in the USA. I was told to particularly be careful of being 'converted' by the Americans to 'engaging in despicable homosexual acts. Implicit in this was the suspicion that I may, in fact, be gay, and that a context such as the USA would allow for an easier performance of my supposed gay identity.

Msibi's account shows the many ways in which homophobic sentiments permeates in the context of higher education for immerging academics under the hospices of care and support. Moreover, this reflection by Msibi to some extend shows how hetero-patriarchal discourses around what it means to be a man in this context are sustained at the demise of other gender performances in rural higher education institutions. Interesting about Msibi's account of the trusted and respected colleagues is that she had suspicions about Msibi's sexuality, and she intended to police him not to fall into the trap of homosexuality while overseas. Gender expressions and sexuality policing are some the thing heteronormative discourses turn to sustain in contested contexts such as higher education. Msibi's account is similar to that of Brown (2024) Katlego's single case study of a cisgender heterosexual male early career scholar; in that societies or colleagues in these cases turn to police individuals who conduct research in sexuality or in support of diverse gender and sexual identities. In the case of Katlego, his research interests on LGBT experiences turned the spotlight on his sexuality being scrutinised. Brown (2024, p. 4) postulates that Katlego's 'colleagues insisted on knowing what interest he had with 'gays and lesbians', as he is a 'straight' man. His focus on LGBT research was perceived as him being a member of this out-group'. The participant in Brown's (2024) single case study validates Francis (2021b) and Msibi's (2011) assertion that people who support and research the inclusion and transformation of lives of minority groups such as the LGBT communities within higher education a large extent, turn to be perceived as entering dangerous terrain, or 'being suspected of deviant sexual behaviour' much like Brown's participant. Msibi (2013) and Katlego's accounts in Brown (2024) show how early-career academics and researchers in higher education engaging in inclusion and transformational research on the experiences of LGBT are perceived.

Meanwhile, Brown (2024), Francis (2021a), and Sithole (2015) argue that higher educational environments need to be spaces that foster and encourage research, conversation, and educational discussion on sexuality and gender diversity in a non-judgemental and mutual respectability manner for all who participates in higher education spaces. However, reinforced heteronormative ideas, socio-cultural practices, ideological contestation, and inequality shapes participation in higher education institution's lecture halls (Francis, 2021b; Ngabaza et al., 2016). The afore discourses that shape that landscape of higher education emanate from broader society or lack thereof interventions or pedagogical strategies are undoubtedly the stumbling blocks to the realisation of full inclusion and transformation of the experiences of diverse gender and sexual identity minorities (Brown & Diale, 2017). Francis (2021a) has utilised an anti-oppressive education approach to his teaching, he argues that this approach enables greater student participation, and creates an environment that addresses how social groups can co-exist. Enabling possibilities of reimaging a just and equal world, and the formulation of healthier relationships between students and academic staff.

Students' experiences in South African higher education institution campuses are shaped by the broader societal constructs and perceptions of being and belonging as these spaces can be lonely and cumbersome (Gordon & Collins, 2013; Ngabaza et al., 2016). However, scholars reported that for the majority of individuals with diverse gender and sexual orientations, their experiences are flowed with pervasive homophobia and heteronormativity highlights (see Brown & Diale, 2017; Jagessar & Msibi, 2015; Naidu & Mutumbara, 2017; Tshilongo & Rothmann, 2019). In their study that explored the realities of transgender students, Buthelezi and Brown (2023) through the use of photovoice and drawings as data generation tools found that transgender students turn to be harassed by security personnel in their endeavours to access higher education institutions facilities. They postulate that rigid identity markers or information found in the access cards of students are incongruent to that of the transgender student, this speaks to aspects of systematic heteronormativity within the university matrix, one participant in Buthelezi and Brown (2023, p. 5) shared that

> [...] I encountered as a student was with my student card, which is titled as Mr, although I physically appear feminine. I was once prohibited to enter the gate, because they [*security guards*] believed that my student card does not belong to me. My student card information requires from me to explain myself at all times [...] I would come across security guards who will harass me because my student card reflected male.

This transgender student's experience highlights one of the many frustrations of gender nonconforming students and they are ill-treated due to a mismatch between the sex assigned at birth and the gender expressions they choose to perform. Moreover, one could also relate the student's frustrations to the sustenance of heteronormativity within the university in that biomatrix system. Student ID biometrics systems in the majority of institutions in South Africa are gender-fixed in comparison to the flexibility in capturing other identity markers such as race or ethnic information, thus hampering LGBT social inclusion in many ways (Buthelezi & Brown, 2023).

Resident life plays a pertinent role in enabling students' sense of belonging and experiencing the fulfilment of their human right to safety and security. However, Vincent and Munyuki (2017) emphasise some higher education spaces are epicentres of compulsory heteronormativity and heterosexuality contributing to an environment where gendered violence and homophobia are perpetuated. In their study that gathered data using narrative interviews with 14 LGBT students at a South African higher education institution found that while some of their fellow students enjoyed the advantages of feeling at home in higher education residence life, LGBT students described experiences of 'discomfort, alienation, ostracism and nonbelonging' (Vincent & Munyuki, 2017, p. 20). The afore students' experiences provide different understanding of higher education residence life as these are spaces perceived to be safe, conducive for learning and allowing for diverse expressions. These hostile experiences are also visible in Jagessar and Msibi (2015) in their study at one of the Institutions located in Kwa-Zulu Natal and Tshilongo and Rothmann (2019) one of the campuses of the North West University. Not forgetting Lesch et al. (2017) findings at Stellenbosch University. While it's not possible to generalise the research findings of these scholars in their different contexts, they provide an understanding of how homonormative principles do not challenge prevailing heteronormative and heterosexual assumptions at institutions of higher learning (Butler et al., 2003; Jagessar & Msibi, 2015). Instead, LGBT students in these studies advocate for assimilation into the existing heterosexual context, maintaining heterosexuality as the normative ideal. This standpoint has the potential to reinforce a marginalised LGBT community and cultivate a privatised LGBT culture. For example, research conducted on sexual minority students at the University of KwaZulu-Natal demonstrates how gay and lesbian students may inadvertently internalise, normalise, and trivialise heteronormative or homophobic treatment, unintentionally prioritising heterosexuality over homosexuality (Jagessar & Msibi, 2015). Correspondingly, similar findings in the experiences of same-sex student couples at Stellenbosch University underscore the enduring prevalence of heterosexual hegemony, despite the university's efforts to promote inclusivity. Notably, lesbian students navigate between visibility and invisibility, aiming to encourage positive behaviour while avoiding homophobia (Lesch et al., 2017).

These authors articulate the connection between compulsory heteronormativity and heterosexuality in universities, contributing to an environment where gender violence and homophobia are perpetuated. The collective research paints a troubling picture of the reality faced by LGBT students in South African higher education, emphasising the imperative for systemic changes to confront and dismantle the entrenched homophobia and heteronormativity within these academic institutions. The studies underscore the significance of cultivating inclusive and supportive environments that acknowledge and respect diverse gender and sexual identities in the higher education landscape. In the subsequent section, we explore ways in which inclusivity in higher education can be expanded to be responsive to sexual and gender-diverse identities.

## Discussion of Findings

The landscape of South African higher education has been shaped by a complex interplay of historical inequities, progressive constitutional ideals, and ongoing struggles for authentic inclusion. While significant strides have been made in addressing issues of accessibility and representation for marginalised groups based on race, disability, and to some extent, gender, the experiences of individuals with diverse sexual orientations and gender identities remain largely unexamined and unaccounted for within the realm of inclusive education (Koenane, 2013; Msibi, 2013; Salmi & D'Addio, 2021; Sithole, 2015). As the preceding discussions have illuminated, the lived realities of LGBT students and staff in South African universities are marked by pervasive homophobia, heteronormativity, and compulsory heterosexuality, which serve to perpetuate a culture of exclusion, marginalisation, and invisibility (Brown & Diale, 2017; Jagessar & Msibi, 2015; Naidu & Mutumbara, 2017; Tshilongo & Rothmann, 2019). Despite the constitutional protections and legislative policies that enshrine the rights of LGBT individuals, the deeply entrenched sociocultural norms and values that privilege heterosexuality and gender conformity continue to shape the academic landscape, creating barriers to authentic inclusion and belonging (Francis, 2021a; Human Sciences Research Council, 2016; Louw, 2005).

The accounts of early-career academics and researchers who engage in scholarship on LGBT experiences and advocate for inclusivity further underscore the challenges and risks associated with challenging heteronormativity within higher education spaces (Brown, 2024; Msibi, 2013). The policing of gender expressions and sexuality, the questioning of research interests, and the suspicion of deviant sexual behaviour serve as stark reminders of the pervasive homophobic sentiment that permeates academia, even under the guise of care and support (Brown, 2024; Francis, 2021b; Msibi, 2012). Moreover, the experiences of transgender students, as highlighted by Buthelezi and Brown (2023), reveal the systemic heteronormativity embedded within university structures and practices. The rigid gender binary enforced through student identification systems and the harassment faced by gender non-conforming individuals expose the urgent need for a critical interrogation of the institutional matrix that upholds exclusionary norms and hinders LGBT social inclusion.

The hostile and alienating experiences of LGBT students in university residence life, as documented by Vincent and Munyuki (2017), Jagessar and Msibi (2015), Tshilongo and Rothmann (2019), and Lesch et al. (2017), further underscore the pervasive nature of compulsory heteronormativity and heterosexuality in higher education spaces. The discomfort, ostracism, and non-belonging felt by LGBT students in these supposedly safe and conducive learning environments serve as a stark reminder of the urgent need for systemic change and the cultivation of inclusive and supportive spaces that acknowledge and respect diverse gender and sexual identities.

To truly embrace the principles of inclusive education and social justice, it is imperative for South African universities to move beyond the narrow confines of physical accessibility and representation, towards a more comprehensive and intersectional approach that dismantles the systemic barriers and challenges the dominant discourses that perpetuate exclusion and marginalisation (Ahmed, 2022; Donohue & Bornman, 2014; Fraser, 2001). The prevailing discourses of inclusion, social inclusion, and social justice education in South African higher education institutions warrant critical examination and problematisation. While these discourses have gained traction as moral imperatives and vehicles for redressing historical inequities, their application and impact remain limited and contested, particularly in relation to sexual and gender diversity (Tienda, 2013; UN, 2016).

The dominant framing of inclusion in higher education has primarily focussed on addressing issues of physical accessibility and support services for students with disabilities, with important gains made through infrastructure adaptations, assistive technologies, and alternative teaching and assessment practices (Howell & Lazarus, 2003; Republic of South Africa, 2018; Walton & Rusznyak, 2020). However, this medicalised approach, which targets fixed bodily states, fails to fully recognise and address the situational and fluid barriers faced by individuals experiencing socioeconomic, epistemic, linguistic, or cultural alienation within university contexts (Donohue & Bornman, 2014; Walton & Lloyd, 2011). Moreover, the discourse of social inclusion, while laudable in its intent, often falls short in its application and impact. The emphasis on helping vulnerable and disadvantaged individuals fit into existing environments, rather than committing to institutional transformation and consciousness-raising, serves to perpetuate the marginalisation of minority groups (Ahmed, 2022; Walton & Lloyd, 2011). The tokenistic addition of diverse groups without disrupting the underlying norms and power structures that uphold exclusion fails to bring about authentic integration and valuing of difference (Ahmed, 2022; Fraser, 2001).

Similarly, the discourse of social justice education, while rooted in principles of equal rights and non-discrimination, often fails to engage critically with the complex power dynamics and privilege that permeate higher education spaces (Mafumo, 2010). The celebratory recognition of multiculturalism and diversity, devoid of a commitment to redistribution and systemic change, risks sliding into superficial messaging rather than transformative action (Ahmed, 2022; Leibowitz, 2016; Tobbell et al., 2021).

To move towards a more substantive and socially just framing of inclusion, it is necessary to embrace an intersectional approach that acknowledges and addresses the multiple, concurrent systems of advantage and disadvantage that shape students' experiences (Rodó-Zárate, 2023; Walton & Lloyd, 2011). This requires a critical interrogation of the power and privilege dynamics that permeate higher education spaces, and a commitment to redistributing access, resources, and status to foster belonging and capabilities for those historically excluded (Gidley et al., 2010; Leibowitz, 2016; Mafumo, 2010).

To widen inclusive education and strengthen meaningful responses to sexual and gender diversity in South African higher education, the following strategies are proposed:

1. *Policy review and reform*: Conduct a comprehensive review of existing institutional policies and practices to identify and rectify any discriminatory or exclusionary language, procedures, or assumptions. Develop explicit anti-discrimination policies that protect the rights of LGBT students and staff and establish clear reporting mechanisms for incidents of harassment, violence, or discrimination (Matthyse, 2017).
2. *Curriculum transformation*: Engage in a critical examination of curricula across disciplines to identify and challenge heteronormative biases, assumptions, and omissions. Incorporate LGBT perspectives, histories, and contributions into course content, promoting visibility, validation, and critical engagement with diverse identities and experiences (Francis, 2017; Msibi, 2013).

3. *Capacity building and training*: Implement mandatory sensitisation and capacity-building programs for all university stakeholders, including administrators, faculty, staff, and students, to raise awareness about sexual and gender diversity, challenge stereotypes and prejudices, and promote understanding and allyship (Nduna et al., 2017; Nkosi & Masson, 2017).
4. *Support services and resources*: Establish dedicated support services and resources for LGBT students and staff, such as counselling, peer support networks, and information and referral services. Provide access to safe spaces, both physical and virtual, where LGBT individuals can find support, community, and refuge from hostile environments (Matthyse, 2017; Msibi, 2013).
5. *Inclusive residence life*: Review and revise student housing policies and practices to ensure inclusivity and respect for diverse gender identities and sexual orientations. Provide gender-neutral housing options and bathroom facilities, and train residence staff to be sensitive to the unique needs and challenges faced by LGBT students (Vincent & Munyuki, 2017).
6. *Collaborative research and partnerships*: Foster collaborations and partnerships with LGBT community organisations, advocacy groups, and research institutions to promote knowledge sharing, best practices, and resource mobilisation. Engage in participatory research projects that centre the voices and experiences of LGBT individuals in higher education, informing evidence-based interventions and policy recommendations (Nkosi & Masson, 2017).
7. *Accountability and monitoring*: Establish robust accountability mechanisms to ensure the effective implementation and monitoring of inclusive policies and practices. Conduct regular assessments and surveys to gather data on the experiences and needs of LGBT students and staff, informing continuous improvement efforts (Ngabaza, 2022).
8. *Intersectional approach*: Adopt an intersectional lens that recognises and addresses the compounding effects of multiple forms of oppression and marginalisation. Acknowledge and respond to the unique experiences and needs of LGBT individuals who navigate additional challenges based on their race, socioeconomic status, ability, or other marginalised identities (Msibi, 2013; Nkosi & Masson, 2017).
9. *Institutional culture change*: Foster a culture of inclusivity, respect, and social justice within the university community. Encourage open dialogue, critical reflection, and proactive engagement with issues of sexual and gender diversity. Celebrate and affirm LGBT identities and experiences through inclusive events, campaigns, and initiatives (Msibi, 2013; Nduna et al., 2017).
10. *Leadership and advocacy*: Encourage university leadership to take a proactive and visible stance in support of LGBT inclusion and social justice. Engage in advocacy efforts to challenge discriminatory policies, practices, and discourses at the institutional, community, and national levels (Msibi, 2013).

The journey towards widening inclusive education and strengthening meaningful responses to sexual and gender diversity in South African higher education is complex, ongoing, and fraught with challenges. It requires a critical interrogation of the dominant discourses and assumptions that shape the academic landscape, and a commitment to systemic transformation that redistributes power, resources, and opportunities for authentic inclusion and belonging. By troubling the discourses of inclusion, social inclusion, and social justice education, and embracing an intersectional approach that acknowledges and addresses the multiple, concurrent systems of advantage and disadvantage, universities can move towards a more substantive and socially just framing of inclusive education.

The proposed strategies, encompassing policy reform, curriculum transformation, capacity building, support services, inclusive residence life, collaborative research, accountability, intersectionality, institutional culture change, and leadership and advocacy, provide a comprehensive roadmap for widening inclusion and strengthening responses to sexual and gender diversity in higher education. However, it is important to recognise that this work is not a one-time endeavour, but an ongoing process that requires sustained commitment, resource allocation, and the active participation of all stakeholders. It demands a willingness to engage in difficult conversations, challenge entrenched norms and power structures, and imagine new possibilities for creating truly inclusive and transformative educational spaces.

Ultimately, the goal of widening inclusive education for sexual and gender diversity in South African higher education is not only to create safer and more equitable spaces within university walls but also to contribute to the broader societal project of dismantling oppression, challenging heteronormativity, and achieving social justice for all. By nurturing a generation of students, scholars, and leaders who embrace diversity, challenge exclusion, and advocate for the rights and dignity of LGBT individuals, universities can play a pivotal role in shaping a future where all individuals, regardless of their sexual orientation or gender identity, can thrive, belong, and reach their full potential.

## Conclusion

This chapter has critically examined the complex landscape of sexual and gender diversity inclusion within South African higher education institutions. By interrogating the lived experiences of LGBT students and staff, analysing institutional policies and practices, and situating these within broader sociocultural contexts, we have illuminated the persistent challenges and emerging opportunities for fostering authentic inclusion. Our analysis reveals a stark disconnect between South Africa's progressive constitutional ideals and the everyday realities faced by LGBT individuals in university spaces. The pervasive influence of heteronormativity, compulsory heterosexuality, and deeply ingrained societal prejudices continue to shape institutional cultures, policies, and interpersonal dynamics. This manifests in myriad forms of exclusion, from overt discrimination and harassment to more subtle mechanisms of othering and invisibility. Drawing on these insights, we propose a multifaceted approach to widening inclusion that encompasses systemic, cultural, and pedagogical interventions. This approach moves beyond narrow conceptions of access or accommodation to address the root causes of exclusion and marginalisation. Importantly, we argue that meaningful inclusion necessitates a paradigm shift from viewing LGBT individuals as subjects of tolerance or accommodation to recognising them as integral contributors to the intellectual and social fabric of higher education. This shift requires sustained commitment from institutional leadership, ongoing capacity building for all stakeholders, and mechanisms for accountability and continuous improvement.

## References

Ahmed, S. (2022). The marginalised and critical theory: Dialectics of universalism. *International Critical Thought*, *12*(2), 305–326.

Artiles, A. J., & Dyson, A. (2005). Inclusive education in the globalization age: The promise of comparative cultural-historical analysis. In D. Mitchell (Ed.), *Contextualizing inclusive education: Evaluating old and new international perspectives* (pp. 37–62). Routledge.

Bacchi, C., & Eveline, J. (2010). *Mainstreaming politics: Gendering practices and feminist theory*. University of Adelaide Press.

Badat, S. (2015). Institutional combinations and the creation of a new higher education institutional landscape in post-1994 South Africa. In A. Curaj, L. Georghiou, J. C. Harper, & E. Egron-Polak (Eds.), *Mergers and alliances in higher education* (pp. 175–201). Springer.

Bam, A., Kriger, S., & Cottle, Z. (2023). A (mis) guidance of disabled youth: Post-secondary schooling transition experiences in South Africa. *African Journal of Disability (Online)*, *12*, 1–11.

Bearman, M., Smith, C. D., Carbone, A., Slade, S., Baik, C., Hughes-Warrington, M., & Neumann, D. L. (2012). Systematic review methodology in higher education. *Higher Education Research & Development*, *31*(5), 625–640.

Booth, A., Sutton, A., & Papaioannou, D. (2016). *Systematic approaches to a successful literature review* (2nd ed.). Sage.

Braun, V., & Clarke, V. (2022). Conceptual and design thinking for thematic analysis. *Qualitative Psychology*, *9*(1), 3–12.

Brown, A. (2024). Shifting professional and personal identities of the cisgender scholar doing LGBT research. *African Journal of Career Development*, *6*(1), 1–8.

Brown, A., & Diale, B. M. (2017). "You should wear to show what you are": Same-sex sexuality student teachers troubling the heteronormative professional identity. *Gender Questions*, *5*(1), 1–19.

Butler, A., Alpaslan, A., Allen, J. G., & Astbury, G. (2003). Gay and lesbian youth experiences of homophobia in South African secondary education. *Journal of Gay & Lesbian Issues in Education*, *1*(2), 3–28. https://doi.org/10.1300/J367v01n02_02

Buthelezi, J., & Brown, A. (2023). In (ex) clusion of transgender students in South African higher education institutions. *Transformation in Higher Education*, *8*, 11.

Byron, K. (2017). From infantilizing to world making: Safe spaces and trigger warnings on campus. *Family Relations*, *66*(1), 116–125.

DePalma, R., & Francis, D. (2014). Silence, nostalgia, violence, poverty…: What does 'culture' mean for South African sexuality educators? *Culture, Health & Sexuality*, *16*(5), 547–561.

Donohue, D., & Bornman, J. (2014). The challenges of realising inclusive education in South Africa. *South African Journal of Education*, *34*(2), 1–14.

Falconer, E., & Taylor, Y. (2017). Negotiating queer and religious identities in higher education: Queering 'progression' in the 'university experience'. *British Journal of Sociology of Education*, *38*(6), 782–797.

Fourie, M. (1999). Institutional transformation at South African universities: Implications for academic staff. *Higher Education*, *38*, 275–290.

Francis, D. A. (2017). *Troubling the teaching and learning of gender and sexuality diversity in South African education*. Palgrave Macmillan.

Francis, D. A. (2021a). 'A Gay Agenda': Troubling compulsory heterosexuality in a South African university classroom. *Teaching Sociology*, *49*(3), 278–290. https://doi.org/10.1177/0092055X211022472

Francis, D. A. (2021b). 'Oh my word; for us African gays it's another story.' Revealing the intersections between race, same sex-sexuality and schooling in South Africa. *Race Ethnicity and Education*, *24*(1), 1–17. https://doi.org/10.1080/13613324.2019.1679752

Fraser, N. (2001). Social justice in the knowledge society: Redistribution, recognition, and participation. In *Gut zu Wissen conference paper*, Heinrich Böll Stiftung (vol. 5, pp. 1–13).

Gidley, J. M., Hampson, G. P., Wheeler, L., & Bereded-Samuel, E. (2010). From access to success: An integrated approach to quality higher education informed by social inclusion theory and practice. *Higher Education Policy*, 23, 123–147.

Gordon, S. F., & Collins, A. (2013). 'We face rape. We face all things': Understandings of gender based violence amongst female students at a South African university: Original contributions. *African Safety Promotion*, 11(2), 93–106.

Gough, D., Oliver, S., & Thomas, J. (Eds.). (2017). *An introduction to systematic reviews* (2nd ed.). Sage.

Howell, C., & Lazarus, S. (2003). Access and participation for students with disabilities in South African higher education: Challenging accepted truths and recognising new possibilities. *Perspectives in Education*, 21(3), 59–74.

Jagessar, V., & Msibi, T. (2015). "It's not that bad": Homophobia in the residences of a university in KwaZulu-Natal, Durban, South Africa. *Agenda*, 29(1), 63–73.

Koenane, M. L. J. (2013). Xenophobic attacks in South Africa–An ethical response: Have we lost the underlying spirit of Ubuntu? *International Journal of Science, Commerce and Humanities*, 1(6), 106–111.

Leibowitz, B. (2016, August). Power, knowledge and learning: A humble contribution to the decolonisation debate. In *Keynote address delivered at the 10th annual teaching & learning conference*, University of KwaZulu-Natal (Vol. 16, pp. 31–42).

Lesch, E., Brits, S., & Naidoo, N. T. (2017). 'Walking on eggshells to not offend people': Experiences of same-sex student couples at a South African university. *South African Journal of Higher Education*, 31(4), 127–149.

Lourens, H. (2015). *The lived experiences of higher education for students with a visual impairment: A phenomenological study at two universities in the Western Cape, South Africa* [Doctoral dissertation, Stellenbosch University, Stellenbosch].

Louw, S. (2024). Die konstruksie van Afrikaanse manlikheid in tydskrifte:'n Fokus op seksualiteit. *Stilet: Tydskrif van die Afrikaaanse Letterkundevereniging*, 36(1), 3–33.

Lythreatis, S., Singh, S. K., & El-Kassar, A. N. (2022). The digital divide: A review and future research agenda. *Technological Forecasting and Social Change*, 175, 1–11.

Mafumo, T. N. (2010). *Managing racial integration in South African public schools: In defense of democratic action* [Doctoral dissertation, University of Stellenbosch, Stellenbosch].

Martin, A. J., Sperling, R. A., & Newton, K. J. (Eds.). (2020). *Handbook of educational psychology and students with special needs*. Routledge.

Matthyse, G. (2017). Heteronormative higher education: Challenging this status quo through LGBTIQ awareness-raising. *South African Journal of Higher Education*, 31(4), 112–126.

Msibi, T. (2011). The lies we have been told: On (homo) sexuality in Africa. *Africa today*, 58(1), 55–77.

Msibi, T. (2012). 'I'm used to it now': Experiences of homophobia among queer youth in South African township schools. *Gender and Education*, 24(5), 515–533.

Msibi, T. (2013). Queering transformation in higher education. *Perspectives in Education*, 31(2), 65–73.

Naidu, M., & Mutumbara, V. (2017). Questioning heteronormative higher education spaces: Experiences of lesbian women at a South African university. *South African Journal of Higher Education*, 31(4), 34–52.

Nakidien, T., Singh, M., & Sayed, Y. (2021). Teachers and teacher education: Limitations and possibilities of attaining SDG 4 in South Africa. *Education Science*, 11(2), 1–13.

Nduna, M., Mthombeni, A., Mavhandu-Mudzusi, A. H., & Mogotsi, I. (2017). Studying sexuality: LGBTI experiences in institutions of higher education in Southern Africa. *South African Journal of Higher Education*, 31(4), 1–13.

Ngabaza, S., Shefer, T., & Macleod, C. I. (2016). "Girls need to behave like girls you know": the complexities of applying a gender justice goal within sexuality education in South African schools. *Reproductive Health Matters*, 24(48), 71–78.

Ngabaza, S. (2022). Parents resist sexuality education through digital activism. *Journal of Education*, 89, 84–104.

Nkosi, S., & Masson, F. (2017). 'Christianity and homosexuality: Contradictory or complementary? A qualitative study of the experiences of Christian homosexual university students. *South African Journal of Higher Education*, 31(4), 72–93.

Petticrew, M., & Roberts, H. (2006). *Systematic reviews in the social sciences: A practical guide*. Blackwell Publishing.

Republic of South Africa. (2018). *Strategic disability policy framework in the post-school education and training system*. Department of Higher Education and Training (DHET). Retrieved November 30, 2023, from http://www.dhet.gov.za/SiteAssets/Gazettes/Approved%20Strategic%20Disability%20Policy%20Framework%20Layout220518.pdf

Rodó-Zárate, M. (2023). Intersectionality and the spatiality of emotions in feminist research. *The Professional Geographer*, 75(4), 676–681.

Salmi, J., & D'Addio, A. (2021). Policies for achieving inclusion in higher education. *Policy Reviews in Higher Education*, 5(1), 47–72.

Sithole, S. (2015). Challenges faced by gay, lesbian, bisexual and transgender (GLBT) students at a South African university. *TD: The Journal for Transdisciplinary Research in Southern Africa*, 11(4), 193–219.

StatsSA. (2019). *Education series volume V: Higher education and skills in South Africa, 2017*. Statistics South Africa.

Sutherland, C., Roberts, B., Gabriel, N., Struwig, J., & Gordon, S. (2016). *Progressive prudes: A survey of attitudes towards homosexuality & gender non-conformity in South Africa*. The Other Foundation.

Tienda, M. (2013). Diversity≠inclusion: Promoting integration in higher education. *Educational Researcher*, 42(9), 467–475.

Tobbell, J., Burton, R., Gaynor, A., Golding, B., Greenhough, K., Rhodes, C., & White, S. (2021). Inclusion in higher education: an exploration of the subjective experiences of students. *Journal of Further and Higher Education*, 45(2), 284–295.

Tshilongo, T., & Rothmann, J. (2019). A sociological exploration of the need for safe spaces for lesbian and gay students on a South African university campus. *Transformation in Higher Education*, 4(1), 1–12.

UN. (2016). *One humanity: Shared responsibility*. Report of the Secretary-General for the World Humanitarian Summit. UN. http://sgreport.worldhumanitariansummit.org

Vincent, L., & Chiwandire, D. (2019). Funding and inclusion in higher education institutions for students with disabilities. *African Journal of Disability*, 8(1), 1–12.

Vincent, L. D., & Munyuki, C. (2017). 'It's tough being gay'. Gay, lesbian and bisexual students' experiences of being 'at home' in South African university residence life. *South African Journal of Higher Education*, 31(4), 14–33.

Walker, M. (2018). Aspirations and equality in higher education: Gender in a South African University. *Cambridge Journal of Education*, 48(1), 123–139.

Walton, E., & Lloyd, G. (2011). An analysis of metaphors used for the inclusive education in South Africa. *Acta Academica*, 43(3), 1–31.

Walton, E., & Rusznyak, L. (2020). Cumulative knowledge-building for inclusive education in initial teacher education. *European Journal of Teacher Education*, 43(1), 18–37.

Wolbring, G., & Lillywhite, A. (2021). Equity/equality, diversity, and inclusion (EDI) in universities: The case of disabled people. *Societies*, 11(2), 1–34.

Chapter 14

# Leveraging Assistive Technologies to Advocate for Accessibility for Students with Disabilities, an Inclusive Curriculum Practice

*Mohau Ben Manyarela, Mochina Mphuthi and Ntsoaki Joyce Malebo*

Central University of Technology, Free State, South Africa

## Abstract

This systematic review addresses the pivotal role of assistive technologies (AT) in enhancing accessibility and inclusivity within higher education curricula for students with disabilities. It critically evaluates how these technologies are integrated into educational frameworks, identifying both the advancements and the persisting barriers that affect their effective utilisation. AT are heralded as crucial for enabling access yet are often deployed without a cohesive framework, leading to significant disparities in their effectiveness across different educational settings. Qualitative in-depth analysis reveals that while AT offer potential enhancements in accessibility, their integration is frequently hampered by inadequate professional development for educators and a lack of systemic support. These deficiencies contribute to the uneven implementation of inclusive practices, particularly affecting students from socioeconomically disadvantaged backgrounds who may need more access to necessary technological resources. Furthermore, the review explores the variance in the application of these technologies within different socio-cultural and infrastructural contexts, emphasising the need for contextually adapted solutions to bridge the accessibility gap in diverse educational landscapes. Given the findings, this review advocates for robust policy reforms and strategic educational practices to foster a more inclusive learning environment. It calls for comprehensive training programmes for educators, enhanced support for the development and maintenance of AT, and a greater alignment of these initiatives with the principles of Universal Design for Learning (UDL).

*Keywords*: Assistive technologies; curriculum practice; inclusive education; Universal Design for Learning; learning

## Introduction

Higher education is experiencing growth in number of students with disabilities and those with learning barriers, which requires institutions to develop an inclusive learning environment. Mpofu (2023) hails AT as a panacea for enabling access to learning for students with disabilities, however, Batty and Reilly (2023) caution that significant barriers persist in integrating these technologies into a genuinely inclusive curriculum. Beyene et al. (2023) emphasise that while AT are available, their deployment in educational settings often lacks a cohesive framework, leaving many students underserved. This disconnect points to a broader systemic issue, where the potential of technology to support diverse learning needs still needs to be fully realised (Beyene et al., 2023).

Moreover, integrating AT into the curriculum is not just a logistical challenge but a pedagogical one. This is supported by O'Sullivan et al. (2023) in their claim that educational institutions frequently struggle with adapting teaching methodologies to incorporate technological aids effectively. This inadequacy may lead to a disjointed educational experience for students requiring these technologies. Furthermore, Al-Dababneh and Al-Zboon (2022) argue that the absence of comprehensive training for educators on using AT exacerbates this issue, suggesting a gap in professional development. In line with this narrative, Park et al. (2022) highlight the critical need for curriculum developers to consider AT not as supplementary but as integral to curriculum design, ensuring all students have equal access to learning opportunities.

Various studies have been conducted on leveraging AT to advocate for accessibility for students with disabilities within an inclusive curriculum practice. For instance, Danemayer et al. (2021) examined the disparity in access to AT across different socioeconomic groups. The study revealed that students from lower socioeconomic backgrounds are less likely to benefit from these technologies due to resource limitations in their educational environments. The study argued for a more equitable distribution of resources to ensure that all students, regardless of their economic status, have access to necessary technologies. This study underlines the need for policy adjustments to bridge this gap and promote inclusivity.

Similarly, Atanga et al. (2020) focussed on the training aspect of educators in the use of AT. The study determined that many teachers are not adequately prepared to integrate these tools into their teaching practices effectively. The lack of proficiency limits the potential benefits of AT, creating an uneven playing field for students with disabilities. Patel advocated for comprehensive training programmes as part of continuing professional development for educators. This approach would enhance educators' capabilities, thereby improving the overall effectiveness of AT in the classroom and ensuring that students with disabilities receive the support they need.

In addition to educator's adequate training, a study by Helena Martins et al. (2018) explored the need for establishing an inclusive higher education, and the findings identified attitude and culture within higher education as some of the barriers to the use of assistive devices as enablers to student learning. Moriña (2019) also discovered that over and above the needs of students with disabilities, barriers of negative attitude and culture pose a significant obstacle impacting students' experience, fear of judgement, and feelings of frustration.

In the African context, Nkomo and Dube (2022) explored how AT are utilised within schools in rural areas of South Africa. Their research highlighted significant infrastructure and internet connectivity challenges that hinder the effective use of such technologies in these regions. The findings reveal that despite the potential of AT to transform educational access, their impact is curtailed by foundational issues such as unreliable electricity and internet services. The study firmly concluded that infrastructural improvements are a prerequisite for the successful integration of AT in education.

Furthermore, Adebayo and Ayorinde (2022) investigated the role of government policy in supporting the use of AT in Nigerian schools. The study noted that while there are policies in place intended to promote inclusivity, their implementation is often inconsistent and lacks rigorous enforcement. The study calls for a more substantial commitment from government bodies to draft inclusive policies and ensure their effective implementation. By doing so, the gap between policy and practice can be bridged, fostering a more inclusive educational environment for students with disabilities across Africa (Makoelle & Makhalemele, 2020).

Despite the growing body of research on leveraging AT in education, there remains a noticeable gap in systematic evaluations of these studies, particularly from an African perspective. Many of the existing studies, while insightful, are fragmented and lack a cohesive synthesis that could provide a comprehensive understanding of how AT can be leveraged to maximise access to learning for students with disabilities. This systematic review is essential to bridge this gap by consolidating existing research, highlighting regional disparities, and underscoring the unique needs and solutions applicable to African settings. Consequently, this review aims to inform policymakers and educators, guiding more effective strategies for integrating AT into the curriculum to enhance accessibility for students with disabilities genuinely.

This systematic review aims to respond to the following research question: 'How can AT be leveraged to enhance accessibility and inclusivity in the higher education curriculum for students with disabilities?' To conduct this systematic study, Mphuthi (2024) recommends the use of the PICo framework in a qualitative review. PICo is an abbreviation for Population, Interest, and Context to provide guidelines to interrogate the literature to respond to the identified research question which guided the study.

Research question using the PICo Framework:

- Population (P): Students with disabilities.
- Interest (I): Leveraging AT.
- Context (Co): Inclusivity and access in higher education curriculum practice.

In answering the research question, the study aims to guide policymakers and educational leaders in formulating strategies that mitigate current barriers and enhance the overall educational experiences of students with disabilities. This systematic approach to integrating AT within the curriculum is crucial for achieving true educational equity and inclusivity.

## Theoretical Framework

This chapter is guided by the UDL, a framework developed by researchers at the Center for Applied Special Technology in the 1990s (Rose et al., 2005). Courtad (2019) argues that UDL is based on the premise that educational environments and products should be designed from the outset to accommodate all kinds of learners, thus minimising the need for subsequent modifications. According to Rose et al. (2006), the framework outlines three primary principles for achieving this: providing multiple means of representation to give learners various ways of acquiring information and knowledge, offering multiple means of action and expression to provide learners alternatives for demonstrating what they know, and supplying multiple means of engagement to tap into learners' interests, offering appropriate challenges, and increasing motivation.

UDL is highly relevant to this study as it directly addresses the need for educational practices that include AT to enhance accessibility for students with disabilities. By applying UDL principles, the study aims to explore and advocate for curriculum designs that inherently consider all students' diverse needs and abilities, thereby reducing learning barriers. This theory addresses the main problem by suggesting that if educational materials and environments are flexible and accommodating from the start, they can better serve a broader range of variability in learner abilities and preferences, including those requiring AT. Thus, UDL promotes a more inclusive educational landscape and ensures that all students have equitable access to learning opportunities.

## Methodology and Design

This systematic chapter employed a qualitative methodology to investigate deeply the varied experiences and contextual factors influencing the use of AT in the curriculum practice in educational settings. By synthesising qualitative studies, the chapter aimed to uncover patterns and themes that reveal the complexities of implementing inclusive practices. This approach gave a comprehensive understanding of the practical challenges and successes encountered in diverse educational environments (Tran et al., 2023).

## Inclusion and Exclusion Criteria

For this systematic chapter, the inclusion criteria were qualitative studies focussed on the use of AT in educational settings and specifically addressed the incorporation of these technologies within the framework of UDL. Studies were also required to be published in English, conducted within the last 10 years, and involve primary secondary and higher educational settings. The exclusion criteria ruled out studies that were purely quantitative or theoretical, did not directly involve AT, or fell outside the scope of educational settings. Additionally, studies not accessible in full text, such as abstracts or conference proceedings without detailed results, and research conducted more than ten years ago were excluded to ensure the relevance and recency of the data analysed.

## Search Strategy

For the systematic chapter, a comprehensive search strategy was employed across several academic databases, including Google Scholar, ProQuest, Elsevier, EBSCOHost, and Web of Science (Fundoni et al., 2023). The search combined vital terms related to AT and inclusive education within the context of UDL. The terms were combined using Boolean operators to refine the search and ensure comprehensive coverage of relevant literature. Initial searches were followed by a chapter of reference lists in identified articles to capture additional studies that may not have appeared in the database searches.

Tables 14.1 and 14.2 include specific and broad terms to comprehensively cover the study's thematic scope across different academic databases, ensuring a robust search for relevant literature from 2014 to 2024.

## Study Selection

The study selection for this systematic review involved a meticulous process where initially 120,248 articles were identified and subsequently narrowed down through rigorous screening based on relevance, inclusion criteria, and quality assessments (Martinez et al., 2023). Ultimately, 15 articles met all specified criteria, providing

Table 14.1. Search Terms Used.

| Search Terms Table | |
| --- | --- |
| **Concepts** | **Search Terms** |
| Assistive Technologies | ('assistive technologies' OR 'adaptive technologies') |
| Inclusive Education | ('inclusive education' OR 'accessibility') |
| Universal Design | ('Universal Design for Learning' OR 'UDL') |
| Educational Settings | ('education' OR 'school' OR 'classroom') |

Table 14.2. Search Strings.

| Database | Search Strings | Year Filter |
| --- | --- | --- |
| Google Scholar | ('assistive technologies' AND 'inclusive education' AND 'Universal Design for Learning' AND 'students with disabilities') | 2014–2024 |
| ProQuest | ('assistive technologies' AND 'inclusive education' AND 'Universal Design for Learning' AND 'students with disabilities') | 2014–2024 |
| Elsevier | ('assistive technologies' AND 'inclusive curriculum' AND 'Universal Design for Learning' AND ('educational settings' OR 'schools')) | 2014–2024 |
| EBSCOhost | ('assistive technologies' AND 'accessibility' AND 'Universal Design for Learning' AND 'students with disabilities' AND ('primary education' OR 'secondary education')) | 2014–2024 |
| Web of Science | ('assistive technologies' AND 'inclusive practices' AND 'Universal Design for Learning' AND 'students with disabilities' AND 'education') | 2014–2024 |

a robust foundation to explore the effective integration of AT within inclusive educational practices for students with disabilities.

*Identification*

A comprehensive search across multiple databases (Google Scholar, ProQuest, Elsevier, EBSCOhost, and Web of Science) was conducted, yielding a total of 120,248 articles. The searches were executed using specifically designed search strings incorporating terms like 'assistive technologies', 'inclusive education', 'Universal Design for Learning', and 'students with disabilities', relevant to the study's focus from 2014 to 2024.

*Screening*

Out of the initial pool, 118,388 articles were excluded for non-relevance to the desired search terms. This massive filtering was necessary to focus only on articles that directly address the use of AT in educational settings within the specified frameworks and contexts.

*Eligibility*

The remaining 1,860 records were then rigorously screened against inclusion criteria: articles must be peer-reviewed, focussed on the integration of AT within educational curriculum, and relevant to accessibility and inclusivity for students with disabilities. This process led to the exclusion of 1,689 articles that did not meet these specific criteria.

*Inclusion*

The final phase involved a detailed assessment of the remaining 171 articles based on their titles, abstracts, and full texts. This resulted in the exclusion of 151 articles – 98 due to irrelevant titles, 43 for abstracts that failed to substantiate a focus on practical implementations, and 15 for full texts that did not adequately address the research question or were methodologically unsound.

*Included*

Ultimately, 15 articles fully met all the criteria and were included in the systematic review. These articles were deemed most pertinent for a comprehensive understanding of how AT can be effectively leveraged within educational settings to enhance accessibility and inclusivity for students with disabilities.

## Limitations of the Study

This systematic literature review had several limitations that might affect the generalisability and applicability of its findings. Firstly, the review was constrained to articles published between 2014 and 2024, potentially excluding relevant studies that predated this period. Additionally, the focus was strictly on literature available in English, which might have omitted significant contributions in other languages, thereby limiting the cultural diversity and broader applicability of the results. Moreover, while this review concentrated on qualitative research, this may have skewed the findings towards more subjective interpretations and potentially underrepresented quantitative analyses, which could provide different insights into the effectiveness of AT in educational settings. Lastly, the selection of databases, though comprehensive, may not have encompassed all relevant publications, and the time-limited nature of the research might have restricted a more exhaustive search. Despite these limitations, the review aimed to provide a thorough synthesis of the available literature on leveraging AT for inclusivity in educational practices for students with disabilities.

## Ethical Considerations

Conducting a comprehensive literature review entailed adhering to strict ethical standards, even in the absence of primary data collection. The review needed to maintain the highest standards of confidentiality and academic integrity, including proper citation to avoid plagiarism (Guba & Tsivinskaya, 2024). Additionally, ensuring objectivity throughout the review process was paramount to avoid bias in the synthesis of findings Mphuthi (2024). Although this study did not involve direct participation of human subjects, nor did it require ethical approval from an institutional review board, it was imperative to handle the reviewed literature with the utmost respect for the original authors' intellectual property rights. Moreover, the absence of external funding for this study underscored the need for meticulous, unbiased analysis, further emphasising the importance of ethical rigour in the absence of financial influence (Nakitare & Otike, 2023). The findings provided insightful information, showcasing the researcher's commitment to ethical scholarly practices.

## Thematic Analysis

The study employed thematic analysis to systematically evaluate and interpret the data collected from the reviewed articles. According to Christou (2023), thematic analysis is a widely used method for identifying, analysing, and reporting patterns (themes) within data. It provides a flexible and invaluable research tool capable of offering a rich and detailed yet complex account of data (Cernasev & Axon, 2023). Thematic analysis was particularly relevant to this study as it allowed for the extraction of common themes regarding the challenges, opportunities, and best practices associated with the use of AT in higher education. By applying this method, the study looked deeply into the qualitative data to uncover underlying issues and trends that may have yet to be apparent through quantitative methods alone.

## Findings

The systematic review results from the extraction and analysis of findings from 15 studies, each contributing unique insights into the use of AT within inclusive educational settings. This synthesis revealed various perspectives on the challenges and successes associated with implementing AT to enhance accessibility for students with disabilities. The selected studies, published between 2014 and 2024, encompassed a range of geographical locations and educational contexts, providing a comprehensive overview of the topic. Table 14.3 summarises each author's contribution, the specific focus of their study, and key findings, facilitating a clear understanding of the collective evidence and diverse viewpoints in this field.

## Thematic Analysis of Data Extracted from the Articles

### *Theme 1: Integration of Assistive Technologies*

The integration of AT within educational settings is a critical area of focus, emphasised by several studies in the extraction table. Hayhoe (2014) highlights the importance of guiding educators and technologists to develop AT not merely as supplementary tools but as integral components of students' educational experiences. This perspective suggests a shift from traditional uses of AT, where technologies often act as aids external to the regular learning process, to a more embedded approach. By integrating AT into daily educational practices, the goal is to ensure that students with disabilities experience seamless and meaningful participation in all learning activities. This approach requires a comprehensive

Table 14.3. Data Extraction and Analysis Table.

| No. | Author | Topic | Summary of the Findings |
|---|---|---|---|
| 1 | Hayhoe (2014) | The Need for Inclusive Accessible Technologies for Students with Disabilities and Learning Difficulties | Aims to guide educators and technologists on effectively developing AT that are not merely supplementary but integral to students' educational experiences |
| 2 | Kioko and Makoelle (2014) | Inclusion in Higher Education: Learning Experiences of Disabled Students at Winchester University | The study is driven by the belief that inclusive educational practices enhance the participation and success of all students |
| 3 | Ampratwum et al. (2016) | Barriers to the Use of Computer Assistive Technology among Students with Visual Impairment in Ghana: The Case of Akropong School for the Blind | Findings reveal that the primary barriers are related to personal adaptation to the technology rather than external factors |
| 4 | Schock and Lee (2016) | Children's Voices: Perspectives on Using Assistive Technology | This research advocates for more targeted training for educators and a more consistent application of AT to support students with LD, emphasising the need for educational practices that respond more effectively to the diverse needs of learners |
| 5 | Cook, and Polgar (2014) | Assistive Technologies in Urban Settings | Focusses on the deployment of AT in urban educational settings, revealing higher adoption rates compared to rural areas |
| 6 | Boot et al. (2018) | Access to Assistive Technology for People With Intellectual Disabilities: A Systematic Review to Identify Barriers and Facilitators | The review also highlights the critical need for improved policy and systems to support access to AT, emphasising that such enhancements could significantly impact the well-being and inclusion of people with ID in society |

(*Continued*)

Table 14.3. (*Continued*)

| No. | Author | Topic | Summary of the Findings |
|---|---|---|---|
| 7 | Mpu and Adu (2021) | The Challenges of Inclusive Education and Its Implementation in Schools: The South African Perspective | The findings underscored that the educational system still significantly segregates learners with disabilities, primarily due to infrastructural inadequacies and educational practices that fail to accommodate diverse learning needs |
| 8 | Ndlovu (2021) | Challenges of the Universal Design of Learning in South African Higher Education | The chapter calls for a more profound transformation in educational practices to truly realise inclusive education |
| 9 | Ditlhale and Johnson (2022) | Teacher Attitudes Towards Assistive Technology in OdeL Environment | Explores teacher attitudes towards AT, identifying a need for better training and support |
| 10 | Zongozzi (2022) | Accessible Quality Higher Education for Students with Disabilities in a South African Open Distance and e-Learning Institution: Challenges | Explores teacher attitudes towards AT, identifying a need for better training and support |
| 11 | Ochsner, et al. (2022) | Rethinking Assistive Technologies: Users, Environments, Digital Media, and App-Practices of Hearing | Investigates accessibility challenges in higher education, with a focus on the need for better technology integration |
| 12 | Makoelle and Mosito (2023) | Preparations of Pre-service Teachers for Inclusive Classrooms | Findings emphasise the significance of adapting teaching methods and attitudes to meet the needs of all students, particularly those with special educational needs and disabilities |
| 13 | Smith et al. (2024) | Innovations in Assistive Technologies in Higher Education | Emphasises that AT are not merely supportive tools but are central to enabling persons with disabilities to live independently and participate fully in all aspects of life |

Table 14.3. (*Continued*)

| 14 | Schwab et al. (2024) | Inclusion Does Not Solely Apply to Students with Disabilities | The findings suggest a need for educational frameworks that support diverse learning needs across the entire student body, advocating for an inclusive approach in teacher training programmes |
|---|---|---|---|
| 15 | Timuş et al. (2024) | Explores the Perceptions of Faculty in the EU and US Regarding the Implementation of UDL and Inclusive Pedagogy in Higher Education | The study's findings emphasise the importance of these pedagogical approaches in enhancing educational accessibility and equity |

understanding of both the technological and pedagogical aspects of AT use, suggesting a need for collaboration between educators, technologists, and disability experts to create environments that genuinely cater to the diverse needs of all students.

Similarly, Schock and Lee (2016) advocate for targeted training for educators to ensure a consistent and effective application of AT in supporting students with learning disabilities (LD). Their research underscores the necessity for educational practices to adapt to the diverse needs of learners, which the strategic use of AT can significantly facilitate. The call for more structured educator training reflects an understanding that the successful integration of AT depends heavily on teachers' ability to operate and incorporate these technologies into their teaching strategies. Both Hayhoe, Schock and Lee point towards an educational landscape where AT serves as a bridge, not a barrier, enhancing the learning experience for students with disabilities by making educational content accessible and engaging.

## *Theme 2: Barriers to Accessibility*

The barriers to accessibility in educational settings, particularly in AT use, represent a significant challenge, as highlighted by several studies. Ampratwum et al. (2016) focussed on the use of computer-AT at the Akropong School for the Blind in Ghana, identifying that primary barriers are related more to personal adaptation to technology rather than external factors. This indicates that the difficulties often lie in the availability of technologies and the user's ability to effectively engage with these tools due to insufficient training or familiarity. Such insights emphasise the need for comprehensive user-oriented training programmes that address the technical skills and the confidence required to navigate these technologies efficiently.

Additionally, Mpu and Adu (2021) discuss the systemic barriers within the South African educational system that segregate learners with disabilities, highlighting infrastructural inadequacies and educational practices that fail to accommodate diverse learning needs. These barriers are not just physical but are also embedded in the attitudes and practices of the educational institutions themselves. The findings from their study suggest that overcoming these barriers requires not only policy changes but also a shift in educational culture towards more inclusive practices. These studies together illustrate the multifaceted nature of accessibility barriers in education, spanning from personal to systemic levels. Addressing these barriers calls for a holistic approach that includes policy reform, educational training, and infrastructure development to create genuinely inclusive learning environments.

These findings from the studies of Ampratwum et al. (2016) and Mpu and Adu (2021) highlight critical areas for intervention to enhance the accessibility of education through AT and inclusive practices. Overcoming these barriers is essential for ensuring that all students, particularly those with disabilities, have equal opportunities to benefit from educational advancements.

### *Theme 3: Teacher Training and Attitudes*

The third theme of Teacher Training and Attitudes encompasses significant aspects of educational practices that influence the success of inclusive schooling and the integration of AT. This theme is highlighted in studies where the focus is on the preparedness and mind-set of teachers towards accommodating diverse learning needs. Schock and Lee (2016) emphasise the necessity for more targeted training for educators to enable a more consistent application of AT to support students with LD. Their research points out that while AT can provide substantial aid to students, its effectiveness largely depends on the teachers' ability to implement these technologies appropriately within the curriculum. This calls for enhanced training programmes that equip teachers with the necessary technical skills and pedagogical strategies tailored towards inclusivity.

Furthermore, Ditlhale and Johnson (2022) explore teacher attitudes towards AT in an Open and Distance Learning (ODeL) environment, identifying a pressing need for better training and support. Their findings suggest teachers need more confidence in using AT, primarily due to inadequate training. This affects their attitudes towards implementing such technologies, often leading to underutilisation in educational settings. Both studies underscore the critical role of teacher training in shaping the educational landscape to be more inclusive. By improving teacher training, educational institutions can enhance teachers' attitudes towards and proficiency in using AT, thereby fostering an environment more conducive to learning for all students.

These insights suggest that to address the challenges posed by diverse educational needs effectively, it is crucial to focus on teachers' attitudes and competencies. Professional development programmes that emphasise inclusivity and provide practical training on AT can bridge the gap between the potential benefits of technology in education and the current reality of its underutilisation due to training deficiencies.

### Theme 4: Educational Equity and Inclusivity

The theme of Educational Equity and Inclusivity is central to the discussions surrounding the broader goals of inclusive education. This theme captures the essential challenge of creating educational systems that not only accommodate but actively support the diversity of student needs across various spectrums, including cultural, physical, and cognitive differences. The studies by Schwab et al. (2024) and Timuş et al. (2024) offer profound insights into how inclusivity is perceived and implemented across different educational settings and regions.

Schwab et al. (2024) investigate the perceptions of inclusion beyond just students with disabilities, advocating for educational frameworks that support diverse learning needs across the entire student body. Their study highlights the necessity for teacher training programmes to embed inclusivity as a fundamental principle, ensuring that all students, regardless of their educational needs or backgrounds, are equally supported. This approach challenges the traditional norms of education systems and calls for a paradigm shift towards genuine inclusivity where every student's needs are met.

Similarly, Timuş et al. (2024) explore faculty perceptions in the EU and US regarding the implementation of UDL and inclusive pedagogy. Their findings emphasise the importance of these approaches in enhancing educational accessibility and equity, suggesting that inclusive pedagogies are critical in meeting the diverse needs of students in higher education. The study points to the need for ongoing adjustments and reforms in teaching practices and curriculum designs to accommodate and celebrate diversity within educational institutions.

Both sets of research advocate for systemic changes that go beyond mere accommodation. They call for a rethinking of educational practices to ensure that inclusivity and equity are not just add-ons but are integrated into the core functioning of educational institutions. These changes are crucial for dismantling barriers to education that students from diverse backgrounds often face, thus promoting a more equitable and inclusive educational environment where all students have the opportunity to succeed.

### Theme 5: Diverse Needs in Inclusive Settings

The theme of Diverse Needs in Inclusive Settings highlights the importance of understanding and addressing the varied requirements of students within educational environments that aim to be genuinely inclusive. This theme is underscored by several authors' work emphasising the necessity to tailor educational practices to suit a wide array of learning preferences, cultural backgrounds, and ability levels.

The study by Makoelle and Mosito (2023) examined how pre-service teachers are prepared to manage classrooms that include students with special educational needs and disabilities alongside their peers. Their findings highlight the importance of training teachers to adapt their teaching methods and attitudes to meet the diverse needs of all students, emphasising that effective inclusive education depends not only on physical accessibility but also on curriculum and pedagogical inclusivity. This involves a comprehensive approach to teacher education that integrates principles of diversity and inclusion from the outset, preparing teachers to recognise and respond to the different ways students engage with and process information.

Furthermore, the systematic review by Boot et al. (2018) identifies barriers and facilitators to individuals with intellectual disabilities accessing AT. This study broadens the discussion of diversity to include technological access, pointing out that true inclusivity must consider how different groups access and use technology as part of their learning experience. The findings advocate for policies and practices that not only provide technologies but also ensure these tools are effectively integrated into learning environments in ways that respect and enhance the capabilities of all users.

These studies collectively argue for a more nuanced understanding of what it means to create inclusive settings. They suggest that educational strategies should be robust and flexible enough to cater to the full spectrum of student needs. This approach not only benefits those with recognised disabilities but also enhances the learning environment for all students by fostering a culture of adaptability, respect, and support for diverse learning styles and needs. By doing so, educational institutions can move closer to achieving true inclusivity, where every student has the opportunity to thrive based on their unique strengths and challenges.

### *Theme 6: Policy and System Enhancements*

The Policy and System Enhancements theme centres on the necessity for refined policies and improved systemic support as crucial steps towards facilitating inclusive education and the effective use of AT. This theme is prominently discussed in the research of Boot et al. (2018) and the study conducted by Mpu and Adu (2021), each pointing out the vital role that robust policies and systemic frameworks play in enabling and sustaining educational inclusivity.

Boot et al. (2018) investigate the systemic barriers to accessing AT for people with intellectual disabilities, emphasising the critical need for policies that not only make these technologies available but also ensure they are integrated into educational and social systems in meaningful ways. Their review underscores the gap between the potential benefits of AT and their actual impact, largely attributed to deficiencies in policy frameworks that need to adequately support their deployment and maintenance. The study calls for a comprehensive overhaul of policy frameworks to ensure they more effectively address the specific needs and circumstances of users, enhancing the accessibility and utility of technological aids.

Similarly, Mpu and Adu (2021) explore the challenges of implementing inclusive education in South African schools, revealing that practical implementation needs to catch up despite the progressive policies aimed at promoting inclusivity. They highlight the disconnection between policy intentions and classroom realities, particularly noting that infrastructural inadequacies and entrenched educational practices often undermine these policies. This study suggests that for policies to be truly effective, they must be accompanied by rigorous implementation strategies and ongoing monitoring to ensure they bring about the desired changes in educational practices.

These insights from the literature suggest that while policies are essential for setting the goals and frameworks for inclusive education and technology use, their effectiveness ultimately depends on the systems put in place to implement and sustain them. Enhanced policies must be supported by concrete systemic changes that include adequate funding, professional development for educators, and robust support structures to bridge the gap between policy and practice. By focussing on policy enhancement and systemic overhaul, educational institutions and governments must effectively foster environments that genuinely support diversity, accessibility, and inclusion.

## Implications of the Study

When examined through the lens of UDL, the theoretical implications of the identified themes underline the necessity of adopting a holistic and flexible approach to education that proactively accommodates diverse learner needs. UDL advocates for the development of a curriculum that provides multiple means of representation, expression, and engagement to ensure that all students, regardless of their abilities or backgrounds, have equal opportunities to learn and succeed (Meyer et al., 2014). The themes relating to the Integration of AT and Diverse Needs in Inclusive Settings particularly resonate with the UDL principle of providing multiple means of representation. These themes highlight the critical role of AT in removing barriers to access and participation in the learning process. By embedding these technologies into the curriculum design, as Hayhoe (2014) and Schock and Lee (2016) suggested, educators can ensure that instructional materials are accessible and applicable to all students, thus aligning with UDL's goal of fostering an inclusive educational environment.

Furthermore, the themes of teacher training and attitudes and policy and system enhancements reveal the importance of the other two UDL principles: providing multiple means of action and expression, as well as multiple means of engagement. The need for enhanced teacher training, as discussed by Ditlhale and Johnson (2022), reflects the necessity for educators to be equipped with the skills to use AT and the pedagogical strategies that support diverse expressions and actions from students. This is crucial for fostering an educational setting where students feel competent and motivated to participate, aligning with UDL's emphasis on engagement. Moreover, the emphasis on policy enhancements highlights the systemic support required to uphold these principles effectively across educational systems, ensuring that inclusivity is not merely aspirational but a practical reality (Boot et al., 2018; Mpu & Adu, 2021).

Lastly, the analysis of educational equity and Inclusivity within the framework of UDL underscores the theoretical implication that education systems must transcend traditional approaches to teaching and learning that cater predominantly to the majority. By implementing UDL, educational institutions commit to a paradigm where every student's learning needs are anticipated and valued as inherently equal. This approach challenges the status quo and promotes a culture of inclusivity that is dynamic and responsive to the evolving educational landscape. The synthesis of these themes through the UDL framework suggests a transformative shift in educational practices, advocating for a more compassionate, equitable, and inclusive approach to education that truly embodies the principles of UDL (Smith et al., 2024; Timuş et al., 2024).

These findings collectively highlight how UDL's theoretical underpinnings can guide and enhance the practical application of the themes identified, providing a robust framework for addressing the challenges and opportunities in modern education.

## Conclusion

This chapter intended to show how AT can be used to enhance the participation of students with disabilities in the higher education curriculum in and accessible and equitable manner. The findings from the systematic literature review reveal that there are challenges to the incorporation of AT however with more research and deeper analysis of different educational contexts indicate that this concept is possible. The study also advocates for a more comprehensive original research on use of AT to enhance learning for students with disabilities.

## Recommendations

To effectively advance the integration of UDL principles and AT within educational frameworks, several strategic recommendations are proposed. Firstly, enhanced professional development is crucial. Educational institutions should commit to ongoing professional development for educators that emphasises the practical application of UDL principles. This training should incorporate hands-on experiences with AT and adaptive teaching strategies to ensure that educators are fully equipped to meet the diverse needs of their students.

Secondly, systemic policy reform is necessary. Policymakers must ensure that educational policies are not only inclusive by design but are also robustly implemented. This involves providing adequate funding for the necessary technologies and resources, as well as establishing clear guidelines for their use in educational settings. Such measures will help to ensure that the policies achieve their intended outcomes of inclusivity and accessibility.

Thirdly, fostering cross-sector collaboration is essential. Collaboration between educational institutions, technology developers, and policymakers can drive innovation and ensure that technological solutions are effectively integrated into educational practices. This partnership can lead to the development of more sophisticated and user-friendly AT that can be seamlessly incorporated into the curriculum.

Lastly, continuous research and the establishment of feedback loops must be considered. Continued research into the effectiveness of UDL implementations and AT should be encouraged. Additionally, establishing feedback loops within educational systems will allow for the ongoing refinement of strategies and practices based on actual classroom experiences. This iterative process is vital for ensuring that educational practices continually evolve to meet the changing needs of students. By following these recommendations, educational institutions can significantly enhance their capacity to provide inclusive and accessible education for all students.

## References

Adebayo, E. O., & Ayorinde, I. T. (2022). Efficacy of assistive technology for improved teaching and learning in computer science. *International Journal of Education and Management Engineering*, *12*(5), 9–17.

Al-Dababneh, K. A., & Al-Zboon, E. K. (2022). Using assistive technologies in the curriculum of children with specific learning disabilities served in inclusion settings: teachers' beliefs and professionalism. *Disability and Rehabilitation: Assistive Technology*, *17*(1), 23–33.

Ampratwum, J., Offei, Y. N., & Ntoaduro, A. (2016). Barriers to the use of computer assistive technology among students with visual impairment in Ghana: The case of Akropong School for the Blind. *Journal of Education and Practice*, *7*(29), 58–61.

Atanga, C., Jones, B. A., Krueger, L. E., & Lu, S. (2020). Teachers of students with learning disabilities: Assistive technology knowledge, perceptions, interests, and barriers. *Journal of Special Education Technology*, *35*(4), 236–248.

Batty, L., & Reilly, K. (2023). Understanding barriers to participation within undergraduate STEM laboratories: Towards development of an inclusive curriculum. *Journal of Biological Education*, *57*(5), 1147–1169.

Beyene, W. M., Mekonnen, A. T., & Giannoumis, G. A. (2023). Inclusion, access, and accessibility of educational resources in higher education institutions: Exploring the Ethiopian context. *International Journal of Inclusive Education*, *27*(1), 18–34.

Boot, F. H., Owuor, J., Dinsmore, J., & MacLachlan, M. (2018). Access to assistive technology for people with intellectual disabilities: A systematic review to identify barriers and facilitators. *Journal of Intellectual Disability Research*, *62*(10), 900–921.

Cernasev, A., & Axon, D. R. (2023). Research and scholarly methods: Thematic analysis. *Journal of the American College of Clinical Pharmacy*, *6*(7), 751–755.

Christou, P. A. (2023). How to use thematic analysis in qualitative research. *Journal of Qualitative Research in Tourism*, *1*, 1–17.

Cook, A. M., & Polgar, J. M. (2014). *Assistive technologies-e-book: Principles and practice*. Elsevier Health Sciences.

Courtad, C. A. (2019). Making your classroom smart: Universal design for learning and technology. In V. Uskov, R. Howlett, & L. Jain (Eds.), *Smart education and e-learning 2019* (vol. 144, pp. 501–510). Springer Singapore.

Danemayer, J., Boggs, D., Smith, E. M., Ramos, V. D., Battistella, L. R., Holloway, C., & Polack, S. (2021). Measuring assistive technology supply and demand: A scoping review. *Assistive Technology*, *33*(suppl), S35–S49.

Ditlhale, T. W., & Johnson, L. R. (2022). Assistive technologies as an ODeL strategy in promoting support for students with disabilities. *Technology and Disability*, *34*(3), 153–163.

Fundoni, M., Porcu, L., & Melis, G. (2023). Systematic literature review. In P. Foroudi, & C. Dennis (Eds.), *Researching and Analysing Business: Research Methods in Practice*. Taylor & Francis.

Guba, K. S., & Tsivinskaya, A. O. (2024). Ambiguity in ethical standards: Global versus local science in explaining academic plagiarism. *Science and Engineering Ethics*, *30*(1), 4.

Hayhoe, S. (2014). The need for inclusive accessible technologies for students with disabilities and learning difficulties. In L. Burke (Ed.), *Learning in a digitalized age: Plugged in, turned on, totally engaged?* (pp. 257–274). John Catt Educational Publishing.

Helena Martins, M., Borges, M. L., & Gonçalves, T. (2018). Attitudes towards inclusion in higher education in a Portuguese university. *International Journal of Inclusive Education, 22*(5), 527–542.

Kioko, V. K., & Makoelle, T. M. (2014). Inclusion in higher education: Learning experiences of disabled students at Winchester University. *International Education Studies, 7*(6), 106–116.

Makoelle, T. M., & Makhalemele, T. (2020). Teacher leadership in South African schools. *International Journal of Management in Education, 14*(3), 293–310.

Makoelle, T. M., & Mosito, C. P. (2023). Pre-service teacher preparation for inclusive teaching in South Africa. In G. Boadu, G. Odhiambo, & P. Marandi (Eds.), *Practices and perspectives of teaching and teacher education in Africa* (pp. 1–23). IGI Global.

Martinez, E. C., Valdés, J. R. F., Castillo, J. L., Castillo, J. V., Montecino, R. M. B., Jimenez, J. E. M., Escamilla, D. A., & Diarte, E. (2023). Ten steps to conduct a systematic review. *Cureus, 15*(12).

Meyer, A., Rose, D. H., & Gordon, D. (2014). *Universal design for learning: Theory and practice*. CAST Professional Publishing.

Moriña, A. (2019). Inclusive education in higher education: challenges and opportunities. In M. R. Coleman, & M. Shevlin (Eds.), *Postsecondary educational opportunities for students with special education needs* (pp. 3–17). Routledge.

Mphuthi, M. (2024). The role of the life orientation curriculum in curbing learner behaviour that triggers school violence. *Perspectives in Education, 42*(1), 53–70.

Mpofu, J. (2023). An afro-centric approach to inclusive education. In M. O. Maguvhe, & M. M. Masuku (Eds.), *Using African epistemologies in shaping inclusive education knowledge* (pp. 69–86). Springer Nature Switzerland.

Mpu, Y., & Adu, E. O. (2021). The challenges of inclusive education and its implementation in schools: The South African perspective. *Perspectives in Education, 39*(2), 225–238.

Nakitare, J., & Otike, F. (2023). Plagiarism conundrum in Kenyan universities: An impediment to quality research. *Digital Library Perspectives, 39*(2), 145–165.

Ndlovu, S. (2021). Challenges of the Universal Design of Learning in South African Higher Education. In A. P. Ndofirepi, & E. T. Gwaravanda (Eds.), *Mediating learning in higher education in Africa* (pp. 98–117). Brill.

Nkomo, D., & Dube, B. (2022). Modelling inclusive education in rural schools. In M. O. Maguvhe, & M. M. Masuku (Eds.), *Handbook of research on creating spaces for African epistemologies in the inclusive education discourse* (pp. 260–273). IGI Global.

Ochsner, B., Spöhrer, M., & Stock, R. (2022). Rethinking assistive technologies: Users, environments, digital media, and app-practices of hearing. *Nanoethics, 16*(1), 65–79.

O'Sullivan, K., McGrane, A., Long, S., Marshall, K., & Maclachlan, M. (2023). Using a systems thinking approach to understand teachers perceptions and use of assistive technology in the republic of Ireland. *Disability and Rehabilitation: Assistive Technology, 18*(5), 502–510.

Park, J., Bagwell, A. F., Bryant, D. P., & Bryant, B. R. (2022). Integrating assistive technology into a teacher preparation program. *Teacher Education and Special Education, 45*(2), 141–159.

Rose, D. H., Harbour, W. S., Johnston, C. S., Daley, S. G., & Abarbanell, L. (2006). Universal design for learning in postsecondary education: Reflections on principles and their application. *Journal of Postsecondary Education and Disability, 19*(2), 135–151.

Rose, D. H., Hasselbring, T. S., Stahl, S., & Zabala, J. (2005). Assistive technology and universal design for learning: Two sides of the same coin. In D. L. Edyburn, K. Higgins, & R. Boone (Eds.), *Handbook of special education technology research and practice* (pp. 507–518).

Schock, R. E., & Lee, E. A. (2016). Children's voices: Perspectives on using assistive technology. *Exceptionality Education International, 26*(1), 76–94.

Schwab, S., Resch, K., & Alnahdi, G. (2024). Inclusion does not solely apply to students with disabilities: Pre-service teachers' attitudes towards inclusive schooling of all students. *International Journal of Inclusive Education, 28*(2), 214–230.

Smith, E. M., Huff, S., Wescott, H., Daniel, R., Ebuenyi, I. D., O'Donnell, J., Maalim, M., Zhang, W., Khasnabis, C., & MacLachlan, M. (2024). Assistive technologies are central to the realization of the Convention on the Rights of Persons with Disabilities. *Disability and Rehabilitation: Assistive Technology, 19*(2), 486–491.

Timuş, N., Bartlett, M. E., Bartlett, J. E., Ehrlich, S., & Babutsidze, Z. (2024). Fostering inclusive higher education through universal design for learning and inclusive pedagogy–EU and US faculty perceptions. *Higher Education Research & Development, 43*(2), 473–487.

Tran, N. H. N., Amado, C. A. D. E. F., & Santos, S. P. D. (2023). Challenges and success factors of transnational higher education: A systematic review. *Studies in Higher Education, 48*(1), 113–136.

Zongozzi, J. N. (2022). Accessible quality higher education for students with disabilities in a South African open distance and e-learning institution: Challenges. *International Journal of Disability, Development and Education, 69*(5), 1645–1657.

Chapter 15

# Inclusion in Higher Education During Natural Disruptions: Lessons from the COVID-19 Pandemic

*Maitumeleng Albertina Nthontho[a] and Pontsho Moepya[b]*

[a]*North-West University, South Africa*
[b]*University of Pretoria, South Africa*

## Abstract

This book chapter explores how the COVID-19 pandemic has impacted inclusive education in higher education, with specific reference to students who are from low-income and poor backgrounds. The study that underpins this chapter followed a qualitative research approach with the autobiographical narrative as a data collection device. Autobiographical narratives were collected from a lecturer and a postgraduate student who was pursuing studies during the outbreak of the COVID-19 pandemic and beyond. The main study findings reveal that the COVID-19 pandemic exposed the inequalities that exist within higher education institutions. For instance, programmes in some institutions experienced setbacks while other institutions adapted easily and faster. In addition, the findings exposed the digital divide among communities, with students from poor backgrounds experiencing exclusion and mental health among academics and students becoming evident. Therefore, the study recommends that the mitigation strategies should aim at empowering disadvantaged students and their communities.

*Keywords*: COVID-19; inclusion; inequality; higher education; digital divide; digital teaching and learning; socio-economic backgrounds

## Introduction

The COVID-19 pandemic has significantly impacted higher education institutions around the world (Bao, 2020). Its effects include widespread disruptions in teaching and learning, research as well as student support services (Ali, 2020). One of the key areas affected by the pandemic is the issue of inclusion in higher education (Ajani & Gamede, 2021). Inclusion in higher education refers to the practice of ensuring that all students, regardless of their background, abilities, or circumstances, have equal access to and opportunities for success within the higher education environment (Salmi, 2023). In the South African context, the COVID-19 pandemic, and the shift to emergency remote teaching and online learning highlighted issues of the disparities of inclusion, access, and exacerbated existing inequalities in higher education (Menon & Motala, 2022). Marongwe and Garidzirai (2021) highlight that

> a call that was made by the Department of Higher Education and Training (DHET) and mandated universities to adopt remote learning to save the academic year, was a blanket statement that did not consider the context of different universities' backgrounds, given the inequalities that existed before the outbreak of COVID-19.

With that said, the shift to digital teaching and learning due to the COVID-19 pandemic widened the already existing gap between the *haves*, those with access to technological resources, and *have-nots*, those without access to technological resources – *digital divide* (Menon & Motala, 2022). The digital divide adds to the already existing disparities within South African communities. Mr. Thabo Mbeki, former president of South Africa, once described South Africa as a country with two faces due to inequalities that exist between the Black rural communities – *have-nots* and the *haves*, largely populated by White communities with Black rural communities most affected by lack of economic, physical, educational, communication, and other infrastructure resources (Marongwe & Garidzirai, 2021; Mbeki, 1998). As such, many students, particularly those from underprivileged backgrounds experienced challenges such as a lack of teaching and learning resources, technological gadgets, and internet connections to continue with their studies remotely (Czerniewicz et al., 2020) and that meant automatic exclusion from the teaching and learning (Menon & Motala, 2022).

Ajani and Gamede (2021) concur that students from disadvantaged backgrounds have limited access to quality education due to lack and inadequate facilities. They struggle with irregular electricity supply, poor network coverage that does not allow them to efficiently access remote learning, while some of them don't have relevant gargets such as laptops and smartphones, and those that have, find it difficult to access the internet resulting in them missing much of the teaching and learning (Ajani & Gamede, 2021).

This book chapter explores how the COVID-19 pandemic has impacted inclusive education in higher education, with specific reference to students who are from low-income and poor backgrounds. To do so, the authors adopted Warschauer's

(2003) framework as the lens that guided them to conclude the extent to which students from unprivileged backgrounds were affected by online learning because of the COVID-19 pandemic. The book chapter also discusses strategies and best practices that institutions have employed to address these challenges and to support inclusive education during times of disruption. Lessons learned from the pandemic can provide valuable insights into how higher education can support diverse student populations during times of crisis and beyond. By looking into the impact of natural disruptions on inclusion in higher education through the equity theory, the authors of this chapter assume that institutions can work towards implementing more equitable and inclusive practices to support all students, regardless of their socio-economic background. Hence the sub-topics that follow are discussed in depth.

## Digitising Higher Education

Higher education and technology were co-existent before the COVID-19 pandemic. Thus, worldwide, higher learning institutions, including those in Africa, have been pacing themselves in the use of technology to fast-track their research, teaching, and learning, as well as responding to societal needs. It is, however, important to mention that while the pace was accommodative depending on affordability due to inequality, the COVID-19 pandemic disrupted the snail-pace and forced higher learning institutions to shift from hybrid to online teaching mode. This massive and emergent shift did not only cause institutions extreme disruptions, but the implications on access to facilities and resources in terms of inclusion and injustices remained crucial (Czerniewicz et al., 2020; Menon & Motala, 2022).

The outbreak of the pandemic and the subsequent lockdown restrictions abruptly disrupted higher education teaching and learning (Ali, 2020) which resulted in Emergency Remote Teaching and Learning (ERTL) that drastically transitioned from hybrid to digital classrooms through the use of several technical tools and Internet-based learning systems (Zhong et al., 2020) such as mobile devices, smartboards, MOOCs, tablets, laptops, simulations, dynamic visualisations, and virtual laboratories (Haleem et al., 2022). The shift to total online teaching and learning to save the academic year was regarded as the only workable solution, it was the panacea to the crisis (Menon & Motala, 2022). However, scholars criticised this view and argued that it would exacerbate and widen existing inequalities as it ignored the lived realities of most students in terms of access to the necessary digital tools and technology and a conducive environment for online teaching and learning (Czerniewicz et al., 2020). The student representative council remained adamant that the shift severely impacted students from various background differently. This is what they stated:

> Universities should assume all students are inherently 'disadvantaged' by the circumstances, whether due to technology access, their home environment, learning styles, or loss of structure. (Chrysanthos, 2020; Essop, 2021)

Although, continuity of learning was a priority, with contact universities rapidly turning digital teaching and learning; it should not be equated to the full teaching and learning experience as it was not the enabler of equity but the excluder of students from poor backgrounds (Essop, 2021; Motala & Menon, 2020). For instance, 'an impoverished black working class and rural students could not learn online without the access to resources such as a laptop and unstable Wi-Fi hotspots, with power outages and in congested, noisy home environments' (Menon & Motala, 2022). Therefore, enabling continuity of teaching through digital teaching and learning perpetuated the existing inequalities and exclusions in higher education institutions (Essop, 2021). Indications are that students lost hope and fear of the future was very prevalent.

Additionally, Mahaye (2020) indicated that some students come from poor, mostly rural areas that are family-oriented, and they live amid their families where spaces for academic activities are not available, while some are from noisy home environments that are not conducive for learning. Furthermore, the impact of the shift to online teaching and learning reflected the inequalities between students from poor backgrounds and those from well-off families and both mirrored apartheid, which meant that the transition was context-dependent and had limitations, thereby challenging students from impoverished backgrounds (Menon & Motala, 2022; Mncube et al., 2021). These challenges may limit the effectiveness of learning technologies or hinder the adoption of digital teaching and learning because of the issues of the digital divide in terms of access to the digital equipment, facilities, and infrastructure necessary to pursue online learning (Ajani & Gamede, 2021; Salmi, 2020).

## COVID-19 and Digital Divide in Higher Education

The digital divide is another challenge to online learning in South Africa and elsewhere (Bagarukayo & Kalema, 2015). Hence the pandemic impacts are not experienced equally the same way in all in institutions of the same context (Essop, 2021; Salmi, 2020). Therefore, the pandemic has called for the reshaping of the higher education fraternity with 'the intersections of equity, inequality, and teaching online for the better tomorrow' (Czerniewicz et al., 2020, p. 2). Research by Essop (2021) suggests that the digital divide is stark in the case of a South Africa context, indicating the fact that 82% of students do not have access to the internet or household computers, internet usage is 26.3% as against a global average of 51.4% and internet penetration is 47%, with significant inequalities between urban and rural areas (Essop, 2021).

Similarly, in their study, Marongwe and Garidzirai (2022) found that rural students were affected by the lockdown compared to urban students. In the same vein, Czerniewicz et al. (2020), Menon and Motala (2021), and Ajani and Gamede (2021) found that in 15 diverse universities in South Africa, the students from disadvantaged groups; low-income and poor backgrounds were the most affected. Essop (2021) further indicates that the transition challenges experienced by students in South African institutions were the outcomes of the deep-seated inequalities between the historically white or advantaged institutions and the historically black or disadvantaged institutions which are the legacy of the apartheid past. Research evidence suggests that some of the institutions were able to transition to digital teaching and learning by mid-April (two weeks after the announcement of the lockdown measures by the President) while others began online teaching and learning in June and July which extended the academic year to March 2021 (Czerniewicz et al., 2020; Mahaye, 2020).

In South Africa, the extent of the digital divide is illustrated by the fact that, although in terms of place of residence, 97.5% of students live in municipalities where more than 50% of households have access to electricity, just over half (53.15%) live in municipalities where between 10% and 20% of households have internet access and just under half in municipalities where between 30% and 47% of households have access to a suitable device – either a laptop or tablet (Essop, 2021). According to Tate and Warschauer (2022), to effectively engage in online learning, students need access to appropriate hardware (e.g., Chromebooks and laptops), reliable and robust internet access, and a quiet environment in which to study. The need for digital devices and internet access to support online learning has been widely discussed under the umbrella of the 'digital divide' by economists, researchers of educational technology, and educators alike. With this stated, higher learning institutions must ensure that students have access to laptops and tablets, data packages, and equipment in response to the pandemic (Menon & Motala, 2022).

## Warschauer's Framework of 2003

In a world where digital education has been exciting to watch, with new advances rapidly growing, Warschauer's framework of 2003 became relevant to be used as a theory that can guide the focus the study that underpins this chapter. The framework ensures that diverse contexts of students are accommodated in preparing for online teaching modalities. For instance, factors of creating equitable access during the pandemic include physical resources – space, hardware, and internet, of which students from poor and low-income backgrounds did not have; a challenged that severely affected them; while others had a smooth transition to the digital teaching and learning (Mukhtar et al., 2020; UNESCO, 2020).

The worldwide progress in digital education has also been exciting to watch, with new advances rapidly growing. In digital era, teaching and learning has taken another turn – Digitised teaching and learning (DTL) has become more prevalent in higher learning institutions as new technology is introduced. Following the onset of the COVID-19 pandemic, DTL is being used as an alternative mode of teaching and learning that can be considered in other future unknown challenges. While increased access to information through digital platforms can be liberating, this is only true if someone is physically able to access those platforms – i.e. via the Internet, mobile phones, computers, etc. On the contrary, for those who lack access, such digital solutions serve as another form of exclusion from the global information society (De Klerk & Palmer, 2022). Considering existing unequal access to digital resources experienced by different social groups, along with the effects that this gap has on existing socio-economic, the question is 'How well the higher learning institutions can respond to the ever-growing need for digital education solutions post-pandemic while they maintain inclusivity, in the context of already struggling education systems?' To respond to this question, the authors adopted Warschauer's (2003) framework to discuss ways to address challenges of exclusion experienced by students from poor backgrounds during the COVID-19 pandemic. The framework also guides in how equity in online teaching and learning, can be addressed as well as directions for research.

Warschauer's (2003) framework conceptualises the term 'equity' as the main aspect of inclusion and access in higher learning institutions. During the COVID-19 pandemic, the shift to ERTL brought to the fore the inequities that existed prior to the pandemic (Menon & Motala, 2022). According to Tate and Warschauer (2022), equitable learning occurs when every learner belongs, contributes, and thrives, regardless of race/ethnicity or socio-economic status. Equity, however, does not mean that all students obtain equal education outcomes, but rather that differences in students' outcomes are unrelated to their background or to economic and social circumstances over which students have no control (The Organisation for Economic Cooperation and Development [OECD], 2018).

To narrow the scope of our discussion, we concur with Warschauer's (2003) factors of creating equitable access to emergency response to digital learning during the pandemic and online teaching and learning in future namely physical resources – space, hardware, and software or internet. At a minimum, to have a successful online learning, students need a reliable internet-enabled computer, a physical learning space, and a distraction-free environment (Tate & Warschauer, 2022). Finding an appropriate physical learning space, free from noise or distraction at home, is difficult for students coming from disadvantaged backgrounds such as informal settlements and large-membered families (Mahaye, 2020). The need for physical conducive space ensures that there is no distractions and interruptions during the online teaching and learning (Ajani & Gamede, 2021). In addition to conducive space for digital learning, disparities on physical access to computer and internet remains a concern and the reasons involve issues of economics, politics, infrastructure, culture, and education (Warschauer, 2003).

## Methodological Underpinnings

The study that underpins this chapter followed a qualitative research approach with the autobiographical narrative as a data collection device. The motive behind this choice is influenced by a need for the chapter to focus on where the story unfolded, the events that took place, and the reactions thereof (Cooper & Lilyea, 2022). The focus is on the social, cultural, and institutional context, within which the experiences were constituted, shaped, expressed, and enacted (Munro, 2011). The autobiographical narrative design therefore engaged the lecturer and a postgraduate student who was pursuing the studies since the outbreak of the COVID-19 pandemic and beyond. The purpose is to enable these practitioners to reflect and introspect processes throughout this journey to gather their personal stories, perceptions, and insights related to their experiences 'now' and 'beyond' the pandemic. This research design enabled these participants to relate their experiences highlighting significant moments, challenges encountered, learning opportunities, and transformative aspects of their roles.

The narrative in this study intended to elicit in-depth information regarding their experiences during the digital teaching and learning at a South African university. The researchers who by default are the authors of this paper hope that the insights drawn from this study benefit higher education institutions through self-reflection. The findings thereof would contribute significantly to this emerging body of knowledge. While conducting the autobiographic narrative inquiry, the researchers tend to be influenced by their memories and interpretations (Walker, 2017). To address this challenge, they read the narratives, collaborated with the participants, and had in-depth conversations with them to co-construct the narratives of their experiences. The researchers further engaged the participants in data analysis for an accurate interpretation of their stories. Data were analysed thematically; the researchers worked with the data, organised it and broke it down into meaningful units, synthesised it, and then identified 'thematising meanings' (Clarke & Braun, 2013).

Before conducting the study, the researchers approached the participants to explain the study's intentions and who agreed to participate. The participants sent their narratives to the researchers via email and gave them consent to use their narratives while at the same time, they were open to providing more information and clarifications if necessary. Clandinin and Caine (2008) attest that researchers ought to be thoughtful and vigilant in using autobiography narrative as a research inquiry. Therefore, the researchers were careful in composing the research text by considering anonymity and confidentiality paramount (Creswell & Creswell, 2018) and used pseudonyms to conceal the actual identities of the participants and the concerned university.

## Research Findings: Digital Teaching and Learning During COVID-19

Academic activities such as teaching and learning were not spared disturbance and destruction by the COVID-19 pandemic. Higher learning institutions had to swiftly respond to this unexpected crisis. As a result, the shift occurred as higher learning institutions were forced to shift from hybrid to fully online education theories and models within a short time to curb the spread of coronavirus (Baticulon, 2021). Consequently, the crisis-response migration due to the pandemic should not be equated with effective online education or digital transformation of universities but rather be seen from the perspective of emergency remote teaching platforms (Adedoyin et al., 2020).

Research evidence revealed that 'online education' is deeply constrained by inadequate planning and designs of instructions with several available theories and models. There is not enough evidence that higher learning institutions had ample time to plan, design, and develop online instructional programmes due to the pandemic (Ferri et al., 2020). Policymakers and higher education institutions were subjected to uncertainties during the abrupt shift as the process of the COVID-19 pandemic did not allow time for planning (Opere, 2021). The experience, however, differed between countries and institutions. For instance, while the phasing in of online teaching and learning was slower than anticipated in some institutions, due to the lack of appropriate infrastructure development and training of lecturers (Alex, 2022), others switched most of their programmes to an online format very quickly (Mahaye, 2020). These disparities did not manifest themselves between institutions only, but also between students and academics.

Research, globally, indicates frustrations experienced by students due to the digital teaching and learning imposed on them by the COVID-19 pandemic and circumstances of inequalities. Students from some of the South African universities had these experiences to share.

> 'I ... could not go home during hard lockdown because of circumstances. For instance, I don't own a laptop, so I make use of the university computer lab. Going home would mean putting my studies on hold and that would mean a wasted academic year', expressed a student from one university.

The student from the other university said,

> My life is at a halt; I am worried about my degree. I am a final-year student in education apparently, they don't consider us essential students only medical students are considered essential. It is very difficult to study from home, where I live with 14 people and share a bedroom with 4 of them. There is no privacy, no space for me to quietly sit and do my schoolwork. I am very worried that my grades will decrease or whether I will make it or not. There is too much noise at home. So COVID-19 just ruined my life.

> 'The COVID-19 pandemic has cost us a lot especially us from the rural areas with no internet connection or access, it is very difficult, and we are often left behind', indicated a student from another university.

It is important also to highlight that some universities established initiatives meant to assist needy students. Such initiatives included lending them laptops, providing them with monthly data bundles. The selection criterion was, however, not communicated leaving other students unassisted.

> 'My supervisor submitted my name for the laptop assistance to the faculty. We have been waiting for the outcome, but I have already lost hope and time is catching up on me… don't think I will ever recover from this setback … eish', lamented a student from a South African university.

Students from other countries also had similar experiences and this is what one of the students at one of the universities in Ghana had to say:

> It did not help because only some people use smartphones and laptops during online learning. As a finance student, I had to learn how to use Sakai to type mathematical equations during an assignment, which was a challenge and caused my average to drop from 3.6 to 3.52. (Acheampong, 2023)

While digital learning exposed students to uncertainties, stress, and anxiety, it awakened skills that most of them were not aware that they possessed, on the other hand. For instance, exercising patience, acquisition of time management skills, independence and organising one's work, and resilience appeared on top of the list.

> 'I had to become much more independent in my work, I had to be much more organised, and I had to manage my time efficiently. When I was at the university, I would just go see my professor, if I had questions. But now if I have any questions, I must send an email and wait for a response, which can be another burden. So instead, I try to first understand by myself. And if I really don't understand, then I ask. I've had to learn to be a bit more independent', emphasised one of the students.

The other student pointed out,

> Being organised is so crucial because I had so many activities demanding my attention. So, if I compromised my organising skill, I could miss deadlines. I know some of my friends who suffered from that. I therefore ensured that I stayed organised and even do work in advance, rather than waiting for the eleventh hour.

> 'We have so many modules to deal with at the same time, and many projects, which can be a big burden because they demand lots of groupwork. Time management, which of course goes with organising remained crucial during the pandemic. Having to deal with group members' schedules and mine at the same time, still having a lot of other schoolwork and family responsibilities to handle, I really needed extra effort to manage my time, or I just won't cope', indicated another student.

The rapid shift from the hybrid to total digital teaching and learning during the COVID-19 pandemic did not only affect students, but academics were also equally affected with individual paths markedly different – much rougher for some than others. Moving most of the programmes to digital format automatically suggested changes in the way academics had to deliver classes as well as the way they needed to guide and support students in preparation for such classes. We cannot turn a blind eye though, to the wide disparities of resources and infrastructure between South African universities and elsewhere. These inequalities already suggest unequal access to such resources by academics. Not only that, their different levels of exposure to technological systems also cannot be overlooked. This means that while the COVID-19 pandemic presented challenges, its severity within the university context meant that academics had to find practical means to navigate their way through their academic responsibilities and other obligations.

To save the academic year from going to a waste, higher learning institutions invested in creating virtual classrooms and trained academics to make the most of the technology, reinvent themselves, and deliver the best possible learning experiences tailored to a live digital format (Alex, 2022). Doing all the administrative processes online and from home was a completely different way of working and as expected academics grappled with uncertainties. The experiences below are a true reflection of how some academics in higher learning institutions found themselves thrown into a deep end whereas others had a completely different experience.

> 'I was appointed as a lecturer amid the COVID-19 pandemic with no training, so most lecturers I worked with, were already schooled about how they had to teach online. And as a new appointee, I did not know anything about online teaching. I then had to do what you call a trial-and-error method. I taught myself online teaching strategies and at times I fumbled in a virtual class with students present', one of the academics shared his online teaching and learning experience.

> Like the above experiences, another novice lecturer said, 'I have not adapted to the online teaching method, I was appointed during the COVID-19 pandemic from a school context, so I am still in a learning process'.

> The other lecturer buttressed, 'Online teaching was a learning process for me. I taught myself most of the online teaching styles and still I was not sure if I was on'. Another lecturer added to these views 'I struggled to adapt, I wished I had someone that could hold my hand and guide me throughout the first few months of my online teaching'.

However, as mentioned earlier, some academics had a different experience altogether. For example, Anna relates her story thus.

> As it turned out, for this past winter semester [2020], I was already scheduled to teach an asynchronous online course. During the pandemic, I taught the courses that I would have taught. So, for me, unlike

for many, the scramble to quickly drop what you were doing for classroom teaching and convert it all instantly to online was not an issue.

Grace narrated, 'Online teaching was not new in this university, my adaption came directly from practicing hybrid teaching, I mean I always enjoyed teaching online'.

'I seem to have adapted well because of the training I received. It started from the university level, then it was cascaded to different departments. In some cases, we had joint training sessions as a faculty where lecturers from different departments came together, and we shared ideas', reiterated the other lecturer.

The online teaching training that I received from the innovation department in the early days of the outbreak assisted me greatly!

Smanga supported, 'Training through the university instructional designers enhanced my online competencies and I think it contributed to the adaptation of online teaching'.

The above scenario, therefore, suggests that there may be opportunities provided by the pandemic and the sudden transition of the mode of learning (Mhlanga & Moloi, 2020; Mpungose, 2020). For instance, the research findings by Mhlanga and Moloi (2020) have revealed that in South Africa, during the lockdown, a variety of the Fourth Industrial Revolution (4IR) tools were unleashed from primary education to higher and tertiary. This suggests that South Africa generally has some pockets of excellence to drive the education sector into the 4IR, which has the potential to increase access (Czerniewicz et al., 2020; Mhlanga & Moloi, 2020).

## Discussions

The findings above advocate that the pandemic can be an opportunity and an exercise for emergency remote teaching to evaluate emerging challenges during emergencies and develop a coherent online education (Ferri et al., 2020). In the African context and other parts of the world, this pandemic has ironically provided possibilities for policy reformulations and entrenching new practices that foreground flexible and equitable forms of provision (Czerniewicz et al., 2020). Online learning during the pandemic has brought into focus numerous examples of extraordinary resilience, unexpected collaboration, and support, including inspiring creativity (Czerniewicz et al., 2020; Mahaye, 2020). Nonetheless, research evidence points out that some students and academics, mostly females, experienced significant mental health challenges due to isolation and lack of physical presence which might have made it harder for the provision of adequate support. Although channels of communication have evolved due to contemporary technology, being physically separated because of the lockdown did contribute to emotional impacts and mental health issues as discussed in the following sections.

## The Impact of COVID-19 Disruptions on Mental Health

Research indicates that a multitude of consequences were encountered during the transition from hybrid, traditional face-to-face to digital teaching and learning on both the students and academic staff (Magomedov et al., 2020; Opere, 2021). One of the most crucial issues that the COVID-19 pandemic raised was student and staff mental health. Many students and staff of all ages experienced mental health challenges during the pandemic, ranging from health anxiety to depression caused by isolation, physical absence, and uncertainty (Rapanta et al., 2020).

According to UNESCO (2020), about 73% of students were reported to have experienced poor mental health because of the COVID-19 pandemic. It must however be emphasised that most mental health issues seemed to be significantly worse among female students. As mentioned by Li (2023) the possible causes of such mental issues are related to social isolation, frustration, uncertainty, and academic stress. The mental health crisis seems to have been one of the major COVID-19 pandemic impacts, not only students experienced these challenges, but academic staff were also equally affected. Although most academic staff used online learning platforms before the pandemic, they were nonetheless accessible and incorporated with conversational teaching. Therefore, with little to no training in online teaching and learning, academic staff found themselves having to adapt without being afforded adequate consideration which was challenging, difficult, and demanding (Lufungulo et al., 2021). Research evidence also suggests that academics were already struggling to combine teaching, research, and service commitments, not to mention the work-life balance, then with the COVID-19-related impacts, were subjected to additional pressure which resulted in immense stress (Ferri et al., 2020; Rapanta et al., 2020).

It is evident that both students and lecturers faced different obstacles in the process of emergent online learning due to the existing limitations related to technological, pedagogical, and socio-economic challenges (Phejane, 2022; Seeletso & Letseka, 2020). Nevertheless, we also need to consider the individual level of resource constraints; not all students and academic staff have access to adequate internet connectivity and access for effective online *e*-learning. The digital gap remains the primary obstacle preventing students from attaining the full potential of *e*-learning, despite the difficulties faced by academic staff adding workloads which resulted in immense pressure (Landa et al., 2021). Most students were not prepared to study online in a short period.

Although some academic staff could afford to purchase bundles of internet services and work from home, others struggled to do so and remained behind with some of their duties, article writing, for instance (Opere, 2021). With this said, due to a lack of resources and limited financial support, access to education is infringed. There is therefore a need for higher learning institutions to offer support in terms of mental health, promoting resilience, as well as providing equitable access of resources within the higher education community during the pandemic.

## Accessibility to Teaching and Learning Resources

In the context of higher learning institutions, there is a critical need for increased investment in upgrading resources, both in universities and at the community level, because of the digital divide (Ali, 2020). As we mentioned earlier on, academic staff and students in some institutions quickly adapted to the online teaching and learning during the pandemic whereas those in other institutions experienced curriculum setbacks. The implication is therefore that while there is still much to be done and the need for further research, this book chapter emphasises the need for both practical and theoretical alternative pathways that can be used to enable university students to realise the full potential of *e*-learning. Higher learning institutions need to plan for hindrances to learning such as a pandemic outbreak, student protests, and others, and make use of technology to expand access through distance learning programmes (El Said, 2021).

To do so, students must be familiarised with online learning to enhance their digital literacy and refine their misperceptions about online learning. The students should also be given mentors who assess their participation and engagement in the online learning, and then assist where there is room for improvement. Moreover, there is a need for proactive intervention through national legislation, which requires mobile providers to support ERTL through zero rating data (Pokhrel & Chhetri, 2021). The higher education stakeholders may negotiate with providers, for instance in the South African context, the National organisations Tertiary Education and Research Network and Universities South Africa can speak to providers such MTN, VODACOM, TELKOM, or CELLC regarding the technical process of 'whitelisting' educational sites. This will assist students with data and minimise financial constraints.

However, the above may not address the lack of devices, smartphones, internet quota, and a stable internet connection which are still critical issues that the universities must assist with from the crisis funding to minimise the financial burden on students who are from poor backgrounds (Ali, 2020). Additionally, planning and preparation should inevitably be done for better online learning in the future since online learning requires more time than face-to-face classes to be well-prepared and ready.

The academic staff should be trained and prepared with sufficient knowledge and skill development opportunities to maximise their practices in carrying out online teaching and learning (Adedoyin et al., 2020; Toquero, 2020). The students must be familiarised with online learning to enhance their technology competencies. Most importantly, future education and training must include the integration of technology in technology-enhanced language learning, information, and communication technology in language learning, and online language learning courses in their curriculum since the need for technology integration in language learning is inevitable (Adnan & Anwar, 2020).

## Conclusions and Recommendations

Inclusive education has been recognised as a human right, so by law, educational provisioning should be inclusive and accessible as suggested by the legislative frameworks. However, online learning because of the COVID-19 pandemic challenged the accessibility and inclusivity of education due to the digital divide. The lack of resources and devices and the issue of connectivity have exposed infrastructural gaps that exist within South African higher learning institutions. This technological lack is historical and manifested through unequal disparities. The advent of the COVID-19 pandemic compounded teaching and learning experiences and caused numerous cases of mental health issues and this was due to limited infrastructure and policies on navigating pandemics within learning environments (Czerniewicz et al., 2020; Mpungose, 2020).

## References

Acheampong, J. O. (2023). The impact of COVID-19 on students' academic performance: The case of the university of Ghana business school, *Cogent Education*, *10*(1), 1–13, doi: 10.1080/2331186X.2023.2186011

Adedoyin, O., & Soykan, E. (2020). COVID-19 pandemic and online learning: The challenges and opportunities. *Interactive Learning Environments*, *31*(2), 863–875. doi: 10.1080/10494820.2020.1813180

Adnan, M., & Anwar, K. (2020). Online learning amid the COVID-19 pandemic: Students' perspectives. *Journal of Pedagogical Sociology and Psychology*, *2*(1), 45–51. https://doi.org/10.33902/JPSP.2020261309

Ajani, O. A., & Gamede, B. T. (2021). Curriculum delivery and digital divide in South African higher institutions during the COVID-19 pandemic: A case of social injustice. *International Journal of Innovation, Creativity and Change*, *15*(8), 590–603. doi:10.5430/ijhe.v10n5p121

Alex, J. K. (2022). Impact of the COVID-19 pandemic on the academic life of higher education students. *South African Journal of Higher Education*, *36*(1), 20–40. doi: 10.20853/36-1-4303

Ali, W. (2020). Online and remote learning in higher education institutes: Necessity in light of COVID-19 pandemic. *Higher Education Studies*, *10*(3), 16–25.

Bagarukayo, B., & Kalema, B. (2015). Evaluation of eLearning usage in South African universities: A critical review. *International Journal of Education and Development using Information and Communication Technology*, *2*(11), 168–183.

Bao, W. (2020). COVID-19 and online teaching in higher education: A case study of Peking University. *Human Behavior and Emerging Technologies*, *2*, 113–115.

Baticulon, R. E., Sy, J. J., Alberto, N. R. I., Baron, M. B. C., Mabulay, R. E. C., Rizada, L. G. T., Tiu, C. J. S., Clarion, C. A. & Reyes, J. C. B. (2021). Barriers to online learning in the time of COVID-19: A national survey of medical students in the Philippines. *Medical Science Educator*, *31*(2), 615–626. doi: 10.1007/s40670-021-01231-z

Chrysanthos, N. (2020). 'You're being watched and recorded, every breath': Students unsettled by exam software. The Sydney Morning Herald, 22 May 2020. Retrieved July 12, 2024 from https://www.smh.com.au/nation al/nsw/you-re-being-watched-and-recorded-every-breath-students-unsettled-by-exam-software 20200519-p54ucb.html

Clandinin, D., & Caine, V. (2008). *Narrative inquiry*. In Lisa M. Given (Ed.), *The Sage encyclopedia of qualitative research methods*. (pp. 542–545). SAGE Publications, Inc. doi: http://dx.doi.org/10.4135/9781412963909.n275

Clarke, V., & Braun, V. (2013). *Successful qualitative research: A practical guide for beginners* (1st ed.). Sage

Cooper, R., & Lilyea, B. V. (2022). I'm interested in autoethnography, but how do i do it? *The Qualitative Report*, *27*(1), 197–208. https://doi.org/10.46743/2160-3715/2022.5288

Czerniewicz, Ll., Agherdien, N., Badenhorst, J., Belluigi, D., Chambers, T., Chili, M., de Villiers, M., Felix, A., Gachago, D., Gokhale, C., Ivala, E., Kramm, N., Madiba, M., Mistri, G., Mgqwashu, E., Pallit, N., Prinsloo, P., Solomon, K., Strydom, S., Swanepoel, M., Waghid, F., & Wissing, G. (2020). A wake-up call: Equity, inequality

and COVID-19 emergency remote teaching and learning. *Postdigital Science and Education, 2*, 946–967.
De Klerk, D. E., & Palmer, J. M. (2022). Technology inclusion for students living with disabilities through collaborative online learning during and beyond COVID-19. *Perspectives in Education, 40*(1), 80–95 http://dx.doi.org/10.18820/2519593X/pie.v40.i1
El Said, G. R. (2021). How did the COVID-19 pandemic affect higher education learning experience? An empirical investigation of learners' academic performance at a university in a developing country. *Advances in Human-Computer Interaction, 2021*(3), 1–10. doi: 10.1155/2021/6649524
Essop, A. (2021). *COVID-19: The "new normal" and the future of higher education.* Internal Report, University of Johannesburg, Johannesburg, South Africa.
Ferri, F., Grifoni, P., & Guzzo, T. (2020). Online learning and emergency remote teaching: Opportunities and challenges in emergency situations. *Societies, 10*(4), 1–18. doi: 10.3390/soc10040086
Haleem, A., Javaid, M., Qadri, M. & Suman, R. (2022). Understanding the role of digital technologies in education: A review. *Sustainable Operations and Computers, 3*(2022), 275–285. doi: 10.1016/j.susoc.2022.05.004
Landa, N., Zhou, S., & Marongwe, N. (2021). Education in emergencies: Lessons from COVID 19 in South Africa. *International Review of Education, 67*, 167–183.
Li, S. (2023). The effect of teacher self-efficacy, teacher resilience, and emotion regulation on teacher burnout: A mediation model. *Front in Psychology, 14*, 1185079.
Lufungulo, E. S., Mwila, K., Mudenda, S., Kampamba, M., Chulu, M., & Hikaambo, C. N. (2021). Online teaching during COVID-19 pandemic in Zambian Universities: Unpacking lecturers' experiences and the implications for incorporating online teaching in the university pedagogy. *Creative Education, 12*, 2886–2904. https://doi.org/10.4236/ce.2021.121221
Mahaye, N. E. (2020). *The impact of COVID-19 pandemic on education: Navigating forward the pedagogy of blended learning.* Department of Education KwaZulu-Natal, South Africa.
Magomedov, A., Khaliev, M. S., & Ibragimova, L. V. (2020). The need for introducing new technology in agriculture to ensure a sustainable future. In *IOP Conference Series: Earth and Environmental Science, 548*(3), 1–4: doi:10.1088/1755-1315/548/3/032026
Marongwe, N., & Garidzirai, R. (2021). Together but not together: Challenges of remote learning for students amid the COVID-19 pandemic in rural South African universities. *Research in Social Sciences and Technology, 6*(3), 213–226. https://doi.org/10.46303/ressat.2021.39
Mbeki, T. M. (1998). *Africa the time has come: Selected speeches of thabo mbeki.* Mafube Publishers.
Menon, K., & Motala, S. (2022). *Pandemic disruptions to access to higher education in South Africa: A dream deferred?* University of Johannesburg, South Africa.
Mhlanga, D., & Moloi, T. (2020). COVID-19 and the digital transformation of education: What are we learning on 4IR in South Africa. *Education Sciences, 10*(7), 1–11. doi:10.3390/educsci10070180.
Mncube, V., Mutongoza, B. H., & Olawale, E. (2021). Managing higher education institutions in the context of COVID-19 stringency: Experiences of stakeholders at a rural South African university. *Perspectives in Education, 39*(1), 390–409.
Motala, S., & Menon, K. (2020). In search of the 'new normal': Reflections on teaching and learning during COVID-19 in a South African University. *Southern African Review of Education, 26*(1), 80–99.
Mpungose, C., B. (2020). Emergent transition from face-to-face to online learning in a South African university in the context of the Coronavirus pandemic. *Humanities and Social Sciences Communications, 7*(113) 1–9. doi: 10.1057/s41599-020-00603-x.
Mukhtar, K., Javed, K., Arooj, M., & Sethi, A. (2020). Advantages, limitations and recommendations for online learning during COVID-19 pandemic era. *Pakistan Journal of Medical Sciences, 36*(4), 27–31. doi:10.12669/pjms.36.COVID19-S4.2785.

OECD. (2018). Equity in education: Breaking down barriers to social mobility. PISA, OECD Publishing. doi:10.1787/9789264073234-en

Opere, W. M. (2021). Negative impacts of the current COVID-19 crisis on science education in Kenya: How certain can we be about the efficacy of the Science learning framework online? *Journal of Microbiology & Biology Education, 22*(1), 1–7. doi:10.1128/jmbe.v22i1.2559

Munro, A. J. (2011). *Autoethnography as a research method in design research at universities.* Faculty of the Arts, Tshwane University of Technology; Design Education Forum of Southern Africa. www.defsa.org.za

Pokhrel, S., & Chhetri, R. (2021). A literature review on the impact of COVID-19 pandemic on teaching and learning. *Higher Education for The Future, 8*(1), 133–141. doi: 10.1177/2347631120983481

Phejane, M. V. (2022). "The new normal": A case study on the emergent transition towards online teaching and learning in internal medicine and anaesthesiology at the University of the Free State; *Perspectives in Education, 40*(1), 164–178.

Rapanta, C., Botturi, L., Goodyear, P., Guàrdia, L., & Koole, M. (2020). Online university teaching during and after the COVID-19 crisis: Refocusing teacher presence and learning activity. *Postdigital Science and Education, 2*, 923–945. doi: 10.1007/s42438-020-00155-y

Salmi, J. (2020). *COVID's lessons for global higher education: Coping with the present while building a more equitable future.* IMF Annual Report. Retrieved from covids-lessons-for-global-higher-education.pdf

Salmi, J. (2023). Equity and inclusion in higher education. International Higher Education, (113), 5–6. https://ejournals.bc.edu/index.php/ihe/article/view/16089

Seeletso, M., & Letseka, M. (2020). Virtual learning: The lacuna for improved access, openness and flexibility in an open and distance learning university. *International Journal of Multidisciplinary Perspectives in Higher Education, 5*(2), 86–99.

Tate, T., & Warschauer, M. (2022). Equity in online learning. *Educational Psychologist, 57*(3), 192–206. https://doi.org/10.1080/00461520.2022.2062597

Toquero, C. M. (2020). Challenges and opportunities for higher education amid the COVID-19 pandemic: The Philippine context. *Pedagogical Research, 5*(4), 1–5. doi: 10.29333/pr/7947.

UNESCO. (2020, March 13). *COVID-19 educational disruption and response.* https://en.unesco.org/themes/education-emergencies/coronavirus-school-closures

Universities South Africa. (2020). *Public universities are readying themselves for virtual teaching and learning during the national lockdown.* Universities South Africa Web Site. Retrieved July 5, 2024, from https://www.usaf.ac.za/universities-coronavirus-covid-19-updates/

Walker, A. (2017). Critical autobiography as research. *The Qualitative Report, 22*(7), 1896–1908. https://doi.org/10.46743/2160-3715/2017.2804

Warschauer, M. (2003). *Technology and social inclusion. In technology and social inclusion.* The MIT Press. https://doi.org/10.7551/mitpress/6699.001.0001

Zhong, B. L., Luo, W., Li, H. M., Zhang, Q. Q., Liu, X. G., & Li, W. T. (2020). Knowledge, attitudes, and practices towards COVID-19 among Chinese residents during the rapid rise period of the COVID-19 outbreak: A quick online cross-sectional survey. *International Journal of Biological Science, 16*(10), 1745–1752.

# Chapter 16

# Conclusion

*Tsediso Michael Makoelle*

Nazarbayev University, Kazakhstan

## Abstract

This chapter reflects on the findings and conclusions from the previous chapters. It is an analytic chapter that discusses the seven cardinal pillars of inclusion in further and higher education that emerged from the discussions in this volume. Based on the research outcomes presented in this volume, lessons and recommendations are drawn.

*Keywords*: Policy; leadership; technology assessment; curriculum; pedagogy

## Introduction

In the introductory chapter, we established that this volume's approach is rooted in a systems-ecological perspective. While we discuss the various components of the system as distinct entities, it's crucial to recognise their interconnectedness. Therefore, based on the discussions in the previous chapters, the emerging conceptual framework for inclusion in higher and further education is built on seven cardinal pillars. Fig. 16.1 provides a comprehensive overview of these cardinal pillars, highlighting their interdependence and the role they play in shaping inclusive education.

Therefore, this chapter reflects on the findings and conclusions in the previous chapters. Based on such reflections, lessons are illuminated about the current state of inclusive further and higher education in South Africa, and some achievements, challenges, and recommendations for the future are foregrounded.

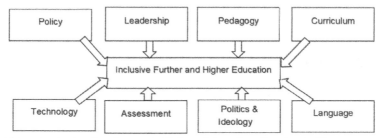

Fig. 16.1. Inclusive Further and Higher Education Cardinal Pillars.

## Inclusive Further and Higher Education: Reflections and Recommendations

According to discussions in this volume, inclusive education in further and higher education points to the fact that the historical context in both political, economic, and ideological influences how inclusion in further and higher education is conceptualised, enacted, and practised. A comparison of literature from countries of the North and those from the South seems to suggest that the history of colonialisation has impacted how education in these two critical levels has been configured and developed (Abdulrahman et al., 2021). As a result, the notions of equity, equality, access, inclusion, and social justice have been impacted by this background. The fact that the nature of further and higher education is part of the broader political and socio-economic context cannot be overlooked. So, inclusion in further and higher education cannot be considered in isolation as it is interwoven with the general socio-economic fibre of the society and the community within which the further and higher education institution is located.

It is evident that the implementation of inclusive education in further and higher education is intertwined with a country's general political and ideological context, as well as the governance, leadership, and institutional culture (O'Donnell, 2016), as framed by contemporary education developments in that context. For instance, South Africa has embarked on the process to redress the past imbalances of the apartheid system. Therefore, any process to implement inclusion in further and higher education cannot disregard this political background. So, inclusion as a social justice endeavour occurs within the realm of the transformation, not only of education but the entire society.

It is evident that ideology and political context impact policy direction in terms of inclusion, equity, and access. However, there is always a gap between policy intentions and the practices on the ground (Slee, 2019). Indications emerging from this volume demonstrate that although there was a concerted effort to develop policies to enable access, equity, and inclusion in South African further and higher education, a gap between policy and practice appears to be wide. According to Watkins et al. (2016), it is imperative to close this gap through systematic support and regular process monitoring. While there are efforts to decolonise further and higher education, the challenges of exclusive practices such as epistemic, language, financial, and other forms of excluding and marginalising practices persist. As a result, Moriña (2019, p. 1) suggests that moving the university towards an inclusive setting requires designing policies, strategies, processes, and actions that contribute to ensuring the success of all the students.

The attempts to prioritise the Indigenous knowledge systems seem to be moving very slowly, taking into account the dominance of Eurocentric-oriented pieces of knowledge (Marovah & Mutanga, 2023). While the curriculum is at the centre of the process to make learning content, its delivery, assessment, and application inclusive, the process by further and higher education institutions to develop an inclusive curriculum is facing many challenges, such as faculty non-preparedness, lack of adequate competencies and skills in developing a curriculum that may respond to the needs of diverse students (Taff & Clifton, 2022). Therefore, professional development of faculty in understanding inclusion, its principles and practices is necessary for them to make pedagogical choices and decisions that may enable and promote inclusion, equity, and educational access (Makoelle & Mosito, 2023). While there are efforts to ensure that language does not become a barrier to access to further and higher education, both English as a medium of instruction and Afrikaans as a medium of instruction have far-reaching implications for access, especially for students from previously disadvantaged backgrounds. Hence, Ngo (2024) proposes trans-languaging as an alternative to one medium of instruction for inclusive classes. While some institutions of further and higher education have disability centres, which in most cases focus on remediation, it is crucial that institutions transition to a centred support approach, which means from a medical model to a social model of support that embraces principles such as the Universal Design for Learning (Bualar, 2018) and Open Education Resources to ensure that institutions of further and higher education respond to the student's educational needs. It is important that institutions of further and higher education adopt a holistic approach to developing inclusive education environments.

While there are attempts to ensure continuous assessment as opposed to summative assessment, the assessment approaches at further and higher education institutions still by and large do not respond to the needs of diverse students. The overemphasis on standardisation creates inflexible methods of assessment that, in some cases, create a barrier to student learning and support. It is, therefore, pivotal that institutions of further and higher learning adopt multiple forms of assessment to cater for the diverse learning needs of students. Kaur et al. (2017) talk about contextually sensitive assessment strategies that are fair and inclusive.

Continuous professional development of faculty is crucial for ensuring that faculty are updated about modern teaching strategies and technologies that may support inclusion, equity, and access. In this volume, the significance of institutions of teacher education that provide higher education for teachers is crucial, taking into account preparing teachers for inclusive teaching through processes such as practicum and pre-service teacher mentoring for inclusive teaching and learning facilitation (Makoelle & Burmistrova, 2021). Therefore, reforming the teacher education curriculum to encompass the ideals of inclusive education is paramount. It is also important that further and higher education develops plans to implement digital inclusive education. The advent of the COVID-19 pandemic left a legacy of blended learning, which explored online and face-to-face learning opportunities. Institutions of further and higher education need to embark on digital transformation that would see not only the application of learning support devices for students but also the creation of a digital ecosystem that creates both virtual and physical inclusive learning environments.

While inclusive education policy was adopted in South Africa, there have been more efforts at the secondary education level to implement it. In further and higher education, there has been a lack of leadership and governance that embraces inclusion but is also willing to lead its implementation. While the discussion on barriers to inclusion is dominated by the disability focus, gender-related exclusions and marginalisation of women in further and higher education manifest in leadership, STEM education, and other male-dominated educational field. There are also challenges to the inclusion of students with diverse gender identities (Elliott et al., 2013).

## Chapter Conclusion

This chapter reflected on the findings and conclusions from the previous chapters. It provided an analytic discussion of the seven cardinal pillars of inclusion in further and higher education that emerged from the discussions in previous chapters. Lessons and recommendations are made based on the research outcomes presented in other chapters. This book, therefore, forms the basis for discussions and debates about equity, access, and inclusion in South African further and higher education. The editors and chapter authors are aware that the further and higher education landscape in South Africa is evolving and changing rapidly as a result of the process of transformation of South African education and its society. Therefore, some findings in the book might need to be more conclusive. However, this book shares valuable insights about inclusion in further and higher education that could inform future research, policy making, and practice.

## References

Abdulrahman, H. K., Adebisi, F. I., Nwako, Z., & Walton, E. (2021). Revisiting (inclusive) education in the postcolony. *Journal of the British Academy, 9*, 47–75.

Bualar, T. (2018). Barriers to inclusive higher education in Thailand: Voices of blind students. *Asia Pacific Education Review, 19*(4), 469–477.

Elliott, C. M., Stransky, O., Negron, R., Bowlby, M., Lickiss, J., Dutt, D., & Barbosa, P. (2013). Institutional barriers to diversity change work in higher education. *Sage Open, 3*(2), 2158244013489686.

Kaur, A., Noman, M., & Nordin, H. (2017). Inclusive assessment for linguistically diverse learners in higher education. *Assessment & Evaluation in Higher Education, 42*(5), 756.

Makoelle, T. M., & Burmistrova, V. (2021). Teacher education and inclusive education in Kazakhstan. *International Journal of Inclusive Education*, 1–17.

Makoelle, T. M., & Mosito, C. P. (2023). Pre-service teacher preparation for inclusive teaching in South Africa. In *Practices and perspectives of teaching and teacher education in Africa* (pp. 1–23). IGI Global Scientific Publishing.

Marovah, T., & Mutanga, O. (2023). Decolonising participatory research: Can Ubuntu philosophy contribute something? *International Journal of Social Research Methodology, 27*(5), 501–516.

Moriña, A. (2019). Inclusive education in higher education: challenges and opportunities. In M. R. Coleman, & M. Shevlin (Eds.), *Postsecondary educational opportunities for students with special education needs* (pp. 3–17). Routledge.

Ngo, P. L. H. (2024). EMI programmes in Vietnamese higher education: A case study of translanguaging practices for inclusive education. *Journal of English as a Lingua Franca, 13*(1), 163–184.

O'Donnell, V. L. (2016). Organisational change and development towards inclusive higher education. *Journal of Applied Research in Higher Education, 8*(1), 101–118.

Slee, R. (2019). Belonging in an age of exclusion. *International Journal of Inclusive Education, 23*(9), 909–922.

Taff, S. D., & Clifton, M. (2022). Inclusion and belonging in higher education: A scoping study of contexts, barriers, and facilitators. *Higher Education Studies, 12*(3), 122–133.

Watkins, A., Meijer, C. J., & Forlin, C. (Eds.). (2016). *Implementing inclusive education: Issues in bridging the policy-practice gap*. Emerald Group Publishing.

Printed and bound by CPI Group (UK) Ltd, Croydon, CR0 4YY
02/07/2025
14698048-0002